# 3rd Workshop on Argument Mining 2016

Held at ACL 2016

Berlin, Germany
12 August 2016

ISBN: 978-1-5108-2767-7

ACL 2016

**The 54th Annual Meeting of the
Association for Computational Linguistics**

**Proceedings of the 3rd Workshop on Argument Mining**

August 12, 2016
Berlin, Germany

# Preface

This third edition of the Workshop on Argument Mining builds on the success of the first and second workshops held at ACL 2014 and NAACL 2015, with an increasing maturity in the work reported. The breadth of papers in the programme this year attests to the range of techniques, the diverse domains and the varied goals that are encompassed in argument (or argumentation) mining.

The focus of argument mining is to tackle the problem of automatic identification of arguments and their internal structure and interconnections.The papers collected here provide a rich exploration of the nature of argumentative structure that can be automatically identified, from identification of the presence of argument, through evidence relationships and types of evidence relationships, argument types and premise types, to highly demanding tasks such as enthymeme reconstruction.

One of the facets that makes argument mining such an exciting and demanding problem is that purely statistical approaches very rapidly reach performance maxima with more knowledge-intensive, linguistically-aware and structurally constrained approaches required as well. Combinations of statistical robustness and structural priors hold particular promise, with early results reported in several of the papers here.

As a very new area, argument mining is also working *ab initio* on challenges such as data availability, annotation standards, corpus definition and publication, as well as quantification, validation and evaluation of results. Again, several papers here are tackling these community-oriented, practical – but vitally important – problems. We are also very pleased to introduce for the first time a special track focusing on an 'Unshared Task' to bootstrap the process of shared data provision for the community. The contributions to this track will lead to a detailed panel discussion with a goal of establishing some initial momentum to what will hopefully become a regular part of the Argument Mining workshop series.

This year also sees a special track on Debating Technologies reflecting the thread of work in the area that focuses on applications of the techniques in solving real problems in man-machine communication, driven in part by commercial R&D and by IBM's Debating Technology team in particular.

We were delighted with the quantity and quality of submissions, and as a result have developed a packed programme. The workshop attracted 31 submissions in total, of which 13 were accepted as full papers, four as short papers and a further three as contributions to the Unshared Task Panel. As the area continues to grow with an increasing number of groups turning their attention to the problems presented by argument mining, we look forward to seeing further growth in the workshop and the community that it supports.

*CAR*
*Dundee, June 2016*

**Organizers:**

Chris Reed, University of Dundee (Chair)
Kevin Ashley, University of Pittsburgh
Claire Cardie, Cornell University
Nancy Green, University of N.C. Greensboro
Iryna Gurevych, Technische Universitat Darmstadt
Diane Litman, University of Pittsburgh
Georgios Petasis, N.C.S.R. Demokritos
Noam Slonim, IBM Research, Israel
Vern Walker, Hofstra University

**Program Committee:**

Stergos Afantenos, IRIT Toulouse
Carlos Alzate, IBM Research, Ireland
Kevin Ashley, University of Pittsburgh
Katarzyna Budzynska, Polish National Academy of Sciences
Elena Cabrio, University of Nice
Claire Cardie, Cornell University
Matthias Grabmair, University of Pittsburgh
Nancy Green, University of N.C. Greensboro
Iryna Gurevych, Technische Universitat Darmstadt
Ivan Habernal, Technische Universitat Darmstadt
Graeme Hirst, University of Toronto
Ed Hovy, CMU
Vangelis Karkaletsis, N.C.S.R. Demokritos
Mitesh Khapra, IBM Research, India
Valia Kordoni, Humboldt Universitat zu Berlin
Jonas Kuhn, Stuttgart University
John Lawrence, University of Dundee
Joao Leite, FCT-UNL – Universidade Nova de Lisboa
Ran Levy, IBM Research, Israel
Beishui Liao, Zhejiang University
Maria Liakata, University of Warwick
Diane Litman, University of Pittsburgh
Bernardo Magnini, FBK Trento
Robert Mercer, University of Western Ontario
Marie-Francine Moens, Katholieke Universiteit Leuven
Huy Nguyen, University of Pittsburgh
Smaranda Muresan, Columbia University
Fabio Paglieri, CNR Italy
Alexis Palmer, Saarland University
Joonsuk Park, Cornell University
Simon Parsons, Kings College London
Georgios Petasis, N.C.S.R. Demokritos
Craig Pfeifer, MITRE
Chris Reed, University of Dundee
Ariel Rosenfeld, Bar-Ilan University

Patrick Saint-Dizier, IRIT Toulouse
Christian Schunn, University Pittsburgh
Jodi Schneider, University Pittsburgh
Noam Slonim, IBM Research, Israel
Christian Stab, Technische Universitat Darmstadt
Manfred Stede, Universitat Potsdam
Benno Stein, Universitat Weimar
Henning Wachsmuth, Universitat Weimar
Marilyn Walker, University of California, Santa Cruz
Vern Walker, Hofstra University
Serena Villata, INRIA Sophia-Antipolis Mediterranee
Lu Wang, Northeastern University
Adam Wyner, University Aberdeen

# Table of Contents


*"What Is Your Evidence?" A Study of Controversial Topics on Social Media*
Aseel Addawood and Masooda Bashir . . . . . . . . . . . . . . . . . . . . . . . . . . . . . . . . . . . . . . . . . . . . . 1

*Summarizing Multi-Party Argumentative Conversations in Reader Comment on News*
Emma Barker and Robert Gaizauskas . . . . . . . . . . . . . . . . . . . . . . . . . . . . . . . . . . . . . . . . . . . . . 12

*Argumentative texts and clause types*
Maria Becker, Alexis Palmer and Anette Frank . . . . . . . . . . . . . . . . . . . . . . . . . . . . . . . . . . . . 21

*Contextual stance classification of opinions: A step towards enthymeme reconstruction in online reviews*
Pavithra Rajendran, Danushka Bollegala and Simon Parsons . . . . . . . . . . . . . . . . . . . . . . . . . 31

*The CASS Technique for Evaluating the Performance of Argument Mining*
Rory Duthie, John Lawrence, Katarzyna Budzynska and Chris Reed . . . . . . . . . . . . . . . . . . . 40

*Extracting Case Law Sentences for Argumentation about the Meaning of Statutory Terms*
Jaromir Savelka and Kevin D. Ashley . . . . . . . . . . . . . . . . . . . . . . . . . . . . . . . . . . . . . . . . . . . . 50

*Scrutable Feature Sets for Stance Classification*
Angrosh Mandya, Advaith Siddharthan and Adam Wyner . . . . . . . . . . . . . . . . . . . . . . . . . . . 60

*Argumentation: Content, Structure, and Relationship with Essay Quality*
Beata Beigman Klebanov, Christian Stab, Jill Burstein, Yi Song, Binod Gyawali
and Iryna Gurevych . . . . . . . . . . . . . . . . . . . . . . . . . . . . . . . . . . . . . . . . . . . . . . . . . . . . . . . . . . . 70

*Neural Attention Model for Classification of Sentences that Support Promoting/Suppressing Relationship*
Yuta Koreeda, Toshihiko Yanase, Kohsuke Yanai, Misa Sato and Yoshiki Niwa . . . . . . . . . 76

*Towards Feasible Guidelines for the Annotation of Argument Schemes*
Elena Musi, Debanjan Ghosh and Smaranda Muresan . . . . . . . . . . . . . . . . . . . . . . . . . . . . . . 82

*Identifying Argument Components through TextRank*
Georgios Petasis and Vangelis Karkaletsis . . . . . . . . . . . . . . . . . . . . . . . . . . . . . . . . . . . . . . . 94

*Rhetorical structure and argumentation structure in monologue text*
Andreas Peldszus and Manfred Stede . . . . . . . . . . . . . . . . . . . . . . . . . . . . . . . . . . . . . . . . . . . 103

*Recognizing the Absence of Opposing Arguments in Persuasive Essays*
Christian Stab and Iryna Gurevych . . . . . . . . . . . . . . . . . . . . . . . . . . . . . . . . . . . . . . . . . . . . . 113

*Expert Stance Graphs for Computational Argumentation*
Orith Toledo-Ronen, Roy Bar-Haim and Noam Slonim . . . . . . . . . . . . . . . . . . . . . . . . . . . . 119

*Fill the Gap! Analyzing Implicit Premises between Claims from Online Debates*
Filip Boltuzic and Jan Šnajder . . . . . . . . . . . . . . . . . . . . . . . . . . . . . . . . . . . . . . . . . . . . . . . . 124

*Summarising the points made in online political debates*
Charlie Egan, Advaith Siddharthan and Adam Wyner . . . . . . . . . . . . . . . . . . . . . . . . . . . . . . 134

*What to Do with an Airport?*
*Mining Arguments in the German Online Participation Project Tempelhofer Feld*
Matthias Liebeck, Katharina Esau and Stefan Conrad . . . . . . . . . . . . . . . . . . . . . . . . . . . . . . 144

*Unshared task: (Dis)agreement in online debates*
Maria Skeppstedt, Magnus Sahlgren, Carita Paradis and Andreas Kerren . . . . . . . . . . . . . . . . . . . . 154

*Unshared Task: Perspective Based Local Agreement and Disagreement in Online Debate*
Chantal van Son, Tommaso Caselli, Antske Fokkens, Isa Maks, Roser Morante, Lora Aroyo and
Piek Vossen . . . . . . . . . . . . . . . . . . . . . . . . . . . . . . . . . . . . . . . . . . . . . . . . . . . . . . . . . . . . . . . . . . . . . . . . . . . . 160

*Unshared Task: A Preliminary Study of Disputation Behavior in Online Debating Forum*
Zhongyu Wei, Yandi Xia, Chen Li, Yang Liu, Zachary Stallbohm, Yi Li and Yang Jin . . . . . . . . 166

# Workshop Program

**Friday, August 12, 2016**

**09:00–09:10**  *Welcome*

**09:10–10:30**  **Session I**

09:10–09:30  *"What Is Your Evidence?" A Study of Controversial Topics on Social Media*
Aseel Addawood and Masooda Bashir

09:30–09:50  *Summarizing Multi-Party Argumentative Conversations in Reader Comment on News*
Emma Barker and Robert Gaizauskas

09:50–10:10  *Argumentative texts and clause types*
Maria Becker, Alexis Palmer and Anette Frank

10:10–10:30  *Contextual stance classification of opinions: A step towards enthymeme reconstruction in online reviews*
Pavithra Rajendran, Danushka Bollegala and Simon Parsons

**10:30–11:00**  *Coffee break*

**11:00–12:30**  **Session II**

11:00–11:20  *The CASS Technique for Evaluating the Performance of Argument Mining*
Rory Duthie, John Lawrence, Katarzyna Budzynska and Chris Reed

11:20–11:40  *Extracting Case Law Sentences for Argumentation about the Meaning of Statutory Terms*
Jaromir Savelka and Kevin D. Ashley

11:40–12:00  *Scrutable Feature Sets for Stance Classification*
Angrosh Mandya, Advaith Siddharthan and Adam Wyner

12:00–12:15  *Argumentation: Content, Structure, and Relationship with Essay Quality*
Beata Beigman Klebanov, Christian Stab, Jill Burstein, Yi Song, Binod Gyawali and Iryna Gurevych

12:15–12:30  *Neural Attention Model for Classification of Sentences that Support Promoting/Suppressing Relationship*
Yuta Koreeda, Toshihiko Yanase, Kohsuke Yanai, Misa Sato and Yoshiki Niwa

**12:30–14:00**   *Lunch*


**14:00–15:30**   **Session III**

14:00–14:20   *Towards Feasible Guidelines for the Annotation of Argument Schemes*
Elena Musi, Debanjan Ghosh and Smaranda Muresan

14:20–14:40   *Identifying Argument Components through TextRank*
Georgios Petasis and Vangelis Karkaletsis

14:40–15:00   *Rhetorical structure and argumentation structure in monologue text*
Andreas Peldszus and Manfred Stede

15:00–15:15   *Recognizing the Absence of Opposing Arguments in Persuasive Essays*
Christian Stab and Iryna Gurevych

15:15–15:30   *Expert Stance Graphs for Computational Argumentation*
Orith Toledo-Ronen, Roy Bar-Haim and Noam Slonim


**15:30–16:00**   *Coffee break*

**Friday, August 12, 2016 (continued)**

**16:00–17:30**   **Session IV - Debating Technologies and the Unshared Task Panel**

16:00–16:20   *Fill the Gap! Analyzing Implicit Premises between Claims from Online Debates*
Filip Boltuzic and Jan Šnajder

16:20–16:40   *Summarising the points made in online political debates*
Charlie Egan, Advaith Siddharthan and Adam Wyner

16:40–17:00   *What to Do with an Airport? Mining Arguments in the German Online Participation Project Tempelhofer Feld*
Matthias Liebeck, Katharina Esau and Stefan Conrad

**17:00–17:25**   ***Panel Discussion: Unshared Task***

*Unshared task: (Dis)agreement in online debates*
Maria Skeppstedt, Magnus Sahlgren, Carita Paradis and Andreas Kerren

*Unshared Task: Perspective Based Local Agreement and Disagreement in Online Debate*
Chantal van Son, Tommaso Caselli, Antske Fokkens, Isa Maks, Roser Morante, Lora Aroyo and Piek Vossen

*Unshared Task: A Preliminary Study of Disputation Behavior in Online Debating Forum*
Zhongyu Wei, Yandi Xia, Chen Li, Yang Liu, Zachary Stallbohm, Yi Li and Yang Jin

**17:25–17:30**   ***Closing Remarks***

**17:30**   ***Close***

# "What is Your Evidence?" A Study of Controversial Topics on Social Media


**Aseel A. Addawood**  **Masooda N. Bashir**

School of Information Sciences
University of Illinois at Urbana-Champaign
Aaddaw2, mnb@illinois.edu



## Abstract

In recent years, social media has revolutionized how people communicate and share information. One function of social media, besides connecting with friends, is sharing opinions with others. Micro blogging sites, like Twitter, have often provided an online forum for social activism. When users debate about controversial topics on social media, they typically share different types of evidence to support their claims. Classifying these types of evidence can provide an estimate for how adequately the arguments have been supported. We first introduce a manually built gold standard dataset of 3000 tweets related to the recent FBI and Apple encryption debate. We develop a framework for automatically classifying six evidence types typically used on Twitter to discuss the debate. Our findings show that a Support Vector Machine (SVM) classifier trained with n-gram and additional features is capable of capturing the different forms of representing evidence on Twitter, and exhibits significant improvements over the unigram baseline, achieving a $F_1$ macro-averaged of 82.8%.


## 1 Introduction

Social media has grown dramatically over the last decade. Researchers have now turned to social media, via online posts, as a source of information to explain many aspects of the human experience (Gruzd & Goertzen, 2013). Due to the textual nature of online users' self-disclosure of their opinions and views, social media platforms present a unique opportunity for further analysis of shared content and how controversial topics are argued. On social media sites, especially on Twitter, user text contains arguments with inappropriate or missing justifications—a rhetorical habit we do not usually encounter in professional writing. One way to handle such faulty arguments is to simply disregard them and focus on extracting arguments containing proper support (Villalba and Saint-Dizier, 2012; Cabrio and Villata, 2012). However, sometimes what seems like missing evidence is actually just an unfamiliar or different type of evidence. Thus, recognizing the appropriate type of evidence can be useful in assessing the viability of users' supporting information, and in turn, the strength of their whole argument.

One difficulty of processing social media text is the fact that it is written in an informal format. It does not follow any guidelines or rules for the expression of opinions. This has led to many messages containing improper syntax or spelling, which presents a significant challenge to attempts at extracting meaning from social media content. Nonetheless, we believe processing such corpora is of great importance to the argumentation-mining field of study. Therefore, the motivation for this study is to facilitate online users' search for information concerning controversial topics. Social media users are often faced with information overload about any given topic, and understanding positions and arguments in online debates can potentially help users formulate stronger opinions on controversial issues and foster personal and group decision-making (Freeley and Steinberg, 2013).

Continuous growth of online data has led to large amounts of information becoming available for others to explore and understand. Several automatic techniques have allowed us to determine different viewpoints expressed in social media text, e.g., sentiment analysis and opinion mining. However, these techniques struggle to identify complex relationships between concepts in the text. Analyzing argumentation from a computational linguistics point of view has led very recently to a new field called argumentation mining (Green et al., 2014).




*Proceedings of the 3rd Workshop on Argument Mining*, pages 1–11,
Berlin, Germany, August 7-12, 2016. ©2016 Association for Computational Linguistics

It formulates how humans disagree, debate, and form a consensus. This new field focuses on identifying and extracting argumentative structures in documents. This type of approach and the reasoning it supports is used widely in the fields of logic, AI, and text processing (Mochales and Ieven, 2009). The general consensus among researchers is that an argument is defined as containing a claim, which is a statement of the position for which the claimant is arguing. The claim is supported with premises that function as evidence to support the claim, which then appears as a conclusion or a proposition (Walton, Reed, & Macagno, 2008; Toulmin, 2003).

One of the major obstacles in developing argumentation mining techniques is the shortage of high-quality annotated data. An important source of data for applying argumentation techniques is the web, particularly social media. Online newspapers, blogs, product reviews, etc. provide a heterogeneous and growing flow of information where arguments can be analyzed. To date, much of the argumentation mining research has been limited and has focused on specific domains such as news articles, parliamentary records, journal articles, and legal documents (Ashley and Walker, 2013; Hachey and Grover, 2005; Reed and Rowe, 2004). Only a few studies have explored arguments on social media, a relatively under-investigated domain. Some examples of social media platforms that have been subjected to argumentation mining include Amazon online product reviews (Wyner, Schneider, Atkinson, & Bench-Capon, 2012) and tweets related to local riot events (Llewellyn, Grover, Oberlander, & Klein, 2014).

In this study, we describe a novel and unique benchmark data set achieved through a simple argument model, and elaborate on the associated annotation process. Unlike the classical Toulmin model (Toulmin, 2003), we search for a simple and robust argument structure comprising only two components: a claim and associated supporting evidence. Previous research has shown that a claim can be supported using different types of evidence (Rieke and Sillars, 1984). The annotation that is proposed in this paper is based on the type of evidence one uses to support a particular position on a given debate. We identify six types, which are detailed in the methods section (Section 3). To demonstrate these types, we collected data regarding the recent Apple/FBI encryption debate on Twitter between January 1 and March 31, 2016. We believe that understanding online users' views on this topic will help scholars, law enforcement officials, technologists, and policy makers gain a better understanding of online users' views about encryption.

In the remainder of the paper, Section 2 discusses survey-related work, Section 3 describes the data and corresponding features, Section 4 presents the experimental results, and Section 5 concludes the paper and proposes future directions.

## 2   Related Work

### 2.1   Argumentation mining

Argumentation mining is the study of identifying the argument structure of a given text. Argumentation mining has two phases. The first consists of argument annotations and the second consists of argumentation analysis. Many studies have focused on the first phase of annotating argumentative discourse. Reed and Rowe (2004) presented Araucaria, a tool for argumentation diagramming that supports both convergent and linked arguments, missing premises (enthymemes), and refutations. They also released the AracuariaDB corpus, which has been used for experiments in the argumentation mining field. Similarly, Schneider et al. (2013) annotated Wikipedia talk pages about deletion using Walton's 17 schemes (Walton 2008). Rosenthal and McKeown (2012) annotated opinionated claims, in which the author expresses a belief they think should be adopted by others. Two annotators labeled sentences as claims without any context. Habernal, Eckle-Kohler & Gurevych (2014) developed another well-annotated corpus, to model arguments following a variant of the Toulmin model. This dataset includes 990 instances of web documents collected from blogs, forums, and news outlets, 524 of which are labeled as argumentative. A final smaller corpus of 345 examples was annotated with finer-grained tags. No experimental results were reported on this corpus.

As far as the second phase, Stab and Gurevych (2014b) classified argumentative sentences into four categories (none, major claim, claim, premise) using their previously annotated corpus (Stab and Gurevych 2014a) and reached a 0.72 macro-F1

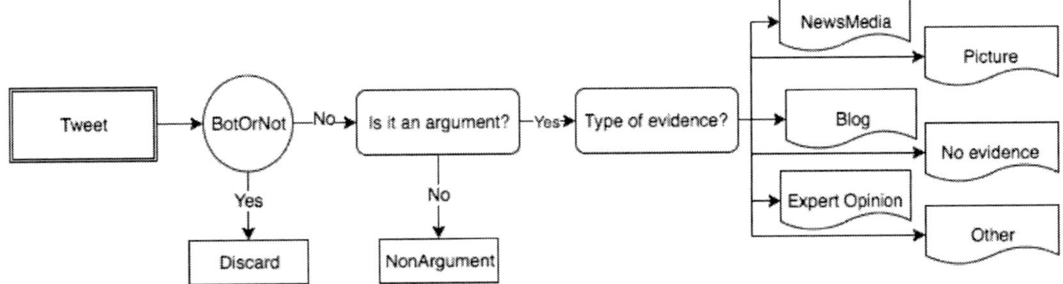



Figure 1: flow chart for annotation

score. Park and Cardie (2014) classified propositions into three classes (unverifiable, verifiable non-experimental, and verifiable experimental) and ignored non-argumentative text. Using multi-class SVM and a wide range of features (n-grams, POS, sentiment clue words, tense, person) they achieved a 0.69 Macro F1.

The IBM Haifa Research Group (Rinott et al., 2015) developed something similar to our research; they developed a data set using plain text in Wikipedia pages. The purpose of this corpus was to collect context-dependent claims and evidence, where the latter refers to facts (i.e., premises) that are relevant to a given topic. They classified evidence into three types (study, expert, anecdotal). Our work is different in that it includes more diverse types of evidence that reflect social media trends while the IBM Group's study was limited to looking into plain text in Wikipedia pages.

## 2.2 Social Media As A Data Source For Argumentation Mining

As stated previously there are only a few studies that have used social media data as a source for argumentation mining. Llewellyn et al. (2014) experimented with classifying tweets into several argumentative categories, specifically claims and counter-claims (with and without evidence), and used verification inquiries previously annotated by Procter, Vis, and Voss (2013). They used unigrams, punctuations, and POS as features in three classifiers. Schneider and Wyner (2012) focused on online product reviews and developed a number of argumentation schemes—inspired by Walton et al. (2008)—based on manual inspection of their corpus.

By identifying the most popular types of evidence used in social media, specifically on Twitter, our research differs from the previously mentioned studies because we are providing a social media annotated corpus. Moreover, the annotation is based on the different types of premises and evidence used frequently in social media settings.

## 3 Data

This study uses Twitter as its main source of data. Crimson Hexagon (Etlinger & Amand, 2012), a public social media analytics company, was used to collect every pubic post from January 1, 2016 through March 31, 2016. Crimson Hexagon houses all public Twitter data going back to 2009. The search criterion for this study was searching for a tweet that contains the word "encryption" anywhere in its text. The sample only included tweets from accounts that set English as their language; this was filtered in when requesting the data. However, some users set their account language to English, but constructed some tweets in a different language. Thus, forty accounts were removed manually, leaving 531,593 tweets in our dataset.

Although most Twitter accounts are managed by humans, there are other accounts managed by automated agents called social bots or Sybil accounts. These accounts do not represent real human opinions. In order to ensure that tweets from such accounts did not enter our data set, in the annotation procedure, we ran each Twitter user through the Truthy BotOrNot algorithm (Davis et al., 2016). This cleaned the data further and excluded any user with a 50% or greater probability of being a bot. Overall, 946 (24%) bot accounts were removed.

# 4 Methodology

## 4.1 Coding Scheme

In order to perform argument extraction from a social media platform, we followed a two-step approach. The first step was to identify sentences containing an argument. The second step was to identify the evidence-type found in the tweets classified as argumentative. These two steps were performed in conjunction with each other. Annotators were asked to annotate each tweet as either having an argument or not having an argument. Then they were instructed to annotate a tweet based on the type of evidence used in the tweet. Figure 1 shows the flow of annotation.

After considerable observation of the data, a draft-coding scheme was developed for the most used types of evidence. In order to verify the applicability and accuracy of the draft-coding scheme, two annotators conducted an initial trial on 50 randomized tweets to test the coding scheme. After some adjustments were made to the scheme, a second trial was conducted consisting of 25 randomized tweets that two different annotators annotated. The resulting analysis and discussion led to a final revision of the coding scheme and modification of the associated documentation (annotation guideline). After finalizing the annotation scheme, two annotators annotated a new set of 3000 tweets. The tweets were coded into one of the following evidence types.

**News media account (*NEWS*)** refers to sharing a story from any news media account. Since Twitter does not allow tweets to have more than 140 characters, users tend to communicate their opinions by sharing links to other resources. Twitter users will post links from official news accounts to share breaking news or stories posted online and add their own opinions. For example:

*Please who don't understand encryption or technology should not be allow to legislate it. There should be a test... https://t.co/I5zkvK9sZf*

**Expert opinion (*EXPERT*)** refers to sharing someone else's opinion about the debate, specifically someone who has more experience and knowledge of the topic than the user. The example below shows a tweet that shares a quotation from a security expert.

*RT @ItIsAMovement "Without strong encryption, you will be spied on systematically by lots of people" - Whitfield Diffie*

**Blog post (*BLOG*)** refers to the use of a link to a blog post reacting to the debate. The example below shows a tweet with a link to a blog post. In this tweet, the user is sharing sharing a link to her own blog post.

*I care about #encryption and you should too. Learn more about how it works from @Mozilla at https://t.co/RTFiuTQXyQ*

**Picture (*PICTURE*)** refers to a user sharing a picture related to the debate that may or may not support his/her point of view. For example, the tweet below shows a post containing the picture shown in figure 2.

*RT @ErrataRob No, morons, if encryption were being used, you'd find the messages, but you wouldn't be able to read them*

According to the police report and interviews with officials, none of the attackers' emails or other electronic communications have been found, prompting the authorities to conclude that the group used encryption. What kind of encryption remains unknown, and is among the details that Mr. Abdeslam's capture could help reveal.

Figure 2: an example of sharing a picture as evidence

**Other (*OTHER*)** refers to other types of evidence that do not fall under the previous annotation categories. Even though we observed Twitter data in order to categorize different, discrete types of evidence, we were also expecting to discover new types while annotating. Some new types we found while annotating include audio, books, campaigns, petitions, codes, slides, other social media references, and text files.

**No evidence (*NO EVIDENCE*)** refers to users sharing their opinions about the debate without having any evidence to support their claim. The example below shows an argumentative tweet from a user who is in favor of encryption. However, he/she does not provide any evidence for his/her stance.

*I hope people ban encryption. Then all their money and CC's can be stolen and they'll feel better knowing terrorists can't keep secrets.*

**Non Argument (*NONARG*)** refers to a tweet that does not contain an argument. For example, the following tweet asks a question instead of presenting an argument.

*RT @cissp_googling what does encryption look like*

Another NONARG situation is when a user shares a link to a news article without posting any opinions about it. For example, the following tweet does not present an argument or share an opinion about the debate; it only shares the title of the news article, "Tech giants back Apple against FBI's 'dangerous' encryption demand," and a link to the article.

*Tech giants back Apple against FBI's 'dangerous' encryption demand #encryption https://t.co/4CUushsVmW*

Retweets are also considered NONARG because simply selecting "retweet" does not take enough effort to be considered an argument. Moreover, just because a user retweets something does not mean we know exactly how they feel about it; they could agree with it, or they could just think it was interesting and want to share it with their followers. The only exception would be if a user retweeted something that was very clearly an opinion or argument. For example, someone retweeting Edward Snowden speaking out against encryption backdoors would be marked as an argument. By contrast, a user retweeting a CNN news story about Apple and the FBI would be marked as NONARG.

**Annotation discussion.** While annotating the data, we observed other types of evidence that did not appear in the last section. We assumed users would use these types of evidence in argumentation. However, we found that users mostly use these types in a non-argumentative manner, namely as a means forwarding information. The first such evidence type was "scientific paper," which refers to sharing a link to scientific research that was published in a conference or a journal. Here is an example:

*A Worldwide Survey of Encryption Products. By Bruce Schneier, Kathleen Seidel & Saranya Vijayakumar #Cryptography https://t.co/wmAuvu6oUb*

The second such evidence type was "video," which refers to a user sharing a link to a video related to the debate. For example, the tweet below is a post with a link to a video explaining encryption.

*An explanation of how a 2048-bit RSA encryption key is created https://t.co/JjBWym3poh*

## 4.2 Annotation results

The results of the annotation are shown in Table 1 and Table 2. The inter-coder reliability was 18%

and 26% for the two tasks, respectively, yielding a 70% inter-annotator observed agreement for both tasks. The unweighted Cohen's Kappa score was 0.67 and 0.79, respectively, for the two tasks.

| Argumentation classification | Class distribution |
|---|---|
| Argument (ARG) | 1,271 |
| Non argument (NONARG) | 1,729 |
| Total | 3000 |

Table 1: Argumentation classification distribution over tweets

| Evidence type | Class distribution |
|---|---|
| No evidence | 630 |
| News media accounts | 318 |
| Blog post | 293 |
| Picture | 12 |
| Expert opinion | 11 |
| Other | 7 |
| Total | 1,271 |

Table 2: Evidence type distribution over tweets

## 5 Experimental Evaluation

We developed an approach to classify tweets into each of the six major types of evidence used in Twitter arguments.

## 5.1 Preprocessing

Due to the character limit, Twitter users tend to use colloquialisms, slang, and abbreviations in their tweets. They also often make spelling and grammar errors in their posts. Before discussing feature selection, we will briefly discuss how we compensated for these issues in data preprocessing. We first replaced all abbreviations with their proper word or phrase counterparts (e.g., 2night => tonight) and replaced repeated characters with a single character (e.g., haaaapy => happy). In addition, we lowercased all letters (e.g., ENCRYPTION => encryption), and removed all URLs and mentions to other users after initially recording these features.

## 5.2 Features

We propose a set of features to characterize each type of evidence in our collection. Some of these features are specific to the Twitter platform. However, others are more generic and could be applied to other forums of argumentation. Many features follow previous work (Castillo, Mendoza, & Poblete, 2011; Agichtein, Castillo, Donato, Gionis, & Mishne, 2008). The full list of features appears in appendix A. Below, we identify four types of features based on their scope: Basic, Psychometric, Linguistic, and Twitter-specific.

**Basic Features** refer to N-gram features, which rely on the word count (TF) for each given unigram or bigram that appears in the tweet.

**Psychometric Features** refer to dictionary-based features. They are derived from the linguistic enquiry and word count (LIWC). LIWC is a text analysis software originally developed within the context of Pennebaker's work on emotional writing (Pennebaker & Francis, 1996; Pennebaker, 1997). LIWC produces statistics on eighty-one different text features in five categories. These include psychological processes such as emotional and social cognition, and personal concerns such as occupational, financial, or medical worries. In addition, they include personal core drives and needs such as power and achievement.

**Linguistic Features** encompass four types of features. The first is grammatical features, which refer to percentages of words that are pronouns, articles, prepositions, verbs, adverbs, and other parts of speech or punctuation. The second type is LIWC summary variables. The newest version of LIWC includes four new summary variables (analytical thinking, clout, authenticity, and emotional tone), which resemble "person-type" or personality measures.

The LIWC webpage ("Interpreting LIWC Output", 2016) describes the four summary variables as follows. *Analytical thinking* "captures the degree to which people use words that suggest formal, logical, and hierarchical thinking patterns." *Clout* "refers to the relative social status, confidence, or leadership that people display through their writing or talking." *Authenticity* "is when people reveal themselves in an authentic or honest way," usually by becoming "more personal, humble, and vulnerable." Lastly, with *emotional tone,*

"although LIWC includes both positive emotion and negative emotion dimensions, the tone variable puts the two dimensions into a single summary variable."

The third type is sentiment features. We first experimented with the Wilson, Wiebe & Hoffmann (2005) subjectivity clue lexicon to identify sentiment features. However, we decided to use the sentiment labels provided by the LIWC sentiment lexicon. We found it provides more accurate results than we would have had otherwise. For the final type, subjectivity features, we did use the Wilson et al. (2005) subjectivity clue lexicon to identify the subjectivity type of tweets.

**Twitter-Specific Features** refer to characteristics unique to the Twitter platform, such as the length of a message and whether the text contains exclamation points or question marks. In addition, these features encompass the number of followers, number of people followed ("friends" on Twitter), and the number of tweets the user has authored in the past. Also included is the presence or not of URLs, mentions of other users, hashtags, and official account verification. We also considered a binary feature for tweets that share a URL as well as the title of the URL shared (i.e., the article title).

## 6 Experimental results

Our first goal was to determine whether a tweet contains an argument. We used a binary classification task in which each tweet was classified as either argumentative or not argumentative. Some previous research skipped this step (Feng and Hirst, 2011), while others used different types of classifiers to achieve a high level of accuracy (Reed and Moens, 2008; Palau and Moens, 2009).

In this study, we chose to classify tweets as either containing an argument or not. Our results confirm previous research showing that users do not frequently utilize Twitter as a debating platform (Smith, Zhu, Lerman & Kozareva, 2013). Most individuals use Twitter as a venue to spread information instead of using it as a platform through which to have conversations about controversial issues. People seem to be more interested in spreading information and links to webpages than in debating issues.

As a first step, we compared classifiers that have frequently been used in related work: Naïve Bayes

| Feature Set | Decision tree | | | SVM | | | NB | | |
|---|---|---|---|---|---|---|---|---|---|
| | Pre. | Rec. | $F_1$ | Pre. | Rec. | $F_1$ | Pre. | Rec. | $F_1$ |
| UNI (*Base*) | 72.5 | 69.4 | 66.3 | 81 | 78.5 | 77.3 | 69.7 | 67.3 | 63.9 |
| All features | 87.3 | 87.3 | 87.2 | 89.2 | 89.2 | **89.2** | 79.3 | 79.3 | 84.7 |

Table 3: Summary of the argument classification results in %

(NB) approaches as used in Teufel and Moens (2002), Support Vector Machines (SVM) as used in Liakata et al. (2012), and Decision Trees (J48) as used in Castillo, Mendoza, & Poblete (2011). We used the Weka data mining software as used in Hall et al. (2009) for all approaches.

Before training, all features were ranked according to their information gain observed in the training set. Features with information gain less than zero were excluded. All results were subject to 10-fold cross-validation. Since, for the most part, our data sets were unbalanced, we used the "Synthetic Minority Oversampling TEchnique" (SMOTE) approach (Chawla, Bowyer, Hall & Kegelmeyer, 2002). SMOTE is one of the most renowned approaches to solve the problem of unbalanced data. Its main function is to create new minority class examples by interpolating several minority class instances that lie together. After that, we randomized the data to overcome the problem of over-fitting the training data.

**Argument classification** Regarding our first goal of classifying tweets as argumentative or non-argumentative, Table 3 shows a summary of the classification results. The best overall performance was achieved using SVM, which resulted in a 89.2% $F_1$ score for all features compared to basic features, unigram model. We can see there is a significant improvement from just using the baseline model.

**Evidence type classification** our second goal was for evidence type classification, results across the training techniques were comparable; the best results were again achieved by using SVM, which resulted in a 78.6% F1 score. Table 4 shows a summary of the classification results. The best overall performance was achieved by combining all features.

In table 5, we computed Precision, Recall, and F1 scores with respect to the top-used three evidence types, employing one-vs-all classification problems for evaluation purposes. We chose the top-used evidence types since other types were too small and could have led to biased sample data. The results show that the SVM classifier achieved a $F_1$ macro-averaged score of 82.8%. As the table shows, the baseline outperformed Linguistic and Psychometric features. This was not expected. However, Basic features (N-gram) had very comparable results to those from combining all features. In other words, the combined features captured the characteristics of each class. This shows

| Feature Set | Decision tree | | | SVM | | | NB | | |
|---|---|---|---|---|---|---|---|---|---|
| | Pre. | Rec. | $F_1$ | Pre. | Rec. | $F_1$ | Pre. | Rec. | $F_1$ |
| UNI (*Base*) | 59.1 | 61.1 | 56.3 | 63.7 | 62.1 | 56.5 | 27.8 | 31.6 | 19.4 |
| All features | 76.8 | 77 | 76.9 | 78.5 | 79.5 | **78.6** | 62.4 | 59.4 | 52.5 |

Table 4: Summary of the evidence type classification results in %

| Feature Set | NEWS vs. All | | | BLOG vs. All | | | NO EVIDENCE vs. All | | | Macro Average F1 |
|---|---|---|---|---|---|---|---|---|---|---|
| | Pre. | Rec. | $F_1$ | Pre. | Rec. | $F_1$ | Pre. | Rec. | $F_1$ | |
| UNI (*Base*) | 76.8 | 74 | 73.9 | 67.3 | 64.4 | 63.5 | 78.5 | 68.7 | 65.6 | 67.6 |
| Basic Features | 842 | 81.3 | 81.3 | 85.2 | 83 | 82.9 | 80.1 | 75.5 | 74.4 | 79.5 |
| Psychometric Features | 62 | 61.7 | 57.9 | 64.6 | 63.7 | 63.5 | 59.2 | 58.9 | 58.6 | 60 |
| Linguistic Features | 65 | 65.3 | 64.2 | 69.1 | 69 | 69 | 63.1 | 62.6 | 62.4 | 65.2 |
| Twitter-Specific Features | 65.7 | 65.2 | 65 | 63.7 | 63.6 | 63.6 | 68.7 | 68.1 | 67.9 | 65.5 |
| All features | 84.4 | 84 | **84.1** | 86 | 85.2 | **85.2** | 79.3 | 79.3 | **79.3** | **82.8** |

Table 5: Summary of evidence type classification results using one-vs-all in %

that we can distinguish between classes using a concise set of features with equal performances.

## 6.1 Feature Analysis

The most informative features for the evidence type classification are shown in Table 6. There are different features that work for each class. For example, Twitter-specific features such as title, word count, and WPS are good indicators of the NEWS evidence type. One explanation for this is that people often include the title of a news article in the tweet with the URL, thereby engaging the aforementioned Twitter-specific features more fully.

Another example is that linguistic features like grammar and sentiments are essential for using the BLOG evidence type. The word "wrote," especially, appears often to refer to someone else's writing, as in the case of a blog. The use of the BLOG evidence type also seemed to correlate with emotional tone and negative emotions, which is a combination of positive and negative sentiment. This may suggest that users have strong negative opinions toward blog posts.

| Feature Set | All Features |
|---|---|
| NEWS vs. All | Word count, title, personal pronoun, common adverbs, WPS, "iphone", "nsa director" |
| BLOG vs. All | Emotional Tone, 1st person singular, negation, colon, conjunction, "wrote", negative emotions, "blog" |
| NO EVI-DENCE vs. All | Title, 1st person singular, colon, Impersonal pronouns, discrepancies, insight, differentiation (cognitive processes), period, adverb, positive emotion |

Table 6: Most informative features for combined features for evidence type classification

Concerning the NO EVIDENCE type, a combination of linguistic features and psychometric features best describe the classification type. Furthermore, in contrast with blogs, users not using any evidence tend to express more positive emotions. That may imply that they are more confident about their opinions. There are, however, mutual features used in both BLOG and NO EVIDENCE types as 1st person singular and colon. One explanation for this is that since blog posts are often written in a less formal, less evidence-based manner than news articles, they are comparable to tweets that lack

sufficient argumentative support. One further shared feature is that "title" appears frequently in both NEWS and NO EVIDENCE types. One explanation for this is that "title" has a high positive value in NEWS, which often involves highlighting the title of an article, while it has a high negative value in NO EVIDENCE since this type does not contain any titles of articles.

As Table 5 shows, "all features" outperforms other stand-alone features and "basic features," although "basic features" has a better performance than the other features. Table 7 shows the most informative feature for the argumentation classification task using the combined features and unigram features. We can see that first person singular is the strongest indication of arguments on Twitter, since the easiest way for users to express their opinions is by saying "I ...".

| Feature set | Features |
|---|---|
| Unigram | I'm, surveillance, love, I've, I'd, privacy, I'll, hope, wait, obama |
| All | 1st person singular, RT, personal pronouns, URL, function words, user mention, followers, auxiliary verbs, verb, analytic |

Table 7: Most informative features argumentation classification

## 7 Conclusions and future work

In this paper, we have presented a novel task for automatically classifying argumentation on social media for users discussing controversial topics like the recent FBI and Apple encryption debate. We classified six types of evidence people use in their tweets to support their arguments. This classification can help predict how arguments are supported. We have built a gold standard data set of 3000 tweets from the recent encryption debate. We find that Support Vector Machines (SVM) classifiers trained with n-grams and other features capture the different types of evidence used in social media and demonstrate significant improvement over the unigram baseline, achieving a macro-averaged F1 score of 82.8 %.

One consideration for future work is classifying the stance of tweets by using machine learning techniques to understand a user's viewpoint and opinions about a debate. Another consideration for future work is to explore other evidence types that may not be presented in our data.

## Acknowledgments

We would like to thank Andrew Marturano and Amy Chen for assisting us in the annotation process.

## References


Agichtein, E., Castillo, C., Donato, D., Gionis, A., & Mishne, G. (2008, February). Finding high-quality content in social media. In *Proceedings of the 2008 International Conference on Web Search and Data Mining* (pp. 183-194). ACM.

Ashley, K. D., & Walker, V. R. (2013). From InformaNon Retrieval (IR) to Argument Retrieval (AR) for Legal Cases: Report on a Baseline Study.

Cabrio, E., & Villata, S. (2012, July). Combining textual entailment and argumentation theory for supporting online debates interactions. In *Proceedings of the 50th Annual Meeting of the Association for Computational Linguistics: Short Papers-Volume 2* (pp. 208-212). Association for Computational Linguistics.

Castillo, C., Mendoza, M., & Poblete, B. (2011, March). Information credibility on twitter. In *Proceedings of the 20th international conference on World wide web* (pp. 675-684). ACM.

Chawla, N. V., Bowyer, K. W., Hall, L. O., & Kegelmeyer, W. P. (2002). SMOTE: synthetic minority over-sampling technique. *Journal of artificial intelligence research*, 321-357.

Davis, C. A., Varol, O., Ferrara, E., Flammini, A., & Menczer, F. (2016, April). BotOrNot: A System to Evaluate Social Bots. In *Proceedings of the 25th International Conference Companion on World Wide Web* (pp. 273-274). International World Wide Web Conferences Steering Committee.

Etlinger, S., & Amand, W. (2012, February). Crimson Hexagon [Program documentation]. Retrieved April, 2016, from http://www.crimsonhexagon.com/wp-co tent/uploads/2012/02/CrimsonHexagon_Altimeter_W ebinar_111611.pdf

Feng, V. W., & Hirst, G. (2011, June). Classifying arguments by scheme. In *Proceedings of the 49th Annual Meeting of the Association for Computational Linguistics: Human Language Technologies-Volume 1* (pp. 987-996). Association for Computational Linguistics.

Freeley, A., & Steinberg, D. (2013). *Argumentation and debate*. Cengage Learning.

Green, N., Ashley, K., Litman, D., Reed, C., & Walker, V. (2014). *Proceedings of the First Workshop on Argumentation Mining*. Baltimore, MD: Association for Computational Linguistics.

Gruzd, A., & Goertzen, M. (2013, January). Wired academia: Why social science scholars are using social media. In *System Sciences (HICSS), 2013 46th Hawaii International Conference on* (pp. 3332-3341). IEEE.

Habernal, I., Eckle-Kohler, J., & Gurevych, I. (2014, July). Argumentation Mining on the Web from Information Seeking Perspective. In *ArgNLP*.

Hachey, B., & Grover, C. (2005, March). Sequence modelling for sentence classification in a legal summarisation system. In *Proceedings of the 2005 ACM symposium on Applied computing* (pp. 292-296). ACM.

Hall, M., Frank, E., Holmes, G., Pfahringer, B., Reutemann, P., & Witten, I. H. (2009). The WEKA data mining software: an update. *ACM SIGKDD explorations newsletter, 11*(1), 10-18.

Interpreting LIWC Output. Retrieved April 17, 2016, from http://liwc.wpengine.com/interpreting-liwc-output/

Liakata, M., Saha, S., Dobnik, S., Batchelor, C., & Rebholz-Schuhmann, D. (2012). Automatic recognition of conceptualization zones in scientific articles and two life science applications. *Bioinformatics, 28*(7), 991-1000.

Llewellyn, C., Grover, C., Oberlander, J., & Klein, E. (2014). Re-using an Argument Corpus to Aid in the Curation of Social Media Collections. In *LREC* (pp. 462-468).

Mochales, R., & Ieven, A. (2009, June). Creating an argumentation corpus: do theories apply to real arguments?: a case study on the legal argumentation of the ECHR. In *Proceedings of the 12th International Conference on Artificial Intelligence and Law* (pp. 21-30). ACM.

Palau, R. M., & Moens, M. F. (2009, June). Argumentation mining: the detection, classification and structure of arguments in text. In *Proceedings of the 12th international conference on artificial intelligence and law* (pp. 98-107). ACM.

Park, J., & Cardie, C. (2014, June). Identifying appropriate support for propositions in online user comments. In *Proceedings of the First Workshop on Argumentation Mining* (pp. 29-38).

Pennebaker, J. W. (1997). Writing about emotional experiences as a therapeutic process. *Psychological science, 8*(3), 162-166.

Pennebaker, J. W., & Francis, M. E. (1996). Cognitive, emotional, and language processes in disclosure. *Cognition & Emotion, 10*(6), 601-626.

Procter, R., Vis, F., & Voss, A. (2013). Reading the riots on Twitter: methodological innovation for the analysis of big data. *International journal of social research methodology, 16*(3), 197-214.

Reed, C., & Rowe, G. (2004). Araucaria: Software for argument analysis, diagramming and representation. *International Journal on Artificial Intelligence Tools, 13*(04), 961-979.

Rieke, R. D., & Sillars, M. O. (1984). *Argumentation and the decision making process*. Addison-Wesley Longman.

Rinott, R., Dankin, L., Alzate, C., Khapra, M. M., Aharoni, E., & Slonim, N. (2015, September). Show Me Your Evidence–an Automatic Method for Context Dependent Evidence Detection. In *Proceedings of the 2015 Conference on Empirical Methods in NLP (EMNLP), Lisbon, Portugal* (pp. 17-21).

Rosenthal, S., & McKeown, K. (2012, September). Detecting opinionated claims in online discussions. In *Semantic Computing (ICSC), 2012 IEEE Sixth International Conference on* (pp. 30-37). IEEE.

Schneider, J., & Wyner, A. (2012). Identifying Consumers' Arguments in Text. In *SWAIE* (pp. 31-42).

Schneider, J., Samp, K., Passant, A., & Decker, S. (2013, February). Arguments about deletion: How experience improves the acceptability of arguments in ad-hoc online task groups. In *Proceedings of the 2013 conference on Computer supported cooperative work* (pp. 1069-1080). ACM.

Smith, L. M., Zhu, L., Lerman, K., & Kozareva, Z. (2013, September). The role of social media in the discussion of controversial topics. In *Social Computing (SocialCom), 2013 International Conference on* (pp. 236-243). IEEE.

Stab, C., & Gurevych, I. (2014a). Annotating Argument Components and Relations in Persuasive Essays. In *COLING* (pp. 1501-1510).

Stab, C., & Gurevych, I. (2014b). Identifying Argumentative Discourse Structures in Persuasive Essays. In *EMNLP* (pp. 46-56).

Teufel, S., & Kan, M. Y. (2011). *Robust argumentative zoning for sensemaking in scholarly documents* (pp. 154-170). Springer Berlin Heidelberg.

Teufel, S., & Moens, M. (2002). Summarizing scientific articles: experiments with relevance and rhetorical status. *Computational linguistics, 28*(4), 409-445.

Toulmin, S. E. (2003). *The uses of argument*. Cambridge University Press.

Villalba, M. P. G., & Saint-Dizier, P. (2012). Some Facets of Argument Mining for Opinion Analysis. *COMMA, 245*, 23-34.

Walton, D., Reed, C., & Macagno, F. (2008). *Argumentation schemes*. Cambridge University Press.

Wilson, T., Wiebe, J., & Hoffmann, P. (2005, October). Recognizing contextual polarity in phrase-level sentiment analysis. In *Proceedings of the conference on human language technology and empirical methods in natural language processing* (pp. 347-354). Association for Computational Linguistics.

Wyner, A., Schneider, J., Atkinson, K., & Bench-Capon, T. J. (2012). Semi-Automated Argumentative Analysis of Online Product Reviews. *COMMA, 245*, 43-50.

## Appendix A. Feature types used in our Model

| Type | Feature | Description |
|---|---|---|
| **Basic Features** | Unigram | Word count for each single word that appears in the tweet |
| | Bigram | Word count for each two words that appears in the tweet |
| **Psychometrics Features** | Perceptual process | Percentage of words that refers to multiple sensory and perceptual dimensions associated with the five senses. |
| | Biological process | Percentage of words related to body, health, sexual and Ingestion |
| | Core Drives and Needs | Percentage of words related to personal drives as power, achievement, reward and risk |
| | Cognitive Process-es | Percentage of words related to causation, discrepancy, tentative, certainty, inhibition and inclusive. |
| | Personal Concerns | Percentage of words related to work, leisure, money, death, home and religion |
| | Social Words | Percentage of words that are related to family and friends |
| **Linguistic Features** | Analytical Think-ing | Percentage of words that captures the degree to which people use words that suggest formal, logical, and hierarchical thinking patterns |
| | Clout | Percentage of words related to the relative social status, confidence, or leadership that people display through there writing or talking. |
| | Authenticity | Percentage of words that reveals people in an authentic or honest way, they are more personal, humble, and vulnerable |
| | Emotional Tone | Percentage of words related to the emotional tone of the writer which is a combination of both positive emotion and negative emotion dimensions. |
| | Informal Speech | Percentage of words related to informal language markers as assents, fillers and swears words |
| | Time Orientation | Percentage of words that refer to Past focus, present focus and future focus. |
| | Grammatical | Percentage of words that refer to personal pronouns, impersonal pronouns, articles, prepositions, auxiliary verbs, common adverbs, punctuation |
| | Positive emotion | Percentage of positive words in a sentence |
| | Negative emotion | Percentage of negative words in a sentence |
| | Subjectivity type | Subjectivity type derived by Wilson et al. (2005) lexicon |
| | Punctuation | Percentage of punctuation in text including periods, commas, colons, semicolons etc. |
| **Twitter-specific Features** | RT | 1.0 if the tweet is a retweet |
| | Title | 1.0 if the tweet contains a title to the article title |
| | Mention | 1.0 if the tweet contains a mention to another user '@' |
| | Verified account | 1.0 if the author has a 'verified' account |
| | URL | 1.0 if the tweet contains a link to a URL |
| | Followers | Number of people this author is following at posting time |
| | Following | Number of people following this author at posting time |
| | Posts | Total number of user's posts |
| | hashtag | 1.0 if the tweet contains a hashtag '#' |
| | WC | Word count of the tweet |
| | Words>6 letters | Count of words with more then six letters |
| | WPS | Count of words per sentence |
| | QMark | Percentage of words contains question mark |
| | Exclam | Percentage of words contains exclamation mark |

# Summarizing Multi-Party Argumentative Conversations in Reader Comment on News

**Emma Barker** and **Robert Gaizauskas**
Department of Computer Science
University of Sheffield
{e.barker, r.gaizauskas}@sheffield.ac.uk

## Abstract

Existing approaches to summarizing multi-party argumentative conversations in reader comment are extractive and fail to capture the argumentative nature of these conversations. Work on argument mining proposes schemes for identifying argument elements and relations in text but has not yet addressed how summaries might be generated from a global analysis of a conversation based on these schemes. In this paper we: (1) propose an issue-centred scheme for analysing and graphically representing argument in reader comment discussion in on-line news, and (2) show how summaries capturing the argumentative nature of reader comment can be generated from our graphical representation.

## 1  Introduction

A very common feature of on-line news is a reader comment facility that lets readers comment on news articles and on previous readers' comments. What emerges are *multi-party conversations*, typically argumentative, in which, for example, readers question, reject, extend, offer evidence for, explore the consequences of points made or reported in the original article or in earlier commenters' comments. See, e.g. *The Guardian* on-line.

One problem with such conversations is that they can rapidly grow to hundreds or thousands of comments. Few readers have the patience to wade through this much content, a task made all the more difficult by lack of explicit topical structure. A potential solution is to develop methods to summarize comment automatically, allowing readers to gain an overview of the conversation.

Various researchers have already proposed methods to automatically generate summaries of reader comment (Khabiri et al., 2011; Ma et al., 2012; Llewellyn et al., 2014). These authors adopt broadly similar approaches: first reader comments are topically clustered, then comments within clusters are ranked and finally one or more top-ranked comments are selected from each cluster, yielding an extractive summary. A major drawback of such summaries is that they fail to capture the essential argument-oriented nature of these multi-way conversations, since single comments taken from clusters do not reflect the argumentative structure of the conversation. I.e. such summaries do not identify the *issues* about which commenters are arguing, the alternative *viewpoints* commenters take on the issues or key *evidence* supporting one viewpoint or another, which a truly informative summary must do.

By contrast, researchers working on argument mining from social media, including reader comment and on-line debate, have articulated various schemes defining argument elements and relations in argumentative discourse (e.g. Ghosh et al. (2014), Habernal et al. (2014), Swanson et al. (2015)). If such elements and relations could be automatically extracted then they could potentially serve as a basis for generating a summary that better reflects the argumentative content of reader comment. Indeed, several of these authors have cited summarization as a motivating application for their work. However, to the best of our knowledge none have proposed how, given a formal analysis of an conversation in response to a news article, one might produce a summary of that conversation. This is a non-trivial issue.

In this paper we make two main contributions. First (Section 2) we present a light-weight analytical framework consisting of various argument elements and relations, specifically developed to



*Proceedings of the 3rd Workshop on Argument Mining*, pages 12–20,
Berlin, Germany, August 7-12, 2016. ©2016 Association for Computational Linguistics

capture argument in reader comments and news and we show, via an example, how an analysis using this framework may be graphically represented. Secondly (Section 3), we make proposals for how summaries that capture the argument-oriented character of reader comment conversations could be derived from the graphical representation of the argument structure of a set of comments and the article, as presented in Section 2.

## 2 A Framework for Characterising Argument in Comment on News

### 2.1 Issues, Viewpoints and Assertions

From an idealised perspective, commenters address *issues*, hold *viewpoints* on issues and make *assertions*, which serve many purposes including directly expressing a viewpoint and providing evidence for an assertion (or viewpoint). Of course reader comments may also have other functions, e.g. expressing emotions or making jokes, but here we are primarily interested in their argumentative content. We expand on these terms as follows[1]:

**Assertions**  A comment typically comprises one or more assertions – propositions that the commenter puts forward and believes to be true. Each assertion has a particular role in the local discourse. We find relations between assertions made within a comment, between assertions made in different comments and between assertions in comments and assertions in the article. Key relations between assertions include: *rationale* (one provides evidence to support another); *agree/disagree* (one agrees or disagrees with another).

**Viewpoints**  Disagreement or contention between comments is a pervasive feature of reader comment and news. When an assertion made by one comment is contradicted by or contends i) an assertion expressed in another comment, or ii) an assertion reported in or entailed by something reported in the news article, each opposed assertion expresses a *viewpoint*. It follows that whether or not an assertion expresses a viewpoint is an emergent property of the discourse and only relative to the local discourse; it is not an inherent feature of the assertion itself.

---

[1]We would like to thank one our reviewers for pointing out close similarities between the framework we describe here and the IBIS framework of Kunz and Rittel (1970). In particular they share the ideas that issues are questions, are key primitive elements in a theory of argumentative discourse and emerge dynamically and recursively in argument.

**Issues**  Implicitly related to notion of viewpoint is that of *issue*. We can think of an issue as a question or problem to which there are two or more contending answers. The space of possible answers is the set of related but opposed viewpoints expressed in the comment set. I.e. an issue is that which a viewpoint is a viewpoint *on*.

Issues may be expressed in various ways, e.g. (1) via a "whether or not"-type expression, e.g. *whether or not to lower the drinking age*; (2) via a yes-no question, e.g. *Should Britain leave the EU?*; (3) via a "which X?"-type expression when there are more than two alternatives, e.g. *Which was the best film of 2015?*. However, issues are rarely explicitly articulated in reader comments or in the initial news article. Rather, as the dialogue evolves, a set of assertions made by commenters may indicate a space of alternative, opposed viewpoints, and an issue can then be recognised.

*Sub-issues* frequently emerge within the discussion of an issue, i.e. issues have a recursive nature. When evidence proposed as support for a viewpoint on an issue is contended, the two contending comments, which may in turn attract further comments, become viewpoints on a new issue, subordinate to the first. Sub-sub-issues may arise below sub-issues and so on.

### 2.2 A Graphical Representation

In the previous sub-section we defined the key concepts in our approach to analysing argument in comment on news. To demonstrate how they can be used to analyse a particular news article plus comment set we propose a graphical representation of the argument structure, with indices that anchor the representation in textual elements. A graphical approach is well-suited to the task of identifying structural relations between elements in a scheme, particularly when some of the elements are abstractions not themselves directly represented in the text (as is widely recognised in the argumentation community (Reed et al., 2007; Conklin and Begeman, 1988)).

We introduce our graphical representation via an example. Figure 1 shows an extract from a *Guardian* news article about the controversy surrounding a town council's decision to reduce the frequency of bin collection, and 11 (of 248) comments posted in response to the article. Figure 2 shows a partial depiction of the issues, viewpoints and rationales and argumentative structure in this

| | | | |
|---|---|---|---|
| [S0] **Rubbish?** [S1] **Bury council votes to collect wheelie bins just once every three weeks** ||||
| [S2] Locals fear the new move will lead to an increase in fly-tipping and attract foxes and vermin, but the council insists it will make the borough more environmentally friendly. [S3] Is it just a desperate cost cutting measure? . . . ||||
| [S4] A council in Greater Manchester is to be the first in England to start collecting wheelie bins only once every three weeks, scrapping the current fortnightly collection. [S5] The controversial decision was unanimously passed by councillors in Bury on Wednesday night, despite fears fly tipping would increase. [S6] One councillor who voted for the motion accused her opponents of "scaremongering" after they warned rubbish would pile up and attract vermin. [S7] Another argued the money saved could be spent on more social workers. ||||
| [S8] It affects the grey bins used for general household waste which can't be recycled . . . [S9] The Labour-run council claims the move is part of a strategy to turn Bury into a "zero waste borough", boost recycling and save money on landfill fees . . . [S10] Many residents feel it is simply a desperate cost saving measure, after the town hall was told to make more than £32m of cuts over the next two years . . . ||||

| Id | Poster | Reply | Comment |
|---|---|---|---|
| 1 | A | | I can't see how it won't attract rats and other vermin. I know some difficult decisions have to be made with cuts to funding, but this seems like a very poorly thought out idea. |
| 2 | B | 2 → 1 | Plenty of people use compost bins and have no trouble with rats or foxes. |
| 3 | C | 3 → 2 | If they are well-designed and well-managed- which is very easily accomplished. If 75% of this borough composted their waste at home then they could have their bins collected every six-weeks. It's amazing what doesn't need to be put into landfill. |
| 4 | D | 4 → 1 | It won't attract vermin if the rubbish is all in the bins. Is Bury going to provide larger bins for families or provide bins for kitchen and garden waste to cut down the amount that goes to landfill? Many people won't fill the bins in 3 weeks - even when there was 5 of us here, we would have just about managed. |
| 5 | E | 5 → 1 | Expect Bury to be knee deep in rubbish by Christmas it's a lame brained Labour idea and before long it'll be once a month collections. I'm not sure what the rubbish collectors will be doing if there are any. We are moving back to the Middle Ages, expect plague and pestilence. |
| 6 | F | | Are they completely crazy? What do they want a new Plague? |
| 7 | G | 7 → 6 | Interesting how you suggest that someone else is completely crazy, and then talk about a new plague. |
| 8 | H | 8 → 7 | Do you think this is a good idea? We struggle with fortnightly collection. This is tantamount to a dereliction of duty. What are taxpayers paying for? I doubt anyone knew of this before casting their vote. |
| 9 | I | 9 → 8 | I think it is an excellent idea. We have fortnightly collection, and the bin is usually half full or less[family of 5].. Since 38 of the 51 council seats are held by Labour, it seems that people did vote for this. Does any party offer weekly collections? |
| 10 | G | 10 → 8 | I don't think it's a good idea. But..it won't cause a plague epidemic. |
| 11 | G | 11 → 9 | I live by myself, so my bin is going to be smaller ..but I probably have more bin-space-per-person. And I recycle everything I can possibly recycle, and make sure nothing slips through the net. Yet I almost fill my bin with food waste and the odd bit of unrecyclable packaging in a fortnight.. How are you keeping your bin so empty? |

Figure 1: Part of a news article (top) and comments responding to it (bottom). Comments are taken from two threads in sequence but some intermediate comments have been omitted. Full article and comments at: `http://gu.com/p/4v2pb/sbl`.

example as a directed graph.

Nodes in the graph represent issues, viewpoints or assertions. Issues are distinguished by italics, e.g. *Is reducing bin collection to once every 3 weeks a good idea?* Nodes inside dashed boxes are implicit parts of the argument, i.e. are not directly expressed in the comments or article but are implied by them and allow other nodes which are explicit to be integrated into the overall argument structure. Nodes are labelled with abstract glosses of content explicitly or implicitly mentioned in the article, with repeated content represented only once. For nodes that are expressed or signalled in the news article or comments, a list of article sentence [sn] and comment [cn] indices is given, grounding the argument graph in the text.

Relations between nodes are indicated by directed edges in the graph. Orange edges indicate that the assertion at the tail of arrow is a viewpoint on the issue at the head, e.g. [less frequent collection] "will attract vermin" or "will not attract vermin". Blue edges indicate the assertion at the tail provides a rationale for the assertion at the head.

To create such a graph manually is a laborious process of iterative refinement: (1) Look for textual units expressing contention in the article. When spotted, formulate initial glosses of opposed viewpoints. (2) Read the comments in turn, by thread, looking for textual units expressing contention between comments or comments and the article. When spotted, formulate/refine glosses for opposed viewpoints (*will attract vermin/won't attract vermin*) and propose a potential issue. (3) Group similar and related comment together – requires re-reading earlier content to assess similarity and may result in refining earlier glosses of viewpoints and issues. (4) As rationale relations are recognised, add these in beneath viewpoint or

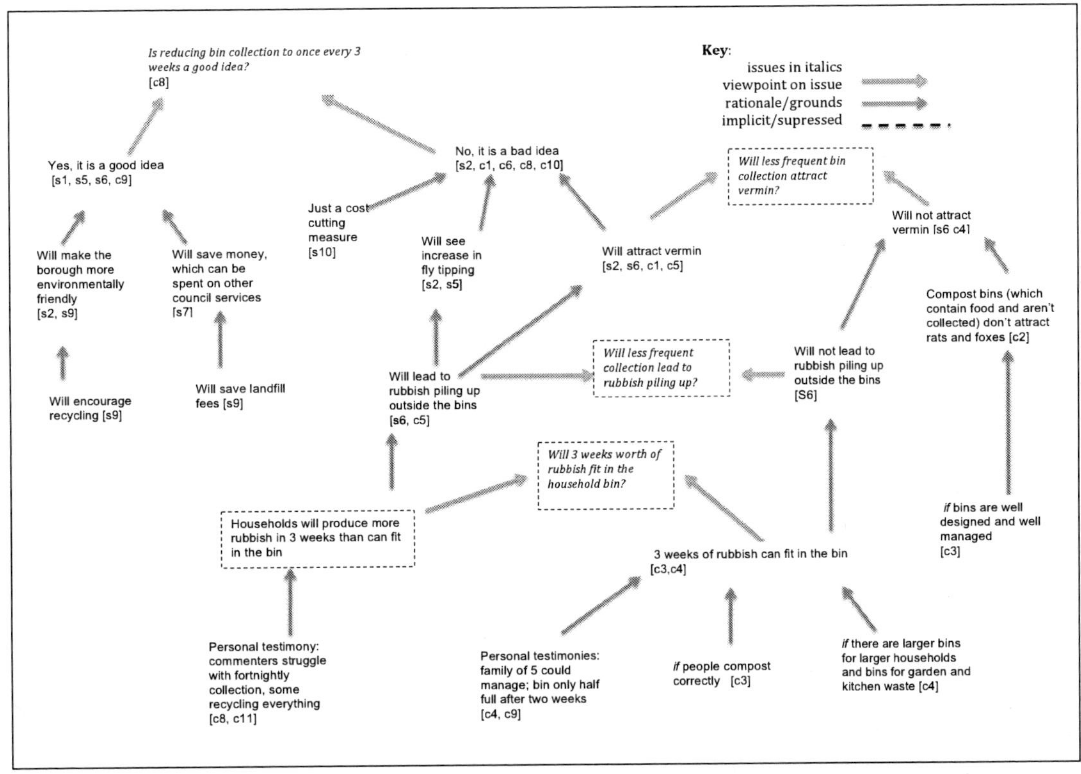


Figure 2: Argument graph for the article and comment subset shown in Figure 1

rationale nodes already in the graph. Implicit assertions or viewpoints may need to be added to capture the structure of the argument (e.g. *households will produce more rubbish in 3 weeks than can fit in the bin*). This should only be done when necessary to integrate parts of the argument that are explicit (i.e. not all implicit assertions need to be made explicit).

## 3 Generating Summaries from Argument Graphs

Argument graphs show the issues raised, viewpoints taken and rationales given across a (possibly very large) set of comments. Such a graph reveals the argumentative structure of the comment set in relation to the article, something that should be reflected in any argument-oriented summary. But clearly it contains far too much information to appear in a summary. How, then, can we use the graph structure and the information it contains to produce a summary?

The argument graph itself could be used as a *visual* presentation mechanism for the argumentative content of the comments and article. The user could, e.g., be allowed to expand or collapse nodes on demand, starting from the top-most issues(s) and viewpoints. While this is a promising line of work, here we focus on how to generate a *textual* summary from an argument graph. In the next subsection we discuss features of the graph one could take into account to generate a summary. Then we present two heuristic algorithms for generating summaries that exploit these features and illustrate the output of one of them by using it (manually) to produce a summary from an extended version of the argument graph presented in Figure 2. Finally, we compare that summary with a human summary of the same article and comments produced in a less prescriptive way.

### 3.1 Features for Summarization

Given an argument graph as presented in Section 2.2, a summarization algorithm could exploit both quantitative features of nodes in the graph as well as structural relations between nodes.

Features of *issue* nodes to use include:

**Issue Index Count** Number of comments or article sentences explicitly mentioning the issue.

| Issue Id | Textual Gloss of Issue | Issue Index Count | Max Issue Depth | Sub Node Count | Sub Issue Count | Total Index Count |
|---|---|---|---|---|---|---|
| 1 | Is reducing bin collection to once every 3 weeks a good idea? | 1 | 7 | 31 | 7 | 58 |
| 2 | Will less frequent bin collection attract vermin? | 0 | 6 | 21 | 5 | 38 |
| 3 | Will less frequent collection lead to rubbish piling up? | 0 | 4 | 15 | 3 | 24 |
| 4 | Will 3 weeks of rubbish fit in the bin? | 0 | 4 | 13 | 2 | 21 |
| 5 | Will reducing collection encourage recycling? | 0 | 3 | 10 | 2 | 13 |
| 6 | Can people recycle/compost more rubbish than they do? | 0 | 2 | 7 | 1 | 11 |
| 7 | Are vermin attracted by the type of rubbish in the black/grey bin? | 0 | 1 | 2 | 0 | 5 |
| 8 | Do people in flats have composting facilities? | 0 | 1 | 2 | 0 | 4 |

Table 1: Issues in Bin Collection Article and First 30 Comments

| Id | Issue | Textual Gloss of Viewpoint on Issue | VPt Index Count | Total Index Count | Evid. Count | Total Evid. Count | Max VPt Depth | Evid. Nodes Contd |
|---|---|---|---|---|---|---|---|---|
| 1 | 1 | No it is a bad idea | 6 | 21 | 3 | 7 | 4 | 4 |
| 2 | 1 | Yes it is a good idea | 4 | 14 | 3 | 7 | 4 | 2 |
| 3 | 2 | Will attract vermin | 4 | 12 | 2 | 4 | 3 | 3 |
| 4 | 2 | Will not attract vermin | 3 | 19 | 3 | 10 | 5 | 4 |
| 5 | 3 | Will lead to rubbish piling up | 2 | 5 | 1 | 2 | 2 | 1 |
| 6 | 3 | Will not lead to rubbish piling up | 1 | 12 | 1 | 6 | 4 | 2 |
| 7 | 4 | 3 weeks of rubbish can fit in the bin | 2 | 11 | 3 | 5 | 3 | 1 |
| 8 | 4 | 3 weeks of rubbish cannot fit in the bin | 0 | 3 | 1 | 1 | 1 | 0 |
| 9 | 5 | Reducing collection will encourage recycling | 1 | 6 | 2 | 3 | 2 | 1 |
| 10 | 5 | Reducing collection will not encourage recycling | 0 | 5 | 1 | 3 | 2 | 2 |
| 11 | 6 | People don't recycle/compost everything they can | 3 | 4 | 1 | 2 | 1 | 0 |
| 12 | 6 | People recycle/compost everything they can already | 1 | 5 | 2 | 2 | 1 | 1 |
| 13 | 7 | Black/grey bins contain the type of rubbish that attracts vermin | 3 | 3 | 0 | 0 | 0 | 0 |
| 14 | 7 | Black/grey bins contain packaging that does not attract vermin | 2 | 2 | 0 | 0 | 0 | 0 |
| 15 | 8 | People in flats don't have composting facilities | 3 | 3 | 0 | 0 | 0 | 0 |
| 16 | 8 | People in flats have composting facilities | 1 | 1 | 0 | 0 | 0 | 0 |

Table 2: Viewpoints (VPts) in Bin Collection Article and First 30 Comments

**Maximum Issue Depth** Count of all levels below an issue.

**Sub-Node Count** Count of all viewpoint and rationale nodes below the issue node. including points of contention.

**Sub-Issue Count** Count of all issues below a given issue.

**Total Index Count** Count of all indices on the issue itself and all sub-nodes.

Maximum Issue Depth, together with the Sub-node Count give a broad indication of the structural character of the argument. A shallow depth score of say 2, with a high number of nodes suggest that there are lots of different reasons given for supporting or not supporting something, but no complex case given to explain or justify the support for these positions. Sub-issue Count is indicative of the degree of contention on an issue and Total Index Count indicates the volume of explicit comment relating to an issue, i.e. is an indication of the number of participants in the conversation saying things related to the issue. Table 1, which is meant to be indicative only, shows these counts for a version of the argument graph of Figure 2 extended to include 30 comments (two full threads).

Features of *viewpoint* nodes to use include:

**Viewpoint Index Count** Count of the indices of comments or article sentences that directly support the viewpoint.

**Viewpoint Total Index Count** Count of all indices on the viewpoint, both direct and indirect; i.e. indices on the viewpoint and indices on all rationale nodes supporting the high level viewpoint (excludes indices on nodes contending any of the lower level rationales).

**Evidence Count** Count of the number of rationale nodes directly below a viewpoint.

**Total Evidence Count** Count of all nodes playing a role in supporting the viewpoint.

**Maximum Viewpoint Depth** Count of the levels of rationale given below the viewpoint.

**Evidence Nodes Contended** Count of the number of direct contentions to rationales supporting a viewpoint.

Viewpoint Index Count shows the strength of direct support for a viewpoint. Viewpoint Total Index Count provides an indication of both direct support for the viewpoint and support for the supporting arguments. Together, Evidence Count, Total Evidence Count and Maximum Viewpoint Depth indicate the structural complexity and detail of the supporting case. Evidence Nodes Contended indicates the degree to which rationales for a viewpoint are contended by counter arguments. Table 2 shows these counts for the extended version of the argument graph shown in Figure 2.

Table 2 defines measures relating to the position and popularity of issue and viewpoint nodes in an argument graph. The same measures can be calculated for *evidence* nodes.

### 3.2   Algorithms for Summarization

The counts specified in the previous section together with the structure of the argument graph can be used in many different ways to generate summaries. Here we mention just two as an indication of the space of possibilities. [2]

**Simple Issue-oriented Summarizer**   One simple baseline is to list issues discussed, up to the summary length limit, ordered by whichever quantitative measure for issues is felt to best indicate significance. Choosing an ordering measure like Total Index Count places value on the number of commenters discussing the issue; choosing Sub-Node Count favours more elaborated arguments and Sub-Issue Count favours issues that give rise to more contention. In the example shown in Table 1 the various measures all correlate closely so the choice of which measure to use is arbitrary; however this need not always be the case.

---

[2] One important technical observation should be made In the example above the argument graph is a connected graph in which there is a unique issue node (the *root issue*): (1) to which all other nodes are connected either via viewpoint or rationale relations or via issues arising from contention of a rationale node otherwise related to the root issue, and (2) none of whose viewpoint nodes are rationales for other nodes in the argument. In Figure 2, e.g., while no issue node has a parent, the issue *Is reducing bin collection to once every 3 weeks a good idea?* is unique in that none of its viewpoint nodes is a rationale for any other node in the graph. In the general case, comment sets can give rise to multiple, unrelated root issues. We do not discuss such cases here, i.e. we assume the graph to be summarised is a connected graph with a single root issue. However, the algorithms discussed below could easily be extended to accommodate the more general case, e.g. by distributing the total summary length between each root-dominated sub-graph, possibly allowing "larger" sub-graphs, as determined by one of the measures above, a greater proportion of overall summary length.

---

**Algorithm 1** Single Issue Summarizer

**Require:** An argument graph $G$; issue $I$ in $G$; comparison functions $f_S(.,.)$, $f_E(.,.)$ for ordering viewpoint and rationale nodes respectively; a measure $Threshold_E$ on evidence nodes

1:   $Summary \leftarrow []$
2:   $Summary \mathrel{+}= I$
3:   $S \leftarrow$ list of the viewpoints on $I$ ordered by $f_S$
4:   **for each** viewpoint $s$ in $S$ **do**
5:      $Summary \mathrel{+}= s$
6:      $R_s \leftarrow$ list of rationales for $s$ ordered by $f_E$
7:      **for each** rationale node $r_s$ in $R_s$ **do**
8:         **if** $f_E(Threshold_E, r_s)$ **then**
9:            $Summary \mathrel{+}= r_s$
10:         **end if**
11:     **end for**
12: **end for**

---

**Simple Argument-Oriented Summarizer**   The simple issue-oriented approach ignores information about viewpoints and rationales and about which sub-issues relate to which specific dominating issues. A more interesting approach to summarization should take this into account. One way to do this is shown in Algorithm 1, which outlines the logic for selecting the content for inclusion in an argument-oriented summary of one issue. Given an argument graph and an issue, the algorithm starts by including the issue in the summary, then for each viewpoint on the issue adds that viewpoint in an order defined over some feature of viewpoints (e.g. Total Index Count). As each viewpoint is added, evidence nodes for the viewpoint are added, ordered by some node feature (e.g. Evidence Nodes Contended), provided their count on this feature exceeds a threshold.

Algorithm 1 only summarizes a single issue. It could be used to generate a high level summary of an argument graph by calling it with the root node. Or, it could be extended to cover more of the graph in various ways. For example, after line 9, when the decision to add an evidence node $r_s$ to the summary has been made, $r_s$ could be checked to see if it is a viewpoint on a issue, i.e. if it has been contended. If yes, it could be added to a list $SubI$ of sub-issues to report in the summary. After line 12, $SubI$ could be sorted by some measure of importance and, possibly, thresholded or truncated to shorten it. The algorithm

| **Summary 1** (97 words) Many commenters were unhappy with the less frequent collections; some were struggling already with the fortnightly collection and were concerned with vermin or overflowing bins. A few commenters, however, countered that black bins were for non-food waste that would not attract vermin. Other commenters thought fewer collections were manageable if people recycled their food waste, garden waste, and any other recycleable materials. Few commenters, however, pointed out the lack of composting facilities for those living in some areas or flats. The council should provide more education and services in these areas to encourage more people to recycle. | **Summary 2** (112 words) The central issue discussed was whether reducing bin collection to once every 3 weeks is a good idea. Some argued it was a bad idea because it would lead to vermin being attracted and to an increase in flying tipping. Others argued it was a good idea as it would save money that could be spent on other council services and would make the borough more environmentally. Whether the proposal would lead to vermin being attracted was debated. Some argued they would because the proposal would lead to rubbish piling up in the streets. Others argued it would not as the proposal would not lead to rubbish piling up in the streets. |
| --- | --- |

Figure 3: A human authored summary (Summary 1) and a potential automatic summmary (Summary 2) of the first 30 comments on the Bury Bin Collection Article

could then be called recursively on each of the issues in $SubI$ or $SubI$ could be returned and added to an agenda maintained by a higher level controlling algorithm, which calls Algorithm 1 iteratively on each of the issues in its agenda. Of course the summary must not exceed its length limit.

The algorithm only selects the content for inclusion in a summary and ignores details of how it is to be realised. A more or less mechanical surface realisation process could be used to generate a summary like that shown in Figure 3, Summary 2. In this summary for the extended argument graph underlying Tables 1 and 2, we assume the root issue has been summarised (sentences 1-3) and that one further issue (2) has also been chosen for inclusion using the sort of extension to the algorithm described in the last paragraph (sentences 4-6).

### 3.3 Comparison with Human Summaries

Figure 3 shows a human-authored summary of the first 30 comments on the bin collection article, created as part of a corpus of gold standard reader comment summaries (SENSEI Project, 2016). Annotators created the gold standard summaries using a novel 3 stage method: (1) each comment in the source set is annotated with a *label* (i.e. a mini-summary of the main points in the comment); (2) related labels are sorted into groups that the annotator believes will be helpful for writing an overview summary and a group label is produced to indicate common content in the group; (3) based on the analysis and annotations created in stages (1) and (2), an overview summary is written, which should identify the main points raised in the discussion, different views, areas of consensus, the proportion of comments addressing a topic or sharing a view, and strong feelings shown.

The human summary sentences shown above correspond very closely to elements in the graph-

ical representation of the same 30 comments and while the summary addresses only a subset of the graph nodes, it does not introduce any additional content. This is a promising, if weak, form of validation as it suggests that summaries read off our argument graph using the algorithm of the last section are very similar to those produced by humans, given only modest direction. Further comparison of our gold standard human summaries with graphical representations of the same source texts might provide additional insights into how to refine algorithms for summary content selection.

## 4   Related Work

In recent years various authors have begun work on argument mining in on-line discussion forums (e.g., Cabrio and Vilatta (2012); Boltužić and Šnajder (2014); Swanson et al. (2015)) and reader comment on news (e.g., Sobhani et al. (2015); Carstens and Toni (2015); Sardianos et al. (2015)). While sharing some features, such as allowing multiple participants to exchange views, make claims and supply supporting arguments, these two sources of argumentative discourse also exhibit notable differences. For instance, in on-line discussion forums such as *debatepedia.org* or *convinceme.net*, debates are topically organized or tagged with key words, e.g. *climate change*, and a debate is typically framed by a starting motion or question and an example of a supporting or counter statement (similar to our notion of issue and viewpoint). In reader comment this structured information is missing and the debate is framed solely by a document (the article), with issues, as we define them, rarely explicitly signalled in the article or comments. Thus, the task of structuring the debate by discovering the issues, which our framework addresses, is a challenge of particular importance for reader comment.

Many authors propose models of argumentation and associated annotation schemes, e.g. Ghosh et al. (2014), Swanson et al. (2015), Carstens and Toni (2015). These models/schemes specify a set of argumentative elements and relations between them and, as noted by Peldszus and Stede (2013), approaches to argument mining typically address the subtasks of identifying, classifying and relating argumentative discourse units (ADUs) according to the types of ADU and argumentative relation specified in whatever model/scheme has been adopted. Our framework too relies upon defining and operationalising the identification of similar argument elements and relations (viewpoints and rationales in our case). However, with the exception of Kunz and Rittel (1970) we are not aware of any argumentation model that puts the notion of issue in the form of a question at the centre of the model and organises argument elements and relations around it.

Aside from differences in the text type addressed (reader comment rather than on-line debate) and the prominence given to notion of issue in our anaytical framework, our principal difference to other work in argument mining is the task we focus on: summarization. Some authors have cited summarization as a motivating end-user task, e.g. Swanson et al. (2015) and Misra et al. (2015). However, both these works aim at summarising an argument on a single topic like "gun control" across multiple dialogues and do not address the summarization of single, multi-party argumentative conversations that may address multiple issues, such as those found in reader comments. To the best of our knowledge no one has addressed the form that an end-user overview summary of reader comment might take or how it might be generated from the abstract representation of an argument, as we do in this paper.

## 5   Discussion and Future Work

In this paper we have defined notions of *issue*, *viewpoint* and *assertion* as part of a framework for analysing argumentative conversations such as those that appear in response to news articles in on-line news. We introduced a graphical representation for representing these argument elements and relations between them, such as *viewpoint-on* holding between viewpoints and issues and *rationale-for* holding between assertions and viewpoints/other assertions. We also discussed how an argument graph can be used to generate summaries of argumentative conversations, proposing features that could be extracted from an argument graph to assist in selecting content to be summarised and sketching two basic summarization algorithms suggestive of the space of possible algorithms that could be developed.

We are fully aware that our analytical framework, graphical representation and proposals for summarization algorithms are theoretical preliminaries and, while grounded in extensive observation and analysis of data, need to be implemented and empirically evaluated to be validated. This forms the core of our current and future work. Specifically we need to further develop, implement and evaluate (1) methods for reliably extracting an argument graph from news articles and comments (2) summarization algorithms of the sort outlined above. Building argument graphs is the greater of these challenges and is perhaps best approached by factoring it into sub-tasks, such as *candidate assertion detection, argumentative relation detection* and *issue identification*. Candidate assertion detection involves segmenting the text into clauses that could play a role in the argument. Argumentative relation detection involves identifying various relations between candidate assertions, such as identity, disagreement or contradiction and evidence or support. Issue identification involves detecting a disagreement or contradiction relation between assertions and establishing sufficient supporting argumentation for the opposed assertions and/or repetition across multiple participants in the conversation to deem them an issue. Building components to carry out these sub-tasks is likely to require the creation of annotated resources for training and testing. Existing supervised learning techniques can then be brought to bear. As well as implementing our proposals, further work should be carried out to refine and validate our analytical framework, e.g., by getting multiple analysts to generate argument graphs for a corpus of comment sets.

While these challenges are substantial we believe the proposals made in this paper provide a realistic framework to progress work on summarization of multi-party argumentative conversations.

**Acknowledgements**   The authors would like to thank the European Commission for supporting this work, carried out as part of the FP7 SENSEI project, grant reference: FP7-ICT-610916.

## References

Filip Boltužić and Jan Šnajder. 2014. Back up your stance: Recognizing arguments in online discussions. In *Proceedings of the First Workshop on Argumentation Mining*, pages 49–58.

Elena Cabrio and Serena Villata. 2012. Combining textual entailment and argumentation theory for supporting online debates interactions. In *The 50th Annual Meeting of the Association for Computational Linguistics, Proceedings of the Conference*, pages 208–212.

Lucas Carstens and Francesca Toni. 2015. Towards relation based argumentation mining. In *Proceedings of the 2nd Workshop on Argumentation Mining*, pages 29–34, Denver, CO, June. Association for Computational Linguistics.

Jeff Conklin and Michael L. Begeman. 1988. gIBIS: A hypertext tool for exploratory policy discussion. *ACM Trans. Inf. Syst.*, 6(4):303–331.

Debanjan Ghosh, Smaranda Muresan, Nina Wacholder, Mark Aakhus, and Matthew Mitsui. 2014. Analyzing argumentative discourse units in online interactions. In *Proceedings of the First Workshop on Argumentation Mining*, pages 39–48.

Ivan Habernal, Judith Eckle-Kohler, and Iryna Gurevych. 2014. Argumentation mining on the web from information seeking perspective. In *Proceedings of the Workshop on Frontiers and Connections between Argumentation Theory and Natural Language Processing*, pages 26–39.

Elham Khabiri, James Caverlee, and Chiao-Fang Hsu. 2011. Summarizing user-contributed comments. In *Proceedings of The Fifth International AAAI Conference on Weblogs and Social Media (ICWSM-11)*, pages 534–537.

Werner Kunz and Horst W. J. Rittel. 1970. Issues as elements of information systems. Working Paper No. 131, Institute of Urban and Regional Development, Univ. of California, Berkeley, Calif.

Clare Llewellyn, Claire Grover, and Jon Oberlander. 2014. Summarizing newspaper comments. In *Proceedings of the Eighth International Conference on Weblogs and Social Media, ICWSM 2014*, pages 599–602.

Zongyang Ma, Aixin Sun, Quan Yuan, and Gao Cong. 2012. Topic-driven reader comments summarization. In *Proceedings of the 21st ACM international Conference on Information and Knowledge Management*, CIKM '12, pages 265–274.

Amita Misra, Pranav Anand, Jean E. Fox Tree, and Marilyn Walker. 2015. Using summarization to discover argument facets in online ideological dialog. In *Proceedings of the 2015 Conference of the North American Chapter of the Association for Computational Linguistics: Human Language Technologies*, pages 430–440.

Andreas Peldszus and Manfred Stede. 2013. From argument diagrams to argumentation mining in texts: A survey. *International Journal of Cognitive Informatics and Natural Intelligence (IJCINI)*, 7(1):1–31.

SENSEI Project. 2016. The SENSEI corpus of human summaries of reader comment conversations in online news. Available from: nlp.shef.ac.uk/sensei/.

Chris Reed, Douglas Walton, and Fabrizio Macagno. 2007. Argument diagramming in logic, law and artificial intelligence. *Knowledge Engineering Review*, 22(1):87–109.

Christos Sardianos, Ioannis Manousos Katakis, Georgios Petasis, and Vangelis Karkaletsis. 2015. Argument extraction from news. In *Proceedings of the 2nd Workshop on Argumentation Mining*, pages 56–66.

Parinaz Sobhani, Diana Inkpen, and Stan Matwin. 2015. From argumentation mining to stance classification. In *Proceedings of the 2nd Workshop on Argumentation Mining*, pages 67–77.

Reid Swanson, Brian Ecker, and Marilyn Walker. 2015. Argument mining: Extracting arguments from online dialogue. In *Proceedings of the SIGDIAL 2015 Conference*, pages 217–226.

# Argumentative texts and clause types

**Maria Becker, Alexis Palmer, and Anette Frank**
Leibniz ScienceCampus *Empirical Linguistics and Computational Language Modeling*
Department of Computational Linguistics, Heidelberg University
Institute of German Language, Mannheim
`{mbecker,palmer,frank}@cl.uni-heidelberg.de`

## Abstract

Argumentative texts have been thoroughly analyzed for their argumentative structure, and recent efforts aim at their automatic classification. This work investigates linguistic properties of argumentative texts and text passages in terms of their semantic clause types. We annotate argumentative texts with *Situation Entity* (SE) classes, which combine notions from lexical aspect (states, events) with genericity and habituality of clauses. We analyse the correlation of SE classes with argumentative text genres, components of argument structures, and some functions of those components. Our analysis reveals interesting relations between the distribution of SE types and the argumentative text genre, compared to other genres like fiction or report. We also see tendencies in the correlations between argument components (such as premises and conclusions) and SE types, as well as between argumentative functions (such as support and rebuttal) and SE types. The observed tendencies can be deployed for automatic recognition and fine-grained classification of argumentative text passages.

## 1 Introduction

In this study we annotate a corpus of short argumentative texts with semantic clause types drawn from work in theoretical linguistics on modes of discourse. The aim is to better understand the linguistic characteristics of argumentative text passages. Our study suggests that these clause types, as linguistic features of argumentative text passages, could be useful for automatic argument mining – for identifying argumentative regions of text, for identifying premises and conclusions/claims, or for classifying the argumentative functions served by premises.

Specifically, this is an empirical investigation of the semantic types of clauses found in **argumentative text passages**, using the inventory of clause types developed by Smith (2003) and extended in later work (Palmer et al., 2007; Friedrich and Palmer, 2014). **Situation entity (SE) types** describe how clauses behave in discourse, and as such they are aspectual rather than ontological categories. Individual clauses of text evoke different types of situations (for example, states, events, generics, or habituals), and the situations evoked in a text passage are linked to the text type of the passage. For more detail see Section 2. Furthermore, SE types are recognizable (and annotatable) through a combination of linguistic features of the clause and its main verb, and models have recently been released for their automatic classification (Friedrich et al., 2016).

Our approach is the first we know of to link clause type to argumentative structure, although features of the verb have been widely used in previous work for classifying argumentative vs. non-argumentative sentences. For example, Moens et al. (2007) include verb lemmas and modal auxiliaries as features, and Florou et al. (2013) find that, for Greek web texts related to public policy issues, tense and mood features of verbal constructions are helpful for determining the role of the sentences within argumentative structures.

Our analysis is performed on German texts. Taking the argumentative microtext corpus (Peldszus and Stede, 2015a) as a set of prototypical argumentative text passages, we annotated each clause with its SE type (Section 3).[1] In this way we are able to investigate which SE types are most prevalent in argumentative texts and, further, to link the clause

---

[1] The segmentation of microtexts into clauses is discussed in Section 3.2.

21

*Proceedings of the 3rd Workshop on Argument Mining*, pages 21–30,
Berlin, Germany, August 7-12, 2016. ©2016 Association for Computational Linguistics

type (via SE label) to the argumentation graphs provided with the microtext corpus (Section 4). We additionally provide SE annotations for a number of non-argumentative (or at least only partially argumentative) German texts, in order to contrast SE type distributions across these text types.

This annotation case study addresses the following questions:

1. Do argumentative text passages differ from non-argumentative text passages with respect to clause type?
2. Do particular clause types correlate with particular elements in the argumentation graphs?
3. Do particular clause types correlate with particular functions of argument components?

Recently, systems have been developed for automatically deriving full argumentative structures from text. Peldszus and Stede (2015b) present a system for automatic argument structure prediction, the first for the microtext corpus. The linguistic features used by the system include discourse connectives, lemmas and parts-of-speech, verb morphology, and dependency patterns. Stab and Gurevych (2016) develop an end-to-end argument structure parser for persuasive texts. The parser performs the entire task pipeline, including segmentation of texts into argumentative vs. non-argumentative components, using sequence labeling at the token level in order to accurately model sentences containing multiple argument components. The features used vary with the particular task, with structural, syntactic, lexical, and lexico-syntactic, as well as discourse connective, features.

None of these systems have investigated **semantic features from the perspective of the clause**. We propose, based on the outcomes from our annotation and analysis, that SE types are worth exploring as features for argument mining.

## 2 Theoretical background

The phrase *situation entity* refers to the fact that clauses of text evoke situations within a discourse. For example, the previous sentence describes two situations: (i) the meaning of *situation entity*, and (ii) what clauses of text do, in general. The second situation is embedded as part of the first. Notions related to SE type have been widely studied in theoretical linguistics (Vendler, 1957; Verkuyl, 1972; Dowty, 1979; Smith, 1991; Asher, 1993; Carlson and Pelletier, 1995, among others) and have

seen growing interest in computational linguistics (Siegel and McKeown, 2000; Zarcone and Lenci, 2008; Herbelot and Copestake, 2009; Reiter and Frank, 2010; Costa and Branco, 2012; Nedoluzhko, 2013; Friedrich and Pinkal, 2015, for example).

### 2.1 Situation entity types

We directly follow Friedrich and Palmer (2014) for the inventory of SE types, described below.

The inventory of SE types starts with states and events, including a subtype of events for attributional statements. REPORT-type clauses such as (3) do not necessarily refer to an actual event of speaking but rather indicate a source of information.

1. STATE (S) *Armin has brown eyes.*
2. EVENT (E) *Bonnie ate three tacos.*
3. REPORT (R) *The agency said applications had increased.*

Phenomena such as modality, negation, future tense, and conditionality, when coupled with an EVENT-type clause, cause a coercion to STATE. In brief, such phenomena refer to actual or potential states of the world rather than actual events. Several examples appear below.

- E → S: *Carlo should get the job.*
- E → S: *Darya did not answer.*
- E → S: *If he wins the race, …*

An important distinction for argumentative texts, as we will see, is between generic sentences and generalizing sentences, or habituals. While the former predicate over classes or kinds, the latter describe regularly-occurring events, such as habits of individuals.

4. GENERIC SENTENCE (GEN): *Birds can fly. / Scientific papers make arguments.*
5. GENERALIZING SENTENCE (GS): *Fei travels to India every year.*

The next category of SE types is broadly referred to as *Abstract Entities*. This type of clause presents semantic content in a manner that draws attention to its epistemic status. We focus primarily on a small subset of constructions - factive and propositional predicates with clausal complements. Of course a wide range of linguistic constructions can be used to convey such information, and to address them all would require a comprehensive treament of subjective language. In the examples below, the matrix clause is in both cases a STATE, and the embedded clause (in italics) is both an EVENT and either a FACT, PROPOSITION, or RE-SEMBLANCE-type situation entity. Note that in the RESEMBLANCE case, it is unclear whether or not the embedded event took place.

6. FACT (F): Georg knows that *Reza won the competition.*
7. PROPOSITION (P): Georg thinks that *Reza won the competition.*
8. RESEMBLANCE (RES): Reza looks like *he won the competition.*

The first sentence of this section, for example, would be segmented and labeled as shown below.

(i) The phrase *situation entity* refers to the fact [S]
(ii) that clauses of text evoke situations within a discourse. [F, GEN]

The first segment is a STATE, and the embedded clause is both a FACT, by virtue of being the complement clause following *the fact that*, and a GENERIC SENTENCE, by virtue of predicating over a class of entities (*clauses of text*).

Finally, the labels QUESTION and IMPERATIVE are added to allow complete annotation of texts. Although they fulfill important and varied rhetorical functions, neither of these clause types directly evoke situations.

9. QUESTION (Q): *Why do you torment me so?*
10. IMPERATIVE (IMP): *Listen to this.*

## 2.2 Discourse modes

The inventory of SE types is motivated by theoretical work (Smith, 2003; Smith, 2005) which aims to determine which specific linguistic features of text passages allow human readers to distinguish, e.g. narrative passages from argumentative passages. Smith identifies five **modes of discourse**: Narrative, Description, Report, Information, and Argument/Commentary. Each mode is linked to linguistic characteristics of the *clauses* which compose the passages.

The set of SE types outlined above allows a complete, comprehensive description of these five discourse modes. The discourse modes approach is related to that of Argumentative Zoning (Teufel, 2000; O'Seaghdha and Teufel, 2014), in which linguistic features of scientific texts are used to distinguish genre-specific types of text passages, such as Methods or Results. Going back to discourse modes, Smith's claim, supported by manual textual analysis, is that different modes show different characteristic distributions of SE types.

Previous work shows that this claim is supported at the level of genre (Palmer and Friedrich, 2014), taking genre as an approximation of discourse mode. This approximation is problematic, though, because texts of any genre are in fact composed of multiple text passages which instantiate different discourse modes. In this study we focus down to the level of the text passage, offering the first empirical analysis of argumentative text passages from the perspective of clause types. The analysis looks at German texts, both contrasting purely argumentative texts with mixed texts and, further, analyzing the correlations between SE annotations and argument structure graphs.

## 3 Data

In this section we describe the corpus of texts we annotate with SE types and the process used for annotating the texts. Section 3.3 presents the first step of the analysis, comparing the distribution of SE types in the argumentative microtexts to those for texts from other genres.

### 3.1 Argumentative microtext corpus

Our data includes the whole argumentative microtext corpus (Peldszus and Stede, 2015a) which consists of 112 German texts.[2] Each microtext is a short, dense argument written in response to a question on some potentially controversial topic (e.g. "Should intelligence services be regulated more tightly by parliament?"). The writers were asked to include a direct statement of their main claim as well as at least one objection to that claim. The texts, each of which contains roughly 5 argumentative segments (and no irrelevant segments), were first written in German and professionally translated into English.

An example text from the corpus appears in Table 1, segmented into **argumentative discourse units (ADUs)** as in the original corpus version.

The texts in the corpus are manually annotated according to a scheme based on Freeman's theory of the macro-structure of argumentation (Freeman, 1991; Freeman, 2011) for representing text-level argumentation structure. This scheme represents

---

[2]https://github.com/peldszus/arg-microtexts

| SE | German/English |
|----|-----------------|
| GS | Die Geheimdienst müssen dringend stärker vom Parlament kontrolliert werden,<br>*Intelligence services must urgently be regulated more tightly by parliament;* |
| S | das sollte jedem nach den Enthüllungen von Edward Snowden klar sein.<br>*this should be clear to everyone after the disclosures of Edward Snowden.* |
| S | Die betreffen zwar vor allem die britischen und amerikanischen Geheimdienste,<br>*Granted, those concern primarily the British and American intelligence services,* |
| GEN | aber mit denen arbeiten die Deutschen Dienste bekanntermaßen eng zusammen.<br>*but the German services evidently do collaborate with them closely.* |
| GS | Deren Werkzeuge, Daten und Knowhow wird schon lange zu unserer Überwachung genutzt.<br>*Their tools, data and expertise have been used to keep us under surveillance for a long time.* |

Table 1: Sample microtext (`micro_b005`), both German and English versions, with SE labels.

an **argument**, consisting of one conclusion and one or more premises, as a "hypothetical exchange" (Peldszus and Stede, 2013a) between the **proponent** and the **opponent**, who respectively defend or question a specific claim. Note that Peldszus and Stede (2013a) use the term "argument" to describe the complex of premises put forward in favor of a conclusion, while premises and conclusions are propositions expressed in the text.

The microtexts are segmented into "elementary units of argumentation" (sometimes called ADUs as above), which consist of either the conclusion or a single premise. Each ADU corresponds to a structural element in an argument graph (Figure 1). In these texts, **conclusions** are only associated with the proponent, but **premises** can be associated with either the proponent or the opponent.

Round nodes in the graph are proponent nodes (premises or conclusions) while square ones are opponent nodes (premises only). In addition, several different supporting and attacking moves (also called "argumentative functions" of a segment (Peldszus and Stede, 2013b)) are labelled and represented by the arcs connecting the nodes. The most frequent argumentative functions are:

- **support:** a premise supporting a conclusion
- **rebuttal:** a premise which attacks a conclusion or premise by challenging the acceptability of the proposition being attacked
- **undercut:** a premise which attacks by challenging the acceptability of an inference between two propositions

The argument graph for our sample text appears in Figure 1. Here we see that the second segment supports the conclusion (first segment), while the third segment undercuts segment two. This undercutting move itself is then undercut by the fourth segment (a proponent node), which is in turn supported by segment five.

## 3.2 Annotation process

The granularity of situation-evoking clauses is different from that of ADUs, requiring that the texts be re-segmented prior to SE annotation. Table 3 illustrates a microtext with more SE segments than ADUs. For segmentation we use DiscourseSegmenter (Sidarenka et al., 2015), a python package offering both rule-based and machine-learning based discourse segmenters.[3] After preprocessing texts with the Mate Tools,[4] we use DiscourseSegmenter's rule-based segmenter (`edseg`), which employs German-specific rules to determine the boundaries of elementary discourse units in texts. Because DiscourseSegmenter occasionally over-split segments, we did a small amount of post-processing. On average, one ADU contains 1.16 SE segments. Table 2 shows the number of segments of each type, as well as the distribution of both argument components and SE types over the segments.

In addition to labeling each segment with its SE type, we also annotate three important verb- or clause-level features: (a) lexical aspect (dynamic/stative) of the main verb, (b) whether the main referent of the clause is generic or non-

[3] `https://github.com/WladimirSidorenko/DiscourseSegmenter`

[4] `http://www.ims.uni-stuttgart.de/forschung/ressourcen/werkzeuge/matetools.html`

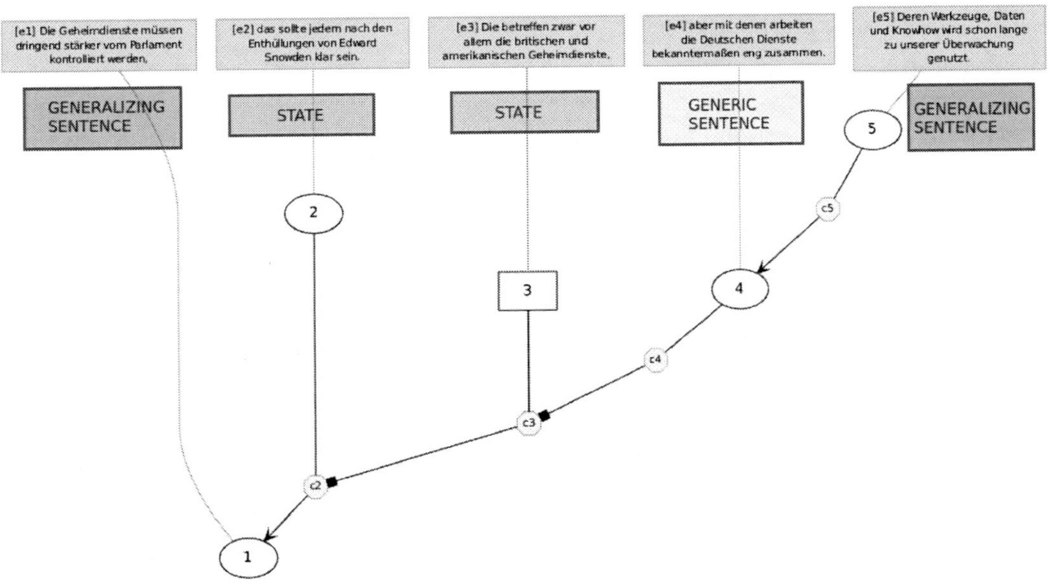



Figure 1: Argument graph for sample microtext (`micro_b005`), with SE labels added.

| #texts=112 | #ADUs=576 | | #SE Segs=668 | | | | | |
|---|---|---|---|---|---|---|---|---|
| | concl./premise | 112 / 464 | state | 212 (0.32) | generic | 320 (0.48) | question | 10 (0.01) |
| | prop./opp. | 451 / 125 | event | 57 (0.09) | generalizing | 67 (0.10) | resemblance | 2 (0.00) |

Table 2: Microtext corpus used for this analysis (percentages in brackets). ADUs are the argument component segments in the original data; SE Segs are situation entity segments.

| | German/English (+SE-Labels) |
|---|---|
| CONCL. | Alternative Heilpraktiken sollten genauso wie ärztliche Behandlungen bezuschusst werden, (GEN) <br> *Alternative treatments should be subsidized in the same way as conventional treatments,* |
| PREMISE | weil beide Wege zur Verhinderung, Minderung oder Heilung einer Krankheit führen könnten. (GEN) <br> *since both methods can lead to the prevention, mitigation or cure of an illness.* |
| PREMISE | Zudem müsste es im Sinne der Krankenkassen liegen, (GEN) \\ Naturheilpraktiken als ärztliche Behandlung anzuerkennen, (GEN) <br> *Besides it should be in the interest of the health insurers* \\ *to recognize alternative medicine as treatment,* |
| PREMISE | da eine Chance der Genesung besteht. (ST) <br> *since there is a chance of recovery.* |
| PREMISE | Es spielt dabei doch keine Rolle, (GS) \\ dass die Behandelnden nicht den Ärzte-Status" tragen. (GEN) <br> *It doesn't matter after all* \\ *that those who administer the treatment don't have 'doctor status'.* |

Table 3: Sample microtext (`micro_b010`), both German and English versions, with SE labels.

generic, and (c) whether the clause is habitual (a pattern of occurrences), episodic (a fixed number of occurrences), or static (an attribute, characteristic, or quality). Using these feature values in a decision tree has been shown to improve human agreement on the SE type annotation task (Friedrich and Palmer, 2014).

**Annotators and annotator training.** Each text was annotated by two trained (but novice) student annotators and one expert annotator. Following Mavridou et al. (2015), with a modified and translated version of an existing SE annotation manual,[5] student annotators were trained on a set of longer texts from different genres, automatically segmented as described above: fiction (47 segments), reports (42 segments), TED talks (50 seg-

<hr>

[5] www.coli.uni-saarland.de/projects/ sitent/page.php?id=resources

ments), and commentary (127 segments).

**Inter-annotator agreement.** We compute agreement separately for SE type and for the three features introduced above, as shown in Table 4 (reported as Cohen's Kappa). Numbers in brackets represent IAA for the training texts.

| level | Observed Agreement | Chance Agreement | Cohen's Kappa |
|---|---|---|---|
| Main Referent | 0.62 (0.76) | 0.50 (0.57) | 0.23 (0.45) |
| Aspect | 0.84 (0.91) | 0.50 (0.52) | 0.69 (0.81) |
| Habituality | 0.68 (0.70) | 0.26 (0.27) | 0.57 (0.58) |
| Situation Entity | 0.52 (0.61) | 0.21 (0.22) | 0.40 (0.50) |

Table 4: Inter-annotator agreement on microtexts (and training texts).

The table shows that the IAA for our training set is (slightly) better than the IAA we gained for the microtexts. The best results we obtained in the category Aspect (0.69 K), the worst in the category Main Referent (0.23 K).

**Error Analysis.** As reported by several studies (Peldszus and Stede, 2013b), the annotation of argumentative texts is a difficult task for humans. Our annotators often disagreed about the genericity of the Main Referent (binary: generic/non-generic). The SE-labels that caused most disagreement among the annotators are STATE vs. GENERIC SENTENCE (39% of all disagreements regarding SE-type), followed by STATE vs. GENERALIZING SENTENCE (22%).
This first annotation round suggests that we might benefit from:

1. adapting the SE annotation scheme for (purely) argumentative texts; and
2. training annotators specifically to deal with (purely) argumentative texts.

Given the relatively low agreement, for the analysis we produce a gold standard annotation by re-annotating all segments for which the two student annotators disagree about the SE type label. This third annotation is done by an expert annotator (one of the authors). For the segments which needed re-annotation, the expert annotator agreed with one of the two student annotators regarding SE label 87% of the time.

### 3.3 Distributions

One key claim of Smith (2003) is that text passages in different discourse modes have different

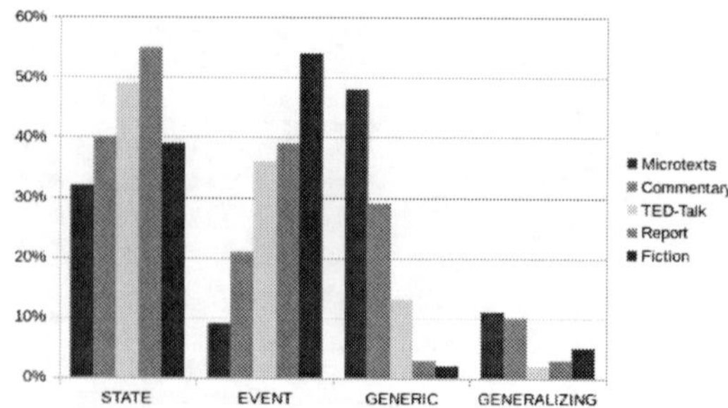


Figure 2: Distribution of SE types in all genres.

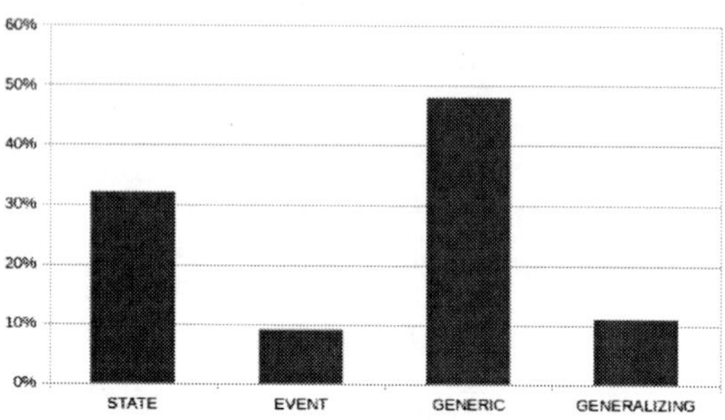


Figure 3: Distribution of SE types in microtexts.

predominant SE types. We investigate this claim by comparing the distribution of SE types in the microtext subcorpus to those in the training texts (see Figure 2). The microtexts (Figure 3), which can be described as 'purely' argumentative texts, are characterized by a high proportion of generic and generalizing sentences and very few events, while reports and talks, for example, contain a high proportion of states. Fiction is characterized by a high number of events. The genre commentary, which contains many argumentative passages but is not as 'purely' argumentative as the microtexts, is most likely to be comparable to the microtexts. This finding suggests that SE types could be helpful for modeling argumentative regions of text.

## 4 Analysis

**Extraction of argument graphs.** As a next step, we look at the correspondences between SE type labels and various aspects of the argument graph components (ADUs):

- conclusion vs. premise
- proponent premise vs. opponent premise
- support vs. attack by rebuttal vs. attack by undercut

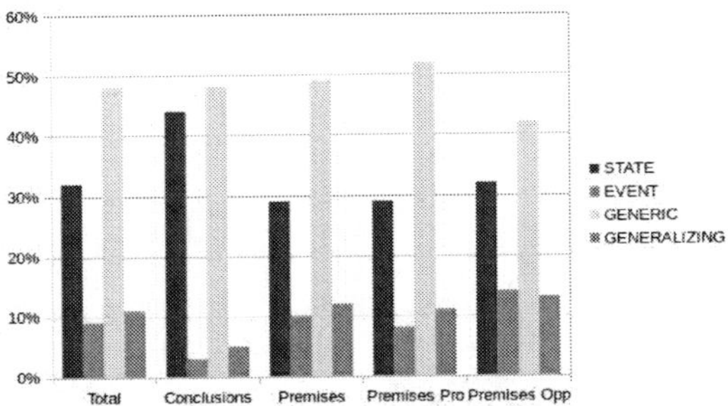

Figure 4: Correlations between SE types and argument components.

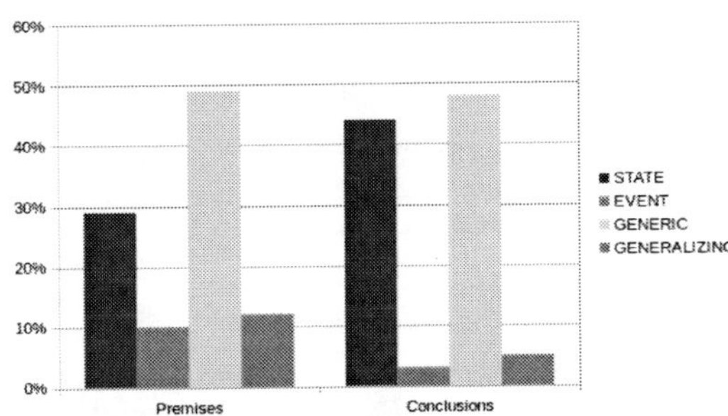

Figure 5: Correlations between SE types and conclusions/premises.

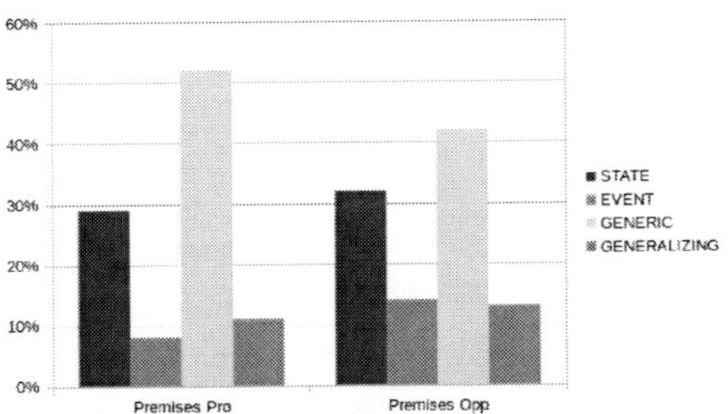

Figure 6: Correlations between SE types and proponent/opponent argument components.

For this analysis, we match the ADU segments extracted from the argument graphs to the situation segments produced by our own segmentation routine. Because the segments of the microtext corpus (ADUs) sometimes contain several situation segments, it can happen that several SE labels are assigned to one ADU. The results of these analyses are presented below.

### 4.1 Correlations between SE types and argument components

The mapping of the two sets of annotations reveals interesting correlations between SE types and argument components. Figure 4 shows the overall distribution of SE types over specific argument components. First, conclusions are almost exclusively either GENERIC SENTENCES (48%) or STATES (44%), while premises also consist of GENERALIZING SENTENCES (12%) and EVENTS (10%).

An example of a generic conclusion is given below:

GEN: *Nicht jeder sollte verpflichtet sein, den Rundfunkbeitrag zu bezahlen.* (Translation: *Not everyone should be obliged to pay the TV & radio licence.*)

Figure 5, where all premises are contrasted with all conclusions, shows this difference even more clearly. The STATE label is more frequent for conclusions (44%) than for premises (29%). On the other hand, premises contain 10% EVENT labels, while there are only 3% EVENT labels in the set of conclusions.

The SE types also correspond to the distinction between premises that support a conclusion ("pro"-label) and premises that attack a conclusion ("opp"-label), as Figure 6 indicates. First, proponent ADUs contain more GENERIC SENTENCE labels (52%) than opponent units (42%). Furthermore, the STATE and EVENT labels are more frequent within opponent units (32% and 14%), while they make up only 29% and 8% in proponent units.

To illustrate this, below we show an extract of an argument consisting of a stative opponent premise (in bold face) attacking a conclusion:

*Die Krankenkassen sollten Behandlungen beim Natur- oder Heilpraktiker nicht zahlen, **es sei denn der versprochene Effekt und dessen medizinischer Nutzen sind handfest nachgewiesen.*** (Translation: *Health insurance companies should not cover treatment in complementary medicine **unless the promised effect and its medical benefit have been concretely proven.***)

Of course, the corpus on which these investigations are carried out is quite small, and the phenomena we observe can be interpreted solely as tendencies. Nevertheless, we hypothesize that the prevalence of the GENERIC SENTENCE and GENERALIZING SENTENCE labels, as well as the absence (or rareness) of the EVENT label are indicators for

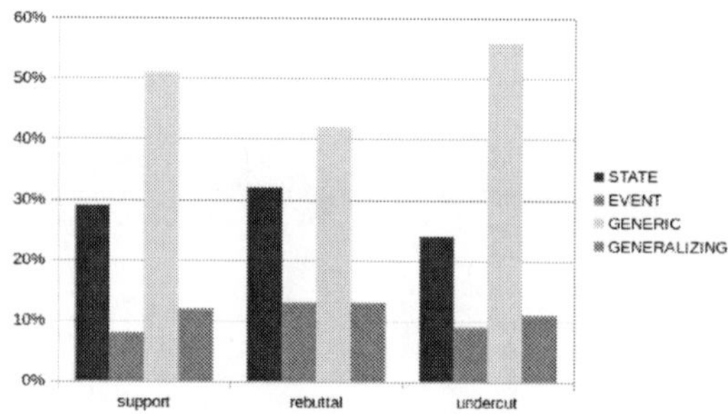

Figure 7: Correlations between SE types and argumentative functions

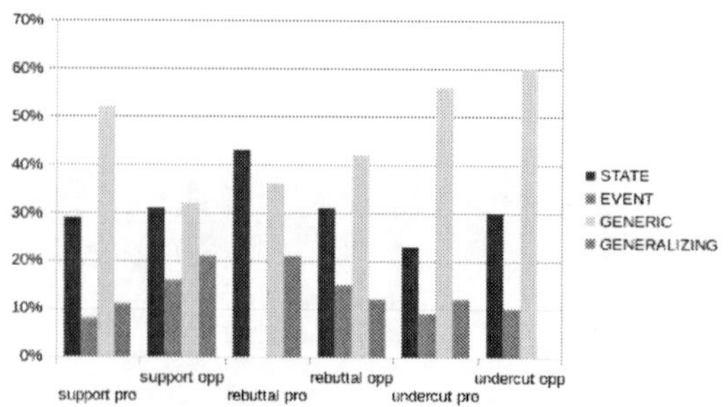

Figure 8: Correlations between SE types and argumentative functions with regard to pro/opp

argumentative text passages. Furthermore, such prevalences (or also rarenesses) can be interpreted as indicators for particular argument components such as proponent premises or conclusions.

## 4.2 Correlations between SE types and argumentative functions

There are also some interesting correlations between SE types and the argumentative functions of premises. In this study we focus on the three most frequent functions in our data, namely support, rebuttal and undercut. Table 5 gives an overview of their distribution within the microtexts.

| function | pro/opp | n |
|---|---|---|
| support | proponent | 250 |
| support | opponent | 13 |
| rebut | proponent | 12 |
| rebut | opponent | 96 |
| undercut | proponent | 51 |
| undercut | opponent | 12 |

Table 5: Distribution of argumentative functions within the microtexts.

It is worth mentioning that the rebuttals in the microtext corpus seem to differ slightly from all of the other segments in terms of the frequency of the label GENERIC SENTENCE. While this is by far the most frequent label in the microtexts (overall frequency of 48%), here it has only a frequency of 42%, followed by the label STATE with a frequency of 32% (see Figure 7). Rebuttals are less strongly biased toward GENERIC SENTENCES, compared to other argumentative functions. In contrast, supporting and undercutting moves are characterized by an above-average number of GENERIC SENTENCES

(51% and 56%).

To give a better idea of how rebuttals of different SE types look, below we show two examples, one a STATE and the other one GENERIC SENTENCE:

*Die Krankenkassen sollten Behandlungen beim Natur- oder Heilpraktiker nicht zahlen, **es sei denn der versprochene Effekt und dessen medizinischer Nutzen sind handfest nachgewiesen.*** (STATE)
(Translation: *Health insurance companies should not cover treatment in complementary medicine**unless the promised effect and its medical benefit have been concretely proven.***)

***Ja, seinen Müll immer ordentlich zu trennen ist nervig und mühselig.** [...] Aber immer noch wird in Deutschland viel zu viel Mll produziert.* (GENERIC SENTENCE)
(Translation: ***Yes, it's annoying and cumbersome to separate your rubbish properly all the time.** [...] But still Germany produces way too much rubbish.*)

Finally, Figure 8 shows the distribution of SE types among the different argumentative functions, separated into proponent and opponent premises.

According to this distribution, support moves, for example, can be distinguished by SE type into premises supporting the opponent and those supporting the proponent. While proponent support premises contain clearly more GENERIC SENTENCES (52%) than STATES (29%), the number of GENS and STATES within opponent support premises is almost equal (32% and 31%).

The following is a generic premise that supports the proponent, contrasted with a STATE premise supporting the opponent:

*Mit der BA-Arbeit kann man jedoch die Inter-
essen und die Fachkenntnisse besonders gut zeigen.
**Schlielich ist man nicht in jedem Fach sehr gut.***
(GENERIC SENTENCE)

(Translation: *With a BA dissertation one can,
however, demonstrate interests and subject matter
expertise particularly well. **After all one doesn't
excel in every subject.***)

*Es bleibt jedoch fragwürdig, ob die tatsächliche
Durchführung derartiger Kontrollen auch gle-
ichzeitig zur stärkeren Einhaltung von Gesetzen
fhrt, **denn jetztendlich liegt diese Entscheidung
in den Händen des jeweiligen Regierungschefs.***
(STATE)

(Translation: *Yet it remains questionable
whether the actual implementation of such supervision would at the same time lead to a stronger
observance of laws, **as ultimately this decision
is in the hands of the respective government
leaders.***)

These results suggest that SE types could be
helpful even for a finer-grained analysis of argumentative functions. Nonetheless we would reiter-
ate here that our results are based on a small dataset
only and need to be confirmed by further experiments. Therefore, annotations of larger texts with
a mixture of argumentative and non-argumentative
passages are already underway.

## 5 Conclusion

This paper presents an annotation study whose goal
is to dig into the usefulness of semantic clause types
(in the form of situation entity labels) for mining
argumentative passages and modeling argumentative regions of text. This is the first study to label
argumentative texts (microtexts, in this case) with
situation entity types at the clause level. We have
explored the correlation of SE classes with argumentative text genres, particularly in comparison
to non-argumentative texts. We have also looked at
the correlations between SE types and both specific
argument components (premise vs. conclusion, proponent vs. opponent) and specific argumentative
functions (support, rebuttal, undercut).

We do our analysis on German texts, but we fully
expect that the results should carry over to other
languages, as the link between SE type distribution
and discourse mode has been shown to hold cross-

linguistically. Due to the small dataset, our results
can be interpreted solely as tendencies which have
to be confirmed by more extensive studies in the
future. Nonetheless there is some evidence that
the observed tendencies can be deployed for automatic recognition and fine-grained classification of
argumentative text passages.

In addition to the ongoing annotation work
which will give us more data to analyze, we intend
to cross-match SE types with the newly-available
discourse structure annotations for the microtext
corpus (Stede et al., 2016). We would additionally
explore the role of modal verbs within this intersection of SE type and argument structure status.
The end goal of this investigation, of course, is to
deploy automatically-labeled SE types as features
for argument mining.

## Acknowledgments

We want to thank Michael Staniek for building
up the annotation tool and preprocessing the texts.
Sabrina Effenberger and Rebekka Sons we thank
for the annotations and their helpful feedback on
the annotation manual. We would also like to thank
the reviewers for their insightful comments and
suggestions on the paper.
This research is funded by the Leibniz Science-
Campus *Empirical Linguistics and Computational
Language Modeling*, supported by Leibniz Association grant no. SAS-2015-IDS-LWC and by the
Ministry of Science, Research, and Art of Baden-
Württemberg.

## References

Nicholas Asher. 1993. *Reference to Abstract objects
in Discourse*. Kluwer Academic Publishers.

Gregory N. Carlson and Francis Jeffry Pelletier, editors.
1995. *The Generic Book*. University of Chicago
Press.

Francisco Costa and António Branco. 2012. Aspectual type and temporal relation classification. In
*Proceedings of the 13th Conference of the European
Chapter of the Association for Computational Linguistics*, pages 266–275. Association for Computational Linguistics.

David Dowty. 1979. *Word Meaning and Montague
Grammar*. Reidel.

Eirini Florou, Stasinos Konstantopoulos, Antonis
Kukurikos, and Pythagoras Karampiperis. 2013. Argument extraction for supporting public policy formulation. In *Proceedings of the 7th Workshop on*

*Language Technology for Cultural Heritage, Social Sciences, and Humanities.*

James B. Freeman. 1991. *Dialectics and the Macrostructure of Argument*. Foris.

James B. Freeman. 2011. *Argument Structure: Representation and Theory*, volume 18 of *Argumentation Library*. Springer.

Annemarie Friedrich and Alexis Palmer. 2014. Situation entity annotation. In *Proceedings of the Linguistic Annotation Workshop VIII*.

Annemarie Friedrich and Manfred Pinkal. 2015. Discourse-sensitive Automatic Identification of Generic Expressions. In *Proceedings of the 53rd Annual Meeting of the Association for Computational Linguistics (ACL)*, Beijing, China, July.

Annemarie Friedrich, Alexis Palmer, and Manfred Pinkal. 2016. Situation entity types: automatic classification of clause-level aspect. In *Proceedings of ACL 2016*.

Aurelie Herbelot and Ann Copestake. 2009. Annotating genericity: How do humans decide? (A case study in ontology extraction). *Studies in Generative Grammar 101*, page 103.

Kleio-Isidora Mavridou, Annemarie Friedrich, Melissa Peate Sorensen, Alexis Palmer, and Manfred Pinkal. 2015. Linking discourse modes and situation entities in a cross-linguistic corpus study. In *Proceedings of the EMNLP Workshop LSDSem 2015: Linking Models of Lexical, Sentential and Discourse-level Semantics*.

Marie-Francine Moens, Erik Boiy, Raquel Mochales Palau, and Chris Reed. 2007. Automatic detection of arguments in legal texts. In *Proceedings of ICAIL 2007*.

Anna Nedoluzhko. 2013. Generic noun phrases and annotation of coreference and bridging relations in the Prague Dependency Treebank. In *Proceedings of the 7th Linguistic Annotation Workshop and Interoperability with Discourse*, pages 103–111.

Diarmuid O'Seaghdha and Simone Teufel. 2014. Unsupervised learning of rhetorical structure with untopic models. In *Proceedings of COLING*.

Alexis Palmer and Annemarie Friedrich. 2014. Genre distinctions and discourse modes: Text types differ in their situation type distributions. In *Proceedings of the Workshop on Frontiers and Connections between Argumentation Theory and NLP*.

Alexis Palmer, Elias Ponvert, Jason Baldridge, and Carlota Smith. 2007. A sequencing model for situation entity classification. In *Proceedings of ACL*.

Andreas Peldszus and Manfred Stede. 2013a. From argument diagrams to argumentation mining in texts: A survey. *International Journal of Cognitive Informatics and Natural Intelligence (IJCINI)*, 7(1):1–31.

Andreas Peldszus and Manfred Stede. 2013b. Ranking the annotators: An agreement study on argumentation structure. In *Proceedings of the 7th Linguistic Annotation Workshop and Interoperability with Discourse*, pages 196–204, Sofia, Bulgaria, August. Association for Computational Linguistics.

Andreas Peldszus and Manfred Stede. 2015a. An annotated corpus of argumentative microtexts. In *Proceedings of the First European Conference on Argumentation: Argumentation and Reasoned Action*.

Andreas Peldszus and Manfred Stede. 2015b. Joint prediction in MST-style discourse parsing for argumentation mining. In *Proceedings of EMNLP*.

Nils Reiter and Anette Frank. 2010. Identifying Generic Noun Phrases. In *Proceedings of the 48th Annual Meeting of the Association for Computational Linguistics*, pages 40–49, Uppsala, Sweden, July. Association for Computational Linguistics.

Uladzimir Sidarenka, Andreas Peldszus, and Manfred Stede. 2015. Discourse Segmentation of German Texts. *Journal for Language Technology and Computational Linguistics*, 30(1):71–98.

Eric V. Siegel and Kathleen R. McKeown. 2000. Learning methods to combine linguistic indicators: Improving aspectual classification and revealing linguistic insights. *Computational Linguistics*, 26(4):595–628.

Carlota S. Smith. 1991. *The Parameter of Aspect*. Kluwer.

Carlota S Smith. 2003. *Modes of discourse: The local structure of texts*, volume 103. Cambridge University Press.

Carlota S Smith. 2005. Aspectual entities and tense in discourse. In *Aspectual inquiries*, pages 223–237. Springer.

Christian Stab and Iryna Gurevych. 2016. Parsing argumentation structures in persuasive essays. arXiv preprint, under review, April.

Manfred Stede, Stergos Afantenos, Andreas Peldszus, Nicholas Asher, and Jeremy Perret. 2016. Parallel discourse annotations on a corpus of short texts. In *Proceedings of LREC*.

Simone Teufel. 2000. *Argumentative zoning: Information extraction from scientific text*. Ph.D. thesis, University of Edinburgh.

Zeno Vendler, 1957. *Linguistics in Philosophy*, chapter Verbs and Times, pages 97–121. Cornell University Press, Ithaca, New York.

H.J. Verkuyl. 1972. *On the Compositional Nature of the Aspects*. Reidel.

Alessandra Zarcone and Alessandro Lenci. 2008. Computational models of event type classification in context. In *Proceedings of LREC2008*.

# Contextual stance classification of opinions:
## A step towards enthymeme reconstruction in online reviews


**Pavithra Rajendran**
University of Liverpool

**Danushka Bollegala**
University of Liverpool

**Simon Parsons**
King's College London



## Abstract

Enthymemes, that are arguments with missing premises, are common in natural language text. They pose a challenge for the field of argument mining, which aims to extract arguments from such text. If we can detect whether a premise is missing in an argument, then we can either fill the missing premise from similar/related arguments, or discard such enthymemes altogether and focus on complete arguments. In this paper, we draw a connection between explicit vs. implicit opinion classification in reviews, and detecting arguments from enthymemes. For this purpose, we train a binary classifier to detect explicit vs. implicit opinions using a manually labelled dataset. Experimental results show that the proposed method can discriminate explicit opinions from implicit ones, thereby providing encouraging first step towards enthymeme detection in natural language texts.


## 1 Introduction

Argumentation has become an area of increasing study in artificial intelligence (Rahwan and Simari, 2009). Drawing on work from philosophy, which attempts to provide a realistic account of human reasoning (Toulmin, 1958; van Eemeren et al., 1996; Walton and Krabbe, 1995), researchers in artificial intelligence have developed computational models of this form of reasoning. A relatively new sub-field of argumentation is *argument mining* (Peldszus and Stede, 2013), which deals with the identification of arguments in text, with an eye to extracting these arguments for later processing, possibly using the tools developed in other areas of argumentation.

Examining arguments that are found in natural language texts quickly leads to the recognition that many such arguments are incomplete (Lippi and Torroni, 2015a). That is if you consider an argument to be a set of *premises* and a *conclusion* that follows from those premises, one or more of these elements can be missing in natural language texts. A premise is a statement that indicates support or reason for a conclusion. In the case where a premise is missing, such incomplete arguments are known as *enthymemes* (Walton, 2008). One classic example is given below.

***Major premise*** *All humans are mortal (unstated).*

***Minor premise*** *Socrates is human (stated).*

***Conclusion*** *Therefore, Socrates is mortal (stated).*

According to Walton, enthymemes can be completed with the help of common knowledge, echoing the idea from Aristotle that the missing premises in enthymemes can be left implicit in most settings if they represent familiar facts that will be known to those who encounter the enthymemes. Structured models from computational argumentation, which contain structures that mimic the syllogisms and argument schemes of philosophical argumentation will struggle to cope with enthymemes unless we can somehow provide the unstated information.

Several authors have already grappled with the problem of handling enthymemes and have represented shared common knowledge as a solution to reconstruct these enthymemes (Walton, 2008; Black and Hunter, 2012; Amgoud and Prade, 2012; Hosseini et al., 2014).

In this paper, we argue that there exists a close relationship between detecting whether a particular statement conveys an explicit or an implicit opinion, and whether there is a premise that supports the conclusion (resulting in a argument) or




*Proceedings of the 3rd Workshop on Argument Mining*, pages 31–39,
Berlin, Germany, August 7-12, 2016. ©2016 Association for Computational Linguistics

not (resulting in an enthymeme). For example, consider the following two statements $S_1$ and $S_2$:

$S_1 = $ *I am extremely disappointed with the room.*

$S_2 = $ *The room is small.*

Both $S_1$ and $S_2$ express a negative sentiment towards the room aspect of this hotel. In $S_1$, the stance of the reviewer (whether the reviewer is in favour or against the hotel) is explicitly stated by the phrase *extremely disappointed*. Consequently, we refer to $S_1$ as an *explicitly opinionated* statement about the room. However, to interpret $S_2$ as a negative opinion we must possess the knowledge that being small is often considered as negative with respect to hotel rooms, whereas being small could be positive with respect to some other entity such as a mobile phone. The stance of the reviewer is only implicitly conveyed in $S_2$. Consequently, we refer to $S_2$ as an *implicitly opinionated* statement about the room. Given the conclusion that this reviewer did not like this room (possibly explicitly indicated by a low rating given to the hotel), the explicitly opinionated statement $S_1$ would provide a premise forming an argument, whereas the implicitly opinionated statement $S_2$ would only form an enthymeme. Thus:

**Argument**

***Major premise*** *I am extremely disappointed with the room.*

***Conclusion*** *The reviewer is not in favour of the hotel.*

whereas:

**Enthymeme**

***Major premise*** *A small room is considered bad (unstated).*

***Minor premise*** *The room is small.*

***Conclusion*** *The reviewer is not in favour of the hotel.*

Our proposal for enthymeme detection via opinion classification is illustrated in Figure 1, and consists of the following two steps. This assumes a separate process to extract the ("predefined") conclusion, for example from the rating that the hotel is given.

**Step-1** Opinion structure extraction

    a. Extract statements that express *opinions* with the help of local sentiment (positive or negative) and discard the rest of the statements.

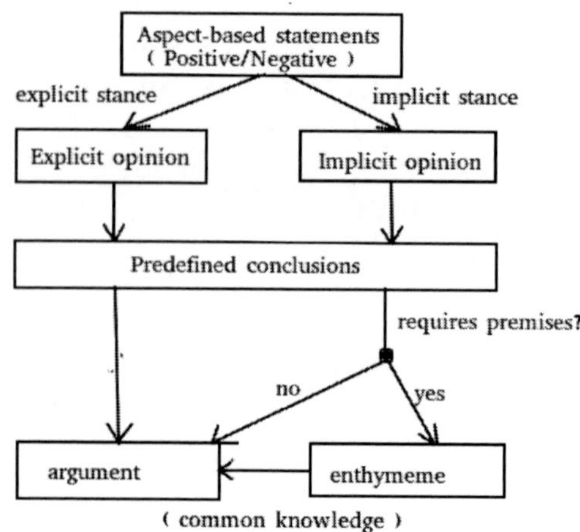


Figure 1: The relationship between explicit/implicit opinions and arguments/enthymemes.

    b. Perform an aspect-level analysis to obtain the aspects present in each statement and those statements that include an aspect are considered and the rest of the statements are discarded.

    c. Classify the *stance* of statements as being explicit or implicit.

**Step-2** Premise extraction

    a. Explicit opinions paired with the predefined conclusions can give us complete arguments.

    b. Implicit opinions paired with the predefined conclusions can either become arguments or enthymemes. Enthymemes require additional premises to complete the argument.

    c. Common knowledge can then be used to complete the argument.

This process uses both opinion mining and stance detection to extract arguments, but it still leaves us with enthymemes. Under some circumstances, it may be possible to combine explicit and implicit premises to complete enthymemes.

To see how this works, let us revisit our previous example. The explicitly opinionated statement *"I am extremely disappointed with the room"* can be used to complete an argument that has premise *"the rooms are small and dirty"*, which was extracted from the review, and a conclusion that *"The hotel is not favored"* which comes from the fact that the review has a low rating.

While developing this approach is our long-term goal, this paper has a much more limited focus. In particular we consider Step 1(c), and study the classification of opinions into those with explicit stance and those with implicit stance.

We focus on user reviews such as product reviews on Amazon.com, or hotel reviews on TripAdvisor.com. Such data has been extensively researched for sentiment classification tasks (Hu and Liu, 2004; Lazaridou et al., 2013). We build on this work, in particular, aspect-based approaches. In these approaches, sentiment classification is based around the detection of terms that denote *aspects* of the item being reviewed — the battery in the case of reviews of portable electronics, the room and the pool in the case of hotel reviews — and whether the sentiment expressed about these aspects is positive or negative.

Our contributions in this paper are as follows:

- As described above, we propose a two-step framework that identifies opinion structures in aspect-based statements which help in detecting enthymemes and reconstructing them.

- We manually annotated a dataset classifying opinionated statements to indicate whether the author's stance is explicitly or implicitly indicated.

- We use a supervised approach using the SVM classifier to automatically identify the opinion structures as *explicit* and *implicit* opinions using the $n$-grams, part of speech (POS) tags, SentiWordNet scores and noun-adjective patterns as features.

## 2  Related work

Argument mining is a relatively new area in the field of computational argumentation. It seeks to automatically identify arguments from natural language texts, often online texts, with the aim of helping to summarise or otherwise help in processing such texts. It is a task which, like many natural language processing tasks, varys greatly from domain to domain. A major part of the challenge lies in defining what we mean by an argument in unstructured texts found online. It is very difficult to extract properly formed arguments in online discussions and the absence of proper annotated corpora for automatic identification of these arguments is problematic.

According to Lippi and Torroni (2015a) who have made a survey of the various works carried out in argument mining so far with an emphasis on the different machine learning approaches used, the two main approaches in argument mining relate to the extraction of abstract arguments (Cabrio and Villata, 2012; Yaglikci and Torroni, 2014) and structured arguments.

Much recent work in extracting structured arguments has concentrated on extracting arguments pertaining to a specific domain such as online debates (Boltužić and Šnajder, 2014), user comments on blogs and forums (Ghosh et al., 2014; Park and Cardie, 2014), Twitter datasets (Llewellyn et al., 2014) and online product reviews (Wyner et al., 2012; Garcia-Villalba and Saint-Dizier, 2012). Each of these work target on identifying the kind of arguments that can be detected from a specific domain.

Ghosh et al. (2014) analyse target-callout pairs among user comments, which are further annotated as stance/rationale callouts. Boltuzic and Snaider (2014) identify argument structures that they propose can help in stance classification. Our focus is not to identify the stance but to use the stance and the context of the relevant opinion to help in detecting and reconstructing enthymemes present in a specific domain of online reviews.

Lippi and Torroni (2015b) address the domain-dependency of previous work by identifying claims that are domain-independent by focussing on rhetoric structures and not on the contextual information present in the claim.

Habernal et al. (2014) consider the context-independent problem using two different argument schemes and argues that the best scheme to use varies depending upon the data and problem to be solved. In this paper, we address a domain-dependent problem of identifying premises with the help of stance classification. We think that claim identification will not solve this problem, as online reviews are rich in descriptive texts that are mostly premises leading to a conclusion as to whether a product/service is good or bad.

There are a few papers that have concentrated on identifying enthymemes. Feng and

Hirst (2011) classify argumentation schemes using explicit premises and conclusion on the Araucaria dataset, which they propose to use to reconstruct enthymemes. Similar to (2011), Walton (2010) investigated how argumentation schemes can help in addressing enthymemes present in health product advertisements. Amgoud et al. (2015) propose a formal language approach to construct arguments from natural language texts that are mostly enthymemes. Their work is related to mined arguments from texts that can be represented using a logical language and our work could be useful for evaluating (Amgoud et al., 2015) on a real dataset. Unlike the above, our approach classifies stances which can identify enthymemes and implicit premises that are present in online reviews.

Research in opinion mining has started to understand the argumentative nature of opinionated texts (Wachsmuth et al., 2014a; Vincent and Winterstein, 2014). This growing interest to summarise what people write in online reviews and not just to identify the opinions is much of the motivation for our paper.

## 3 Method

### 3.1 Manual Annotation of Stance in Opinions

We started with the ArguAna corpus of hotel reviews from TripAdvisor.com (Wachsmuth et al., 2014b) and manually separated those statements that contained an aspect and those that did not. This process could potentially be carried out automatically using opinion mining tools, but since this information was available in the corpus, we decided to use it directly. We found that many of the individual statements in the corpus directly refer to certain aspects of the hotel or directly to the hotel itself. These were the statements we used for our study. The rest were discarded.[1]

Each statement in the corpus was previously annotated as positive, negative or objective (Wachsmuth et al., 2014b). Statements with a positive or negative sentiment were more opinion-oriented and hence we discarded the statements that were annotated as objective. A total of 180 reviews then gave us 784 opinions. Before we annotated the statements, we needed to define the possi-

ble (predefined) conclusions for the hotel reviews, and these were:

**Conclusion 1** The reviewer is in favor of an aspect of the hotel or the hotel itself.

**Conclusion 2** The reviewer is against an aspect of the hotel or the hotel itself.

We then annotated each of the 784 opinions with one of these conclusions. This was done to make the annotation procedure easier, since each opinion related to the conclusion forms either a complete argument or an enthymeme. During the annotation process, each opinion was annotated as either explicit or implicit based on the stance definitions given above. The annotation was carried out by a single person and the ambiguity in the annotation process was reduced by setting out what kind of statements constitute explicit opinions and how these differ from implicit opinions. These are as follows:

***General expressive cues*** Statements that explicitly express the reviewer's views about the hotel or aspects of the hotel. Example indicators are *disappointed, recommend, great*.

***Specific expressive cues*** Statements that point to conclusions being drawn but where the reasoning is specific to a particular domain and varies from domain to domain. Examples are *"small size batteries"* and *"rooms are small"*. Both represent different contextual notions, where the former suggests a positive conclusion about the battery and the latter suggests a negative conclusion about the room. Such premises need additional support.

***Event-based cues*** Statements that describe a situation or an incident faced by the reviewer and needs further explanation to understand what the reviewer is trying to imply.

Each statement in the first category (general expressive) is annotated as an explicit opinion and those that match either of the last two categories (specific expressive, event-based) were annotated as non-explicit opinions. The non-explicit opinions were further annotated as having a neutral or implicit stance. We found that there were statements that were both in favor of and against the hotel and we annotated such ambiguous statements as being neutral.

---

[1] The remaining statements could potentially be used, but it would require much deeper analysis in order to construct arguments that are relevant to the hotels. The criteria for our current work is to collect simpler argument structures that can be reconstructed easily, and so we postpone the study of the rest of the data from the reviews for future work.

| Explicit stance | Implicit stance |
| --- | --- |
| i would not choose this hotel again. | the combination of two side jets and one fixed head led to one finding the entire this bathroom flooded upon exiting the shower. |
| great location close to public transport and chinatown. | the pool was ludicrously small for such a large property, the sun loungers started to free up in the late afternoon. |
| best service ever | the rooms are pretentious and boring. |

Table 1: A few examples of statements from the hotel data that are annotated with explicit and implicit stances.

From the manually annotated data, 130 statements were explicit, 90 were neutral and the rest were implicit. In our experiments, we focussed on extracting the explicit opinions and implicit opinions and thus ignored the neutral ones. Table 1 shows examples of statements annotated as explicit and implicit.

As shown in Figure 1, explicit opinions with their appropriate conclusions can form complete arguments. This is not the case for implicit opinions. Implicit opinions with their appropriate conclusions may form complete arguments or they may require additional premises to entail the conclusion. In this latter case, the implicit opinion and conclusion form an enthymeme. As discussed above, we may be able to use related explicit opinions to complete enthymemes. When we look to do this, we find that the explicit opinions in our dataset fall into two categories:

**General** These explicit opinions are about an aspect category, which in general, can be related to several sub-level aspects within the category.

**Specific** These explicit opinions are about a specific aspect and hence can only be related to that particular aspect.

To illustrate the difference between the two kinds of explicit claim, let us consider three examples given below.

- A1 : "The front desk staffs completely ignored our complaints and did nothing to make our stay better". *(implicit)*

- A2 : "The front desk staff are worst". *(specific explicit)*

- A3 : "I am disappointed with the overall customer service!" *(general explicit)*

In this case, both the specific opinion A2: "The front desk staff are worst", and the general opinion A3: "I am disappointed with the overall customer service" will work to complete the argument because the aspect *front desk staff* of the specific explicit opinion A2 matches that of the implicit statement A1. However, if the implicit statement was about another aspect (say the room cleaning service), then A2 woud not match the aspect, whereas the more general statement A3 would.

Having sketched our overall approach to argument extraction and enthymeme completion, we turn to the main contribution of the paper — an exploration of stance classification on hotel review data, to demonstrate that Step 1(c) of our process is possible.

### 3.2 Learning a Stance Classifier

Since we wish to distinguish between explicit and implicit stances, we can consider the task as a binary classification problem. In this section we describe the features that we considered as input to a range of classifiers that we used on the problem. Section 4 describes the choice of classifiers that we used.

The following are a set of features that we used.

**Baseline** As a baseline comparison, statements containing words from a list of selected cues such as excellent, great, worst etc. are predicted as explicit and those that do not contain words present in the cue list are predicted as implicit. The criteria followed here is that the statement should contain atleast one cue word to be predicted as explicit. The ten most important cue words were considered.

**N-grams (Uni, Bi)** Unigrams (each word) and bigrams (successive pair of words).

**Part of Speech (POS)** The NLTK[2] tagger helps in tagging each word with its respective part of speech tag and we use the most common tags (noun, verb and adjective) present in the explicit opinions as features.

---

[2]Natural Language Toolkit, www.nltk.org

| Classifier | Explicit | Implicit |
|---|---|---|
| Logistic Regression | 0.44 | 0.86 |
| MultinomialNB | 0.27 | 0.85 |
| Linear SVM | **0.75** | **0.90** |

Table 2: F1-scores of 5-fold cross validation results performed with different classifiers. The bold figures are the highest in each column.

**Part of Speech (POS Bi)** As for POS, but we consider the adjacent pairs of part of speech tags as a feature.

**SentiWordNet score (senti)** We used the Senti-WordNet (Baccianella et al., 2010) lexical resource to assign scores for each word based on three sentiments i.e positive, negative and objective respectively. The positive, negative and objective scores sum up to 1. We use the individual lemmatized words in a statement as an input and obtain the scores for each of them. For each lemmatized word, we obtain the difference between their positive and negative score. We add up the computed scores for all the words present in a statement and average it which gives the overall statement score as a feature.

**Noun-Adjective patterns** Both the statements in general expression cues and specific expressions cues contain combinations of noun and adjective pairs. For every noun present in the text, each combination of adjective was considered as a noun-adjective pair feature.

In addition to these features, each token is paired with its *term frequency*, defined as:

$$\frac{number\ of\ occurrences\ of\ a\ token}{total\ number\ of\ tokens} \quad (1)$$

Thus rather than a statement containing several instances of a common term (like "the"), it will contain a single instance, plus the term frequency.

## 4 Experiments

Having covered the features we considered, this section describes the experimental setup and the results we obtained. We used the scikit-learn toolkit library to conduct three experiments.

### 4.1 Classifier

The first experiment was to train different classifiers — Logistic Regression, Multinomial Naive Bayes and Linear SVM — using the basic unigrams and bigrams as features and determine the best classifier for our task. Table 2 gives the 5 cross-fold validation F1-score results with the linear SVM classifier performing best. We used the scikit-learn GridSearchcv function to perform an evaluative search on our data to get the best regularization parameter value for the linear SVM classifier. This was C=10.

### 4.2 Training data

Having picked the classifier, the second experiment was to find the best mix of data to train on. This is an important step to take when we have data that is as unbalanced, in terms of the number elements of each type of data we are classifying, as the data we have here. The manually annotated statements were divided into two sets — training set and test set. We collected 30 explicit and 150 implicit opinions as the test set. These were not used in training. We gathered the remaining 100 explicit opinions and created a training set using these statements and a variable-sized set of implicit opinions. For each such training set, we ran a 5 fold cross-validation and also tested it against the test set that we had created. We use the linear SVM classifier to train and test the data with the basic features (unigrams and bigrams respectively). The mean F1-scores for the cross-validation on different train sets and the F1-scores on the test set for both explicit and implicit opinions are shown in Figure 2. The plot also contains the false positive rate for the test set with respect to different training sets.

### 4.3 Features

Given the results of the second experiment, we can identify the best size of training set, in terms of the number of explicit and implicit opinions. Considering Figure 2, we see that a training set containing 100 explicit and 250 implicit opinions will be sufficient. With this mix, the false positive rate is close to minimum, and the performance on the test set is close to maximum. We then carried out a third experiment to find the best set of features to identify the stances. To do this we ran a 5 fold cross-validation on the training set using the all the features described in Section 3.2 — in other words we expanded the feature set from just unigrams and bigrams — using both individual features and sets of features. We also performed the same experiment using these different features on

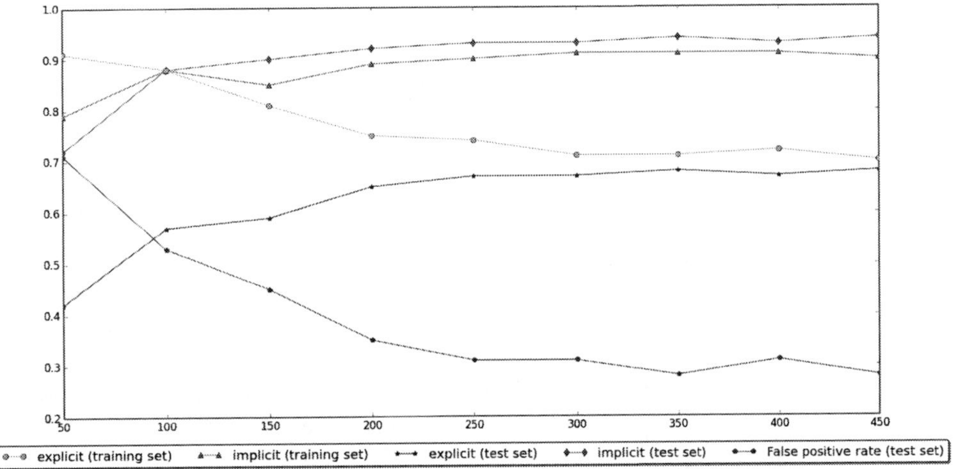


Figure 2: The results of the experiment to identify the best mix of explicit and implicit stances for training. The training set contained 100 explicit stances and as many implicit stances as indicated on the x-axis. The graph shows the cross-validation F1 scores for the training sets, and the corresponding F1 scores obtained on the test set. False positive rates for the test set with respect to each training set are also plotted.

the test set.

## 4.4 Results

Table 3 contains the results for the third experiment. The best performance results are highlighted — the highest values in each of the first four columns (classification accuracy) are in bold, as is the lowest value in the final column (false positive rate). We see that the basic features, unigrams and bigrams, give good results for both the cross-validation of the training set and for the test set. We also see that while the sentiment of each statement was useful in determining whether a statement is an opinion (and thus the statement is included in our data), sentiment does not help in distinguishing the explicit stance from the implicit stance which is why there is no improvement with the SentiWordNet scores as features. This is because both positive and negative statements can be either implicit or explicit. In contrast, the special features that include the noun-adjective patterns along with unigrams and bigrams gave the best performance for the test set, and also produced the lowest false positive rate.

## 4.5 Top 10 features

The linear SVM classifier gives the best performance results and thus we use the weights of the classifier for identifying the most important features in the data. The classifier is based on the following decision function:

$$y(\boldsymbol{x}) = \boldsymbol{w}^\top \boldsymbol{x} + b \tag{2}$$

where $w$ is the weight vector and $b$ is the bias value. Support vectors represent those weight weight vectors that are non-zero, and we can use these to obtain the most important features. Table 4 gives the most important 10 features identified in this way for both explicit and implicit opinions.

## 5 Conclusion

In this paper, we focus on a specific domain of online reviews and propose an approach that can help in enthymemes detection and reconstruction. Online reviews contain aspect-based statements that can be considered as stances representing for/against views of the reviewer about the aspects present in the product or service and the product/service itself. The proposed approach is a two-step approach that detects the type of stances based on the contextual features, which can then be converted into explicit premises, and these premises with missing information represents enthymemes. We also propose a solution using the available data to represent common knowledge that can fill in the missing information to

| Features | Training set | | Test set | | |
|---|---|---|---|---|---|
| | *F1 Score* | | *F1 Score* | | *False positive rate* |
| | Explicit | Implicit | Explicit | Implicit | |
| Baseline | 0.73 | 0.88 | 0.67 | 0.92 | 0.41 |
| Uni | 0.74 | **0.90** | 0.65 | 0.92 | 0.40 |
| Uni +Bi | 0.75 | **0.90** | 0.70 | **0.94** | 0.30 |
| Uni + Bi + POS | 0.74 | 0.90 | 0.68 | 0.93 | 0.33 |
| Uni + Bi + POS + POS Bi | 0.72 | 0.89 | **0.71** | **0.94** | **0.26** |
| Uni + Bi + POS + POS Bi + Senti | 0.66 | 0.89 | 0.68 | 0.94 | 0.3 |
| Uni + Bi + POS + Senti | 0.73 | **0.90** | 0.70 | **0.94** | 0.31 |
| Uni + Bi + Noun-Adj patterns | **0.77** | **0.90** | **0.72** | **0.94** | **0.26** |

Table 3: The results of the experiment to identify the best feature set. The table gives the F1 scores for training set and test set using different sets of features. False positive rate on the test set is also listed. All results were obtained using the Linear SVM classifier except the baseline classifier. The bold numbers are the highest classification rates in each column, or the lowest false positive rate for the column, as appropriate.

| Explicit | Weight | Implicit | Weight |
|---|---|---|---|
| excellent | 4.18 | Adj + Noun | -1.26 |
| location | 3.43 | the hotel | -1.25 |
| great | 2.55 | nice star | -1.23 |
| experience | 2.02 | fairly | -1.08 |
| recommend | 1.91 | hotel the | -1.03 |
| was excellent | 1.84 | helpful + Noun | -0.96 |
| hotel | 1.61 | location but | -0.95 |
| service | 1.48 | hotel with | -0.94 |
| extremely | 1.45 | advice stay | -0.94 |
| was great | 1.43 | hotel stars | -0.94 |

Table 4: List of the 10 most important features present in explicit and implicit stances with their weights

complete the arguments. The first-step requires automatic detection of the stance types — explicit and implicit, which we have covered in this paper. We use a supervised approach to classify the stances using a linear SVM classifier, the best performance results on the test set with a macro-averaged F1-scores of 0.72 and 0.94 for explicit and implicit stances respectively. These identified implicit stances are then explicit premises of either complete arguments or enthymemes. (If they are premises of complete arguments, there are other, additional premises.) The identified explicit stances can then represent common knowledge information for the implicit premises, thus becoming explicit premises to fill in the gap present in the respective enthymemes.

## 6 Future work

The next steps in this work take us closer to the automatic reconstruction of enthymemes. The first of these steps is to look to refine our identification of explicit premises (and thus complete arguments, circumventing the need for enthymeme reconstruction). The idea here is that we believe that since we are currently looking only at the sentence level, we may be misclassifying some sentences as expressing implicit opinions when they include both implicit and explicit opinions. To refine the classification, we need to examine sub-sentential clauses of the sentences in the reviews to identify if any of them express explicit opinions. If no explicit opinions are expressed in any of the sub-sentential clauses, then the whole sentence can be correctly classified as a implicit opinion, and along with the predefined conclusion will become an enthymeme. The second of the steps towards enthymeme reconstruction is to look to use related explicit opinions to complete enthymemes, as discussed in Section 3.1. Here the distinction between general and specific opinions becomes important, since explicit general opinions might be combined with any implicit opinion about an aspect in the same aspect category, while explicit specific opinions can only be combined with implicit opinions that relate to the same aspect. Effective combination of explicit general opinions with related implicit opinions requires a detailed model which expresses what "related" means for the relevant domain. We expect the development of this model to be as time-consuming as all work formalising a domain. Another issue in enthymeme reconstruction is evaluating the output of the process. Identifying whether a given enthymeme has been successfully turned into a complete argument is a highly subjective task, which will likely require careful human evaluation. Performing this at a suitable scale will be challenging.

## References

Leila Amgoud and Henri Prade. 2012. Can AI models capture natural language argumentation? In *IJCINI'12*, pages 19–32.

Leila Amgoud, Philippe Besnard, and Anthony Hunter. 2015. Representing and reasoning about arguments mined from texts and dialogues. In *ECSQARU'15*, pages 60–71.

Stefano Baccianella, Andrea Esuli, and Fabrizio Sebastiani. 2010. Sentiwordnet 3.0: An enhanced lexical resource for sentiment analysis and opinion mining. In *LREC'10*, pages 2200–2204.

Elizabeth Black and Anthony Hunter. 2012. A relevance-theoretic framework for constructing and deconstructing enthymemes. *J. Log. Comput.*, 22(1):55–78.

Filip Boltužić and Jan Šnajder. 2014. Back up your stance: Recognizing arguments in online discussions. In *ACL'14*, pages 49–58.

Elena Cabrio and Serena Villata. 2012. Combining textual entailment and argumentation theory for supporting online debates interactions. In *ACL'12*, pages 208–212.

Vanessa Wei Feng and Graeme Hirst. 2011. Classifying arguments by scheme. In *ACL'11*, pages 987–996.

Maria Paz Garcia-Villalba and Patrick Saint-Dizier. 2012. A framework to extract arguments in opinion texts. In *IJCINI'12*, volume 6, pages 62–87.

Debanjan Ghosh, Smaranda Muresan, Nina Wacholder, Mark Aakhus, and Matthew Mitsui. 2014. Analyzing argumentative discourse units in online interactions. In *ACL'14*, pages 39–48.

Ivan Habernal, Judith Eckle-Kohler, and Iryna Gurevych. 2014. Argumentation mining on the web from information seeking perspective. In *Proceedings of the Workshop on Frontiers and Connections between Argumentation Theory and Natural Language Processing*, pages 26–39.

Seyed Ali Hosseini, Sanjay Modgil, and Odinaldo Rodrigues. 2014. Enthymeme construction in dialogues using shared knowledge. In *COMMA'14*, pages 325–332.

Minqing Hu and Bing Liu. 2004. Mining opinion features in customer reviews. In *AAAI'04*, pages 755–760.

Angeliki Lazaridou, Ivan Titov, and Caroline Sporleder. 2013. A Bayesian model for joint unsupervised induction of sentiment, aspect and discourse representations. In *ACL'13*, pages 1630–1639.

Marco Lippi and Paolo Torroni. 2015a. Argument mining: A machine learning perspective. In *TAFA'15*, pages 163–176.

Marco Lippi and Paolo Torroni. 2015b. Context-independent claim detection for argument mining. In *IJCAI'15*, pages 185–191.

Clare Llewellyn, Claire Grover, Jon Oberlander, and Ewan Klein. 2014. Re-using an argument corpus to aid in the curation of social media collections. In *LREC'14*, pages 462–468.

Joonsuk Park and Claire Cardie. 2014. Identifying appropriate support for propositions in online user comments. In *ACL'14*, pages 29–38.

Andreas Peldszus and Manfred Stede. 2013. From argument diagrams to argumentation mining in texts: A survey. In *IJCINI'13*, volume 7, pages 1–31.

Iyad Rahwan and Guillermo R. Simari, editors. 2009. *Argumentation in Artificial Intelligence.* Springer Verlag, Berlin, Germany.

Stephen Toulmin. 1958. *The Uses of Argument.* Cambridge University Press, Cambridge, England.

Frans H. van Eemeren, Rob Grootendorst, Francisca S. Henkemans, J. Anthony Blair, Ralph H. Johnson, Erik C. W. Krabbe, Christian Plantin, Douglas N. Walton, Charles A. Willard, John Woods, and David Zarefsky. 1996. *Fundamentals of Argumentation Theory: A Handbook of Historical Backgrounds and Contemporary Developments.* Lawrence Erlbaum Associates, Mahwah, NJ.

Marc Vincent and Grégoire Winterstein. 2014. Argumentative insights from an opinion classification task on a French corpus. In *New Frontiers in Artificial Intelligence*, pages 125–140.

Henning Wachsmuth, Martin Trenkmann, Benno Stein, and Gregor Engels. 2014a. Modeling review argumentation for robust sentiment analysis. In *ICCL'14*, pages 553–564.

Henning Wachsmuth, Martin Trenkmann, Benno Stein, Gregor Engels, and Tsvetomira Palakarska. 2014b. A review corpus for argumentation analysis. In *IC-CLITP'14*, pages 115–127.

Douglas N. Walton and Erik C. W. Krabbe. 1995. *Commitment in Dialogue: Basic Concepts of Interpersonal Reasoning.* State University of New York Press, Albany, NY, USA.

Douglas N. Walton. 2008. The three bases for the enthymeme: A dialogical theory. *J. Applied Logic*, 6(3):361–379.

Douglas Walton. 2010. The structure of argumentation in health product messages. *Argument & Computation*, 1(3):179–198.

Adam Wyner, Jodi Schneider, Katie Atkinson, and Trevor J. M. Bench-Capon. 2012. Semi-automated argumentative analysis of online product reviews. In *COMMA'12*, pages 43–50.

Nefise Yaglikci and Paolo Torroni. 2014. Microdebates app for Android: A tool for participating in argumentative online debates using a handheld device. In *ICTAI'14*, pages 792–799.

# The CASS Technique for
# Evaluating the Performance of Argument Mining


**Rory Duthie[1], John Lawrence[1], Katarzyna Budzynska[1,2], and Chris Reed[1]**

[1]Centre for Argument Technology, University of Dundee, Scotland
[2]Institute of Philosophy and Sociology, Polish Academy of Sciences, Poland



## Abstract

Argument mining integrates many distinct computational linguistics tasks, and as a result, reporting agreement between annotators or between automated output and gold standard is particularly challenging. More worrying for the field, agreement and performance are also reported in a wide variety of different ways, making comparison between approaches difficult. To solve this problem, we propose the CASS technique for combining metrics covering different parts of the argument mining task. CASS delivers a justified method of integrating results yielding confusion matrices from which CASS-$\kappa$ and CASS-$F1$ scores can be calculated.


## 1 Introduction

To calculate the agreement, or similarity, between two different argumentative structures is an important and commonly occurring task in argument mining. For example, measures of similarity are required to determine the efficacy of annotation guidelines via inter-annotator agreement, and to compare test analyses against a gold standard, whether these test analyses are produced by students, or automated argument mining techniques (*cf.* (Moens, 2013; Peldszus and Stede, 2013)).

To find the the similarity of automatic and manually segmented texts and what impact these segments have on agreement between annotations for an overall argument structure, is a complex task. Similar to these problems is the task of evaluating the argumentative structure of annotations using pre-segmented text. Despite the relative ease of manually analysing these situations, arguments with long relations can easily make this task complex.

Commonly to find the agreement of manual annotators or the effectiveness of an automatic solution, two scores are given, Cohen's kappa (Cohen, 1960), which takes into account the observed agreement between two annotators and the chance agreement, giving an overall kappa value for agreement, and $F1$ score (Rijsbergen, 1979), which is the harmonic mean of the precision and recall of an algorithm. The way in which these scores are utilised can over penalise differences in argumentative structures. In particular, if used incorrectly, Cohen's kappa can penalise doubly (penalise for segmentation and penalise segmentation in argumentative structures) if not split into separate tasks or penalise too harshly when annotations have only slight differences, again if the calculation is not split by argumentative structure. When using the $F1$ score the same problems arise without split calculations.

To combat these issues this paper introduces two advances: first, the definition of an overall score, the Combined Argument Similarity Score (CASS), which incorporates a separate segmentation score, propositional content relation score and dialogical content relation score; and second, the deployment of an automatic system of comparative statistics for calculating the agreement between annotations over the two steps needed to ultimately perform argument mining: manual annotations compared with manual annotations (corpora compared with corpora) and automatic annotations evaluated against a gold standard (automatically created argument structures compared with a manually annotated corpus).

## 2 Related Work

Creating the CASS technique and an automatic system to calculate it, is based on theories established in linguistics and computational linguistics.




*Proceedings of the 3rd Workshop on Argument Mining*, pages 40–49,
Berlin, Germany, August 7-12, 2016. ©2016 Association for Computational Linguistics

In (Afantenos et al., 2012), a discourse graph is considered and split into discourse units and relations, to calculate agreement using $F1$ score. This gives what is described as a "brutal estimation" which gives an underestimation of the agreement. To combat this it is suggested that reasoning over the structures is needed.

In (Artstein and Poesio, 2008) a survey is given of agreement values in computational linguistics. Different measures of the statistics both Cohen's kappa and Krippendorff's alpha (Krippendorff, 2007) along with other variations are considered for different tasks. On the task of segmentation, it is noted that kappa in any form does not account for near misses (where a boundary missed by a word or two words) and that instead other measures (see Section 4) should be considered. On the topic of relations and discourse entities, again kappa in its various forms and alpha are considered. For both relations and discourse entities the kappa score is low overall because partial agreement is not considered. Instead the idea of a partial agreement coefficient is introduced as being applicable.

In (Habernal and Gurevych, 2016), Krippendorff's unitized alpha ($\alpha_U$) is proposed as an evaluation method, to take into account both labels and boundaries of segments by reducing the task to a token level. The $\alpha_U$ is calculated over a continuous series of documents removing the need for averaging on a document level, but is dependent on the ordering of documents where the error rate of ordering is low.

Finally, in (Kirschner et al., 2015) methods for calculating inter-annotator agreement are specified: adapted percentage agreement (APA), weighted average and a graph based technique (see also Section 3.2).

APA takes the total number of agreed annotations and divides it by the total number of annotations, on a sentence level of argument but not corrected for chance. Chance is taken into account, when performing the weighted average. A weight is provided for the distance between related propositions when the distance is not greater than six. Meaning any relation with a distance greater than six is discounted. This is justified with only 5% of relations having a distance greater than two. Chance is accounted for by using this weighted average for multi-annotator kappa and $F1$ score. Finally, a graph based approach is defined, where the distance between nodes is taken for each annotation with each node distance as a fraction. The distance is added, then multiplied by the overall number of edges giving a normalised score for both annotations, not considering the direction or types of relations or any unconnected propositions. The harmonic mean is then taken to provide the agreement between the annotations.

Results are also provided when considering relation types for weighted average and nodes with distance less than six for inter-annotator agreement on propositional content nodes for a pre-segmented text.

If we consider the papers submitted to the 2nd workshop on argumentation mining, we can see there is an inconsistency in the area when calculating inter-annotator agreement and overall argument mining results. To calculate the agreement between annotators, three papers used Cohen's kappa (*cf.* (Bilu et al., 2015; Carstens and Toni, 2015; Sobhani et al., 2015)), three papers used inter-annotator agreement as a percentage (*cf.* (Green, 2015; Nguyen and Litman, 2015; Kiesel et al., 2015)), two used precision and recall (*cf.* (Sardianos et al., 2015; Oraby et al., 2015)) and three others used different methods (*cf.* (Kirschner et al., 2015; Yanase et al., 2015; Reisert et al., 2015)). To calculate the results of argument mining, four papers used accuracy (*cf.* (Bilu et al., 2015; Kiesel et al., 2015; Nguyen and Litman, 2015; Yanase et al., 2015)) and five papers used precision, recall and $F1$ score (*cf.* (Lawrence and Reed, 2015; Sobhani et al., 2015; Park et al., 2015; Nguyen and Litman, 2015; Peldszus and Stede, 2015)) with one paper using a macro-averaged $F1$. What is required in the area of argument mining is a coherent model to give results for both annotator agreement but also the results of argument mining.

In the area of text summarization, Recall-Oriented Understudy for Gisting Evaluation (ROUGE) (Lin, 2004) was created exactly for the purpose of having a coherent measure to allow systems in the Document Understanding Conference (DUC) to be evaluated. In creating the CASS technique we aim to emulate ROUGE, and provide consistency in the area of argument mining.

## 3 Foundation

### 3.1 Representing Argument

Arguments in argument mining can be represented in many forms which is particularly important for the development of the CASS technique, as this score must be applicable to different ways of representing argument.

**Scheme for Argumentative Microtexts.** In (Peldszus and Stede, 2013) an annotation scheme was defined which was incorporated in a corpus of 122 argumentative microtexts (Peldszus and Stede, 2015). In this annotation scheme an argument is defined as a non-empty premise, that is a premise which holds some form of relation which supports a conclusion. Graphically this is represented by proposition nodes and support relations, with support relations represented as an arrow between the node and its conclusion.

The scheme defined builds on and extends the work of (Freeman, 2011). Support relations are defined in the most basic way, as an argument in the form of premise and conclusion. This accompanied by attack relations where rebutting is defined for when an argument is attacked directly and undercutting when a premise is attacked. Counter attacks then allow rebuttals of an attack support, the undercutting of an attack support and a counter consideration argument. Each microtext is pre-segmented to avoid bias from annotators segmenting text in their own style, with rules defined in the scheme which allow annotators to change the segmentation.

**Internet Argument Corpus (IAC).** Argument data is also represented use quote-response pairs (QR pairs) in the IAC (Walker et al., 2012). The IAC provides 390,704 individual posts automatically extracted from an Internet forum. Each post is related to a response which is provided through a tree structure of all the posts on the forum.

QR pairs work with a pre-defined segmentation which can allow annotators to identify relations between a quote (post) and a response. Relations can be on a number of levels with the most basic of these, agree and disagree, to the more complex, sarcasm where an annotator decides if a response is of sarcastic manner using their own intuition where a formal definition or annotation is near impossible without being present during the vocalisation of the point.

**Argument Interchange Format (AIF).** Argument data can also be represented according to the AIF (Chesñevar et al., 2006) implemented in the AIFdb[1] database (Lawrence et al., 2012). The

AIF was developed as a means of describing argument networks that would provide a flexible, yet semantically rich, specification of argumentation structures. Central to the AIF core ontology are two types of nodes: Information- (I-) nodes (propositional contents) and Scheme (S-) nodes (relations between contents). I-nodes represent propositional information contained in an argument, such as a conclusion, premise etc. A subset of I-nodes refers to propositional reports specifically about discourse events: these are L-nodes (locutions).

S-nodes capture the application of *schemes* of three categories: argumentative, illocutionary and dialogical. Amongst argumentative patterns there are inferences or reasoning (RA-nodes), conflict (CA-nodes) and rephrase (MA-nodes). Dialogical transitions (TA-nodes) are schemes of interaction or protocol of a given dialogue game which determine possible relations between locutions. Illocutionary schemes are patterns of communicative intentions which speakers use to introduce propositional contents.[2] Illocutionary connections (YA-nodes) can be either anchored (associated, assigned) in locutions or in transitions. In the first case (see e.g. asserting, challenging, questioning), the locution provides enough information to reconstruct illocutionary force and content. Illocutionary connections are anchored in a transition when we need to know what a locution is a response to and to understand an illocution or its content. AIFdb Corpora allows for operation with either an individual NodeSet, or any grouping of NodeSets captured in a corpus. By integrating closely with the OVA+ (Online Visualisation of Argument) analysis tool (Janier et al., 2014), AIFdb Corpora allows for the rapid creation of large corpora compliant with AIF.

AIFdb provides the largest publicly available dataset comprising multiple corpora of analysed argumentation; and in addition AIF works as an interlingua facilitating translation from other representation languages with both the IAC and Microtext corpora in AIF format, for example. For both of these reasons, we have used AIF for our examples here (although the CASS technique itself is largely independent of annotation scheme).

---



[2] Illocutionary schemes are based on illocutionary forces defined in (Searle, 1969; Searle and Vanderveken, 1985).

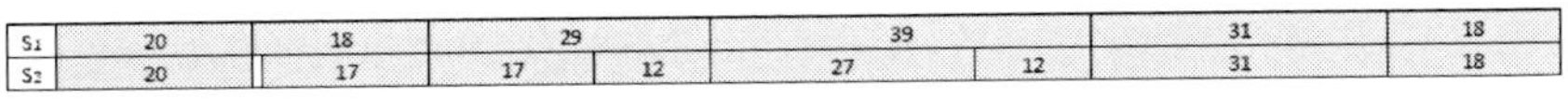

| $S_1$ | 20 | 18 | 29 | | 39 | | 31 | 18 |
|---|---|---|---|---|---|---|---|---|
| $S_2$ | 20 | 17 | 17 | 12 | 27 | 12 | 31 | 18 |

Figure 1: Segmentation boundaries and mass for first and second annotators.

### 3.2 Comparing Analysis

Calculating the inter-annotator agreement of manual analysis, can be problematic when using traditional methods such as Cohen's kappa. In (Kirschner et al., 2015, p.3), the authors highlight this challenge: "as soon as the annotation of one entity depends on the annotation of another entity, or some entities have a higher overall probability for a specific annotation than others, the measures may yield misleadingly high or low values. (...) Therefore, many researchers still report raw percentage agreement without chance correction."

In the comparative statistics module we look to extend the solution in (Kirschner et al., 2015) in seven ways, by: (i) Calculating the segmentation differences between two annotations; (ii) Calculating propositional content relations using confusion matrices, accounting for all the nodes within an argument map and accounting for a differing segmentation; (iii) Calculating dialogical content relations (if they are contained in an argument map) using confusion matrices, accounting for all the nodes within an argument map and accounting for a differing segmentation; (iv) Defining the CASS technique to allow calculation scores to be combined; (v) Allowing the use of any metric for the CASS technique, which uses a confusion matrix, to give consistency to the area of argument mining; (vi) Providing results for not just inter-annotator agreement, but also, the comparison of manually annotated corpora against corpora automatically created by argument mining; (vii) Allowing the comparison of analysis given in different annotation schemes but migrated to AIF (e.g. compare text annotated in IAC to the annotation scheme from the Microtext corpus).

## 4 Comparative Statistics: Segmentation

Comparative statistics can provide for a number of cases with two main motivations: evaluation of automatic annotations against manual gold standards, and comparison of multiple manual annotations. The calculation is given between two separate annotations[3] $A_1$ and $A_2$ available in two separate corpora in AIFdb.

To account for a differing segmentation which does not doubly penalise the argument structure, the agreement calculation involves smaller subcalculations which can give an overview of the full agreement between annotators. Segmentation agreement considers the number of possible segments on which two annotators agree. A segmentation which differs between annotations can have a substantial effect on argument structure, such as the assignment of relations between proposition. An example is provided in Figure 1 where segmentation is given for a first annotator ($S_1$) and a second annotator ($S_2$). In this case the two annotations give segments which resemble very similar mass(the number of words in a segment), however, more boundaries are placed in $S_2$ when compared to $S_1$ with a difference in granularity and a boundary misplaced by a word.

Three techniques are provided to tackle this problem with each recognising that a near miss (two segments that differ by a small margin, e.g. a word) should not be as heavily penalised as a full miss on the placement of segment boundaries. Performing the same calculation with $F1$ score or Cohen's kappa would result in a heavily penalised segmentation.

The $P_k$ statistic (Beeferman et al., 1999), involves sliding a window of length $k$ (where $k$ is half the average segment size) over the segmented text. For each position of the window, the words at each end of the window are taken and the segment in which they lie is considered.

The WindowDiff statistic (Pevzner and Hearst, 2002), takes into account situations in which $P_k$ fails. In $P_k$ false negatives are penalised more than false positives, thus the agreement value could be unfair. The WindowDiff statistic remedies this by taking into account the number of reference boundaries and comparing this to the number of hypothesised boundaries.

The segmentation similarity statistic ($S$)(Fournier and Inkpen, 2012), again takes into account perceived failings of the $P_k$ and WindowDiff statistics. Where both WindowDiff and $P_k$ use fixed sized windows, which can adversely

---

[3]Throughout this paper $A$ is used to denote annotation, $l$ denotes a locution, $p$ a propositional content node, $ta$ a transition node and $ra$ a propositional content relation.

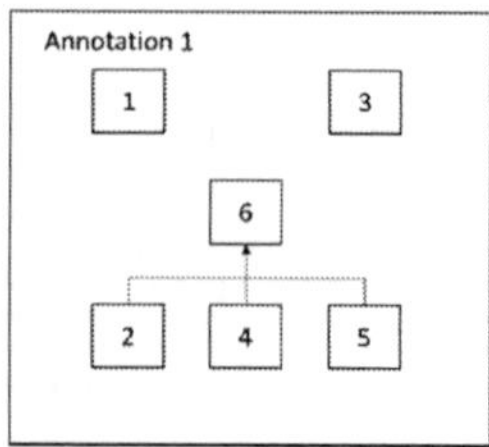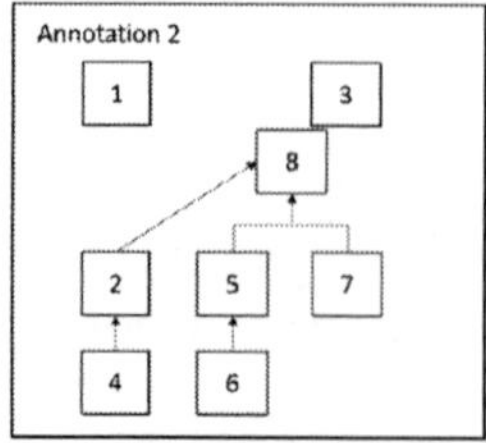



Figure 2: Propositional Content Relations for an annotation from AIFdb with first and second annotators.[4]

affect the outcome of an agreement calculation, $S$ proposes that a minimum edit distance, scaled to the overall segmentation size, is considered. This edit distance allows near misses to be penalised but not to the same degree as a full miss.

## 5 Comparative Statistics: Propositional Relations

To compare relations it is important to calculate the agreement between each of the individual items which are annotated within an argument analysis. By providing calculations for individual items in an annotation we take into account that segmentation's may differ but do not penalise on this basis.

In the case of analysis with a differing segmentation, we use a guaranteed matching formula. This formula makes use of the Levenshtein distance (Levenshtein, 1966), where each locution or proposition in an annotation is compared with every locution or proposition in a second annotation. The Levenshtein distance for each comparison is taken and normalised, this is extended by using the position of words within the annotations taken from the original text. The position of words in the original text is important to correctly match propositions and locutions and therefore a proposition or locution which does not have matching positional words cannot be a match. In this situation the Levenshtein distance is increased (moved to zero) to account for a non-match. Each calculation taken is then stored in a matrix. The matrix is then traversed to find the smallest distance (highest value between zero and one), selecting the pair of locutions or propositions. This is continued until all nodes are matched or there are no matches which can be made, thus giving a Pareto optimal

solution, a solution for which any match between propositions and locutions makes those individual matches consistent without making any other match worse and vice-versa.

An agreement calculation is given for all propositional content relations (support and attack relations). This calculation is based on the location of support and attack nodes within an analysis and the nodes to which they are connected. For a full agreement between annotators, a support or attack node must be connected between two propositions $p_i$, $p_j$, with these propositions being a match in $A_1$ and $A_2$. A support or attack node also has full agreement when one annotation is more fine grained but holds the same propositional content as the other annotation. For example, if annotation $A_1$ contains a support node which begins its relation in $p_{bc}$ and gives a relation between $p_{bc}$ and $p_a$, then this is the same as if $A_2$ had a support node with two separate propositions, $p_b$ and $p_c$ and related to $p_a$. This notion is extended when considering Figure 1 and Figure 2.

The differing segmentation in Figure 1 has an effect on the comparison between propositions. When considering propositions, non-identical propositions lead to a near zero similarity on support relations between these annotations. This is however an unintuitive approach to take, as the overall argumentative structure is penalised doubly (if we consider the segmentation and argumentative structure as different tasks) by the differing segmentation.

This is demonstrated in Figure 2 where the two annotators agree that there is a convergent argument been nodes four and five in annotation 1 and nodes five and seven in annotation 2. Extending this is proposition two of both annotations, where in annotation 1, proposition two is connected to four and five by a convergent argument. Yet in annotation 2, proposition 2 is a separate support relation. In the first instance of a convergent argument, splitting the segmentation calculation from the propositional relation calculation gives a fair representation of the argument structure without penalising for segmentation doubly.

In the second instance of a convergent argument and a separate support relation, there is a slight disagreement between the annotators. Despite both annotators agreeing that proposition two connects to the same node (propositions six in annotation 1 and eight in annotation two being the

---

[4]Numbered nodes represent propositions in the overall text and arrows represent support relations.

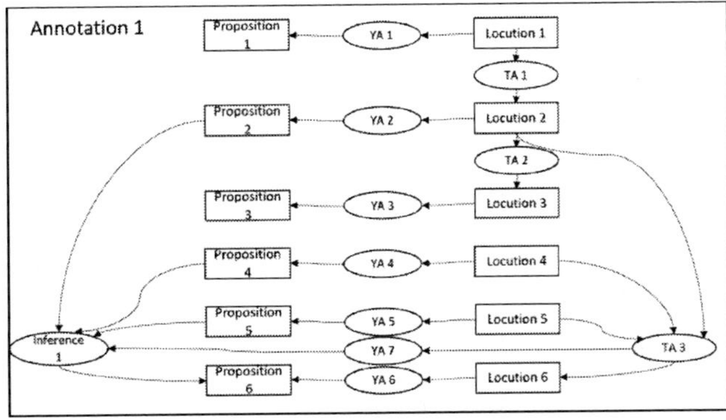


Figure 3: Full AIF IAT diagram for the annotation from the first annotator.

same node) a disagreement is shown because of the connection type if we consider Cohen's kappa or $F1$ score purely. Two options are available when calculating the similarity for this situation, either a similarity of zero is given or two separate calculations could be used with agreement on a premise conclusion basis but no agreement on the type of argument, thus giving a penalty.

To provide a confusion matrix all the possible node pairs to which a propositional content relation could be connected have to be considered. Any node pairs which both annotators have not connected are then counted and all nodes which are matched are counted, giving the observed agreement. All node pairs which the annotators do not agree upon are also counted.

## 6 Comparative Statistics: Dialogical Relations

Dialogical relations consider only the dialogue of an argument with the intentions of the speaker noted. A differing segmentation in various analysis can lead to low kappa or $F1$ scores. By splitting dialogical relations into a separate calculation it removes the double penalty assigned by segmentation. When comparing dialogical relations again we use the Levenshtein distance as described in Section 5.

A calculation is provided for illocutionary connections (YA) anchored in TAs or in Locutions. This calculation involves multiple categories, meaning a multiple category confusion matrix, due to the large number of possible YA-node types which can be chosen by annotators. An agreement is observed when both annotators select the same illocutionary connections. When $A_1$ con-

tains a YA-node which is anchored in $l_i$ and when $A_2$ contains the same YA anchored in $l_i$, then an agreement is observed. This also holds for TA's. The overall calculation then involves a confusion matrix where all disagreements are observed when YA nodes do not match. If we consider Figures 3 and 4 we can see between both annotations that there are a difference of four YA nodes.

A second calculation for YA-nodes, checking the agreement on the propositional content nodes in which they anchor and to where they are anchored (locution or TA), is also given. This calculation involves a multiple category confusion matrix. An example of when agreement is observed is when $A_1$ contains $p_j$ anchored in a YA and the YA anchored in $l_i$ and in $A_2$ the same structure with $p_j$ and $l_i$ is observed with the same YA node. The multi-category confusion matrix is calculated with disagreements observed when propositions and locutions do not match. When considering Figures 3 and 4 we see an example of agreement between the annotators on propositions 1, 2 and 3. Proposition 4, in Figure 3 and proposition 5, in Figure 4 also match and the same for proposition 5, in Figure 3 and proposition 7, in Figure 4. Disagreements are then observed with propositions 4 and 6 in Figure 4.

Three separate calculations are also given for TA-nodes. The first concerns the position of a TA node within locutions. Agreement is observed when $A_1$ contains a TA which is anchored in $l_i$ and anchors $l_j$ and $A_2$ contains the same TA anchored in $l_i$ and anchoring $l_j$. For the final calculation all possible locution pairs are considered to give values for agreements on TA placement, agreements on non-TA placement and disagreements on TA placement. In the examples Figures 3 and 4 there

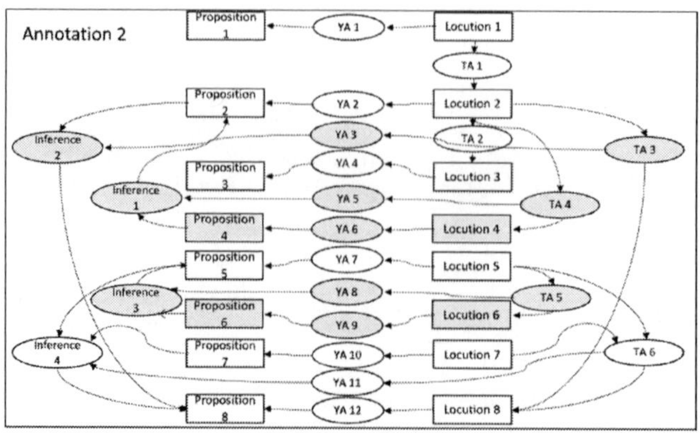


Figure 4: Full AIF IAT diagram for the annotation from the second annotator. Differences from Figure 3 are highlighted.

is a agreement between the annotators on TA 1, 2 and TA 3 in Figure 3 and TA 6, in Figure 4. A second calculation is then given for pairs of propositional content nodes and TA-nodes. When $p_j$ is anchored in $ta_i$ for $A_1$ and the same structure is observed in $A_2$ for the same propositional content node then there is agreement between the annotators. The overall confusion matrix is calculated by considering all pairs of TA-nodes and propositions and all disagreements between annotators. A third and final calculation is given for TA-nodes anchoring propositional content relations. For $A_1$ if $ra_i$ is anchored finally in $ta_i$ and $ra_j$ is anchored finally in $ra_j$, in $A_2$ then agreement is observed. The overall confusion matrix is calculated by considering all possible pairs of TA's and propositional content relations. In Figures 3 and 4 agreement is observed only on inference 1 in Figure 3 and inference 4 in Figure 4. This provides a small penalty between the annotations for the added inference 2 in Figure 4, where earlier in Section 5 no penalty was given.

## 7  Aggregating into the CASS technique

Sections 4, 5 and 6 provide calculations for segmentation, propositional content relations and dialogical content relations. We have defined CASS which incorporates all of these calculation figures to provide a single figure for the agreement between annotators or a manual analysis and an automatic one, using both propositional content relations and dialogical content relations.

$$M = \frac{\sum P + \sum D}{n} \quad (1)$$

$$CASS = 2\frac{M * S}{M + S} \quad (2)$$

In equation 1 the arithmetic mean, $M$, is the the sum of all propositional content calculations, $P$, plus the sum of all dialogical content calculations, $D$, over the total number of calculations made, $n$. We use this figure along with the segmentation similarity score to perform the harmonic mean and provide an overall agreement figure normalised and taking into account any penalties for segmentation errors. Equation 2 gives the CASS technique as the arithmetic mean, $M$, combined with the segmentation similarity, $S$.

The CASS technique allows for any consistent combination of scores to be used as either the propositional content calculations or dialogical calculations. That is to say that the CASS technique is not solely dependent on Cohen's kappa, or $F1$ score and can instead be substituted for any other overall measure. For the purpose of this example we will use the Cohen's kappa metric, as both annotations were annotated manually. We also use the $S$ statistic for segmentation similarity as it handles the errors in $P_k$ and WindowDiff statistics more effectively.

We sum both kappa scores giving an arithmetic mean, M, of 0.43. The $S$ score, 0.95, is then combined with M in equation 2 to give an overall CASS of 0.59. scores this gives a fair representation of the overall agreement between the two annotators. In Table 1 the CASS technique is compared with Cohen's kappa and $F1$ score, where both scores do not take into account the slight difference in argument structure and therefore penalise this.

| Method | Overall Score |
|---|---|
| Cohen's $\kappa$ | 0.44 |
| CASS-$\kappa$ | 0.59 |
| $F1$ score | 0.66 |
| CASS-$F1$ | 0.74 |

Table 1: Scores are provided for Cohen's kappa and $F1$ score, for both segmentation and structure, and CASS with $S$ for segmentation and both kappa and $F1$ for structure.

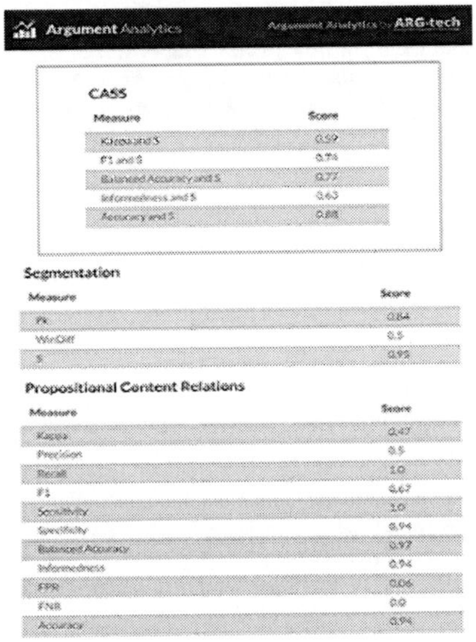

CASS

| Measure | Score |
|---|---|
| Kappa and S | 0.59 |
| F1 and S | 0.74 |
| Balanced Accuracy and S | 0.77 |
| Informedness and S | 0.63 |
| Accuracy and S | 0.88 |

Segmentation

| Measure | Score |
|---|---|
| Pk | 0.84 |
| WinDiff | 0.5 |
| S | 0.95 |

Propositional Content Relations

| Measure | Score |
|---|---|
| Kappa | 0.47 |
| Precision | 0.5 |
| Recall | 1.0 |
| F1 | 0.67 |
| Sensitivity | 1.0 |
| Specificity | 0.94 |
| Balanced Accuracy | 0.97 |
| Informedness | 0.94 |
| FPR | 0.06 |
| FNR | 0.0 |
| Accuracy | 0.94 |

Figure 5: Screenshot of the comparative statistics module within Argument Analytics.

## 7.1 Extending Relation Comparisons

The CASS technique and comparative statistics module caters for the creation of confusion matrices for each calculation, allowing for the adaption of the overall results. This allows kappa, accuracy, precision, recall and $F1$ score all to be calculated, but, other metrics can also be considered for evaluating automatic analyses when using the CASS technique. Balanced accuracy (Brodersen et al., 2010), allows the evaluation of imbalanced datasets. When one class is much larger than the other Balanced Accuracy takes this into account and lowers the score appropriately. Informedness (Powers, 2011), gives the probability that an automatic system is making an informed decision when performing classification. A select set of metrics are part of the comparative statistics module, although, no metric is ruled out from this, allowing any metric employing a confusion matrix to use the CASS technique.

## 7.2 Deployment

Comparative statistics (see Figure 5) is part of the Argument Analytics suite which is to be publicly accessible at http://analytics.arg.tech/. It provides a suite of techniques for analysing sets of AIF data, with components ranging from the detailed statistics required for discourse analysis or argument mining, to graphic visual representations, offering insights in a way that is accessible to a general audience. Modules are available for: viewing simple statistical data, which provides both an overview of the argument structure and frequencies of patterns such as argumentation schemes; dialogical data highlighting the behaviour of participants of the dialogue; and real-time data allowing for the graphical representation of a developing over time argument structure.

## 8 Conclusions

Despite the widespread use of Cohen's kappa and $F1$ score in reporting agreement and performance, they present two key problems when applied to argument mining. First, they do not effectively handle errors of segmentation (or unitization); and second, they are not sensitive to the variety of structural facets of argumentation. These two problems lead to kappa and $F1$ underestimating performance or agreement of argument annotation.

The CASS technique allows for the integration of results for segmentation with those for structural annotation yielding coherent confusion matrices from which new CASS-$\kappa$ and CASS-$F1$ scores can be derived. CASS is straightforward to implement, and we have shown that it can be included in web-based analytics for quickly calculating agreement or performance between online datasets. CASS offers an opportunity for increasing coherence within the community, aiding it to emulate the academic success of other subfields of computational linguistics such as summarization; and its subsequent deployment offers a simple way of applying it to future community efforts such as shared tasks and competitions.

## Acknowledgments

We would like to acknowledge that the work reported in this paper has been supported in part by EPSRC in the UK under grants EP/M506497/1, EP/N014871/1 and EP/K037293/1.

## References

Stergos Afantenos, Nicholas Asher, Farah Benamara, Myriam Bras, Cécile Fabre, Lydia-Mai Ho-Dac, Anne Le Draoulec, Philippe Muller, Marie-Paule Péry-Woodley, Laurent Prévot, et al. 2012. An empirical resource for discovering cognitive principles of discourse organisation: the annodis corpus. In *Proceedings of the Eight International Conference on Language Resources and Evaluation (LREC'12)*. European Language Resources Association (ELRA).

Ron Artstein and Massimo Poesio. 2008. Inter-coder agreement for computational linguistics. *Computational Linguistics*, 34(4):555–596.

Doug Beeferman, Adam Berger, and John Lafferty. 1999. Statistical models for text segmentation. *Machine learning*, 34(1-3):177–210.

Yonatan Bilu, Daniel Hershcovich, and Noam Slonim. 2015. Automatic claim negation: Why, how and when. In *Proceedings of the Second Workshop on Argumentation Mining. Association for Computational Linguistics*, pages 84–93.

K. H. Brodersen, C. S. Ong, K. E. Stephan, and J. M. Buhmann. 2010. The balanced accuracy and its posterior distribution. In *Pattern Recognition (ICPR), 2010 20th International Conference on*, pages 3121–3124.

Lucas Carstens and Francesca Toni. 2015. Towards relation based argumentation mining. In *Proceedings of the Second Workshop on Argumentation Mining. Association for Computational Linguistics*, pages 29–34.

Carlos Chesñevar, Sanjay Modgil, Iyad Rahwan, Chris Reed, Guillermo Simari, Matthew South, Gerard Vreeswijk, Steven Willmott, et al. 2006. Towards an Argument Interchange Format. *The Knowledge Engineering Review*, 21(04):293–316.

Jacob Cohen. 1960. A coefficient of agreement for nominal scales. *Educational and Psychological Measurement*, 20(1):37–46.

Chris Fournier and Diana Inkpen. 2012. Segmentation similarity and agreement. In *Proceedings of the 2012 Conference of the North American Chapter of the Association for Computational Linguistics: Human Language Technologies*, pages 152–161. Association for Computational Linguistics.

James B Freeman. 2011. *Argument Structure: Representation and Theory*. Springer.

Nancy L Green. 2015. Identifying argumentation schemes in genetics research articles. In *Proceedings of the Second Workshop on Argumentation Mining. Association for Computational Linguistics*, pages 12–21.

Ivan Habernal and Iryna Gurevych. 2016. Argumentation mining in user-generated web discourse. *Computational Linguistics*.

Mathilde Janier, John Lawrence, and Chris Reed. 2014. OVA+: An argument analysis interface. In S. Parsons, N. Oren, C. Reed, and F. Cerutti, editors, *Proceedings of the Fifth International Conference on Computational Models of Argument (COMMA 2014)*, pages 463–464, Pitlochry. IOS Press.

Johannes Kiesel, Khalid Al-Khatib, Matthias Hagen, and Benno Stein. 2015. A shared task on argumentation mining in newspaper editorials. In *Proceedings of the Second Workshop on Argumentation Mining. Association for Computational Linguistics*, pages 35–38.

Christian Kirschner, Judith Eckle-Kohler, and Iryna Gurevych. 2015. Linking the thoughts: Analysis of argumentation structures in scientific publications. In *Proceedings of the Second Workshop on Argumentation Mining. Association for Computational Linguistics*, pages 1–11.

Klaus Krippendorff. 2007. Computing Krippendorff's alpha reliability. *Departmental papers (ASC)*, page 43.

John Lawrence and Chris Reed. 2015. Combining argument mining techniques. In *Proceedings of the Second Workshop on Argumentation Mining. Association for Computational Linguistics*, pages 127–136.

John Lawrence, Floris Bex, Chris Reed, and Mark Snaith. 2012. AIFdb: Infrastructure for the Argument Web. In *Proceedings of the Fourth International Conference on Computational Models of Argument (COMMA 2012)*, pages 515–516.

V. I. Levenshtein. 1966. Binary Codes Capable of Correcting Deletions, Insertions and Reversals. *Soviet Physics Doklady*, 10:707.

Chin-Yew Lin. 2004. Rouge: A package for automatic evaluation of summaries. In *Text summarization branches out: Proceedings of the ACL-04 workshop*, volume 8.

Marie-Francine Moens. 2013. Argumentation mining: Where are we now, where do we want to be and how do we get there? In *FIRE '13 Proceedings of the 5th 2013 Forum on Information Retrieval Evaluation*.

Huy V Nguyen and Diane J Litman. 2015. Extracting argument and domain words for identifying argument components in texts. In *Proceedings of the Second Workshop on Argumentation Mining. Association for Computational Linguistics*, pages 22–28.

Shereen Oraby, Lena Reed, Ryan Compton, Ellen Riloff, Marilyn Walker, and Steve Whittaker. 2015. And that's a fact: Distinguishing factual and emotional argumentation in online dialogue. In *Proceedings of the Second Workshop on Argumentation*

*Mining. Association for Computational Linguistics*, pages 116–126.

Joonsuk Park, Arzoo Katiyar, and Bishan Yang. 2015. Conditional random fields for identifying appropriate types of support for propositions in online user comments. In *Proceedings of the Second Workshop on Argumentation Mining. Association for Computational Linguistics*, pages 39–44.

Andreas Peldszus and Manfred Stede. 2013. From argument diagrams to argumentation mining in texts: a survey. *International Journal of Cognitive Informatics and Natural Intelligence (IJCINI)*, 7(1):1–31.

Andreas Peldszus and Manfred Stede. 2015. An annotated corpus of argumentative microtexts. *Proceedings of the First Conference on Argumentation, Lisbon, Portugal, June. to appear.*

Lev Pevzner and Marti A Hearst. 2002. A critique and improvement of an evaluation metric for text segmentation. *Computational Linguistics*, 28(1):19–36.

D.M.W. Powers. 2011. Evaluation: from precision, recall and f-measure to roc, informedness, markedness and correlation. *Journal of Machine Learning Technologies*, 2:27–63.

Paul Reisert, Naoya Inoue, Naoaki Okazaki, and Kentaro Inui. 2015. A computational approach for generating toulmin model argumentation. In *Proceedings of the Second Workshop on Argumentation Mining. Association for Computational Linguistics*, pages 45–55.

C. J. Van Rijsbergen. 1979. *Information Retrieval*. Butterworth-Heinemann, Newton, MA, USA, 2nd edition.

Christos Sardianos, Ioannis Manousos Katakis, Georgios Petasis, and Vangelis Karkaletsis. 2015. Argument extraction from news. In *Proceedings of the Second Workshop on Argumentation Mining. Association for Computational Linguistics*, pages 56–66.

John R. Searle and Daniel Vanderveken. 1985. *Foundations of illocutionary logic*. Cambridge University Press.

John R. Searle. 1969. *Speech acts: An essay in the philosophy of language*. Cambridge University Press.

Parinaz Sobhani, Diana Inkpen, and Stan Matwin. 2015. From argumentation mining to stance classification. In *Proceedings of the Second Workshop on Argumentation Mining. Association for Computational Linguistics*, pages 67–77.

Marilyn A Walker, Jean E Fox Tree, Pranav Anand, Rob Abbott, and Joseph King. 2012. A corpus for research on deliberation and debate. In *LREC*, pages 812–817.

Toshihiko Yanase, Toshinori Miyoshi, Kohsuke Yanai, Misa Sato, Makoto Iwayama, Yoshiki Niwa, Paul Reisert, and Kentaro Inui. 2015. Learning sentence ordering for opinion generation of debate. In *Proceedings of the Second Workshop on Argumentation Mining. Association for Computational Linguistics*, pages 94–103.

# Extracting Case Law Sentences for Argumentation about the Meaning of Statutory Terms


**Jaromír Šavelka**
University of Pittsburgh
4200 Fifth Avenue
Pittsburgh, PA 15260, USA
jas438@pitt.edu

**Kevin D. Ashley**
University of Pittsburgh
4200 Fifth Avenue
Pittsburgh, PA 15260, USA
ashley@pitt.edu



## Abstract

Legal argumentation often centers on the interpretation and understanding of terminology. Statutory texts are known for a frequent use of vague terms that are difficult to understand. Arguments about the meaning of statutory terms are an inseparable part of applying statutory law to a specific factual context. In this work we investigate the possibility of supporting this type of argumentation by automatic extraction of sentences that deal with the meaning of a term. We focus on case law because court decisions often contain sentences elaborating on the meaning of one or more terms. We show that human annotators can reasonably agree on the usefulness of a sentence for an argument about the meaning (interpretive usefulness) of a specific statutory term (kappa>0.66). We specify a list of features that could be used to predict the interpretive usefulness of a sentence automatically. We work with off-the-shelf classification algorithms to confirm the hypothesis (accuracy>0.69).


## 1 Introduction

Statutory law is written law enacted by an official legislative body. A single statute is usually concerned with a specific area of regulation. It consists of provisions which express the individual legal rules (e.g., rights, prohibitions, duties).

Understanding statutory provisions is difficult because the abstract rules they express must account for diverse situations, even those not yet encountered. The legislators use vague (Endicott, 2000) open textured (Hart, 1994) terms, abstract standards (Endicott, 2014), principles, and values (Daci, 2010) in order to deal with this uncertainty.

When there are doubts about the meaning of the provision they may be removed by interpretation (MacCormick and Summers, 1991). Even a single word may be crucial for the understanding of the provision as applied in a particular context.

Let us consider the example rule: "No vehicles in the park."[1] While it is clear that automobiles or trucks are not allowed in the park it may be unclear if the prohibition extends to bicycles. In order to decide if a bicycle is allowed in the park it is necessary to interpret the term 'vehicle'.

The interpretation involves an investigation of how the term has been referred to, explained, interpreted or applied in the past. This is an important step that enables a user to then construct arguments in support of or against particular interpretations. Searching through a database of statutory law, court decisions, or law review articles one may stumble upon sentences such as these:

i. Any mechanical device used for transportation of people or goods is a *vehicle*.
ii. A golf cart is to be considered a *vehicle*.
iii. To secure a tranquil environment in the park no *vehicles* are allowed.
iv. The park where no *vehicles* are allowed was closed during the last month.
v. The rule states: "No *vehicles* in the park."

Some of the sentences are useful for the interpretation of the term 'vehicle' from the example provision (i. and ii.). Some of them look like they may be useful (iii.) but the rest appears to have very little (iv.) if any (v.) value. Going through the sentences manually is labor intensive. The large number of useless sentences is not the only problem. Perhaps, even more problematic is the large redundancy of the sentences.

---

[1] The example comes from the classic 1958 Hart-Fuller debate over the interpretation of rules.




*Proceedings of the 3rd Workshop on Argument Mining*, pages 50–59,
Berlin, Germany, August 7-12, 2016. ©2016 Association for Computational Linguistics

In this paper we investigate if it is possible to retrieve the set of useful sentences automatically. Specifically, we test the hypothesis that by using a set of automatically generated linguistic features about/in the sentence it is possible to evaluate how useful the sentence is for an interpretation of the term from a specific statutory provision.

In Section 2 we describe the new statutory term interpretation corpus that we created for this work. Section 3 describes the tentative set of the features for the evaluation of the sentences' interpretive usefulness. In Section 4 we confirm our hypothesis by presenting and evaluating a rudimentary version of the system (using stock ML algorithms) capable of determining how useful a sentence is for term interpretation.

## 2 Statutory Term Interpretation Data

Court decisions apply statutory provisions to specific cases. To apply a provision correctly a judge usually needs to clarify the meaning of one or more terms. This makes court decisions an ideal source of sentences that possibly interpret statutory terms. Legislative history and legal commentaries tentatively appear to be promising sources as well. We will investigate the usefulness of these types of documents in future work. Here we focus on sentences from court decisions only.

In order to create the corpus we selected three terms from different provisions of the United States Code, which is the official collection of the federal statutes of the United States.[2] The selected terms were 'independent economic value' from 18 U.S. Code § 1839(3)(B), an 'identifying particular' from 5 U.S. Code § 552a(a)(4), and 'common business purpose' from 29 U.S. Code § 203(r)(1). We specifically selected terms that are vague and come from different areas of regulation. We are aware that the number of terms we work with is low. We did not specify additional terms because the cost of subsequent labeling is high. Three terms are sufficient for the purpose of this paper. For future work we plan to extend the corpus.

For each term we have collected a small set of sentences by extracting all the sentences mentioning the term from the top 20 court decisions retrieved from Court Listener.[3] The focus on the top

---

[2] Available at https://www.law.cornell.edu/uscode/text/

[3] Available at https://www.courtlistener.com/. The search query was formulated as the phrase search for the term and it was limited to the 120 federal jurisdictions. The corpus corresponds to the state of Court Listener database on February

|        | # HV | # CV | # PV | # NV |
|--------|------|------|------|------|
| # HV   | **19** | **1** | **1** | **0** |
|        | (1/4/14) | (0/0/1) | (0/1/0) | (0/0/0) |
| # CV   | **15** | **12** | **9** | **1** |
|        | (1/6/8) | (2/0/10) | (1/4/4) | (0/1/0) |
| # PV   | **2** | **27** | **105** | **11** |
|        | (0/0/2) | (11/1/15) | (29/36/40) | (0/3/8) |
| # NV   | **0** | **0** | **4** | **36** |
|        | (0/0/0) | (0/0/0) | (2/2/0) | (5/13/18) |

Table 1: Confusion matrix of the labels assigned by the two annotators (HV: high value, CV: certain value, PV: potential value, NV: no value; the number in bold is the total count and the numbers in the brackets are the counts for the individual terms: ('independent economic value'/'identifying particular'/'common business purpose')).

20 decisions only reflected the high cost of the labeling. In total we assembled a small corpus of 243 sentences.

Two expert annotators, each with a law degree, classified the sentences into four categories according to their usefulness for the interpretation of the corresponding term:

1. **high value** - This category is reserved for sentences the goal of which is to elaborate on the meaning of the term. By definition, these sentences are those the user is looking for.
2. **certain value** - Sentences that provide grounds to draw some (even modest) conclusions about the meaning of the term. Some of these sentences may turn out to be very useful.
3. **potential value** - Sentences that provide additional information beyond what is known from the provision the term comes from. Most of the sentences from this category are not useful.
4. **no value** - This category is used for sentences that do not provide any additional information over what is known from the provision. By definition, these sentences are not useful for the interpretation of the term.

Eventually, we would like the system to assign a sentence with a score from a continuous interval. Since we cannot ask the human annotators to do the same, we discretized the interval into the four categories for the purpose of the evaluation. There was no time limit imposed on the annotation process.

---

16, 2016, which is the last time we updated the corpus.

| Term | # HV | # CV | # PV | # NV | # Total |
|---|---|---|---|---|---|
| Ind. economic val. | 2 | 5 | 40 | 5 | 52 |
| Identifying part. | 6 | 8 | 40 | 17 | 71 |
| C. business purp. | 20 | 26 | 51 | 23 | 120 |
| Total | 28 | 39 | 131 | 45 | 243 |

Table 2: Distribution of sentences with respect to their interpretive value (HV: high value, CV: certain value, PV: potential value, NV: no value).

Table 1 shows the confusion matrix of the labels as assigned by the two expert annotators. The average inter-annotator agreement was 0.75 with weighted kappa at 0.66. For the 'independent economic value' the agreement was 0.71 and the kappa 0.51, for the 'identifying particular' 0.75 and 0.67, and for the 'common business purpose' 0.75 and 0.68 respectively. The lower agreement in case of the 'independent economic value' could be explained by the fact that this term was the first the annotators were dealing with. Although, we provided a detailed explanation of the annotation task we did not provide the annotators with an opportunity to practice before they started with the annotation. The practice could be helpful and we plan to use it in future additions to the corpus.

After the annotation was finished the annotators met and discussed the sentences for which their labels differed. In the end they were supposed to agree on consensus labels for all of those sentences. For example, the following sentence from the 'identifying particular' part of the corpus was assigned with different labels:

> Here, the district court found that the duty titles were not numbers, symbols, or other *identifying particulars*.

One of the reviewers opted for the 'certain value' label while the other one picked the 'high value' label. In the end the reviewers agreed that the goal of the sentence is not to elaborate on the meaning of the 'identifying particular' and that it provides grounds to conclude that, e.g., duty titles are not identifying particulars. Therefore, the 'certain value' label is more appropriate.

Table 2 reports counts for the consensus labels. The most frequent label (53.9%) is the 'potential value.' The least frequent (11.5%) is the 'high value' label. The distribution varies slightly for the different terms.

## 3 Features for Predicting Interpretive Usefulness of Sentences

For testing the hypothesis we came up with a tentative list of features that could be helpful in predicting the interpretive usefulness of a sentence. We reserve the refinement of this list for future work. In addition, many features were generated with very simple models which leaves space for significant improvements. We briefly describe each of the features in the following subsections.

### 3.1 Source

This category models the relation between the source of the term of interest (i.e., the statutory provision it comes from) and the source of the term as used in the retrieved sentence. To automatically generate this feature we used a legal citation extractor.[4] Each sentence can be assigned with one of the following labels:

1. *Same provision*: This label is predicted if we detect a citation of the provision the term of interest comes from in any of the 10 sentences preceding or following the sentence mentioning the term of interest.

2. *Same section*: We predict this label if we detect a citation of the provision from the same section of the United States Code in the window of 10 sentences around the sentence mentioning the term of interest.

3. *Different section*: This label is predicted if we detect any other citation to the United States Code anywhere in the decision's text.

4. *Different jurisdiction*: We predict this label if we are not able to detect any citation to the United States Code.

The distribution of the labels in this category is summarized in the top left corner of Table 3. We can see that the distribution wildly differs across the terms we work with. For the 'independent economic value' the 'different jurisdiction' (DJR) label is clearly dominant whereas for the 'common business purpose' we predict the 'same provision' (SPR) almost exclusively.

As an example let us consider the following sentence retrieved from one of the decisions:

> The full text of § *1839(3)(B)* is: "[...]".
> [...] Every firm other than the original

---

| | Source | | | | Semantic Similarity | | | | Structural Placement | | | | |
|---|---|---|---|---|---|---|---|---|---|---|---|---|---|
| | SPR | SSC | DSC | DJR | SAM | SIM | REL | DIF | STS | CIT | QEX | HD | FT |
| Ind. economic val. | 9 | 0 | 0 | 43 | 37 | 1 | 14 | 0 | 9 | 29 | 11 | 0 | 3 |
| Identifying part. | 39 | 28 | 0 | 4 | 67 | 0 | 0 | 4 | 29 | 33 | 5 | 0 | 4 |
| C. business purp. | 118 | 0 | 0 | 2 | 118 | 2 | 0 | 0 | 65 | 29 | 24 | 2 | 0 |
| Total | 166 | 28 | 0 | 49 | 224 | 3 | 14 | 4 | 103 | 91 | 40 | 2 | 7 |

| | Syntactic Importance | | | Rhetorical Role | | | | | | | | |
|---|---|---|---|---|---|---|---|---|---|---|---|---|
| | DOM | IMP | NOT | STL | APL | APA | STF | INL | EXP | RES | HLD | OTH |
| Ind. economic val. | 5 | 25 | 22 | 23 | 13 | 0 | 3 | 3 | 2 | 7 | 1 | 0 |
| Identifying part. | 3 | 21 | 47 | 32 | 7 | 1 | 6 | 9 | 5 | 6 | 5 | 0 |
| C. business purp. | 22 | 64 | 34 | 32 | 27 | 1 | 8 | 23 | 14 | 6 | 5 | 4 |
| Total | 30 | 110 | 103 | 87 | 47 | 2 | 17 | 35 | 21 | 19 | 11 | 4 |

| | Attribution | | | | | Assignment/Contrast | | | | | Feature | | |
|---|---|---|---|---|---|---|---|---|---|---|---|---|---|
| | JUD | LEG | PTY | WIT | EXP | NA | ASC | TSC | TSA | TNA | NA | AF | TF |
| Ind. economic val. | 20 | 25 | 7 | 0 | 0 | 52 | 0 | 0 | 0 | 0 | 37 | 0 | 15 |
| Identifying part. | 36 | 32 | 3 | 0 | 0 | 15 | 49 | 0 | 0 | 7 | 28 | 0 | 43 |
| C. business purp. | 87 | 25 | 7 | 0 | 1 | 107 | 8 | 0 | 3 | 2 | 98 | 11 | 11 |
| Total | 143 | 82 | 17 | 0 | 1 | 177 | 57 | 0 | 3 | 9 | 163 | 11 | 69 |

Table 3: The table shows distribution of the features generated for the prediction of sentences' interpretive usefulness.
Source: Same provision (SPR), same section (SSC), different section (DSC), different jurisdiction (DJR).
Semantic similarity: same (SAM), similar (SIM), related (REL), different (DIF).
Structural placement: quoted expression (QEX), citation (CIT), heading (HD), footnote (FT), standard sentence (STS).
Syntactic importance: dominant (DOM), important (IMP), not important (NOT).
Rhetorical role: application of law to factual context (APL), applicability assessment (APA), statement of fact (STF), interpretation of law (INL), statement of law (STL), general explanation or elaboration (EXP), reasoning statement (RES), holding (HLD), other (OTH).
Attribution: legislator (LEG), party to the dispute (PTY), witness (WIT), expert (EXP), judge (JUD).
Assignment/Contrast: another term is a specific case of the term of interest (ASC), the term of interest is a specific case of another term (TSC), the term of interest is the same as another term (TSA), the term of interest is not the same as another term (TNA), no assignment (NA).
Feature assignment: the term of interest is a feature of another term (TF), another term is a feature of the term of interest (AF), no feature assignment (NA).

equipment manufacturer and RAPCO had to pay dearly to devise, test, and win approval of similar parts; the details unknown to the rivals, and not discoverable with tape measures, had considerable "*independent economic value ... from not being generally known*".

Here we detect the citation to the same provision in the sentence mentioning the term of interest. We predict the 'same source' label.

## 3.2 Semantic Similarity

This category is auxiliary to the 'source' discussed in the preceding subsection. Here we model the semantic relationship between the term of interest as used in the statutory provision and in the retrieved sentence. Essentially, we ask if the meaning of the terms is the same and if not how much do the meanings differ. We partially model this feature based on the label in the 'source' category as well as on the cosine similarity between the bag-of-words (TFIDF) representations of the source provision and the retrieved sentence. Each sentence can be assigned with one of the following labels:

1. *Same*: We predict this label if the 'same provision' label was predicted in the source category.
2. *Similar*: We predict this label if the cosine similarity is higher than 0.5.
3. *Related*: We predict this label if the cosine similarity is between 0.25 and 0.5.
4. *Different*: We predict this label if the cosine similarity is lower than 0.25.

By definition this feature is useful only in case the 'same provision' label is not predicted in the 'source' category. The distribution of the labels in this category can be seen in the middle component of the top row in Table 3. As we have predicted the 'same' label in most of the cases, this feature did not prove as very helpful in our experiments (see Section 4). We plan to refine the notion of this feature in future work. For example, we would like to use a more sophisticated representation of the term of interest such as word2vec.

The two following examples show sentences that use the same term with different meaning:

> [...] the information derives independent economic value, actual or potential, from not being generally known to, and not being readily ascertainable through proper means by, the *public*;

> [...] posted in the establishment in a prominent position where it can be readily examined by the *public*;

The first sentence mentions the term 'public' for the purpose of the trade secret protection. The term refers to customers, competitors and the general group of experts on a specific topic. The second sentence uses the term to refer to a general 'public.'

### 3.3 Syntactic Importance

In this category we are interested in how dominant the term is in the retrieved sentence. To model the feature we use syntactic parsing (Chen and Manning, 2014). Specifically, we base our decision on the ratio of the tokens that are deeper in the tree structure (further from the root) than the tokens standing for the term of interest divided by the count of all the tokens. Each sentence can be assigned with one of the following labels:

1. *Dominant*: We predict this label if the ratio is greater than 0.5.
2. *Important*: This label is predicted if the ratio is less than 0.5 but greater than 0.2.
3. *Not important*: We predict this label if the ratio is less than 0.2.

The distribution of the labels in this category is summarized in the left section of the middle row in Table 3. We labeled most sentences as either 'important' or 'not important' (around the same proportion). Only a small number of sentences were labeled with the 'dominant' label.

As an example let us consider the following example sentence with its syntactic tree shown in Figure 1:

> The park where no *vehicles* are allowed was closed during the last month.

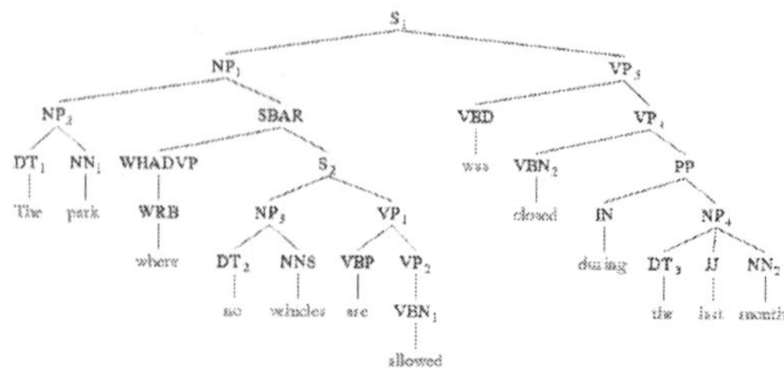

Figure 1:

The syntactic tree contains only one token which is deeper in the structure than the 'vehicle' (the term of interest). Therefore, the ratio is 1/13 and this sentence is labeled as 'not important.'

### 3.4 Structural Placement

This category describes the place of the retrieved sentence and the term of interest in the structure of the document it comes from. To model this feature we use simple pattern matching. Each sentence can be assigned with one of the following labels:

1. *Quoted expression*: We predict this label for a sentence that contains the term of interest in a sequence of characters enclosed by double or single quotes if the sequence starts with a lower case letter.
2. *Citation*: This label is predicted if all the conditions for the 'quoted expression' label are met except that the starting character of the sequence is in upper case.
3. *Heading*: This label is predicted if we detect an alphanumeric numbering token at the beginning of the retrieved sentence.
4. *Footnote*: We predict this label for a sentence that starts a line with a digits enclosed in square brackets.
5. *Standard sentence*: We predict this label if none of the patterns for other labels matches.

The distribution of the labels in this category is shown in the top right corner of Table 3. Almost all the sentences were labeled as the 'standard sentence', the 'citation', or the 'quoted expression.'

Only a very small number of sentences was recognized as the 'heading' or the 'footnote.'

Two examples below show a heading and a footnote correctly recognized in the retrieved sentences:

> A. Related Activities and *Common Business Purpose*

> [5] [...] However, in view of the '*common business purpose*' requirement of the Act, we think [...]

### 3.5 Rhetorical Role

In this category we are interested in the rhetorical role that the retrieved sentence has in the document it comes from. Although, some more sophisticated approaches to automatic generation of this feature have been proposed (Saravanan and Ravindran, 2010; Ravindran and others, 2008; Grabmair et al., 2015) we model it as a simple sentence classification task. We used bag of words (TFIDF weights) representation as features and manually assigned labels for training. Each sentence can be assigned with one of the following labels:

1. *Application of law to factual context*
2. *Applicability assessment*
3. *Statement of fact*
4. *Interpretation of law*
5. *Statement of law*
6. *General explanation or elaboration*
7. *Reasoning statement*
8. *Holding*
9. *Other*

The distribution of the labels in this category is shown in the right part of the middle row in Table 3. Most of the sentences were labeled as the 'statement of law,' the 'application of law,' or the 'interpretation of law.'

### 3.6 Attribution

This category models who has uttered the retrieved sentence. For the purpose of this paper we rely on pattern matching with the assumption that the judge utters the sentence if none of the patterns matches. Each sentence can be assigned with one of the following labels:

1. *Legislator*: We predict this label if we detect a citation to US statutory law followed by a pattern corresponding to citation described in the earlier category.

2. *Party to the Dispute*: We predict this category if we detect a mention of the party (either its name or its role such as plaintiff) followed by one of the specifically prepared list of verbs such as 'contend', 'claim', etc.

3. *Witness*: This label is predicted if we match the word 'witness' followed by one of the verbs from the same set as in case of the preceding label.

4. *Expert*: This label is predicted in the same way as the 'witness' label but instead of the word 'witness' we match 'expert'.

5. *Judge*: We predict this label if none of the patterns for other labels matches.

The distribution of the labels in this category is shown in the bottom left corner of Table 3. We were able to recognize a reasonable number of the 'legislator' labels but apart from that we almost always used the catch-all 'judge' label.

The following example shows a sentence for which we predict the 'party to the dispute' label:

> In support of his contention that Gold Star Chili and Caruso's Ristorante constitute an enterprise, *plaintiff alleges* that Caruso's Ristorante and Gold Star Chili were engaged in the related business activity [...].

### 3.7 Assignment/Contrast

Here we are interested if the term of interest in the retrieved sentence is said to be (or not to be) some other term. To model this category we use pattern matching on the verb phrase of which the term of interest is part (if there is such a phrase in the sentence). Each sentence can be assigned with one of the following labels:

1. *Another term is a specific case of the term of interest*: This label is predicted if one of the specified set of verbs (e.g., may be, can be) is preceded by a noun and followed by a term of interest within a verb phrase.

2. *The term of interest is a specific case of another term*: In case of this label we proceed in the same way as in case of the preceding label but the noun and the term of interest are swapped.

3. *The term of interest is the same as another term*: In case of this label we use a different set of verbs (e.g., is, equals) and we do not care about the order of the term of interest and the noun.

4. *The term of interest is not the same as another term*: We proceed in the same way as in the case of the preceding label but we also require a negation token to occur (e.g., not).

5. *No assignment*: We predict this label if none of the patterns for other labels matches.

The distribution of the labels in this category is shown in the middle part of the bottom row in Table 3. A certain amount of the 'another term is a specific case of the term of interest' was predicted in the 'identifying particular' part of the data set. For the rest of the dataset the catch-all 'no assignment' label was used in most of the cases.

The following example shows a sentence that we labeled with the 'the term of interest is the same as another term' label:

> The Fifth Circuit has held that the *profit motive* is a *common business purpose* if shared.

### 3.8 Feature Assignment

In this category we analyze if the term of interest in the retrieved sentence is said to be a feature of another term (or vice versa). We model this category by pattern matching on the verb phrase of which the term of interest is part. Each sentence can be assigned with one of the following labels:

1. *The term of interest is a feature of another term*: This label is predicted if one of the specified set of verbs (e.g., have) is followed by a term of interest within a verb phrase.

2. *Another term is a feature of the term of interest*: This label is predicted if the term of interest precedes one of the verbs.

3. *No feature assignment*: We predict this label if none of the patterns for other labels matches.

The distribution of the labels in this category is shown in the bottom left corner of Table 3. The 'no feature assignment' label was predicted in approximately 2/3 of the cases and the 'term of interest is a feature of another term' in the rest.

| Classifier | CV | STD | TEST | STD | SIG |
|---|---|---|---|---|---|
| Most frequent | .545 | .025 | .531 | .049 | – |
| Naïve Bayes | .544 | .037 | .611 | .066 | no |
| SVM | .633 | .044 | .657 | .066 | no |
| Random Forest | **.677** | .033 | **.696** | .042 | yes |

Table 4: Mean results from 100 runs of a classification experiment (CV: 10-fold cross validation on the training set, TEST: validation on the test set, SIG: statistical significance)

| Features | CV | STD | TEST | STD |
|---|---|---|---|---|
| -source | **.519** | .05 | .586 | .046 |
| -semantic relationship | .675 | .031 | .694 | .049 |
| -syntactic importance | .532 | .028 | **.521** | .047 |
| -structural placement | .695 | .033 | .708 | .047 |
| -rhetorical role | .687 | .033 | .695 | .049 |
| -attribution | .657 | .034 | .671 | .048 |
| -assignment/contrast | .668 | .032 | .669 | .045 |
| -feature assignment | .662 | .032 | .684 | .047 |

Table 5: Mean results of classification experiment where each line reports the performance when the respective feature was removed.

The following example shows a sentence that we labeled with the 'the term of interest is a feature of another term' label:

> However, Reiser concedes in its brief that the *process* has *independent economic value*.

Here, the independent economic value is said to be an attribute of the process.

## 4 Predicting Usefulness of Sentences for Interpretation of the Terms of Interest

We work with the dataset described in Section 2. The goal is to classify the sentences into the four categories reflecting their usefulness for the interpretation of the terms of interest. As features we use the categories described in Section 3.

The experiment starts with a random division of the sentences into a training set (2/3) and a test set. The resulting training set consists of 162 sentences while there are 81 sentences in the test set. As classification models we train a Naïve Bayes, an SVM (with linear kernel and L2 regularization), and a Random Forest (with 10 estimators and Gini impurity as a measure of the quality of a split) using the scikit-learn library (Pedregosa et al., 2011). We use a simple classifier always predicting the most frequent label as the baseline.

Because our data set is small and the division into the training and test set influences the performance we repeat the experiment 100 times. We report the mean results of 10-fold cross validation on the training set and evaluation on the test set as well as the standard deviations in Table 4.

All the three classifiers outperform the most frequent class baseline. However, due to the large variance of the results from the 100 runs the improvement is statistically significant ($\alpha = .05$) only for the Random Forest which is the best performing classifier overall. With the accuracy of .696 on the test set the agreement of the Random Forest classifier with the consensus labels is quite close to the inter-annotator agreement between the two human expert annotators (.746).

We also tested which features are the most important for the predictions with the Random Forest. We ran the 100-batches of the experiments leaving out one feature in each batch. The results reported in Table 5 show that the source and the syntactic importance were the most important.

## 5 Related Work

Because argumentation plays an essential role in law, the extraction of arguments from legal texts has been an active area of research for some time. Mochales and Moens detect arguments consisting of premises and conclusions and, using different techniques, they organize the individual arguments extracted from the decisions of the European Court of Human Rights into an overall structure (Moens et al., 2007; Mochales and Ieven, 2009; Mochales-Palau and Moens, 2007; Mochales and Moens, 2011). In their work on vaccine injury decisions Walker, Ashley, Grabmair and other researchers focus on extraction of evidential reasoning (Walker et al., 2011; Ashley and Walker, 2013; Grabmair et al., 2015). Bruninghaus and Ashley (2005) and Kubosawa et al. (2012) extract case factors that could be used in arguing about an outcome of the case. In addition, argumentation mining has been applied in a study of diverse areas such as parliamentary debates (Hirst et al., 2014) or public participation in rulemaking (Park et al., 2015).

The task we deal with is close to the traditional NLP task of query-focused summarization of multiple documents as described in Gupta (2010). Fisher and Roark (2006) presented a system based on supervised sentence ranking. Daumé and Marcu (2006) tackled the situation in which the retrieved pool of documents is large. Schiffman and McKeown (2007) cast the task into a question answering problem. An extension introducing interactivity was proposed by Lin et al. (2010).

A number of interesting applications deal with similar tasks in different domains. Sauper and Barzilay (2009) proposed an approach to automatic generation of Wikipedia articles. Demner-Fushman and Lin (2006) described an extractive summarization system for clinical QA. Wang et al. (2010) presented a system for recommending relevant information to the users of Internet forums and blogs. Yu et al. (2011) mine important product aspects from online consumer reviews.

## 6 Discussion and Future Work

The results of the experiments are promising. They confirm the hypothesis even though we used extremely simplistic (sometimes clearly inadequate) approaches to generate the features automatically. We have every reason to expect that improvements in the quality of the feature generation will improve the quality of the interpretive usefulness assessment. We would like to investigate this assumption in future work.

It is also worth mentioning that we used only simple off-the-shelf classification algorithms that we did not tweak or optimize for the task. As in the case of the features, improvements in the algorithms we use would most likely lead to an improvement in the quality of the interpretive usefulness assessment. We plan to focus on this aspect in future work.

The analysis of the importance of the individual features for the success in our task showed that contribution of some of the features was quite limited. We would caution against the conclusion that those features are not useful. It may very well be the case that our simplistic techniques for the automatic generation of those features did not model them adequately. As already mentioned, we plan on improving the means by which the features are generated in future work.

We are well aware of the limitations of the work stemming from the small size of the corpus. This is largely due to the fact that getting the labels is very expensive. Since the nature of this work is exploratory in the sense of showing that the task is (a) interesting and (b) can be automated, we could not afford a corpus of more adequate size. However, since the results of the experiments are promising we plan to extend the corpus.

This work is meant as the first step towards a fully functional and well described framework supporting argumentation about the meaning of statutory terms. Apart from facilitating easier access to law for lawyers, it is our goal to lower the barrier for public officials and other users who need to work with legal texts. In addition, we believe such a framework could support dialogue between lawyers and experts from other fields. There could be a great impact on legal education as well.

## 7 Conclusion

We investigated the possibility of automatic extraction of case law sentences that deal with the meaning of statutory terms. We showed that human annotators can reasonably agree on the interpretive usefulness of a sentence for argumentation about the meaning of a specific statutory term. We specified the list of features that could be useful for a prediction of the interpretive usefulness of a sentence. We used stock classification algorithms to confirm the hypothesis that by using a set of automatically generated linguistic features about/in the sentence it is possible to evaluate how useful the sentence is for an argumentation about the meaning of a term from a specific statutory provision.

## References


Kevin D Ashley and Vern R Walker. 2013. From informanon retrieval (ir) to argument retrieval (ar) for legal cases: Report on a baseline study.

Stefanie Brüninghaus and Kevin D Ashley. 2005. Generating legal arguments and predictions from case texts. In *Proceedings of the 10th international conference on Artificial intelligence and law*, pages 65–74. ACM.

Danqi Chen and Christopher D Manning. 2014. A fast and accurate dependency parser using neural networks. In *EMNLP*, pages 740–750.

Jordan Daci. 2010. Legal principles, legal values and legal norms: are they the same or different? *Academicus International Scientific Journal*, 02:109–115.

Hal Daumé III and Daniel Marcu. 2006. Bayesian query-focused summarization. In *Proceedings of the 21st International Conference on Computational Linguistics and the 44th annual meeting of the Association for Computational Linguistics*, pages 305–312. Association for Computational Linguistics.

Dina Demner-Fushman and Jimmy Lin. 2006. Answer extraction, semantic clustering, and extractive summarization for clinical question answering. In *Proceedings of the 21st International Conference on Computational Linguistics and the 44th annual meeting of the Association for Computational Linguistics*, pages 841–848. Association for Computational Linguistics.

Timothy Endicott. 2000. *Vagueness in Law*. Oxford University Press.

Timothy Endicott. 2014. Law and Language the stanford encyclopedia of philosophy. http://plato.stanford.edu/. Accessed: 2016-02-03.

Seeger Fisher and Brian Roark. 2006. Query-focused summarization by supervised sentence ranking and skewed word distributions. In *Proceedings of the Document Understanding Conference, DUC-2006, New York, USA*. Citeseer.

Matthias Grabmair, Kevin D Ashley, Ran Chen, Preethi Sureshkumar, Chen Wang, Eric Nyberg, and Vern R Walker. 2015. Introducing luima: an experiment in legal conceptual retrieval of vaccine injury decisions using a uima type system and tools. In *Proceedings of the 15th International Conference on Artificial Intelligence and Law*, pages 69–78. ACM.

Vishal Gupta and Gurpreet Singh Lehal. 2010. A survey of text summarization extractive techniques. *Journal of Emerging Technologies in Web Intelligence*, 2(3):258–268.

Herbert L. Hart. 1994. *The Concept of Law*. Clarendon Press, 2nd edition.

Graeme Hirst, Vanessa Wei Feng, Christopher Cochrane, and Nona Naderi. 2014. Argumentation, ideology, and issue framing in parliamentary discourse. In *ArgNLP*.

Shumpei Kubosawa, Youwei Lu, Shogo Okada, and Katsumi Nitta. 2012. Argument analysis. In *Legal Knowledge and Information Systems: JURIX 2012, the Twenty-fifth Annual Conference*, volume 250, page 61. IOS Press.

Jimmy Lin, Nitin Madnani, and Bonnie J Dorr. 2010. Putting the user in the loop: interactive maximal marginal relevance for query-focused summarization. In *Human Language Technologies: The 2010 Annual Conference of the North American Chapter of the Association for Computational Linguistics*, pages 305–308. Association for Computational Linguistics.

D. Neil MacCormick and Robert S. Summers. 1991. *Interpreting Statutes*. Darmouth.

Raquel Mochales and Aagje Ieven. 2009. Creating an argumentation corpus: do theories apply to real arguments?: a case study on the legal argumentation of the echr. In *Proceedings of the 12th International Conference on Artificial Intelligence and Law*, pages 21–30. ACM.

Raquel Mochales and Marie-Francine Moens. 2011. Argumentation mining. *Artificial Intelligence and Law*, 19(1):1–22.

Raquel Mochales-Palau and M Moens. 2007. Study on sentence relations in the automatic detection of argumentation in legal cases. *FRONTIERS IN ARTIFICIAL INTELLIGENCE AND APPLICATIONS*, 165:89.

Marie-Francine Moens, Erik Boiy, Raquel Mochales Palau, and Chris Reed. 2007. Automatic detection of arguments in legal texts. In *Proceedings of the 11th international conference on Artificial intelligence and law*, pages 225–230. ACM.

Joonsuk Park, Cheryl Blake, and Claire Cardie. 2015. Toward machine-assisted participation in erulemaking: an argumentation model of evaluability. In *Proceedings of the 15th International Conference on Artificial Intelligence and Law*, pages 206–210. ACM.

F. Pedregosa, G. Varoquaux, A. Gramfort, V. Michel, B. Thirion, O. Grisel, M. Blondel, P. Prettenhofer, R. Weiss, V. Dubourg, J. Vanderplas, A. Passos, D. Cournapeau, M. Brucher, M. Perrot, and E. Duchesnay. 2011. Scikit-learn: Machine learning in Python. *Journal of Machine Learning Research*, 12:2825–2830.

Balaraman Ravindran et al. 2008. Automatic identification of rhetorical roles using conditional random fields for legal document summarization.

M Saravanan and Balaraman Ravindran. 2010. Identification of rhetorical roles for segmentation and summarization of a legal judgment. *Artificial Intelligence and Law*, 18(1):45–76.

Christina Sauper and Regina Barzilay. 2009. Automatically generating wikipedia articles: A structure-aware approach. In *Proceedings of the Joint Conference of the 47th Annual Meeting of the ACL and the 4th International Joint Conference on Natural Language Processing of the AFNLP: Volume 1-Volume 1*, pages 208–216. Association for Computational Linguistics.

Barry Schiffman, Kathleen McKeown, Ralph Grishman, and James Allan. 2007. Question answering using integrated information retrieval and information extraction. In *HLT-NAACL*, pages 532–539.

Vern R Walker, Nathaniel Carie, Courtney C DeWitt, and Eric Lesh. 2011. A framework for the extraction and modeling of fact-finding reasoning from legal decisions: lessons from the vaccine/injury project corpus. *Artificial Intelligence and Law*, 19(4):291–331.

Jia Wang, Qing Li, Yuanzhu Peter Chen, and Zhangxi Lin. 2010. Recommendation in internet forums and blogs. In *Proceedings of the 48th Annual Meeting of the Association for Computational Linguistics*, pages 257–265. Association for Computational Linguistics.

Jianxing Yu, Zheng-Jun Zha, Meng Wang, and Tat-Seng Chua. 2011. Aspect ranking: Identifying important product aspects from online consumer reviews. In *Proceedings of the 49th Annual Meeting of the Association for Computational Linguistics: Human Language Technologies - Volume 1*, HLT '11, pages 1496–1505, Stroudsburg, PA, USA. Association for Computational Linguistics.

# Scrutable Feature Sets for Stance Classification


**Angrosh Mandya**
Computing Science
University of Aberdeen, UK
angroshmandya@abdn.ac.uk

**Advaith Siddharthan**
Computing Science
University of Aberdeen, UK
advaith@abdn.ac.uk

**Adam Wyner**
Computing Science
University of Aberdeen, UK
azwyner@abdn.ac.uk



## Abstract

This paper describes and evaluates a novel feature set for stance classification of argumentative texts; i.e. deciding whether a post by a user is for or against the issue being debated. We model the debate both as attitude bearing features, including a set of automatically acquired 'topic terms' associated with a Distributional Lexical Model (DLM) that captures the writer's attitude towards the topic term, and as dependency features that represent the points being made in the debate. The stance of the text towards the issue being debated is then learnt in a supervised framework as a function of these features. The main advantage of our feature set is that it is scrutable: The reasons for a classification can be explained to a human user in natural language. We also report that our method outperforms previous approaches to stance classification as well as a range of baselines based on sentiment analysis and topic-sentiment analysis.


## 1 Introduction

In recent years, stance classification for online debates has received increasing research interest (Somasundaran and Wiebe, 2010; Anand et al., 2011; Walker et al., 2012; Ranade et al., 2013; Sridhar et al., 2014). Given a post belonging to a two-sided debate on an issue (e.g. abortion rights; see Table 1), the task is classify the post as for or against the issue. The argumentative nature of such posts makes stance classification difficult; for example, one

has to follow the reasoning quite closely to decide which of the posts in Table 1 argues for or against abortion.

In Table 1, the posts are monologic (independent of each other), but even with the availability of dialogic structure connecting posts, both humans and classifiers experience difficulties in stance classification (Anand et al., 2011), in part because posts that contain rebuttal arguments do not provide clear evidence that they are arguing for or against the main issue being debated. Stance classification is considered particularly challenging however when the posts are monologic since the lack of dialogic structure means all features for classification have to be extracted from the text itself. Indeed studies to classify such independent posts have previously found it difficult to even beat a unigram classifier baseline; for example, Somasundaran and Wiebe (2010) achieved only a 1.5% increase in accuracy from the use of more sophisticated features such as opinion and arguing expressions over a simple unigram model.

In this paper, we propose a new feature set for stance classification of independent posts that, unlike previous work, captures two key characteristics of such debates; namely, writers express their attitudes towards a range of topics associated with the issue being debated and also argue by making logical points. We model the debate using a combination of the following features.

- **topic-stance features** – a set of automatically extracted 'topic terms' (for abortion rights, these would include, for example, 'fetus', 'baby', 'woman' and 'life'), where each topic term is associated with a distributional lexical model (DLM) that captures the writer's stance towards that topic.

- **stance bearing terminology** – words related

60


*Proceedings of the 3rd Workshop on Argument Mining*, pages 60–69,
Berlin, Germany, August 7-12, 2016. ©2016 Association for Computational Linguistics

| FOR ABORTION RIGHTS |
|---|
| If women (not men) are solely burdened by pregnancy, they must have a choice. Men are dominant in their ability to impregnate a woman, but carry no responsibilities afterward. If woman carry the entire burden of pregnancy, they must have a choice. |

| AGAINST ABORTION RIGHTS |
|---|
| Life is an individual right, not a privilege, for unborn humans [...] The right to life does not depend, and must not be contingent, on the pleasure of anyone else, not even a parent or sovereign [...] |

Table 1: Samples from posts arguing for and against abortion rights

    by adjectival modifiers (amod) and the noun compound (nn) relations that carry stance bearing language.

- **logical point features** – features of the form subject-verb-object (SVO) extracted from the dependency parse that capture basic points being made.

- **unigrams and dependency features** – backoff features, useful for classifying short posts lacking other features.

The contributions of this paper are two fold. Using the features listed above, we learn the stance of the debate towards the issue in a supervised setting, demonstrating better classification performance than previous work. Second, we argue that our feature set lends itself to human scrutable stance classification, through features that are human readable.

The paper is organised as follows. In §2, we discuss related work on stance classification. In §3, we describe our methods to model online debates and in §4, we present and discuss the results achieved in this study. In §5, we present our conclusions.

## 2   Related work

Somasundaran and Wiebe (2010) developed a balanced corpus (with half the posts for and the other half against) of political and ideological debates and carried out experiments on stance classification pertaining to four debates on abortion rights, creation, gay rights and gun rights. They achieved an overall accuracy of 63.9% using a sentiment lexicon as well as an ngrams-based lexicon of arguing phrases derived from the manual annota-

tions in the MPQA corpus (Wilson and Wiebe, 2005), barely outperforming a unigram baseline that achieved 62.5%. They also reported performance using the sentiment lexicon alone of only 55.0% and made the point that sentiment features alone were not useful for stance.

More recently, Hasan and Ng (2014) have focused on identifying reasons for supporting or opposing an issue under debate, using a corpus that provides information about post sequence, and with manually annotated reasons. The authors experiment with different features such as n-grams, dependency-based features, frame-semantic features, quotation features and positional features for stance classification of reasons. Nguyen and Litman (2015) proposed a feature reduction method based on the semi-supervised derivation of lexical signals of argumentative and domain content. Specifically, the method involved postprocessing a topic-model to extract argument words (lexical signals of argumentative content) and domain words (terminologies in argument topics).

A larger number of studies have focused on the use of dialogic structure for stance classification. Anand et al. (2011) worked with debates that have rebuttal links between posts. With respect to stance classification, they achieved accuracies ranging from 54% to 69% using such contextual features. Walker et al. (2012) focused on capturing the dialogic structure between posts in terms of agreement relations between speakers. They showed that such a representation improves results as against the use of contextual features alone, achieving accuracies ranging from 57% to 64%. Several others have modelled dialogic structure in more sophisticated ways, reporting further improvements from such strategies (Ranade et al., 2013; Sridhar et al., 2014, for example).

For the related task of opinion mining, dependency parse based features have been shown to be useful. Joshi and Penstein-Rosé (2009) transformed dependency triples into 'composite backoff features' to show that they generalise better than regular dependency features. The composite backoff features replaces either head term or modifier term with its POS tag in a dependency relation to result in two types of features for each relation. Greene and Resnik (2009) focused on 'syntactic packaging' of ideas to identify implicit sentiment. The authors proposed the concept of observable proxies for underlying semantics (OPUS) which involves identifying a set of relevant terms using relative frequency ratio. These terms are used to identify all relations with these terms in the dependency graph, which are further used to define the feature set. Paul and Girju (2010) presented a two-stage approach to summarise multiple contrasting viewpoints in opinionated text. In the first stage they used the topic-aspect model (TAM) for jointly modelling topics and viewpoints in the text. Amongst other features such as bag-of-words, negation and polarity, the TAM model also used the composite backoff features proposed by (Joshi and Penstein-Rosé, 2009).

In summary, many studies on stance classification have focused on the use of dialogic structure between posts (Anand et al., 2011; Walker et al., 2012; Ranade et al., 2013; Sridhar et al., 2014), but there has been less work on exploring feature sets for monologic posts, though a large body of such work exists for the related task of opinion mining. We are unaware of any attention paid to the scrutability of classifiers, though users might well be interested in why a post has been classified in a certain manner. To address these gaps, we consider again the task of stance classification from monologic posts, using the dataset created by Somasundaran and Wiebe (2010). We focus on modelling of the patterns within a post rather than connections between posts, and aim to design a competitive classifier whose decisions can be explained to a user.

## 3  Methods

As described earlier, the goals of this paper are two fold: (1) to develop a classifier for stance classification; and (2) employ the results of classification to create human readable explanations of the reasons for classification. Accordingly, we focus on the following features which lend themselves to human readable explanation, as discussed later: (a) topic-based distributional lexical models; (b) stance bearing relations; (c) points represented as subject-verb-object triplets.

### 3.1  Distributional Lexical Model of Topic

Dependency grammar allows us to identify syntactically related words in a sentence, by modelling the syntactic structure of a sentence using binary asymmetrical relations (De Marneffe and Manning, 2008). We use these relations to build a Distributional Lexical Model (DLM), excluding stop words such as determiners and conjunctions to obtain a set of content words connected to the topic term through syntax. The DLM is constructed in three steps:

*Step 1.* identify topic terms $t_i$ in the sentence;

*Step 2.* for each $t_i$, identify all content words $w_j$ in a dependency relation with $t_i$.

*Step 3.* for each $w_j$, identify all content words $w_k$ in a dependency relation with $w_j$; i.e., identify words that are within two dependency relations of the topic term.

In order to derive the topic terms, we used MALLET (McCallum, 2002), which implements topic modelling using Latent Dirichlet Allocation (LDA) (Blei et al., 2003). Given a set of documents, MALLET produces a set of likely topics where each topic is a distribution over the vocabulary of the document set such that the higher probability words contribute more towards defining the topic. We configured MALLET to produce 10 set of likely topics for the collection of posts for a given political debate, and used the default setting of the top 19 words for each topic. As we required our topic words to be nouns, we filtered the 190 words by part of speech. After further removing repetitions of words in different topics, this resulted in 96, 105, 135, 105 and 110 distinct topic terms for the political debates on abortion rights, creation, gay rights, god and gun rights, respectively. Examples of such topic terms created for the domain of abortion rights are shown in Table 2.

For the sentence and dependency parse shown in Fig. 1 (with punctuation and word positions removed for simplicity), there are three topic terms: 'fetus', 'woman' and 'pregnancy', and the 3-steps above generate the following DLMs:

|           |                                          |
|-----------|------------------------------------------|
| *fetus*:  | 'causes'; 'sickness'; 'discomfort'; 'pain'; 'woman' |
| *woman*:  | 'causes'; 'sickness'; 'discomfort'; 'pain'; 'pregnancy'; 'labor' |
| *pregnancy*: | 'causes'; 'woman'; 'labor' |

```
The fetus causes sickness discomfort and ex-
treme pain to a woman during her pregnancy
and labor.

det(fetus, the)
nsubj(causes, fetus)
dobj(causes, sickness)
dobj(causes, discomfort)
conj_and(sickness, discomfort)
dobj(causes, and)
conj_and(sickness, and)
amod(pain, extreme)
dobj(causes, pain)
conj_and(sickness, pain)
det(woman, a)
prep_to(causes, woman)
poss(pregnancy, her)
prep_during(woman, pregnancy)
prep_during(woman, labor)
conj_and(pregnancy, labor)
```

Figure 1: Dependency Parse (simplified to re-
move punctuation and word positions)

These features facilitate scrutability because
we can explain a classification of a post as
'for abortion rights' with a sentence such as
*"This post is classified as being in favour of
abortion rights because it associates words such
as 'causes', 'sickness', 'discomfort', 'pain' and
'woman' with the term 'fetus'."* Note that
in practice only a few features will select for
a particular stance, and this example (which
uses all the word pairs) is just for illustration.

The process of deriving the model for the
topic term *fetus* from a dependency tree is
graphically shown in Fig. 2. As seen, the word
*causes* (shown in thin dotted lines) is identified in Step 2 and the other words *discomfort,
sickness, pain* and *woman* are obtained in Step
3 (shown in thick dotted lines). Non-content
words are excluded from the model.

This method is aimed at identifying stance
bearing words associated with topic terms in
argumentative posts. The resulting graph for
the post arguing for abortion in Table 4 is

| Abortion Topic Terms |
| --- |
| life; human; conception; embryo; choice; sex; vote; position; birth; rape; war; church; act; evil; fetus; person; body; womb; brain; baby; sperm; egg; cell; logic; people; argument; god; reason; law; woman; pregnancy; children; family; abortion; murder; |

Table 2: Examples of topic terms produced by
MALLET for the domain of abortion rights

shown in Fig. 3, where the labelled arc indicates the sentence in which the relation appears, and the direction of the arrow indicates
whether the topic term precedes or follows the
related word. As seen, a topic word can be
connected to different terms in the graph, e.g.
*pain* and *causes* are connected to *fetus* in sentences 1 and 2.

## 3.2  Stance-bearing terminology

We also consider words connected by adjecti-
val modifier (amod) and noun compound modifier (nn) relations from the dependency graph
as features for the classifier. Given the political debate on abortion rights, phrases such
as 'individual rights', 'personal choices', 'personal decision' and 'unwanted children' are
used primarily in posts arguing for abortion
rights. Similarly, phrases such as 'human life',
'unborn child', 'innocent child' and 'distinct
DNA' provide good indicators that the posts
is arguing against abortion rights. In the example in Fig. 1, the feature 'extreme-pain' is
extracted in this manner. These features could
be used in an explanation in a sentence such
as *"This post is classified as being in favour of
abortion rights because it contains subjective
phrases such as 'extreme pain'."*

## 3.3  Modelling argumentative points

We also extract features aimed at modelling
elementary points made in a debate. We do
this in a limited manner by defining a point
simply as a subject-verb-object triple from the
dependency parse. More sophisticated definitions would not necessarily result in useful features for classification. For the sentence in Fig.
1, the following points are extracted to be used
as features:

```
fetus-causes-sickness
fetus-causes-discomfort
fetus-causes-and
fetus-causes-pain
```

Non-content words are excluded from the
analysis. This analysis could be used to construct explanations such as *"This post is classified as being in favour of abortion rights because it makes points such as 'fetus causes
sickness', 'fetus causes discomfort' and 'fetus
causes pain'."*

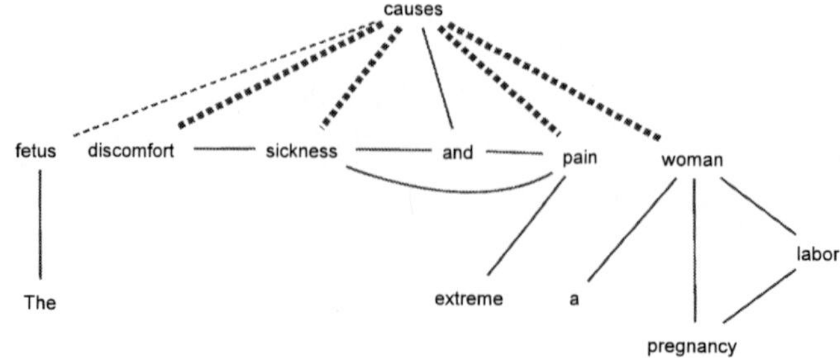

Figure 2: Deriving related words for 'fetus' from the dependency graph.

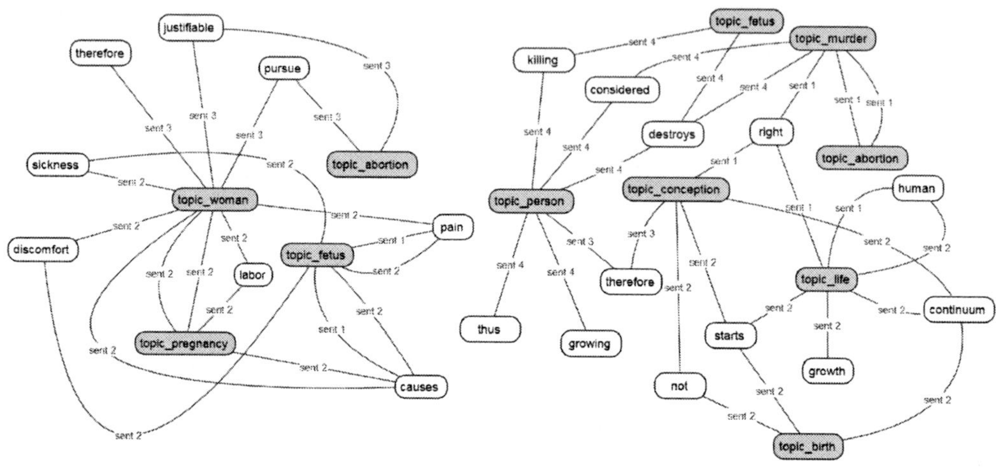

(a) Post arguing for abortion rights

(b) Post arguing against abortion rights

Figure 3: DLM models for the two posts in Table 4

## 3.4 Baselines

In addition to the features proposed above, we experimented with a variety of baselines for comparison.

### 3.4.1 Sentiment model

Our first baseline involved treating stance ('for' or 'against') as sentiment ('positive' or 'negative'). For this purpose, we used the Stanford sentiment tool [1] (Socher et al., 2013) to obtain sentence-level sentiment labels and provide these as features for stance classification of posts.

### 3.4.2 Topic-sentiment model

However, we do not expect a direct equivalence between sentiment and stance; for example, in Table 3, a negative sentiment is expressed in sentences arguing *for* abortion and

a positive sentiment is expressed in sentences arguing *against* abortion. Our second baseline is to therefore model the stance of a post using features that indicate the sentiment of the writer towards key topics related to the issue being debated.

For example, let us consider the two sentences that argue for abortion in Table 3. Using topic modelling, we can identify topic terms such as 'fetus' and 'woman' in sentence 1. Further, using sentiment analysis the sentence can be identified to be negative. By tagging this sentiment to the topic terms contained in the sentence, we can associate a negative sentiment with topic terms 'fetus' and 'human'. Similarly for sentence 2, a negative sentiment can be associated with topic terms such as 'fetus', 'woman' and 'pregnancy'.

This model has the advantage over the sentiment analysis baseline that sentiment is asso-

[1] http://nlp.stanford.edu:8080/sentiment/

| Sentences arguing for abortion rights |
| --- |
| 1. A fetus is no more a human than an acorn is a tree. |
| 2. The fetus causes sickness, discomfort, and and extreme pain to a woman during her pregnancy and labor. |

| Sentences arguing against abortion rights |
| --- |
| 3. A fetus is uniquely capable of becoming a person; deserves rights, it is unquestionable that the fetus, at whatever stage of development, will inevitably develop the traits of a full-grown human person. |
| 4. This is why extending a right to life is of utmost importance; the future of the unborn depends on it. |

Table 3: Example sentences arguing for and against abortion rights

| For abortion rights |
| --- |
| The fetus causes physical pain; the woman has a right to self-defense. The fetus causes sickness, discomfort, and extreme pain to a woman during her pregnancy and labor. It is, therefore, justifiable for a woman to pursue an abortion in self-defense. |

| Against abortion rights |
| --- |
| Human life and a right to life begin at conception; abortion is murder. Human life is continuum of growth that starts at conception, not at birth. The person, therefore, begins at conception. Killing the fetus, thus, destroys a growing person and can be considered murder. |

Table 4: Example posts for and against abortion rights

ciated with topic terms such as 'fetus', rather than the wider issue (abortion) being debated; here, a negative sentiment expressed towards a fetus is not a negative sentiment expressed towards abortion.

Applying the topic-sentiment model to the sentences in Table 3 arguing against abortion, we can associate a positive sentiment for topic terms such as 'fetus', 'person', 'stage', 'development' and 'human' in sentence 3, and for topic terms 'life' and 'unborn' in sentence 4.

We used Mallet as described in §3.1 to derive the topic terms. For an example of a topic-sentiment model, see Fig. 4, which shows the model obtained for the posts in Table 4.

### 3.4.3 Unigram model

We used a third baseline feature set containing all unigrams. The more realistic assumption here (compared to equating stance with sentiment) is that writers use different vocabularies to argue for or against an issue, and therefore a model can be learnt that predicts the likelihood of a class based solely on the words used in the post. As mentioned earlier, previous studies have struggled to outperform such a unigram model (Somasundaran and Wiebe, 2010).

### 3.4.4 Full dependency model

Our proposed feature set for stance classification using a distributional lexical model, stance bearing terminology and points was designed to be scrutable, but therefore made use of only a subset of word-pair features from

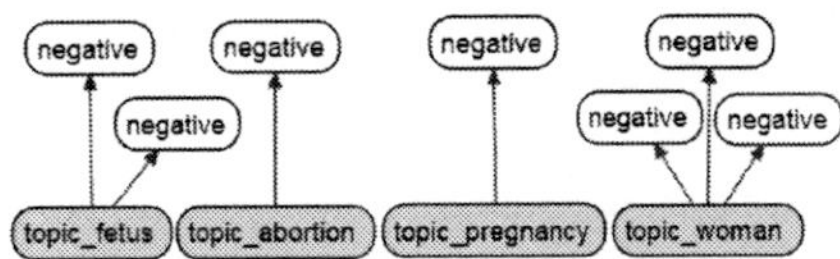


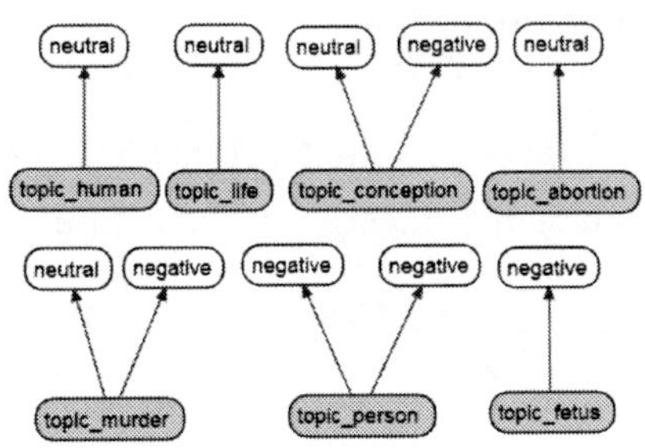


Figure 4: Topic-sentiment model for the two posts in Table 4

the dependency graph. We also evaluated this against a baseline feature set which makes use of all word-pairs obtained from the dependency graph.

## 4 Evaluation

We used the dataset created by Somasundaran and Wiebe (2010) containing monologic posts about five issues: abortion, creation, gay rights, god and gun rights. Somasundaran and Wiebe (2010) reported results on a balanced subset of the corpus with equal numbers of posts for and against each issue. We adopted the same methodology as them to create a balanced subset and evaluated on our balanced dataset containing 4870 posts in total, with

| Feature set | Abortion rights[*] | Creation | Gay rights | Existence of God | Gun rights | Average |
|---|---|---|---|---|---|---|
| **Baselines** | | | | | | |
| B1 | 51.46 | 52.56 | 50.67 | 53.52 | 49.48 | 51.53 |
| B2 | 57.72 | 56.64 | 60.89 | 61.23 | 61.77 | 59.65 |
| B3 | 77.74 | 77.50 | 76.52 | 76.33 | 83.95 | 78.40 |
| B4 | 87.10 | 86.13 | 86.94 | 85.12 | 87.71 | 86.60 |
| **Topic DLM** | | | | | | |
| D1 | 73.37 | 67.48 | 77.87 | 66.34 | 70.98 | 71.20 |
| **SVO, amod and nn** | | | | | | |
| S1 | 70.45 | 72.14 | 72.25 | 67.20 | 72.18 | 70.84 |
| **Combined Models** | | | | | | |
| C1 (D1+S1) | 77.35 | 76.22 | 78.48 | 78.06 | 76.10 | 77.24 |
| C2 (D1+S1+B3) | 84.06 | 82.86 | 82.81 | 83.38 | 88.39 | 84.30 |
| C3 (D1+S1+B3+B4) | 89.40 | 87.99 | 90.18 | 88.05 | 93.51 | 89.26 |

[*]Development set

Table 5: Results of supervised learning experiments using Naive Bayes Multinomial model

1030, 856, 1478, 920 and 586 posts for domains of abortion rights, creation, gay rights, god and gun rights, respectively. We developed our ideas by manual examination of the abortion rights debate, leaving the other four debates unseen. We report results for both the development set and the four unseen test sets.

### 4.1 Classifier and Evaluation Metric

We conducted experiments using Multinomial Naive Bayes classifier implemented in the Weka toolkit (Hall et al., 2009). The Multinomial Naive Bayes model has been previously shown to perform better on text classification tasks with increasing vocabulary size, taking into account word frequencies (McCallum et al., 1998), and this was also our experience. For feature sets produced by each model described in the Methods section, we used the FilteredAttributeEval method available in Weka for feature selection, retaining all features with a score greater than zero. Feature counts were normalised by tf*idf. The performance of the classifier is reported using the accuracy metric, which is most appropriate for a balanced dataset.

### 4.2 Compared Models

Our discussion in §3 results in the following different models for stance classification. We present in the next section, the results of our experiments.

1. Baseline Models:
   B1 Sentence level sentiment features.
   B2 Topic-sentiment features.
   B3 Unigram features.
   B4 Dependency features composed of all word pairs connected by a dependency relation.
2. Distributional Lexical Models (DLM):
   D1 Topic based features resulting from DLM discussed in §3.1.
3. SVO, amod and nn relations based model:
   S1 The subject-verb-object (SVO) triplets, also broken up into SV and VO pairs, and the word pairs obtained from the amod and nn relations in the dependency parse.
4. Combined Models:
   C1 D1+S1 - combining topic based features with SVO triplets and word-pairs from amod and nn relations.
   C2 D1+S1+B3 - combining topic based features with SVO, word-pairs from amod and nn relations, and unigrams.
   C3 D1+S1+B3+B4 - combining topic based features with SVO, word-pairs from amod and nn relations, unigrams and dependency features.

### 4.3 Results and analysis

**Performance of various models:** The 10-fold cross validation results for Multinomial Naive Bayes for different models are reported in Table 5.

As seen in Table 5, the baseline B4 using all relations from the dependency parse performs significantly better compared to other models that focus on selecting specific features for stance classification. The features that we introduce (D1 and S1) become competitive only when combined with one or more baseline models. C3, the best performing model, combines the unigram and dependency baselines with topic DLMs, SVO points, and stance bearing amod and nn relations, and outperforms previously published approaches to stance classification described in §2 by a substantial margin.

With respect to scrutability, the features in C1, as described earlier in this paper, are easily explained in natural language. C2, the first competitive system, extends C1 with unigram features. These can be easily included in an explanation; for example, *"This post is classified as being in favour of abortion rights because it contains words such as 'extreme' and 'pain'."*. C3, which is the best performing classifier, also uses arbitrary dependency features that are harder to use in explanations. However, even when using C3, the classification decision for the vast majority of posts can be explained using features from C2. Table 6 explores the coverage of different features in the dataset, following feature selection.

| Feature set | Coverage |
|---|---|
| **Baselines** | |
| B1 | 100.00% |
| B2 | 32.90% |
| B3 | 74.41% |
| B4 | 75.10% |
| **Topic DLM** | |
| D1 | 37.64% |
| **SVO, amod and nn** | |
| S1 | 40.56% |
| **Combined Models** | |
| C1 (D1+S1) | 54.40% |
| C2 (D1+S1+B3) | 80.45% |
| C3 (D1+S1+B3+B4) | 86.58% |

Table 6: Percentage of posts containing at least one feature for each feature set (following feature selection)

**Poverty of sentiment-based models:** While we expected our baseline model B1 that uses an off the shelf sentiment classifier to perform poorly on this task (see example in §3.4.2 for reasoning), we were slightly surprised by the poor performance of the topic-sentiment models (B2). Clearly there is more to stance classification than sentiment, and more effort into modelling the range of lexical associations with topic terms pays off for the distributional lexical models. The unigram model (B3) performed better than the topic-sentiment models (B2) and the off-the-shelf sentiment analysis tool (B1). This supports the results of Somasundaran and Wiebe (2010), who similarly found that sentiment features did not prove helpful, while unigram features were hard to

beat. We additionally find that dependency features B4 provide an even stronger baseline.

**Comparison with other systems:** Our experiments are directly comparable to Somasundaran and Wiebe (2010) as we report results on the same dataset. Our best scoring system achieves an overall accuracy of 89.26%, in comparison to their overall accuracy of 63.63%, a statistically significant increase ($p < 0.0001$; z-test for difference in proportions). Further, our system performs better for each of the debate issues investigated.

While not directly comparable, our results also compare well to studies in dialogic stance classification. For example, Anand et al. (2011) achieved a maximum of 69% accuracy using contextual features based on LIWC, and Walker et al. (2012) obtained a highest of 64% using information related to agreement relations between speakers. Ranade et al. (2013) achieved 70.3% by focusing on capturing users' intent and Sentiwordnet scores. More recently, Hasan and Ng (2014) achieved an overall accuracy of 66.25% for four domains including abortion and gay rights, using features based on dependency parse, frame-semantics, quotations and position information. Their accuracy for abortion and gay rights was 66.3% and 65.7%, respectively. Our approach, unlike these, focuses on a finegrained modelling of the lexical context of important topic terms, and on dependency relations that relate to points and stance bearing phrases. Our results show that this is indeed beneficial.

### 4.4 Human readable explanations

While previous work in stance classification has primarily focused on the classifier, this is a topic where scrutability is of interest. A user might want to know why a post has been classified in a certain way, and a good response can build trust in the system. The features we have introduced in this paper lend themselves to the generation of explanations. Table 7 shows some example posts (selected to be short due to space constraints), the features (after feature selection) present in the posts, and the generated explanations. The points are generated from the SVO by including all premodifiers of the subject, verb and object in the sentence. The explanation sentence is

**Post:** Abortion is the woman's choice, not the father's The Father should be told that the woman is having an abortion but until he carries and gives birth to his own baby then it is not his choice to tell the woman that she has to keep and give a painful birth to this fetus.
*Points derived using SVO information:* ['Abortion is the woman choice'; 'it is not his choice']; *Unigrams:* ['fetus'; 'woman'; 'choice']; *No other features present*
*Classified Stance:* **For** Abortion rights
**Explanation:** This post has been classified as being in favour of abortion rights because it makes points such as 'abortion is the woman's choice' and 'it is not his choice', and uses vocabulary such as 'fetus', 'woman' and 'choice'.

**Post:** A dog is not a person. Therefore, it does not have rights. Positive feelings about dogs should have no bearing on the discussion. A fetus is not a person. Negative feelings about the metaphysically independent status of women should have no bearing on the discussion.
*Points derived using SVO information:* ['a fetus is not a person'; 'a dog is not a person']; *Unigrams:* ['fetus'; 'independent'; 'bearing']; *No other features present*
*Classified Stance:* **For** Abortion rights
**Explanation:** This post has been classified as being in favour of abortion rights because it makes points such as 'a fetus is not a person' and 'a dog is not a person', and uses vocabulary such as 'fetus', 'independent', and 'bearing'.

**Post:** God exists in the unborn as in the born
*Unigrams:* ['unborn']; *No other features present*
*Classified Stance:* **Against** Abortion rights
**Explanation:** This post has been classified as being against abortion rights because it uses vocabulary such as 'unborn'.

**Post:** Any abortions should not be aloud if you are stupid enough to get pregnant when you do not want a baby or selfish enough not to want to look after it when you find out it may have an illness then it is your own fault why should the life of an innocent unborn child be killed because of your mistake
*amod features:* ['unborn child'; 'innocent child']; *Unigrams:* ['baby'; 'unborn'; 'killed']; *No other features present*
*Classified Stance:* **Against** Abortion rights
**Explanation:** This post has been classified as being against abortion rights because it uses vocabulary such as 'baby', 'unborn' and 'killed' and subjective phrases such as 'unborn child' and 'innocent child'.

Table 7: Examples of explanations generated for stance classification

based on a very simple template that takes as input a list for each feature type, and populates slots based on which features are present.

## 5 Conclusions and future work

In this paper, we presented a new feature set for stance classification in online debates, designed to be scrutable by human users as well as capable of achieving high accuracy of classification. We showed that our proposed model significantly outperforms other approaches based on sentiment analysis and topic-sentiment analysis. We believe our models capture some of the subtleties of argumentation in text, by breaking down the stance towards the debated issue into expressed stances towards a variety of related topics, as well as modelling, albeit in a simple way, the notion of a point. However, this is just a first step; we do not yet model the sequence of points or topic-stance changes in the post, or dialogic structure connecting posts. Finally, stance classification is a staging post to more in-depth argumentation mining. Our ultimate goal is to model a richer argumentative framework including the support and rebuttal of claims, and the changing of opinion by users in online debates.

## Acknowledgements

This work was supported by the Economic and Social Research Council [Grant number ES/M001628/1].

## References

Pranav Anand, Marilyn Walker, Rob Abbott, Jean E Fox Tree, Robeson Bowmani, and Michael Minor. 2011. Cats rule and dogs drool!: Classifying stance in online debate. In *Proceedings of the 2nd workshop on computational approaches to subjectivity and sentiment analysis*, pages 1–9. Association for Computational Linguistics.

David M Blei, Andrew Y Ng, and Michael I Jordan.

2003. Latent dirichlet allocation. *the Journal of machine Learning research*, 3:993–1022.

Marie-Catherine De Marneffe and Christopher D Manning. 2008. The stanford typed dependencies representation. In *Coling 2008: Proceedings of the workshop on Cross-Framework and Cross-Domain Parser Evaluation*, pages 1–8. Association for Computational Linguistics.

Stephan Greene and Philip Resnik. 2009. More than words: Syntactic packaging and implicit sentiment. In *Proceedings of human language technologies: The 2009 annual conference of the north american chapter of the association for computational linguistics*, pages 503–511. Association for Computational Linguistics.

Mark Hall, Eibe Frank, Geoffrey Holmes, Bernhard Pfahringer, Peter Reutemann, and Ian H Witten. 2009. The weka data mining software: an update. *ACM SIGKDD explorations newsletter*, 11(1):10–18.

Kazi Saidul Hasan and Vincent Ng. 2014. Why are you taking this stance? identifying and classifying reasons in ideological debates. In *Proceedings of the 2014 Conference on Empirical Methods in Natural Language Processing (EMNLP)*, pages 751–762, Doha, Qatar, October. Association for Computational Linguistics.

Mahesh Joshi and Carolyn Penstein-Rosé. 2009. Generalizing dependency features for opinion mining. In *Proceedings of the ACL-IJCNLP 2009 Conference Short Papers*, pages 313–316. Association for Computational Linguistics.

Andrew McCallum, Kamal Nigam, et al. 1998. A comparison of event models for naive bayes text classification. In *AAAI-98 workshop on learning for text categorization*, volume 752, pages 41–48. Citeseer.

Andrew Kachites McCallum. 2002. Mallet: A machine learning for language toolkit. http://www.cs.umass.edu/ mccallum/mallet.

Huy V Nguyen and Diane J Litman. 2015. Extracting argument and domain words for identifying argument components in texts. *NAACL HLT 2015*, page 22.

Michael Paul and Roxana Girju. 2010. A two-dimensional topic-aspect model for discovering multi-faceted topics. *Urbana*, 51:61801.

Sarvesh Ranade, Rajeev Sangal, and Radhika Mamidi, 2013. *Proceedings of the SIGDIAL 2013 Conference*, chapter Stance Classification in Online Debates by Recognizing Users' Intentions, pages 61–69. Association for Computational Linguistics.

Richard Socher, Alex Perelygin, Jean Y Wu, Jason Chuang, Christopher D Manning, Andrew Y Ng, and Christopher Potts. 2013. Recursive deep models for semantic compositionality over a sentiment treebank. In *Proceedings of the conference on empirical methods in natural language processing (EMNLP)*, volume 1631, page 1642. Citeseer.

Swapna Somasundaran and Janyce Wiebe. 2010. Recognizing stances in ideological on-line debates. In *Proceedings of the NAACL HLT 2010 Workshop on Computational Approaches to Analysis and Generation of Emotion in Text*, pages 116–124. Association for Computational Linguistics.

Dhanya Sridhar, Lise Getoor, and Marilyn Walker, 2014. *Proceedings of the Joint Workshop on Social Dynamics and Personal Attributes in Social Media*, chapter Collective Stance Classification of Posts in Online Debate Forums, pages 109–117. Association for Computational Linguistics.

Marilyn A Walker, Pranav Anand, Robert Abbott, and Ricky Grant. 2012. Stance classification using dialogic properties of persuasion. In *Proceedings of the 2012 Conference of the North American Chapter of the Association for Computational Linguistics: Human Language Technologies*, pages 592–596. Association for Computational Linguistics.

Theresa Wilson and Janyce Wiebe. 2005. Annotating attributions and private states. In *Proceedings of the Workshop on Frontiers in Corpus Annotations II: Pie in the Sky*, pages 53–60. Association for Computational Linguistics.

# Argumentation: Content, Structure, and Relationship with Essay Quality

**Beata Beigman Klebanov[1], Christian Stab[2], Jill Burstein[1],Yi Song[1],**
**Binod Gyawali[1], Iryna Gurevych[2,3]**
[1] Educational Testing Service
660 Rosedale Rd, Princeton NJ, 08541, USA
{bbeigmanklebanov,jburstein,ysong,bgyawali}@ets.org
[2]Ubiquitous Knowledge Processing Lab (UKP-TUDA)
Department of Computer Science, Technische Universität Darmstadt
[3]Ubiquitous Knowledge Processing Lab (UKP-DIPF)
German Institute for Educational Research
www.ukp.tu-darmstadt.de

## Abstract

In this paper, we investigate the relationship between argumentation structures and (a) argument content, and (b) the holistic quality of an argumentative essay. Our results suggest that structure-based approaches hold promise for automated evaluation of argumentative writing.

## 1 Introduction

With the advent of the Common Core Standards for Education,[1] argumentation, and, more specifically, argumentative writing, is receiving increased attention, along with a demand for argumentation-aware *Automated Writing Evaluation* (AWE) systems. However, current AWE systems typically do not consider argumentation (Lim and Kahng, 2012), and employ features that address grammar, mechanics, discourse structure, syntactic and lexical richness (Burstein et al., 2013). Developments in *Computational Argumentation* (**CA**) could bridge this gap.

Recently, progress has been made towards a more detailed understanding of argumentation in essays (Song et al., 2014; Stab and Gurevych, 2014; Persing and Ng, 2015; Ong et al., 2014). An important distinction emerging from the relevant work is that between argumentative *structure* and argumentative *content*. Facility with the argumentation structure underlies the contrast between (1) and (2) below: In (1), claims are made without support; relationships between claims are not explicit; there is intervening irrelevant material. In (2), the argumentative structure is clear – there is a critical claim supported by a specific reason. Yet,

is it in fact a good argument? When choosing a provider for trash collection, how relevant is the color of the trucks? In contrast, in (3) the argumentative structure is not very explicit, yet the argument itself, if the reader is willing to engage, is actually more pertinent to the case, content-wise. Example (4) has both the structure and the content.

(1) *"The mayor is stupid. People should not have voted for him. His policy will fail. The new provider uses ugly trucks."*

(2) *"The mayor's policy of switching to a new trash collector service is flawed because he failed to consider the ugly color of the trucks used by the new provider."*

(3) *"The mayor is stupid. The switch is a bad policy. The new collector uses old and polluting trucks."*

(4) *"The mayor's policy of switching to a new trash collector service is flawed because he failed to consider the negative environmental effect of the old and air-polluting trucks used by the new provider."*

Song et al. (2014) took the content approach, annotating essays for arguments that are pertinent to the argumentation scheme (Walton et al., 2008; Walton, 1996) presented in the prompt. Thus, a critique raising undesirable side effects (examples 3 and 4) is appropriate for a prompt where a policy is proposed, while the critique in (1) and (2) is not. The authors show, using the annotations, that raising pertinent critiques correlates with holistic essay scores. They build a content-heavy automated model; the model, however, does not generalize

---

[1]www.corestandards.org



*Proceedings of the 3rd Workshop on Argument Mining*, pages 70–75,
Berlin, Germany, August 7-12, 2016. ©2016 Association for Computational Linguistics

well across prompts, since different prompts use different argumentation schemes and contexts.

We take the structure-based approach that is independent of particular content and thus has better generalization potential. We study its relationship with the content-based approach and with overall essay quality. Our contributions are the answers to the following research questions:

1. whether the use of good argumentation structure correlates with essay quality;

2. while structure and content are conceptually distinct, they might in reality go together. We therefore evaluate the ability of the structure-based system to deal with content-based annotations of argumentation.

## 2  Related Work

Existing work in CA focuses on argumentation mining in various genres. Moens et al. (2007) identify argumentative sentences in newspapers, parliamentary records, court reports and online discussions. Mochales-Palau and Moens (2009) identify argumentation structures including claims and premises in court cases. Other approaches focus on online comments and recognize argument components (Habernal and Gurevych, 2015), justifications (Biran and Rambow, 2011) or different types of claims (Kwon et al., 2007). Work in the context of the IBM Debater project deals with identifying claims and evidence in Wikipedia articles (Rinott et al., 2015; Aharoni et al., 2014).

Peldszus and Stede (2015) identify argumentation structures in microtexts (similar to essays). They rely on several base classifiers and minimum spanning trees to recognize argumentative tree structures. Stab and Gurevych (2016) extract argument structures from essays by recognizing argument components and jointly modeling their types and relations between them. Both approaches focus on the structure and neglect the content of arguments. Persing and Ng (2015) annotate argument strength, which is related to content, yet what it is that makes an argument strong has not been made explicit in the rubric and the annotations are essay-level. Song et al. (2014) follow the content-based approach, annotating essay sentences for raising topic-specific critical questions (Walton et al., 2008).

Ong et al. (2014) report on correlations between argument component types and holistic essay scores. They report that rule-based approaches for identifying argument components can be effective for ranking but not rating. However, they used a very small data set. In contrast, we study the relationship between content-based and structure-based approaches and investigate whether argumentation structures correlate with holistic quality of essays using a large public data set.

In the literature on the development of argumentation skills, an emphasis is made on both the structure, namely, the need to support one's position with reasons and evidence (Ferretti et al., 2000), and on the content, namely, on evaluating the effectiveness of arguments. For example, in a study by Goldstein et al. (2009), middle-schoolers compared more and less effective rebuttals to the same original argument.

## 3  Argumentation Structure Parser

For identifying argumentation structures in essays, we employ the system by Stab and Gurevych (2016) as an off-the-shelf argument structure parser. The parser performs the following steps:

**Segmentation**: Separates argumentative from non-argumentative text units; identifies the boundaries of argument components at token-level.

**Classification**: Classifies each argument component as Claim, Major Claim or Premise.

**Linking**: Identifies links between argument components by classifying ordered pairs of components in the same paragraph as either linked or not.

**Tree generation**: Finds tree structures (or forests) in each paragraph which optimize the results of the the previous analysis steps.

**Stance recognition**: Classifies each argument component as either *for* or *against* in order to discriminate between supporting or opposing argument components and argumentative support and attack relations respectively.

## 4  Experiment 1: Content vs Structure

### 4.1  Data

We use data from Song et al. (2014) – essays written for a college-level exam requiring test-takers to criticize an argument presented in the prompt. Each sentence in each essay is classified as generic (does not raise a critical question appropriate for the argument in the prompt) or non-generic (raises an apt critical question); about 40% of sentences are non-generic. Data sizes are shown in Table 1.

| Prompt | Train | | | Test | |
|---|---|---|---|---|---|
| | #Essays | #Sentences | Non-generic | #Essays | #Sentences |
| A | 260 | 4,431 | 42% | 40 | 758 |
| B | 260 | 4,976 | 41% | 40 | 758 |

Table 1: Data description for Experiment 1.

## 4.2 Selection of Structural Elements

We use the training data to gain a better understanding of the relationship between structural and content aspects of argumentation. Each selection is evaluated using kappa against Song et al. (2014) generic vs non-generic annotation.

Our first hypothesis is that any sentence where the parser detected an argument component (any claim or premise) could contain argument-relevant (non-generic) content. This approach yields kappa of 0.24 (prompt **A**) and 0.23 (prompt **B**).

We observed that the linking step in the parser's output identified many cases of singleton claims – namely, claims not supported by an elaboration. For example, *"The county is following wrong assumptions in the attempt to improve safety"* is an isolated claim. This sentence is classified as "generic", since no specific scheme-related critique is being raised. Removing unsupported claims yields kappas of 0.28 (A) and 0.26 (B).

Next, we observed that even sentences that contain claims that are supported are often treated as "generic". Test-takers often precede a specific critique with one or more claims that set the stage for the main critique. For example, in the following 3-sentence sequence, only the last is marked as raising a critical question: *"If this claim is valid we would need to know the numbers. The whole argument in contingent on the reported accidents. Less reported accidents does not mean less accidents."* The parser classified these as Major Claim, Claim, and Premise, respectively. Our next hypothesis is that it is the premises, rather than the claims, that are likely to contain specific argumentative content. We predict that only sentences containing a premise would be "non-generic." This yields a substantial improvement in agreement, reaching kappas of 0.34 (A) and 0.33 (B).

Looking at the overall pattern of structure-based vs content-based predictions, we note that the structure-based prediction over-generates: The ratio of false-positives to false-negatives is 2.9 (A) and 3.1 (B). That is, argumentative structure without argumentative content is about 3 times more common than the reverse. False positives include sentences that are too general (*"Numbers are needed to compare the history of the roads"*) as well as sentences that have an argumentative form, but fail to make a germane argument (*"If accidents are happening near a known bar, drivers might be under the influence of alcohol"*).

Out of all the false-negatives, 30% were cases where the argument parser predicted no argumentative structures at all (no claims of any type and no premises). Such sentences might not have a clear argumentative form but are understood as making a critique in the context. For example, *"What was it 3 or 4 years ago?"* and *"Has the population gone up or down?"* look like fact-seeking questions in terms of structure, but are interpreted in the context as questioning the causal mechanism presented in the prompt. Overall, in 9% of all non-generic sentences the argument parser detected no claims or premises.

## 4.3 Evaluation

Table 2 shows the evaluation of the structure-based predictions (classifying all sentences with a Premise as non-generic) on test data, in comparison with the published results of Song et al. (2014), who used content-heavy features (such as word ngrams in the current, preceding, and subsequent sentence). The results clearly show that while the structure-based prediction is inferior to content-based one when the test data are essays responding to the same prompt as the training data, the off-the-shelf structure-based prediction is on-par with content-based prediction on the cross-prompt evaluation. Thus, when the content is expected to shift, falling back to structure-based prediction is potentially a reasonable strategy.

| System | Train | Test | $\kappa$ |
|---|---|---|---|
| Song et al. (2014) | A | A | .410 |
| Song et al. (2014) | B | B | .478 |
| Song et al. (2014) | A | B | .285 |
| Song et al. (2014) | B | A | .217 |
| Structure-based (Premises) | – | A | .265 |
| Structure-based (Premises) | – | B | .247 |

Table 2: Evaluation of content-based (Song et al., 2014) and structure-based prediction on content-based annotations.

## 5 Experiment 2: Argumentation Structure and Essay Quality

Using argumentation structure and putting forward a germane argument are distinct, not only theoretically, but also empirically, as suggested by the results of Experiment 1. In this section, we evaluate to what extent the use of argumentation structures correlates with overall essay quality.

### 5.1 Data

We use a publicly available set of essays written for the TOEFL test in an argue-for-an-opinion-on-an-issue genre (Blanchard et al., 2013). Although this data was originally used for natural language identification experiments, coarse-grained holistic scores (3-grade scale) are provided as part of the LDC distribution. Essays were written by non-native speakers of English; we believe this increases the likelihood that fluency with argumentation structures would be predictive of the score. We sampled 6,074 essays for training and 2,023 for testing, both across 8 different prompts. In terms of distribution of holistic scores in the training data, 54.5% received the middle score, 11% – the low score, and 34.5% – the high score.

### 5.2 Features for essay scoring

Our set of features has the following essay-level aggregates: the numbers of any argument components, major claims, claims, premises, supporting and attacking premises, arguments against, arguments for, and the average number of premises per claim. Using the training data, we found that 90% Winsorization followed by a log transformation improved the correlation with scores for all features. The correlations range from 0.08 (major claims) to 0.39 (argument components).

### 5.3 Evaluation

To evaluate whether the use of argumentation structures correlates with holistic scores, we estimated a linear regression model using the nine argument features on the training data and evaluated on the test data. We use Cohen's kappa, as well as Pearson's correlation and quadratically-weighted kappa, the latter two being standard measures in essay scoring literature (Shermis and Burstein, 2013). Row "Arg" in Table 3 shows the results; argument structures have a moderate positive relationship with holistic scores.

More extensive use of argumentation structures is thus correlated with overall quality of an argumentative essay. However, argumentative fluency specifically is difficult to disentangle from fluency in language production in general manifested through the sheer length of the essay. In a timed test, a more fluent writer will be able to write more. To examine whether fluency in argumentation structures can explain additional variance in scores beyond that explained by general fluency (as approximated through the number of words in an essay), we estimated a length-only based linear regression model as well as a model that uses all the 9 argument structure features in addition to length. As shown in Table 3, the addition of argumentation structures yields a small improvement across all measures over a length-only model.

| Model | $\kappa$ | $r$ | qwk |
|---|---|---|---|
| Arg | .195 | .389 | .344 |
| Len | .365 | .605 | .518 |
| Arg + Len | .389 | .614 | .540 |

Table 3: Prediction of holistic scores using argument structure features (Arg), length (Len), and argument structure features and length (Arg+Len). "qwk" stands for quadratically weighted kappa.

## 6 Conclusion & Future Work

In this paper, we set out to investigate the relationship between argumentation structures, argument content, and the quality of the essay. Our experiments suggest that (a) more extensive use of argumentation structures is predictive of better quality of argumentative writing, beyond overall fluency in language production; and (b) structure-based detection of argumentation is a possible fallback strategy to approximate argumentative *content* if an automated argument detection system is to generalize to new prompts. The two findings together suggest that the structure-based approach is a promising avenue for research in argumentation-aware automated writing evaluation.

In future work, we intend to improve the structure-based approach by identifying characteristics of argument components that are too general and so cannot be taken as evidence of germane, case-specific argumentation on the student's part (claims like *"More information is needed"*), as well as study properties of seemingly non-argumentative sentences that nevertheless have a potential for argumentative use in context (such as asking fact-seeking questions). We believe this would allow pushing the envelope of structure-based analysis towards identification of arguments that have a higher likelihood of being effective.

## Acknowledgments

The work of Christian Stab and Iryna Gurevych has been supported by the Volkswagen Foundation as part of the Lichtenberg-Professorship Program under grant No. I/82806 and by the German Federal Ministry of Education and Research (BMBF) as a part of the Software Campus project AWS under grant No. 01|S12054.

## References

Ehud Aharoni, Anatoly Polnarov, Tamar Lavee, Daniel Hershcovich, Ran Levy, Ruty Rinott, Dan Gutfreund, and Noam Slonim. 2014. A benchmark dataset for automatic detection of claims and evidence in the context of controversial topics. In *Proceedings of the First Workshop on Argumentation Mining*, pages 64–68, Baltimore, Maryland.

Or Biran and Owen Rambow. 2011. Identifying justifications in written dialogs by classifying text as argumentative. *International Journal of Semantic Computing*, 5(4):363–381.

Daniel Blanchard, Joel Tetreault, Derrick Higgins, Aoife Cahill, and Martin Chodorow. 2013. TOEFL11: A corpus of non-native English. *ETS Research Report Series*, 2013(2):i–15.

Jill Burstein, Joel Tetreault, and Nitin Madnani. 2013. The e-rater automated essay scoring system. In M. Shermis and J Burstein, editors, *Handbook of Automated Essay Evaluation: Current Applications and Future Directions*. New York: Routledge.

Ralph Ferretti, Charles MacArthur, and Nancy Dowdy. 2000. The effects of an elaborated goal on the persuasive writing of students with learning disabilities and their normally achieving peers. *Journal of Educational Psychology*, 93:694–702.

Marion Goldstein, Amanda Crowell, and Deanna Kuhn. 2009. What constitutes skilled argumentation and how does it develop? *Informal Logic*, 29:379–395.

Ivan Habernal and Iryna Gurevych. 2015. Exploiting debate portals for semi-supervised argumentation mining in user-generated web discourse. In *Proceedings of the 2015 Conference on Empirical Methods in Natural Language Processing*, EMNLP ' 15, pages 2127–2137, Lisbon, Portugal.

Namhee Kwon, Liang Zhou, Eduard Hovy, and Stuart W. Shulman. 2007. Identifying and classifying subjective claims. In *Proceedings of the 8th Annual International Conference on Digital Government Research: Bridging Disciplines & Domains*, pages 76–81, Philadelphia, PA, USA.

Hyojung Lim and Jimin Kahng. 2012. Review of Criterion®. *Language Learning & Technology*, 16(2):38–45.

Raquel Mochales-Palau and Marie-Francine Moens. 2009. Argumentation mining: The detection, classification and structure of arguments in text. In *Proceedings of the 12th International Conference on Artificial Intelligence and Law*, ICAIL '09, pages 98–107, Barcelona, Spain.

Marie-Francine Moens, Erik Boiy, Raquel Mochales Palau, and Chris Reed. 2007. Automatic detection of arguments in legal texts. In *Proceedings of the 11th International Conference on Artificial Intelligence and Law*, ICAIL '07, pages 225–230, Stanford, CA, USA.

Nathan Ong, Diane Litman, and Alexandra Brusilovsky. 2014. Ontology-based argument mining and automatic essay scoring. In *Proceedings of the First Workshop on Argumentation Mining*, pages 24–28, Baltimore, MA, USA.

Andreas Peldszus and Manfred Stede. 2015. Joint prediction in mst-style discourse parsing for argumentation mining. In *Conference on Empirical Methods in Natural Language Processing*, EMNLP '15, page (to appear), Lisbon, Portugal.

Isaac Persing and Vincent Ng. 2015. Modeling argument strength in student essays. In *Proceedings of the 53rd Annual Meeting of the Association for Computational Linguistics and the 7th International Joint Conference on Natural Language Processing (Volume 1: Long Papers)*, ACL '15, pages 543–552, Beijing, China.

Ruty Rinott, Lena Dankin, Carlos Alzate Perez, Mitesh M. Khapra, Ehud Aharoni, and Noam Slonim. 2015. Show me your evidence - an automatic method for context dependent evidence detection. In *Proceedings of the 2015 Conference on Empirical Methods in Natural Language Processing*, EMNLP '15, pages 440–450, Lisbon, Portugal.

Mark D. Shermis and Jill Burstein. 2013. *Handbook of Automated Essay Evaluation: Current Applications and Future Directions*. Routledge Chapman & Hall.

Yi Song, Michael Heilman, Beata Beigman Klebanov, and Paul Deane. 2014. Applying argumentation schemes for essay scoring. In *Proceedings of the First Workshop on Argumentation Mining*, pages 69–78, Baltimore, MA, USA.

Christian Stab and Iryna Gurevych. 2014. Annotating argument components and relations in persuasive essays. In *Proceedings of the 25th International*

*Conference on Computational Linguistics*, COLING
'14, pages 1501–1510, Dublin, Ireland, August.

Christian Stab and Iryna Gurevych. 2016. Parsing argumentation structures in persuasive essays. *arXiv preprint arXiv:1604.07370*.

Douglas Walton, Chris Reed, and Fabrizio Macagno. 2008. *Argumentation schemes*. New York, NY: Cambridge University Press.

Douglas Walton. 1996. *Argumentation schemes for presumptive reasoning*. Mahwah, NJ: Lawrence Erlbaum.

# Neural Attention Model for Classification of Sentences that Support *Promoting/Suppressing* Relationship

**Yuta Koreeda, Toshihiko Yanase, Kohsuke Yanai, Misa Sato, Yoshiki Niwa**
Research & Development Group, Hitachi, Ltd.
{yuta.koreeda.pb, toshihiko.yanase.gm, kohsuke.yanai.cs,
misa.sato.mw, yoshiki.niwa.tx}@hitachi.com

## Abstract

Evidences that support a claim "a subject phrase *promotes* or *suppresses* a value" help in making a rational decision. We aim to construct a model that can classify if a particular evidence supports a claim of a *promoting/suppressing* relationship given an arbitrary subject-value pair. In this paper, we propose a recurrent neural network (RNN) with an attention model to classify such evidences. We incorporated a word embedding technique in an attention model such that our method generalizes for never-encountered subjects and value phrases. Benchmarks showed that the method outperforms conventional methods in evidence classification tasks.

## 1 Introduction

With recent trend of big data and electronic records, it is getting increasingly important to collect evidences that support a claim, which usually comes along with a decision, for rational decision making. Argument mining can be utilized for this purpose because an argument itself is an opinion of the author that supports the claim, and an argument usually consists of evidences that support the claim. Identification of a claim has been rigorously studied in argument mining including extraction of arguments (Levy et al., 2014; Boltui and najder, 2014; Sardianos et al., 2015; Nguyen and Litman, 2015) and classification of claims (Sobhani et al., 2015).

Our goal is to achieve classification of positive and negative effects of a subject in a form "a subject phrase $S$ *promotes/suppresses* a value $V$." For example, given a subject $S$ = gambling, a value $V$ = crime and a text $X$ = casino increases theft, we can say that $X$ supports a claim of gambling ($S$) promotes crime ($V$) relationship. Such a technique is important because it allows extracting both sides of an opinion to be used in decision makings (Sato et al., 2015).

We take a deep learning approach for this evidence classification, which has started to outperform conventional methods in many linguistic tasks (Collobert et al., 2011; Shen et al., 2014; Luong et al., 2015). Our work is based on a neural attention model, which had promising result in a translation task (Bahdanau et al., 2015) and in a sentiment classification task (Zichao et al., 2016). The neural attention model achieved these by focusing on important phrases; e.g. when $V$ is economy and $X$ is Gambling boosts the city's revenue., the attention layer focuses near the phrase boosts the city's revenue.

The neural attention model was previously applied to aspect-based sentiment analysis (ABSA) (Yanase et al., 2016), which has some similarity to the evidence classification in that it classifies sentimental polarities towards a subject $S$ given an aspect (corresponding to $V$) (Pontiki et al., 2015). A limitation of (Yanase et al., 2016) was that the learned attention layer is tightly attached to each $S$ or $V$ and does not generalize for never-encountered subjects/values. This means that it requires manually labeled data for all possible subjects and values, which is not practicable. Instead, when we train a model to classify an evidence that supports a claim of a relationship between, for example, gambling and crime, we want the same learned model to work for other $S$ and $V$ pairs such as smoking and health. In other words, we want the model to learn *how* to classify evidences that support a relationship of $S$ and $V$, rather than learning the relationship itself.

In this paper, we propose a neural attention



*Proceedings of the 3rd Workshop on Argument Mining*, pages 76–81,
Berlin, Germany, August 7-12, 2016. ©2016 Association for Computational Linguistics

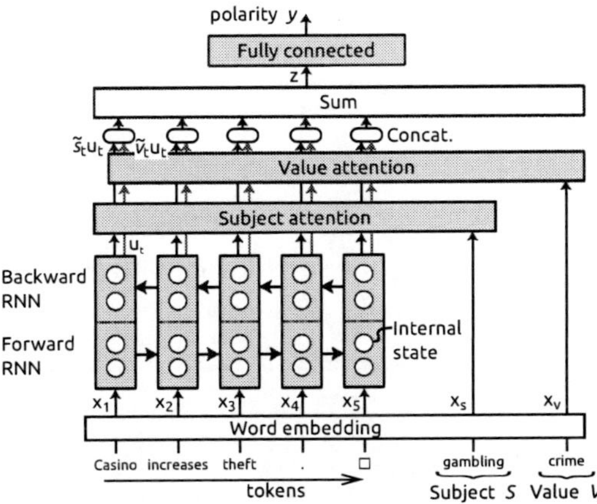



Figure 1: Structure of the proposed bi-directional RNN with word embedding-based attention layer. Colored units are updated during training.

| Subject $S$ | Value $V$ (# of *promoting* / *suppressing* / total labels) |
|---|---|
| *Training data* | |
| national lottery | economy (88 / 57 / 145), regressive tax (4 / 1 / 5) |
| sale of human organ | moral (0 / 6 / 6) |
| generic drug | cost (32 / 87 / 119), poverty (0 / 1 / 1) |
| cannabis | economy (61 / 7 / 68), medicine (215 / 68 / 283) |
| tourism | economy (142 / 11 / 153), corruption (10 / 3 / 13) |
| *Test data* | |
| smoking | income (36 / 33 / 69), disease (158 / 1 / 159) |
| violent video game | crime (36 / 7 / 43), moral (7 / 14 / 21) |

Table 1: Subject phrases and value phrases in the dataset

model that can learn to focus on important phrases from text even when $S$ and $V$ are never encountered, allowing the neural attention model to be applied to the evidence classification. We extend the neural attention model by modeling the attention layer using a distributed representation of words in which similar words are treated in a similar manner. We also report benchmarks of the method against previous works in both neural and lexicon-based approaches. We show that the method can effectively generalize to an evidence classification task with never-encountered phrases.

## 2 Neural Attention Model

Given a subject phrase $S$, a value phrase $V$, and a text $X$, our model aims to classify whether $X$ supports $S$ *promotes* or *suppresses* $V$. A text $X$ is a sequence of word tokens, and the classification result is outputted as a real value $y \in [0.0, 1.0]$ that denotes the *promoting/suppressing* polarity; i.e., $X$ has a higher chance of supporting the *promoting* claim if it is nearer to 1.0 and the *suppressing* claim if it is nearer to 0.0.

Our method is shown in Figure 1. First of all, we apply skip-gram-based word embedding (Mikolov et al., 2013) to each token in $X$ and obtain a varying-length sequence of distributed representations $X = \mathbf{x}_0, \mathbf{x}_1, ..., \mathbf{x}_T$, where $T$ is the number of tokens in the sentence. This is to allow words with similar meaning to be treated in a similar manner.

We also apply word embedding to $S$ and $V$ to obtain $\mathbf{x}_s$ and $\mathbf{x}_v$ respectively. This is a core idea on making attention model generalize to first encountered words. In case there exists more than one word in $S$ and $V$, we take an average of word embedding vectors.

Next, the word vector sequence $X$ is inputted to a recurrent neural network (RNN) to encode contextual information into each token. The RNN calculates an output vector for each $\mathbf{x}_t$ at token position $t$. We use a bi-directional RNN (BiRNN) (Schuster and Paliwal, 1997) to consider both forward context and backward context. A forward RNN processes tokens from head to tail to obtain a forward RNN-encoded vector $\overrightarrow{\mathbf{u}_t}$, and a backward RNN processes tokens from tail to head to obtain a backward RNN-encoded $\overleftarrow{\mathbf{u}_t}$. The output vector is $\mathbf{u}_t = \overrightarrow{\mathbf{u}_t} || \overleftarrow{\mathbf{u}_t}$, where $||$ is the concatenation of vectors. We tested the method with long short-term memory (LSTM) (Sak et al., 2014) and gated recurrent units (GRUs) (Cho et al., 2014) as implementations of RNN units.

Lastly, we filter tokens with $S$ and $V$ to determine the importance of each token and to extract information about the interactions of $S$ and $V$. In the attention layer, attention weight $s_t \in \mathbb{R}$ at each token $t$ is calculated using subject phrase vector $\mathbf{x}_s$. We model attention with Equation (1) in which $W_s$ is a parameter that is updated alongside the RNN during the training.

$$s_t = \mathbf{x}_s^\top W_s \mathbf{u}_t \tag{1}$$

Then, we take the softmax over all tokens in a sentence for normalization.

$$\tilde{s}_t = \frac{\exp(s_t)}{\sum_j \exp(s_j)} \tag{2}$$

| Parameter | BiRNN | BiRNN+ATT |
|---|---|---|
| Dropout rate | 0.7 | 0.5 |
| Learning rate | 0.00075 | 0.0017 |
| RNN model | GRU | LSTM |
| RNN state size | 128 | 64 |
| Mini-batch size | 16 | 32 |
| Training epochs | 6 | 17 |

Table 2: Hyperparameters of BiRNN and BiRNN+ATT (our method)

| | Average AUC-PR | AUC-ROC | Macro prec. | Accuracy |
|---|---|---|---|---|
| BiRNN+ATT | **0.59** | **0.64** | **0.62** | **0.51** |
| BiRNN | 0.57 | 0.59 | 0.54 | 0.45 |
| BoM | 0.58 | 0.57 | 0.49 | 0.22 |
| BoW | 0.56 | 0.61 | 0.56 | 0.42 |

Table 3: Performance of the classifiers. The best result for each metric is shown bold.

The attention $\tilde{v}_t \in \mathbb{R}$ for the value vector is calculated likewise using a parameter $W_v$. $\tilde{s}_t$ and $\tilde{v}_t$ are used as the weight of each token $\mathbf{u}_t$ to obtain sentence feature vector $\mathbf{z}$.

$$\mathbf{z} = \sum_t (\tilde{s}_t \mathbf{u}_t || \tilde{v}_t \mathbf{u}_t) \qquad (3)$$

Finally, the polarity $y$ of the claim is calculated two-layered fully-connected perceptrons with logistic sigmoid functions.

The model is trained by backpropagation using cross entropy as the loss and AdaGrad as the optimizer (Duchi et al., 2011). During training, parameters of fully-connected layers, RNN, $W_s$, and $W_v$ are updated. Note that $\mathbf{x}_s$, $\mathbf{x}_v$ are not updated unlike (Yanase et al., 2016). Dropout (Srivastava et al., 2014) is applied to the input and output of the RNN and gradient norm is clipped to 5.0 to improve the stability.

## 3 Experiments

The purpose of this experiment was to test if the proposed RNN with word embedding-based attention model could perform well in a evidence classification task. We benchmarked our method to the RNN without an attention model and conventional lexicon-based classification methods.

### 3.1 Dataset

We chose seven subject phrases and one or two value phrases for each subject phrase (total of 13 pairs) as shown in Table 1. For each pair of $\mathcal{S}$ and $\mathcal{V}$, we extracted sentences having both $\mathcal{S}$ and $\mathcal{V}$ within two adjacent sentences from Annotated

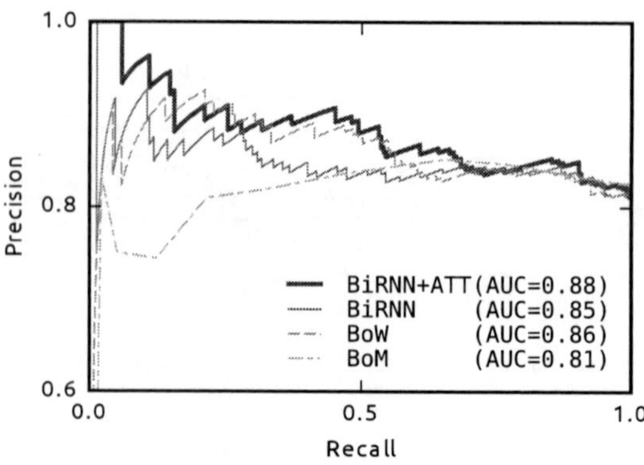

(a) *Promoting*-claim as positive

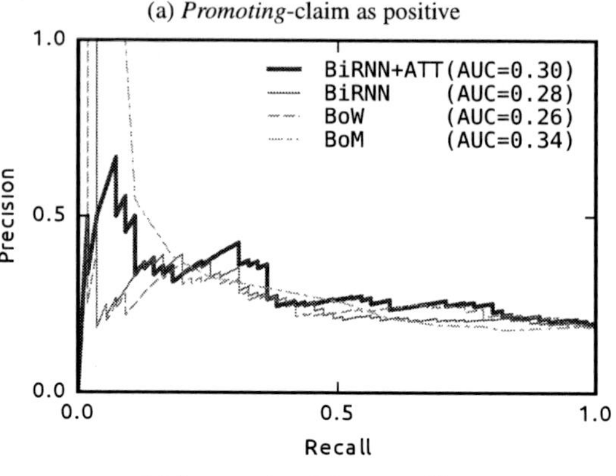

(b) *Suppressing*-claim as positive

Figure 2: Precision-recall curves for the classifications of the evidences

English Gigaword (Napoles et al., 2012). From candidates of 7000 sentences, we manually extracted and labeled 1,085 self-contained sentences that support *promoting/suppressing* relationship. We allowed sentences in which $\mathcal{S}$, $\mathcal{V}$ did not appear. We chose five subject phrases as training data and other two as test data. Notice that only a fraction of the test data had overlapping value phrases with the training data.

### 3.2 Metrics

We compared the methods in terms of the area under a precision-recall curve (AUC-PR) because it represents a method's performance well even when data are skewed (Davis and Goadrich, 2006). The area under a curve is obtained by first calculating precision-recall for every possible threshold (precision-recall curve) and integrating the curve with trapezoidal rule. We took the average AUC-PR for when the *promoting* or *suppressing* claim was taken as positive because it was a binary clas-

| # | | Text |
|---|---|---|
| 1. | $\mathcal{S}$ | Smoking costs some 22 000 Czech citizens their lives every year though the tobacco industry earns huge profits for the nation |
| | $\mathcal{V}$ | Smoking costs some 22 000 Czech citizens their lives every year though the tobacco industry earns huge profits for the nation |
| 2. | $\mathcal{S}$ | For the nation the health costs of smoking far outweigh the economic benefits of a thriving tobacco industry the commentary said |
| | $\mathcal{V}$ | For the nation the health costs of smoking far outweigh the economic benefits of a thriving tobacco industry the commentary said |

Table 4: Visualization of attention in test data with $\mathcal{S}$ =smoking and $\mathcal{V}$ =income. Highlights show $\hat{s}_t$ and $\hat{v}_t$. An underlined word had the smallest cosine distance to $\mathcal{S}$ and $\mathcal{V}$, respectively.

sification task. We calculated the area under a receiver operating characteristic curve (AUC-ROC) in a similar manner as a reference.

Since we formulated the learning algorithm in regression-like manner, we chose the cutoff value with the best macro-precision within the training dataset to obtain predicted label. This was used to calculate the macro-precision, the accuracy and the McNemar's test, which were for a reference.

### 3.3 Baselines

Baselines in this experiment were as follows.

**Bag-of-Words (BoW)** Dictionary of all words in training/test texts, $\mathcal{S}$ and $\mathcal{V}$ were used. The word counts vector was concatenated with one-hot (or $n$-hot in case of a phrase) vectors of $\mathcal{S}$ and $\mathcal{V}$ and used as a feature for a classifier.

**Bag-of-Means (BoM)** The average word embedding (Mikolov et al., 2013) was used as a feature for a classifier.

**BiRNN without attention layer** This was the same as our method except that it took an average of the BiRNN output and concatenated it with the word vector from $\mathcal{S}$ and $\mathcal{V}$ to be fed into the perceptron; i.e., $\mathbf{z} = \mathbf{x}_s || \mathbf{x}_v || \sum_t (\mathbf{u}_t)$.

We tested BoW and BoM with a linear support vector machine (LSVM) and random forest (RF), and BoW with multinomial naïve bayes (NB). We carried out 5-fold cross validation within a training dataset, treating each subject phrase $\mathcal{S}$ as a fold, to determine the best performing hyperparameters and classifiers. The best performing classifier for BoM was RF with 27 estimators. The best performing classifier for BoW was NB with $\alpha = 0.38$ with no consideration of prior probabilities.

### 3.4 System setting

We tuned hyperparameters for our method and the BiRNN in the same manner. The best settings are shown in Table 2.

For the BoM, BiRNN and BiRNN+ATT, we used pretrained word embedding of three hundred dimensional vectors trained with the Google News Corpus[1]. We pretrained the BiRNN and the BiRNN+ATT with the Stanford Sentiment Treebank (Socher et al., 2013) by stacking a logistic regression layer on top of a token-wise average pooling of $\mathbf{u}_t$ and by predicting the sentiment polarity of phrases.

For the BiRNN and BiRNN+ATT, the maximum token size was 40, and tokens that overflowed were dropped.

BiRNN and BiRNN+ATT were implemented with TensorFlow (Abadi et al., 2015).

### 3.5 Results

The average AUC-PRs and reference metrics are shown in Table 3. BiRNN+ATT performed significantly better than baselines with $p = 0.016$ (BiRNN), $p = 1.1 \times 10^{-15}$ (BoM) and $p = 0.010$ (BoW), respectively (McNemar's test). The BiRNN without attention layer was no better than BoW ($p = 0.41$, McNemar's test).

Precision-recall curves of the baselines and our method are shown in Figure 2.

## 4 Discussion

By extending the neural attention model using a distributed representation of words, we were capable of applying the neural attention model to the evidence classification task with never encountered words. The results implied that it learned *how* to classify evidences that support a relationship of $\mathcal{S}$ and $\mathcal{V}$, rather than the relationship itself.

The attention layer selects which part of the sentence the model uses for classification with magnitudes of $\hat{s}_t$ and $\hat{v}_t$ for each token. We visualize the magnitudes of $\hat{s}_t$ and $\hat{v}_t$ on sentences extracted from a test dataset shown in Table 4.

We observed that the attention layers react to the target phrases' synonyms and their qualifiers. For

---

[1] The model retrieved from https://code.google.com/archive/p/word2vec/

example, the value `income` reacted to the word `profit` in Table 4, #1. The classification result and ground truth were both *promoting*. Generalization to similar words was observed for other words such as `Marijuana` ($\mathcal{S}$ = `cannabis`) and `murder` ($\mathcal{V}$ = `crime`). This implies that the attention layers learned to focus on important phrases, which was the reason why the proposed method outperformed conventional BiRNN without an attention layer.

The method failed in Table 4, #2 in which the ground truth was *suppressing* and the method predicted *promoting*. The method shortsightedly focused on the word `benefits` and failed to comprehend longer context. As a future work, we will incorporate techniques that allow our model to cope with a longer sequence of words.

## 5 Conclusion

We proposed a RNN with a word embedding-based attention model for classification of evidences. Our method outperformed the RNN without an attention model and other conventional methods in benchmarks. The attention layers learned to focus on important phrases even if words were never encountered, implying that our method learned *how* to classify evidences that support a claim of a relationship of subject and value phrases, rather than the relationship itself.

## References


[Abadi et al.2015] Martn Abadi, Ashish Agarwal, Paul Barham, Eugene Brevdo, Zhifeng Chen, Craig Citro, Greg S. Corrado, Andy Davis, Jeffrey Dean, Matthieu Devin, Sanjay Ghemawat, Ian Goodfellow, Andrew Harp, Geoffrey Irving, Michael Isard, Yangqing Jia, Rafal Jozefowicz, Lukasz Kaiser, Manjunath Kudlur, Josh Levenberg, Dan Man, Rajat Monga, Sherry Moore, Derek Murray, Chris Olah, Mike Schuster, Jonathon Shlens, Benoit Steiner, Ilya Sutskever, Kunal Talwar, Paul Tucker, Vincent Vanhoucke, Vijay Vasudevan, Fernanda Vigas, Oriol Vinyals, Pete Warden, Martin Wattenberg, Martin Wicke, Yuan Yu, and Xiaoqiang Zheng. 2015. TensorFlow: Large-Scale Machine Learning on Heterogeneous Systems. Software available from tensorflow.org.

[Bahdanau et al.2015] Dzmitry Bahdanau, Kyunghyun Cho, and Yoshua Bengio. 2015. Neural Machine Translation by Jointly Learning to Align and Translate. In *Proceedings of the International Conference on Learning Representations (ICLR 2015)*, San Juan, Puerto Rico, May.

[Boltui and najder2014] Filip Boltui and Jan najder. 2014. Back up your Stance: Recognizing Arguments in Online Discussions. In *Proceedings of the First Workshop on Argumentation Mining*, pages 49–58, Baltimore, Maryland, June. Association for Computational Linguistics.

[Cho et al.2014] Kyunghyun Cho, Bart van Merrienboer, Caglar Gulcehre, Dzmitry Bahdanau, Fethi Bougares, Holger Schwenk, and Yoshua Bengio. 2014. Learning Phrase Representations using RNN EncoderDecoder for Statistical Machine Translation. In *Proceedings of the 2014 Conference on Empirical Methods in Natural Language Processing (EMNLP)*, pages 1724–1734, Doha, Qatar, October. Association for Computational Linguistics.

[Collobert et al.2011] Ronan Collobert, Jason Weston, Lon Bottou, Michael Karlen, Koray Kavukcuoglu, and Pavel Kuksa. 2011. Natural Language Processing (Almost) from Scratch. *J. Mach. Learn. Res.*, 12:2493–2537, November.

[Davis and Goadrich2006] Jesse Davis and Mark Goadrich. 2006. The Relationship Between Precision-Recall and ROC Curves. In *Proceedings of the 23rd International Conference on Machine Learning*, ICML '06, pages 233–240, New York, NY, USA. ACM.

[Duchi et al.2011] John Duchi, Elad Hazan, and Yoram Singer. 2011. Adaptive Subgradient Methods for Online Learning and Stochastic Optimization. *J. Mach. Learn. Res.*, 12:2121–2159, July.

[Levy et al.2014] Ran Levy, Yonatan Bilu, Daniel Hershcovich, Ehud Aharoni, and Noam Slonim. 2014. Context Dependent Claim Detection. In *Proceedings of COLING 2014, the 25th International Conference on Computational Linguistics: Technical Papers*, pages 1489–1500, Dublin, Ireland, August. Dublin City University and Association for Computational Linguistics.

[Luong et al.2015] Thang Luong, Hieu Pham, and Christopher D. Manning. 2015. Effective Approaches to Attention-based Neural Machine Translation. In *Proceedings of the 2015 Conference on Empirical Methods in Natural Language Processing*, pages 1412–1421, Lisbon, Portugal, September. Association for Computational Linguistics.

[Mikolov et al.2013] Tomas Mikolov, Ilya Sutskever, Kai Chen, Greg S Corrado, and Jeff Dean. 2013. Distributed Representations of Words and Phrases and their Compositionality. In C. J. C. Burges, L. Bottou, M. Welling, Z. Ghahramani, and K. Q. Weinberger, editors, *Advances in Neural Information Processing Systems 26*, pages 3111–3119. Curran Associates, Inc.

[Napoles et al.2012] Courtney Napoles, Matthew Gormley, and Benjamin Van Durme. 2012. Annotated Gigaword. In *Proceedings of the Joint Workshop on Automatic Knowledge Base Construction and Web-scale Knowledge Extraction*,

AKBC-WEKEX '12, pages 95–100, Stroudsburg, PA, USA. Association for Computational Linguistics.

[Nguyen and Litman2015] Huy Nguyen and Diane Litman. 2015. Extracting Argument and Domain Words for Identifying Argument Components in Texts. In *Proceedings of the 2nd Workshop on Argumentation Mining*, pages 22–28, Denver, CO, June. Association for Computational Linguistics.

[Pontiki et al.2015] Maria Pontiki, Dimitris Galanis, Haris Papageorgiou, Suresh Manandhar, and Ion Androutsopoulos. 2015. SemEval-2015 Task 12: Aspect Based Sentiment Analysis. In *Proceedings of the 9th International Workshop on Semantic Evaluation (SemEval 2015)*, pages 486–495, Denver, Colorado, June. Association for Computational Linguistics.

[Sak et al.2014] Haim Sak, Andrew Senior, and Franoise Beaufays. 2014. Long Short-Term Memory Based Recurrent Neural Network Architectures for Large Vocabulary Speech Recognition. *arXiv:1402.1128 [cs, stat]*, February. arXiv: 1402.1128.

[Sardianos et al.2015] Christos Sardianos, Ioannis Manousos Katakis, Georgios Petasis, and Vangelis Karkaletsis. 2015. Argument Extraction from News. In *Proceedings of the 2nd Workshop on Argumentation Mining*, pages 56–66, Denver, CO, June. Association for Computational Linguistics.

[Sato et al.2015] Misa Sato, Kohsuke Yanai, Toshinori Miyoshi, Toshihiko Yanase, Makoto Iwayama, Qinghua Sun, and Yoshiki Niwa. 2015. `http://www.aclweb.org/anthology/P15-4019`End-to-end Argument Generation System in Debating. In *Proceedings of ACL-IJCNLP 2015 System Demonstrations*, pages 109–114, Beijing, China, July. Association for Computational Linguistics and The Asian Federation of Natural Language Processing.

[Schuster and Paliwal1997] Mike Schuster and Kuldip K Paliwal. 1997. Bidirectional recurrent neural networks. *Signal Processing, IEEE Transactions on*, 45(11):2673–2681.

[Shen et al.2014] Yelong Shen, Xiaodong He, Jianfeng Gao, Li Deng, and Grgoire Mesnil. 2014. Learning Semantic Representations Using Convolutional Neural Networks for Web Search. In *Proceedings of the 23rd International Conference on World Wide Web*, WWW '14 Companion, pages 373–374, New York, NY, USA. ACM.

[Sobhani et al.2015] Parinaz Sobhani, Diana Inkpen, and Stan Matwin. 2015. From Argumentation Mining to Stance Classification. In *Proceedings of the 2nd Workshop on Argumentation Mining*, pages 67–77, Denver, CO, June. Association for Computational Linguistics.

[Socher et al.2013] Richard Socher, John Bauer, Christopher D. Manning, and Ng Andrew Y. 2013. Parsing with Compositional Vector Grammars. In *Proceedings of the 51st Annual Meeting of the Association for Computational Linguistics (Volume 1: Long Papers)*, pages 455–465, Sofia, Bulgaria, August. Association for Computational Linguistics.

[Srivastava et al.2014] Nitish Srivastava, Geoffrey Hinton, Alex Krizhevsky, Ilya Sutskever, and Ruslan Salakhutdinov. 2014. Dropout: A Simple Way to Prevent Neural Networks from Overfitting. *Journal of Machine Learning Research*, 15:1929–1958.

[Yanase et al.2016] Toshihiko Yanase, Kohsuke Yanai, Misa Sato, Toshinori Miyoshi, and Yoshiki Niwa. 2016. bunji at SemEval-2016 Task 5: Neural and Syntactic Models of Entity-Attribute Relationship for Aspect-based Sentiment Analysis. In *Proceedings of the 10th International Workshop on Semantic Evaluation (SemEval-2016)*, pages 294–300, San Diego, California, June. Association for Computational Linguistics.

[Zichao et al.2016] Yang Zichao, Diyi Yang, Chris Dyer, Xiaodong He, Alex Smola, and Eduard Hovy. 2016. Hierarchical Attention Networks for Document Classification. In *15th Annual Conference of the North American Chapter of the Association for Computational Linguistics: Human Language Technologies*, June.

# Towards Feasible Guidelines for the Annotation of Argument Schemes


**Elena Musi†, Debanjan Ghosh* and Smaranda Muresan†**
†Center of Computational Learning Systems, Columbia University
*School of Communication and Information, Rutgers University
em3202@columbia.edu, debanjan.ghosh@rutgers.edu, smara@ccls.columbia.edu



## Abstract

The annotation of argument schemes represents an important step for argumentation mining. General guidelines for the annotation of argument schemes, applicable to any topic, are still missing due to the lack of a suitable taxonomy in Argumentation Theory and the need for highly trained expert annotators. We present a set of guidelines for the annotation of argument schemes, taking as a framework the *Argumentum Model of Topics* (Rigotti and Morasso, 2010; Rigotti, 2009). We show that this approach can contribute to solving the theoretical problems, since it offers a hierarchical and finite taxonomy of argument schemes as well as systematic, linguistically-informed criteria to distinguish various types of argument schemes. We describe a pilot annotation study of 30 persuasive essays using multiple minimally trained non-expert annotators .Our findings from the confusion matrixes pinpoint problematic parts of the guidelines and the underlying annotation of claims and premises. We conduct a second annotation with refined guidelines and trained annotators on the 10 essays which received the lowest agreement initially. A significant improvement of the inter-annotator agreement shows that the annotation of argument schemes requires highly trained annotators and an accurate annotation of argumentative components (premises and claims).


## 1   Introduction

Argumentation is a type of discourse in which various participants make arguments, presenting some premises in support of certain conclusions, with the aim of negotiating different opinions and reaching consensus (Van Eemeren et al., 2013). The automatic identification and evaluation of arguments require three main stages: 1) the identification, segmentation and classification of argumentative discourse units (ADUs), 2) the identification and classification of the relations between ADUs (Peldszus and Stede, 2013a), and 3) the identification of argument schemes, namely the implicit and explicit *inferential relations* within and across ADUs (Macagno, 2014).

Although considerable steps have been taken towards the first two stages (Teufel and Moens, 2002; Stab and Gurevych, 2014; Cabrio and Villata, 2012; Ghosh et al., 2014; Aharoni et al., 2014; Rosenthal and McKeown, 2012; Biran and Rambow, 2011; Llewellyn et al., 2014), the third stage still constitutes a major challenge because large corpora systematically annotated with argument schemes are lacking. As noticed by Palau and Moens (2009), this is due to the proliferation in Argumentation Theory of different taxonomies of argument schemes based on weak distinctive criteria, which makes it difficult to develop inter-subjective guidelines for annotation. In the *Araucaria* dataset (Reed and Rowe, 2004), for example, two argument scheme sets other than Walton's are used as annotation protocols (Katzav and Reed, 2004; Pollock, 1995).

To overcome this problem, the most successfully applied strategy has been to pre-select from existing larger typologies, such as that of Walton et al. (2008), a subset of argument schemes which is most frequent in a particular text genre, domain or context (Green, 2015; Feng and Hirst, 2011; Song et al., 2014; Schneider et al., 2013) and provide annotators with critical questions as a means to identify the appropriate scheme. Such a bottom up approach allows one to improve the identi-




*Proceedings of the 3rd Workshop on Argument Mining*, pages 82–93,
Berlin, Germany, August 7-12, 2016. ©2016 Association for Computational Linguistics

fication conditions for a set of argument schemes (Walton, 2012), but it is hardly generalizable since it is restricted to specific argumentative contexts. Moreover, while critical questions constitute useful tools to evaluate the soundness of arguments (Song et al., 2014), they are far less suitable as a means to identify the presence of arguments: adopting a normative approach, annotators would conflate the notion of "making an argument" with that of "making a sound argument", while defeasibility should not be considered as an identification condition for the mere retrieval of arguments in texts.

We hypothesize that the *Argumentum Model of Topics* (Rigotti and Morasso, 2010; Rigotti, 2009), an enthymematic approach for the study of the inferential configuration of arguments, has the potential to enhance the recognition of argument schemes. Unlike other approaches (Van Eemeren and Grootendorst, 1992; Walton et al., 2008; Kienpointner, 1987), it offers a *taxonomic hierarchy* of argument schemes based on criteria which are distinctive and mutually exclusive and which appeal to *semantic properties of the state of affairs* expressed by premises/claims, and not to the logical forms (deductive, inductive, abductive) of arguments, whose boundaries are still debated (Section 2). However, even if these semantic properties are linguistically encoded, and hence potentially measurable, they might call for some background knowledge in frame semantics to be identified as well as for quite specific analytic skills. Moreover, the cognitive load requested by the annotation of argument schemes is higher than that needed for the annotation of the argumentative discourse structure (e.g., argument components such as claims and premises, and argument relations such as support/attack). As stated by Peldszus and Stede (2013b) with regard to the annotation of argument structure in short texts, the inter-annotator agreement among minimally trained annotators is bound to be low due to different personal commitments as well as interpretative skills of the texts. We wanted to test whether this conclusion is valid for our annotation task.

We conducted a pilot annotation study using 9 minimally trained non-expert annotators. As a corpus we used 30 short persuasive essays already annotated as to premises, claims and support/attack relations (Stab and Gurevych, 2014). Section 3 presents the set of guidelines and our study. Our findings from measuring the inter-annotator agreement (IAA) support previous findings that annotation of argument schemes would require highly trained annotators (Section 4). We also performed an analysis of confusion matrices to see which argument schemes were more difficult to identify, and which parts of the guidelines might need refinement (Section 4). Another finding of this study is that the identification of argument schemes constitutes a means to refine the annotation of premises and claims (Section 5). We refined the guidelines and tested them through the annotation of the 10 essays which received the lowest inter-annotator agreement using 2 trained non-expert annotators and 1 expert annotator (Section 6). The results show an improvement in the inter-annotator agreement. The confusion matrix suggests that the frequency of non-argumentative relations between premises/claims, claims/major claims highly affects disagreement. The guidelines and the annotated files are available at: `https://github.com/elenamusi/argscheme_aclworkshop2016`.

## 2 Theoretical Background and Framework

As Jacobs (2000, 264) puts it, "arguments are fundamentally linguistic entities that express [...] propositions where those propositions stand in particular inferential relations to one other". These *inferential relations*, namely argument schemes, are textually implicit and have to be reconstructed by the participants of a critical discussion in order to reach agreement or disagreement. In everyday life this happens quite intuitively on the basis of common ground knowledge: everyone would agree that "The sky is blue" does not constitute a premise for the assertion "We cannot make brownies", while the sentence "We ran out of chocolate" does because chocolate is an essential ingredient of brownies. However, to classify the relation between the above given premise-claim pair as an instance of reasoning from the formal cause constitutes a task which lies outside common encyclopedic knowledge. In light of this, a set of guidelines about the explicit and implicit components needed to recognize different types of argument schemes between given pairs of premises and claims has been provided.

## 2.1 The Structure of Argument Schemes following the *Argumentum Model of Topics*

Unlike other contemporary approaches, the *Argumentum Model of Topics* (AMT) does not "conceive of argument schemes as the whole bearing structures that connect the premises to the standpoint or conclusion in a piece of real argumentation" (Rigotti and Morasso, 2010, 483), but as an inference licensed by the combination of both material and procedural premises. Procedural premises are abstract rules of reasoning needed to bridge premises to claims. They include both a broad relation (after which argument schemes are named), which tells us why premises and claims are argumentatively related in a *frame*, and an inferential rule of the implicative type ("if...then"), which further specifies the reasoning at work in drawing a claim from certain premises. Contextual information, necessary to apply abstract rules to a real piece of argumentation, is provided by material premises which include the premise textually expressed and some common ground knowledge about the world. If we consider again the pair of sentences "[We cannot make brownies]CLAIM". "[We ran out of chocolate]PREMISE", the argument scheme connecting them is structured as given in Figure 1. At a structural level, the inferential rule works as a major premise that, combined with the conjunction of the material premises, allows one to draw the conclusion. Among the premises non-textually expressed, while common ground knowledge is per definition accessible to annotators, the inferential rule at work has to be consciously reconstructed.

Figure 1: Inferential configuration of argument according to *Argumentum Model of Topics (AMT)*

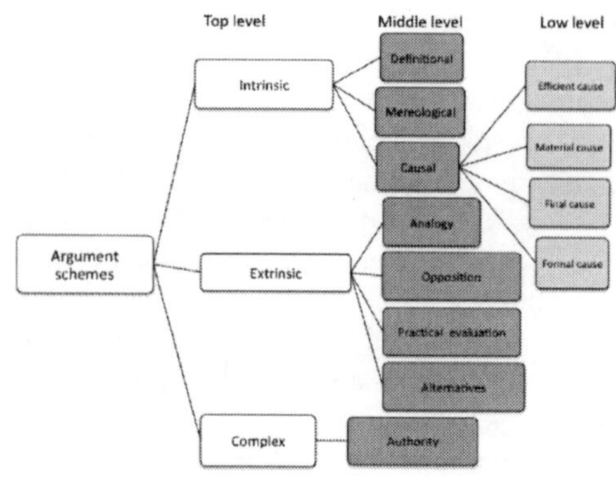


Figure 2: Adopted taxonomy of argument schemes

## 2.2 A Semantically Motivated Taxonomy of Argument Schemes

In this paper, the adopted taxonomy of argument schemes is a simplified version of that elaborated by exponents of the *Argumentum Model of Topics* (Rigotti, 2006; Palmieri, 2014). According to the AMT, argument schemes are organized in hierarchical clusters based on principles relying on frame semantics and pragmatics. As seen in Figure 2, there are three main levels.

At the top level, argument schemes are distinguished into three groups depending on the type of relations linking the State of Affairs (SoA) expressed by the premise to that expressed by the claim:

- *Intrinsic* argument schemes: the SoA expressed by the premise and that expressed by the claim are linked by an ontological relation since they belong to the same *semantic frame*, understood as a unitarian scene featuring a set of participants (Fillmore and Baker, 2010). This entails that the two SoAs take place simultaneously in the real world or that the existence of one affects the existence of the other.

- *Extrinsic* argument schemes: the SoA expressed by the premise and that expressed by the claim belong to different *frames* and are connected by semantic relations that are not ontological. This means that the existence of one SoA is independent from the existence of the other SoA.

- *Complex* argument schemes: the relation between the SoAs expressed by the premise and the claim is not semantic or ontological, but pragmatic. In other words, what guarantees the support of the claim is reference to an expert or an authority.

The middle level refers to the different types of ontological, semantic and pragmatic relations which further specify the top level classes. Each middle level argument scheme is defined by making reference to semantic or pragmatic properties of the propositions constituting the premises and the conclusion. For example, the scheme *Extrinsic:Practical Evaluation* is defined as follows: "the proposition functioning as premise is an evaluation, namely a judgment about something being 'good' or 'bad'. The claim expresses a recommendation/ advice about stopping/continuing/setting up an action".

The low level further specifies the middle level schemes. For example, the *Intrinsic:Causal* argument scheme is further specified following the so-called Aristotelian causes (efficient cause, formal cause, material cause and final cause)[1]. In the annotation protocol, this low level has not been considered since we hypothesize that it will be difficult for annotators to reliably make such fine-grained distinctions, based on results from similar studies using Walton's taxonomy of argument schemes (Song et al., 2014; Palau and Moens, 2009).

## 3 Annotation study

The annotation study has been designed on top of the annotation performed by Stab and Gurevych (2014). In their study, annotators were asked to identify and annotate through the open source annotation tool Brat [2] the argumentative components (premise, claim, major claim), the stance characterizing claims (for/against) and the argumentative relations connecting pairs of argumentative components (supports/against) in 90 short persuasive essays. We selected 30 essays as a sample for our pilot annotation (11 relations for each essay in average). The text genre of short persuasive essays is not bound to the discussion of a specific issue, which would prompt the presence of arguments of the same type, but enables the presence of the entire spectrum of argument schemes.

The annotators involved in the project were nine graduate students with no specific background in Linguistics or Argumentation. Three different annotators have been assigned to the annotation of each essay. The task consisted in annotating the "support" relations between premise-claim, claim-major claim, and premise-premise with one of the middle level argumentation schemes given in Figure 2 or *NoArgument*. For the identification of the middle level argument schemes, annotators were provided with an heuristic procedure and asked to look for linguistic clues as a further confirmation for their choices. We included the label of *NoArgument* to account for potential cases where premises/claims in support of claims/major claims do not actually instantiate any inferential path and cannot, hence, be considered proper arguments. For example, in the following pair of clauses: "[This, therefore, makes museums a place to entertain in people leisure time]PREMISE. [People should perceive the value of museums in enhancing their own knowledge]CLAIM ", the clause annotated as premise simply does not underpin at all the clause annotated as claim. As to the "attacks" relations, which indicate that a statement rebuts another statement, they have not been considered as targets of the annotation since they do not directly instantiate an argument scheme linking the spans of texts annotated as premise/claim and claim/major claim, but a complex refutatory move pointing to the defeasibility of the rebutted statement itself or to that of the premises supporting it. Annotators have independently read the guidelines and proceeded with the annotation without any formal training.

The guidelines contain the description of the key notions of argument, premise, claim and argument schemes' components as well as the AMT taxonomy. Detailed instructions about how to proceed in the annotation of argument schemes and rules were provided as well. The main stages of analysis annotators were asked to go through are the following:

- Identification of the middle level argument scheme linking premises-claims or claims-major claims pairs or recognition of the lack of argumentation in doubtful cases (e.g., *Intrinsic:Definitional*, *Intrinsic:Causal*, *Intrinsic:Mereological*, for a total of 9 choices including *NoArgument*, Figure 2)

- Identification of the inferential rule at work

---

[1] The model presents low level argument schemes for other middle level argument schemes which are not visualized in the Figure 2

[2] http://brat.nlplab.org/

(e.g., Figure 1).

We present these two stages of the annotation process in the next two subsections.

## 3.1 Identification of the Middle Level Argument Schemes

In order to recognize the middle level types of argument schemes, the annotators were asked to browse a set of given identification questions for argument schemes (see Appendix), to choose the question which best matches the pair of argumentative components linked by a "support" relation, and to check if the argumentative components contain linguistic features listed as typical of an argument scheme (see Appendix).

The explanation of the annotation procedure has been backed up by examples. For instance, given the premise-claim pair: "[Due to the increasing number of petrol stations, the competition in this field is more and more fierce]PREMISE, thus [the cost of petrol could be lower in the future]"CLAIM, the annotators were shown which argument scheme was appropriate:

- *Intrinsic:Definitional*: Does the sentence "Due to the increasing number of petrol stations, the competition in this field is more and more fierce" express a definitional property of the predicate "be lower" attributed to the cost of petrol? NO

  **Other linguistic clues**: the premise and the claim usually share the grammatical subject. The verb which appears in the claim expresses a state rather than an action.

- *Intrinsic:Mereological*: Is the fact that "Due to the increasing number of petrol stations, the competition in this field is more and more fierce" or an entity of that sentence (e.g., "the competition") an example/a series of examples/a part of the fact that "the cost of petrol could be lower in the future"? NO

  **Other linguistic clues**: the premise is frequently signaled by the constructions "for example", "as an example", "x proves that".

- *Intrinsic:Causal*: Is the fact that "Due to the increasing number of petrol stations, the competition in this field is more and more fierce" a cause/effect of the fact that "the cost of petrol could be lower in the future" or is it a means to obtain it? YES

**Other linguistic clues**: the claim frequently contains a modal verb or a modal construction ("must", "can", "it is clear/it is necessary"). In the given example, the claim contains the modal verb "could".

As far as linguistic clues are concerned, they have been collected from existing literature about linguistic indicators (Rocci, 2012; Miecznikowski and Musi, 2015; Van Eemeren et al., 2007) and from a preliminary analysis of the considered sample. Annotators have been explicitly warned that the given linguistic indicators, due to their highly polysemous and context sensitive nature, do not represent decisive pointers to the presence of specific arguments schemes, but have to be conceived as supplementary measures.

In presence of difficulties to identify a specific argument scheme applying the given set of identification questions, annotators were instructed to embed the pair of argumentative components under the hypothetical construction "If it is true that [premise/claim], is it then true that [claim/major claim]?" and evaluate its soundness. This simple test was meant to help the annotators checking if an inferential relation connecting the argumentative components is possibly there.

If a premise-claim pair failed the test, annotators were asked to choose the label *NoAgument* and explain why argumentation is not there. In the opposite case, they were told to annotate the pair under analysis as *Ambiguous* and try to identify the top level class of argument schemes applying the following round of identification questions:

- *Intrinsic* argument schemes: Can the state of affairs expressed in the premise and the state of affairs expressed in the claim take place simultaneously in the real world or does the realization of one affects the realization of the other one? If yes, it is an instance of intrinsic argument schemes.

- *Extrinsic* argument schemes: Are the existence of the state of affairs expressed in the premise and that expressed in the claim not simultaneous and independent on each other? If yes, it is an instance of extrinsic argument schemes.

- *Complex* argument scheme: Is the premise a discourse/statement expressed by an expert/an authority/an institution and does the claim coincide with the content of that discourse? If yes, it is an instance of complex argument scheme (authority).

**Example:** Let us consider the example below of a premise supporting a claim.

> "[Knowledge from experience seems a little different from information contained in books]CLAIM . [To cite an example, it is common in books that water boils at 100 Celcius degree. However, the result is not always the same in reality because it also depends on the height, the purity of the water, and even the measuring tool]"PREMISE

To determine whether there is an argument scheme, the annotators could ask themselves: "If it is true that [it is common in books that water boils at 100 Celcius degree. However, the result is not always the same in reality because it also depends on the height, the purity of the water, and even the measuring tool], is it then true that [knowledge from experience seems a little different from information contained in books]?" As the answer is yes, this premise-claim pair is an instance of argument schemes.

When the top level class of argument schemes is concerned, the SoAs expressed by the claim and the premise are simultaneously realized since the premise constitutes an example which shows that what is stated in the claim corresponds to reality. Thus this is an *Intrinsic* scheme. More specifically it is an *Intrinsic: Mereological* scheme (following the questions and the linguistic cues) since a process of induction from an exemplary case to a generalization is at work.

### 3.2  Identification of the Inferential Rule

The last step of the annotation process consisted in the identification of the inferential rule at work for those pairs in which annotators were able to identify a middle level argument scheme. Annotators were provided with representative rules for each argument scheme (see Appendix) such as the following two for the *Intrinsic:Mereological* argument scheme: "if all parts share a property, then the whole will inherit this property"; "if a part of x has a positive value, also x has a positive value".

They were asked either to write down one of the given inferential rules corresponding to the argument scheme or to formulate a rule on their own

if they thought that the provided ones were not fitting. Our hypothesis was that when writing down inferential rules the annotators are forced to control the appropriateness of the chosen argument scheme.

## 4  Evaluation

In order to evaluate the reliability of the annotations we measured the inter-annotators agreement (IAA) using Fleiss' $\kappa$ to account for multiple annotators (Fleiss, 1971). When considering the middle level annotation schemes, the IAA is $\kappa=0.1$, which shows only slight agreement (Landis and Koch, 1977). This finding supports the hypothesis that for annotating argument schemes the IAA is low when using minimally training non-expert annotators. We also measured the IAA between the top level arguments (*Intrinsic, Extrinsic, Complex, NoArgument*), but did not find any significant difference in the Fleiss' $\kappa$ score.

Table 1 represents some descriptive statistics about the annotations. Out of 302 argumentative relations to be annotated, for 30 cases (10%) all three annotators agree, while for 179 cases (59%) at least two out of the three annotators agree. When all three annotators agree the distribution of the argument schemes is: 7 *Intrinsic:Causal*, 9 *Intrinsic:Mereorogical*, 1 *Intrinsic:Definitional*, 6 *Extrinsic:Practical Evaluation* and 7 *NoArgument*. When at least two out of the three annotators agree, the distribution of the argument schemes (majority voting) is: 60 (33.5%) *Intrinsic:Causal*, 46 (25.7%) *Intrinsic:Mereorogical*, 16 (8.9%) *Intrinsic:Definitional*, 28 (15.6%) *Extrinsic:Practical Evaluation*, 3(1%) *Extrinsic:Alternatives'* , 3(1%) *Extrinsic:Opposition* and 23 (12.8%) *NoArgument'*).

When considering the 3 top level argument schemes plus *NoArgument*, out of 302 argumentative relations to be annotated, for 260 instances (86%) at least two annotators agreed. The distribution of majority voting labels in these cases is: 185 (71%) are *Intrinsic*, 52 (20%) are *Extrinsic*, and 23 (8.8%) are *NoArgument*.

One goal of this pilot study was to determine whether confusion exists among particular argument schemes with the aim to improve the guidelines. Table 2 shows the confusion matrix between two argument schemes for all annotators pairs. This confusion matrix is a symmetric one, so we

| Argument Schemes | # of Agreeing Annotators | # of Instances |
|---|---|---|
| Middle | all 3 | 30 |
|  | 2 or more | 179 |
| Top | all 3 | 77 |
|  | 2 or more | 260 |

Table 1: Descriptive Statistics about the annotations

provided only the upper triangular matrix. A detailed discussion is presented in the next section.

## 5 Discussion of the Results

As shown in the previous section, the argument schemes which received the highest IAA were *Intrinsic:Mereological*, *Intrinsic:Causal* among the *Intrinsic* argument schemes, and *Extrinsic:Practical evaluation* for the *Extrinsic* argument scheme. Going through the examples in which all three annotators agreed, our impression is that both the presence of scheme specific linguistic clues and the suitability of inferential rules already offered in the guidelines enhanced the annotators' choices. As to *Intrinsic:Mereological* relations, the frequent presence of constructions such as "for example", "for instance", compatible only with that specific argument scheme, has plausibly fostered its reliable recognition.

In the case of *Intrinsic:Causal* argument schemes, the cited linguistic clues in the guidelines have turned out to be not relevant: modal verbs are not present in the claims/major claims of the pairs annotated as *Intrinsic: Causal* by the majority of annotators. On the other hand, all these examples are instances of inferential rules from the cause to the effect. This suggests that the cause-effect inferential relation is considered as the prototypical type of causal argument schemes.

Only one instance of *Intrinsic:Definitional* argument scheme was recognized by all three annotators. Notions such as that stative predicates as identifiable linguistic clues in the guidelines were probably not informative for every annotator, as shown by the confusion among the *Intrinsic:Definitional* and *Intrinsic:Causal* argument schemes (Table 2).

For *Intrinsic:Mereological* and *Intrinsic:Causal* argument schemes a set of inferential rules was already proposed in the guidelines, as opposed to just one rule given for *Intrinsic:Definitional*. This has probably helped the annotators to check the soundness of the chosen scheme in these cases.

As to *Extrinsic:Practical Evaluation* argument scheme, the recurrent feature which seems to be at the basis of agreement is the presence of a clear evaluation in the premise.

Table 2 shows that, among the three more frequent argument schemes the *Extrinsic:Practical Evaluation* was the one confused the most with another specific argument scheme, namely *Intrinsic: Causal*. From the analysis of the ambiguous cases, two plausible reasons for the confusion have emerged: 1) the presence of the modal verb "should" has been cited in the guideline among the linguistic clues of both argument schemes, and 2) the *Extrinsic:Practical Evaluation* argument scheme shares with the causal argument scheme of the final type the reference to intentionality and, in general, to the frame of human action where consequences of various choices are taken into account. For example, the premise/claim pair "[this kind of ads will have a negative effect to our children] PREMISE. [Advertising alcohol, cigarettes, goods and services with adult content should be prohibited] CLAIM", which is an instance of *Extrinsic:Practical Evaluation* argument scheme, has been confused with the *Intrinsic:Causal* argument scheme licensing the inferential rule "if an action does not allow to achieve the goal, it should not be undertaken". In order to improve the annotation, ambiguous cases of this type will have to be discussed during the training process (see Section 6).

Since the *Extrinsic:Practical Evaluation* argument scheme is the far most frequent *Extrinsic* argument scheme in our sample, improving its identification promises to highly affect the IAA regarding top level *Extrinsic* vs. *Intrinsic* argument schemes.

The *Intrinsic:Causal* argument scheme appears to be frequently confused also with the *Intrinsic:Mereological* argument schemes and vice-versa. This happened mainly in the presence of *Mereological* argument schemes drawing a generalization from a exemplary case (rhetorical induction) such as the following: "[in Vietnam, many cultural costumes and natural scenes, namely drum performance and bay, are being encouraged to preserve and funded by the tourism ministry.] PREMISE [Through tourism industry, many cultural values have been preserved and natural environments have been protected]CLAIM". Some annotators misconceived the SoA expressed by the

| | Intrinsic:Causal | I:Mereorogical | I:Definitional | E:PracticalEvaluation | E:Alternatives | E:Opposition | E:Analogy | NoArgument | C:Authority |
|---|---|---|---|---|---|---|---|---|---|
| I:Causal | 154 | 89 | 45 | 82 | 17 | 17 | 6 | 82 | 5 |
| I:Mereorogical | | 128 | 20 | 47 | 16 | 14 | 14 | 51 | 4 |
| I:Definitional | | | 36 | 26 | 8 | 6 | 5 | 25 | 0 |
| E:Practical Evaluation | | | | 80 | 8 | 8 | 5 | 33 | 1 |
| E:Alternatives | | | | | 6 | 3 | 1 | 17 | 0 |
| E:Opposition | | | | | | 14 | 0 | 13 | 1 |
| E:Analogy | | | | | | | 0 | 4 | 0 |
| NoArgument | | | | | | | | 74 | 1 |
| C:Authority | | | | | | | | | 0 |

Table 2: Confusion Matrix on 30 essays (3 minimally trained non-expert annotators)

premise as an effect of the SoA expressed by the claim. This behavior suggests that the distinction between propositions expressing generalizations and those expressing state of affairs which can be located in space and time was not clear enough in the guidelines.

As to the label *No Argument*, a qualitative analysis of the occurrences showing disagreement has revealed that annotators tried by default to identify an argumentation scheme even when there was none, unless the propositional content of the connected argumentative components was evidently unrelated.

## 6 Annotation with trained annotators

After the initial study, we improved the guidelines keeping only scheme-specific linguistic clues, providing more inferential rules for each argument scheme, stressing the distinction between *Extrinsic:Practical Evaluation* and *Intrinsic:Causal* as well as between *Intrinsic:Mereological* and *Intrinsic:Causal*, and explicitly stating that some "supports" relations in the corpus are not argumentative (some examples have been provided). In order to test the improvement of the guidelines we have performed a further annotation with 2 trained non-expert annotators and 1 expert annotator on the set of essays which received lowest agreement ($\kappa$=-0.01; which indicated poor agreement).

The non-expert annotators went through a two hour training session during which they were asked to annotate 2 essays and received continuous feedback on misunderstandings and/or doubts. The results of the annotation show a shift of the IAA from $\kappa$=-0.01 to $\kappa$=0.311 ("fair agreement") among all three annotators (including the expert).

The IAA among just the two non-expert annotators was similar $\kappa$=0.307. In order to map the disagreement space we have calculated the confusion matrix.

Table 3 shows that in this reduced sample the percentage of relations annotated as *No Argument* is higher compared to the overall sample. Looking at the notes made by the annotators, four main reasons for the non argumentative nature of the relations pop up.

First, among the claims-major claims pairs frequently the propositional content of the claim rephrases that of the major claim, such as in the pair "[There should not be any restriction on artists' work]CLAIM. [The artist must be given freedom]"MAJOR CLAIM. In these cases, the presence of a "supports" relation is justified if redundancy is considered as a stylistic strategy for achieving consensus on a certain stance; however, the claim as a linguistic entity does not work as a argument.

Second, the clause annotated as premise happened to work as an argument only if combined with another clause. This happens bacause the annotation of premises and claims in the original dataset of Stab and Gurevych (2014) was done at the clause level. As recently pointed out by Stede et al. (2016) the mismatch between ADUs, which tend to encompass multiple clauses, and EDUs (elementary discourse units), constitutes one of the major difficulties to overcome in the investigation of the existing intersections between argumentative and discourse relations.

Third, the relation between two argumentative components would have been argumentative if reversed, or if a different claim would have been

| | Intrinsic:Causal | I:Mereorogical | I:Definitional | E:PracticalEvaluation | E:Alternatives | E:Opposition | E:Analogy | NoArgument | C:Authority |
|---|---|---|---|---|---|---|---|---|---|
| I:Causal | 86 | 19 | 10 | 13 | 0 | 1 | 0 | 47 | 0 |
| I:Mereorogical | | 70 | 5 | 1 | 0 | 0 | 0 | 21 | 0 |
| I:Definitional | | | 0 | 1 | 0 | 0 | 0 | 10 | 0 |
| E:PracticalEvaluation | | | | 10 | 0 | 0 | 0 | 9 | 0 |
| E:Alternatives | | | | | 0 | 0 | 0 | 0 | 0 |
| E:Opposition | | | | | | 2 | 0 | 4 | 0 |
| E:Analogy | | | | | | | 0 | 0 | 0 |
| No Argument | | | | | | | | 136 | 0 |
| C:Authority | | | | | | | | | 0 |

Table 3: Confusion Matrix on a set of 10 essays (highly trained annotators: 2 non-experts and 1 expert)

chosen.

Fourth, the clause annotated as premise does not underpin in anyway the clause annotated as claim, but constitutes instead a counterargument.

Although the agreement in the recognition of *No Argument* cases has consistently improved with highly trained annotators (non-expert as well as expert), it still remains a matter of confusion. In particular, the most frequent label chosen instead of *NoArgument* is that of *Intrinsic:Causal* argument scheme. This is probably due to the implicative nature of the proposed test "if the premise is true, then the claim is true", which invites a causal interpretation.

## 7 Conclusion and Future Work

We presented a novel set of guidelines for the annotation of argument schemes based on the *Argumentum Model of Topics*. This framework is advantageous since it offers a hierarchical finite taxonomy of argument schemes based on linguistic criteria which are highly distinctive and applicable to every context. We have conducted a pilot annotation study of 30 short persuasive essays with 9 minimally trained non-expert annotators in order to test the informativeness of the guidelines. The low inter-annotator agreement confirms the difficulties underlined by previous studies for minimally trained annotators to recognize argument schemes. From the qualitative analysis of the confusion matrixes it has emerged that: 1) linguistic indicators of argument schemes constitute useful clues for the annotators only if specific to one argument scheme, otherwise they can be a source of confusion; 2) the reconstruction of inferential rules is highly relevant to enhancing an-

notators' choices and 3) among *Intrinsic:Causal* argument schemes the subtype "Efficient cause" is the easiest to identify. We have improved the guidelines according to these results and tested them on a reduced sample of 10 essays with 2 trained non-expert annotators and one expert annotator. The interannotator agreement has significantly improved (fair agreement). The confusion matrix suggests that the frequency of non argumentative or ambiguous relations is the main cause of disagreement. For future work, we plan to test again the annotation guidelines in a corpus with higher accuracy as to the annotation of argumentative components (premises/claims). A methodological result of the study is that identifying argument schemes constitutes an important tool to verify the presence of argumentative components, and support relations.

## Acknowledgements

This paper is based on work supported partially by the Early Post Doc SNFS Grant for the project "From semantics to argumentation mining in context: the role of evidential strategies as indicators of argumentative discourse relations" and DARPA-DEFT program. The views expressed are those of the authors and do not reflect the official policy or position of the SNFS, Department of Defense or the U.S. Government. We would like to thank the annotators for their work and the anonymous reviewers for their valuable feedback.

## References

Ehud Aharoni, Anatoly Polnarov, Tamar Lavee, Daniel Hershcovich, Ran Levy, Ruty Rinott, Dan Gutfreund, and Noam Slonim. 2014. A benchmark dataset for automatic detection of claims and evidence in the context of controversial topics. In *Proceedings of the First Workshop on Argumentation Mining*, pages 64–68.

Or Biran and Owen Rambow. 2011. Identifying justifications in written dialogs. In *Semantic Computing (ICSC), 2011 Fifth IEEE International Conference on*, pages 162–168. IEEE.

Elena Cabrio and Serena Villata. 2012. Combining textual entailment and argumentation theory for supporting online debates interactions. In *Proceedings of the 50th Annual Meeting of the Association for Computational Linguistics: Short Papers - Volume 2*, ACL '12, pages 208–212, Stroudsburg, PA, USA. Association for Computational Linguistics.

Vanessa Wei Feng and Graeme Hirst. 2011. Classifying arguments by scheme. In *Proceedings of the 49th Annual Meeting of the Association for Computational Linguistics: Human Language Technologies-Volume 1*, pages 987–996. Association for Computational Linguistics.

Charles J Fillmore and Collin Baker. 2010. A frames approach to semantic analysis. *The Oxford handbook of linguistic analysis*, pages 313–339.

Joseph L Fleiss. 1971. Measuring nominal scale agreement among many raters. *Psychological bulletin*, 76(5):378.

Debanjan Ghosh, Smaranda Muresan, Nina Wacholder, Mark Aakhus, and Matthew Mitsui. 2014. Analyzing argumentative discourse units in online interactions. In *Proceedings of the First Workshop on Argumentation Mining*, pages 39–48.

Nancy L Green. 2015. Identifying argumentation schemes in genetics research articles. *NAACL HLT 2015*, page 12.

Scott Jacobs. 2000. Rhetoric and dialectic from the standpoint of normative pragmatics. *Argumentation*, 14(3):261–286.

Joel Katzav and Chris A Reed. 2004. On argumentation schemes and the natural classification of arguments. *Argumentation*, 18(2):239–259.

Manfred Kienpointner. 1987. Towards a typology of argumentative schemes. *Argumentation: Across the lines of discipline*, 3:275–87.

J Richard Landis and Gary G Koch. 1977. The measurement of observer agreement for categorical data. *biometrics*, pages 159–174.

Clare Llewellyn, Claire Grover, Jon Oberlander, and Ewan Klein. 2014. Re-using an argument corpus to aid in the curation of social media collections. In *LREC*, pages 462–468.

Fabrizio Macagno. 2014. Argumentation schemes and topical relations. *Macagno, F. & Walton, D.(2014). Argumentation schemes and topical relations. In G. Gobber, and A. Rocci (eds.), Language, reason and education*, pages 185–216.

Johanna Miecznikowski and Elena Musi. 2015. Verbs of appearance and argument schemes: Italian sembrare as an argumentative indicator. In *Reflections on Theoretical Issues in Argumentation Theory*, pages 259–278. Springer.

Raquel Mochales Palau and Marie-Francine Moens. 2009. Argumentation mining: the detection, classification and structure of arguments in text. In *Proceedings of the 12th international conference on artificial intelligence and law*, pages 98–107. ACM.

Rudi Palmieri. 2014. *Corporate argumentation in takeover bids*, volume 8. John Benjamins Publishing Company.

Andreas Peldszus and Manfred Stede. 2013a. From argument diagrams to argumentation mining in texts: A survey. *International Journal of Cognitive Informatics and Natural Intelligence (IJCINI)*, 7(1):1–31.

Andreas Peldszus and Manfred Stede. 2013b. Ranking the annotators: An agreement study on argumentation structure. In *Proceedings of the 7th linguistic annotation workshop and interoperability with discourse*, pages 196–204.

John L Pollock. 1995. *Cognitive carpentry: A blueprint for how to build a person*. Mit Press.

Chris Reed and Glenn Rowe. 2004. Araucaria: Software for argument analysis, diagramming and representation. *International Journal on Artificial Intelligence Tools*, 13(04):961–979.

Eddo Rigotti and Sara Greco Morasso. 2010. Comparing the argumentum model of topics to other contemporary approaches to argument schemes: the procedural and material components. *Argumentation*, 24(4):489–512.

Eddo Rigotti. 2006. Relevance of context-bound loci to topical potential in the argumentation stage. *Argumentation*, 20(4):519–540.

Eddo Rigotti. 2009. Whether and how classical topics can be revived within contemporary argumentation theory. In *Pondering on problems of argumentation*, pages 157–178. Springer.

Andrea Rocci. 2012. Modality and argumentative discourse relations: a study of the italian necessity modal dovere. *Journal of Pragmatics*, 44(15):2129–2149.

Sara Rosenthal and Kathleen McKeown. 2012. Detecting opinionated claims in online discussions. In *Semantic Computing (ICSC), 2012 IEEE Sixth International Conference on*, pages 30–37. IEEE.

Jodi Schneider, Krystian Samp, Alexandre Passant, and Stefan Decker. 2013. Arguments about deletion: How experience improves the acceptability of arguments in ad-hoc online task groups. In *Proceedings of the 2013 conference on Computer supported cooperative work*, pages 1069–1080. ACM.

Yi Song, Michael Heilman, Beata Beigman, and Klebanov Paul Deane. 2014. Applying argumentation schemes for essay scoring.

Christian Stab and Iryna Gurevych. 2014. Identifying argumentative discourse structures in persuasive essays. In *EMNLP*, pages 46–56.

Manfred Stede, Stergos Afantenos, Andreas Peldszus, Nicholas Asher, and Jérémie Perret. 2016. Parallel discourse annotations on a corpus of short texts.

Simone Teufel and Marc Moens. 2002. Summarizing scientific articles: experiments with relevance and rhetorical status. *Computational linguistics*, 28(4):409–445.

Frans H Van Eemeren and Rob Grootendorst. 1992. *Argumentation, communication, and fallacies: A pragma-dialectical perspective*. Lawrence Erlbaum Associates, Inc.

Frans H Van Eemeren, Peter Houtlosser, and AF Snoeck Henkemans. 2007. *Argumentative indicators in discourse: A pragma-dialectical study*, volume 12. Springer Science & Business Media.

Frans H Van Eemeren, Rob Grootendorst, Ralph H Johnson, Christian Plantin, and Charles A Willard. 2013. *Fundamentals of argumentation theory: A handbook of historical backgrounds and contemporary developments*. Routledge.

Douglas Walton, Christopher Reed, and Fabrizio Macagno. 2008. *Argumentation schemes*. Cambridge University Press.

Douglas Walton. 2012. Using argumentation schemes for argument extraction: A bottom-up method. *International Journal of Cognitive Informatics and Natural Intelligence (IJCINI)*, 6(3):33–61.

## A  Appendix

We report in what follows the "cheat sheet" located at the end of the annotation guidelines which contains i) an identification question, ii) a set of linguistic clues and of iii) inferential relations for each middle level argument scheme. The complete guidelines will be made available.

1. Intrinsic Definition:

   *Does x express a definitional property of the predicate attributed to the grammatical subject in y?*

   Other clues: the premise and the claim usually share the grammatical subject. The verb which appears in the claim expresses a state (*be +noun or be + adjective, consider*) rather than an action.

   Inferential rule: "if x shows typical traits of a class of entities (e.g. positive actions, beneficial decisions), then it is an instance of that class"

2. Intrinsic Mereorogical:

   *Is "the fact that x" or an entity cited in x an example /a series of examples /a part of "the fact that y"?*

   Other clues: the premise is frequently signaled by the constructions *or example, as an example, for instance, x proves that*. In the cases in which induction is at work the premise coincides with the description of a situation that is frequently located in the past.

   Inferential rules:

   - "if all parts share property, then the whole will inherit this property"
   - "if a part of x has a positive value, also x has a positive value"
   - "if something holds/may hold/held for an exemplary case x, it holds/may hold/will hold for all the cases of the same type"
   - "if something holds/may hold/held for a sample of cases of the type x, it holds/may hold/will hold for every case of the type x"

3. Intrinsic Causal:

   *Is x a cause /effect of y or is it a means to obtain y?*

   Other clues: the claim frequently contains a modal verb or a modal construction (*must, can, it is clear /it is necessary*).

   Inferential rules:

   - "if the cause is the case, the effect is the case"
   - "if the effect is the case, the cause is probably the case"
   - "if a quality characterizes the cause, then such quality characterizes the effect too"

- "if the realization of the goal necessitates the means x, x must be adopted"
- "if an action does not allow to achieve the goal, it should not be undertaken"
- "if somebody has the means to achieve a certain goal, he will achieve that goal"

4. Extrinsic Analogy:

*Do x and/or y compare situations happened in different circumstances but similar in some respects?*

Other clues: the premise and /or the claim usually contain comparative conjunctions /constructions (e.g. *as, like, in a similar vein*)

Inferential rules:

- "if the state of affairs x shows a set of features which are also present in the state of affairs y and z holds for x, then z holds for y too"
- "if two events x and y are similar and event x had the consequence z, probably also y will have the consequence z"
- "if two situations x and y are similar in a substantial way and action z was right in the situation x, action y will be right also in the situation y"

5. Extrinsic Opposition:

*does the occurrence of the state of affairs x exclude the occurrence of the state of affairs y? Or does the premise contain entities /events which are opposite with respect entities /events expressed in the claim?*

Other clues: the claim sometimes contain modals which express impossibility (*it is impossible that, it cannot be that*, but it is not always the case.

Inferential rules:

- "If two state of affairs/entities x, y are one the opposite of the other, the occurrence of x excludes the occurrence of y"
- "If two state of affairs x, y are one the opposite of the other, they entail opposite consequences"

6. Extrinsic Alternatives:

*Is/are the state of affairs expressed by x an alternative(s) to the one expressed in y?*

Other clues: the claim frequently contains necessity modals (*must, have to*). The premise states that all possible other alternatives are excluded.

Inferential rules:

- "if all the alternatives to x are excluded, then x is unavoidable"
- "if among a set of alternatives only one is reasonable it has to be undertaken"

7. Extrinsic Practical Evaluation/Termination and setting up:

*Does x express an evaluation and does y express an /a recommendation about stopping /continuing /setting up that action?*

Other clues: the claim usually contains the modal verb *should*.

Inferential rules:

- "if something is of important value, it should not be terminated"
- "if something has a positive value, it should be supported /continued /promoted /maintained"
- "if something has positive effects, it should be supported /continued /promoted /maintained"
- "if something has a negative effect it should be terminated"

8. Complex Authority:

*Is the premise a discourse/statement expressed by a an expert /institution /authority in the field and does the claim coincides with the content of that discourse?*

Other clues: the authority to which the writer appeals is usually introduced by *according to, as shown by, as clarified /explained /declared by.*

Inferential rules:

- "if the institution /expert /authority in the field states that proposition x is true, then x is true"
- "if the institution /expert /authority in the field states event x will occur, then x will probably occur"

# Identifying Argument Components through TextRank

**Georgios Petasis** and **Vangelis Karkaletsis**
Software and Knowledge Engineering Laboratory
Institute of Informatics & Telecommunications
National Center for Scientific Research (N.C.S.R.) "Demokritos"
Athens, Greece.
`{petasis,vangelis}@iit.demokritos.gr`

## Abstract

In this paper we examine the application of an unsupervised extractive summarisation algorithm, TextRank, on a different task, the identification of argumentative components. Our main motivation is to examine whether there is any potential overlap between extractive summarisation and argument mining, and whether approaches used in summarisation (which typically model a document as a whole) can have a positive effect on tasks of argument mining. Evaluation has been performed on two corpora containing user posts from an on-line debating forum and persuasive essays. Evaluation results suggest that graph-based approaches and approaches targeting extractive summarisation can have a positive effect on tasks related to argument mining.

## 1 Introduction

Argumentation is a branch of philosophy that studies the act or process of forming reasons and of drawing conclusions in the context of a discussion, dialogue, or conversation. Being an important element of human communication, its use is very frequent in texts, as a means to convey meaning to the reader. As a result, argumentation has attracted significant research focus from many disciplines, ranging from philosophy to artificial intelligence. Central to argumentation is the notion of argument, which according to (Besnard and Hunter, 2008) is a set of assumptions (i.e. information from which conclusions can be drawn), together with a conclusion that can be obtained by one or more reasoning steps (i.e. steps of deduction). The conclusion of the argument is often called the claim, or equivalently the consequent or the conclusion of the argument. The assumptions are called the support, or equivalently the premises of the argument, which provide the reason (or equivalently the justification) for the claim of the argument. The process of extracting conclusions/claims along with their supporting premises, both of which compose an argument, is known as argument mining (Goudas et al., 2015; Goudas et al., 2014) and constitutes an emerging research field.

Several approaches have been already presented for addressing various subtasks of argument mining, including the identification of argumentative sentences (i.e. sentences that contain argumentation components such as claims and premises), argumentation components, relations between such components, and resources for supporting argument mining, like discourse indicators and other expressions indicating the presence of argumentative components. Proposed methods mostly relate to supervised machine learning exploiting a plethora of features (Goudas et al., 2015), including the combination of several techniques, such as the work presented in (Lawrence and Reed, 2015).

One of the difficulties associated to argument mining relates to the fact that the identification of argument components usually depends on the context in which they appear in. The locality of this context can vary significantly, based not only on the domain, but possibly even to personal writing style. On one hand, discourse indicators, markers and phrases can provide a strong and localised contextual information, but their use is not very frequent (Lawrence and Reed, 2015). On the other hand, the local context of a phrase may indicate that the phrase is a fact, suggesting low or no *argumentativeness* at all, while at the same time, the same phrase may contradict to another phrase several sentences before or after the phrase in question, constituting the phrase under ques-



*Proceedings of the 3rd Workshop on Argument Mining*, pages 94–102,
Berlin, Germany, August 7-12, 2016. ©2016 Association for Computational Linguistics

tion an argumentative component (Carstens and Toni, 2015). While it is quite easy to handle local context through suitable representations and learning techniques, complexity may increase significantly when a broader context is required, especially when relations exist among various parts of a document.

In this paper we want to examine approaches that are able to handle interactions and relations that are not local, especially the ones that can model a document as a whole. An example of a task where documents are modelled in their entirety, is document summarisation (Giannakopoulos et al., 2015). Extractive summarisation typically examines the importance of each sentence with respect to the rest of the sentences in a document, in order to select a small set of sentences that are more "representative" for a given document. A typical extractive summarisation system is expected to select sentences that contain a lot of information in a compact form, and capture the different pieces of information that are expressed in a document. The main idea behind this paper is to examine whether there is any potential *overlap between these sentences* that summarise a document, and *argumentation components* that can exist in a document. Assuming that in a document the author expresses one or more claims, which can be potentially justified through a series of premises or support statements, it will be interesting to examine whether any of these argumentation components will be assessed as significant enough to be included in an automatically generated summary. Will a summarisation algorithm capture at least the claims, and characterise them as important enough to be included in the produced summary?

In order to examine if there is any overlap between extractive summarisation and argument mining (at least the identification of sentences that contain some argumentation components, such as claims), we wanted to avoid any influence from the documents and the thematic domains under examination. Ruling out supervised approaches, we examined summarisation algorithms that are either unsupervised, or can be trained in different domains than the ones they will be applied on. Finally, we opted for an unsupervised algorithm, TextRank (Mihalcea and Tarau, 2004), a graph-based ranking model, which can be applied on extractive summarisation by exploiting "similarity" among sentences, based on their content overlap. We conducted our study on two corpora in English. The first one is a corpus of user generated content, compiled by Hasan and Ng (2014) from online debate forums on four topics: "abortion", "gay rights", "marijuana", and "Obama". The second corpus, compiled by Stab and Gurevych (2014), contains 90 persuasive essays on various topics. Initial results are promising, suggesting that there is an overlap between extractive summarisation and argumentation component identification, and the ranking of sentences from TextRank can help in tasks related to argument mining, possibly as a feature in cooperation with an argumentation mining approach.

The rest of the paper is organised as follows: Section 2 presents an brief overview of approaches related to argument mining, while section 3 presents our approach on applying TextRank for identifying sentences that contain argumentation components. Section 4 presents the experimental setting and evaluation results, with section 5 concluding this paper and proposing some directions for further research.

## 2   Related Work

A plethora of approaches related to argument mining consider the identification of sentences containing argument components or not as a key step of the whole process. Usually labeled as "argumentative" sentences, these approaches model the process of identifying argumentation components as a two-class classification problem. In this category can be classified approaches like (Goudas et al., 2015; Goudas et al., 2014; Rooney et al., 2012), where supervised machine learning has been employed in order to classify sentences into argumentative and non-argumentative ones.

However, there are approaches which try to solve the argument mining problem in a completely different way. Lawrence et al. (2014) combined a machine learning algorithm to extract propositions from philosophical text, with a topic model to determine argument structure, without considering whether a piece of text is part of an argument. Hence, the machine learning algorithm was used in order to define the boundaries and afterwards classify each word as the beginning or end of a proposition. Once the identification of the beginning and the ending of the argument propositions has finished, the text is marked from each starting point till the next ending word.

Another interesting approach was proposed by Graves et al. (2014), who explored potential sources of claims in scientific articles based on their title. They suggested that if titles contain a tensed verb, then it is most likely (actually almost certain) to announce the argument claim. In contrast, when titles do not contain tensed verbs, they have varied announcements. According to their analysis, they have identified three basic types in which articles can be classified according to genre, purpose and structure. If the title has verbs then the claim is repeated in the abstract, introduction and discussion, whereas if the title does not have verbs, then the claim does not appear in the title or introduction but appears in the abstract and discussion sections.

Another field of argument mining that has recently attracted the attention of the research community, is the field of argument mining from online discourses. As in most cases of argument mining, the lack of annotated corpora is a limiting factor. In this direction, Hasan and Ng (2014), Houngbo and Mercer (2014), Aharoni et al. (2014), Green (2014), Stab and Gurevych (2014), and Kirschner et al. (2015) focused on providing corpora spanning from online posts to scientific publications that could be widely used for the evaluation of argument mining techniques. In this context, Boltužić and Šnajder (2014) collected comments from online discussions about two specific topics and created a manually annotated corpus for argument mining. In addition, they used a supervised model to match user-created comments to a set of predefined topic-based arguments, which can be either attacked or supported in the comment. In order to achieve this, they used textual entailment features, semantic text similarity features, and one "stance alignment" feature.

One step further, Trevisan et al. (2014) described an approach for the analysis of German public discourses, exploring *semi-automated* argument identification by exploiting discourse analysis. They focused on identifying conclusive connectors, substantially adverbs (i.e. "hence", "thus", "therefore"), using a multi-level annotation. Their approach consists of three steps, which are performed iteratively (manual discourse linguistic argumentation analysis, semi-automatic text mining (PoS-tagging and linguistic multi-level annotation) and data merge) and their re-sults show the argument-conclusion relationship is most often indicated by the conjunction because followed by "since", "therefore" and "so".

Ghosh et al. (2014) attempted to identify the argumentative segments of texts in online threads. Expert annotators have been trained to recognise argumentative features in full-length threads. The annotation task consisted of three subtasks: In the first subtask, annotators had to identify "Argumentative Discourse Units" (ADUs) along with their starting and ending points. Secondly, they had to classify the ADUs according to the "Pragmatic Argumentation Theory" (PAT) into "Callouts" and "Targets". As a final step, they indicated the link between the "Callouts" and "Targets". In addition, a hierarchical clustering technique has been proposed that assess how difficult it is to identify individual text segments as "Callouts".

Levy et al. (2014) defined the task of automatic claim detection in a given context and outlined a preliminary solution, aiming to automatically pinpoint context dependent claims (CDCs) within topic-related documents. Their supervised learning approach relies on a cascade of classifiers. Assuming that the articles examined are relatively small set of relevant free-text articles, they provided either manually or automatic retrieval methods. More specifically, the first step of their approach is to identify sentences containing CDCs in each article. As a second step a classifier is used in order to identify the exact boundaries of the CDCs in sentences identified as containing CDCs. As a final step, each CDC is ranked in order to isolate the most relevant CDCs to the corresponding topic.

Finally, Carstens and Toni (2015) focus on extracting argumentative relations, instead of identifying the actual argumentation components. Despite the fact that few details are provided and their approach seems to be concentrated in pairs of sentences, the presented approach is similar to the approach presented in this paper in the sense that both concentrate on relations as the primary starting point for performing argument mining.

## 3 Extractive Summarisation and Argumentative Component Identification

### 3.1 The TextRank Algorithm

TextRank is a graph-based ranking model, "which can be used for a variety of natural language processing applications, where knowledge drawn from an entire document is used in making local ranking/selection decisions" (Mihalcea and Tarau, 2004). The main idea behind TextRank is to extract a graph from the text of a document, using textual fragments as vertices. What constitutes a vertex depends on the task the algorithm is applied on. For example, for the task of keyword extraction vertices can be words, while for summarisation the vertices can be whole sentences. Once the vertices have been defined, edges can be added between two vertices according to the "similarity" among text units represented by vertices. Again, "similarity" depends on the task. As a last step, an iterative graph-based ranking algorithm (a slightly modified version of the PageRank algorithm (Brin and Page, 1998)) is applied, in order to score vertices, and associate a value (score) to each vertex. These values attached to each vertex are used for the ranking/selections decisions.

In the case of (extractive) summarisation, TextRank can be used in order to extract a set of sentences from a document, which can be used to form a summary of the document (either through post-processing of the extracted set of sentences, or by using the set of sentences directly as the summary). In such a case, the following steps are applied:

- The text of a document is tokenised into words and sentences.
- The text is converted into a graph, with each sentence becoming a vertex of the graph (as the goal is to rank entire sentences).
- Connections (edges) between sentences are established, based on a "similarity" relation. The edges are *weighted* by the "similarity" score between the two connected vertices.
- The ranking algorithm is applied on the graph, in order to score each sentence.
- Sentences are sorted in reversed order of their score, and the top ranked sentences are selected for inclusion into the summary.

The notion of "similarity" in TextRank is defined as the overlap between two sentences, which can be simply determined as the number of common words between the two sentences. Formally, given two sentences $S_i$ and $S_j$, of sizes $N$ and $M$ respectively, with each sentence being represented by a set of words $W$ such as $S_i = W_1^i, W_2^i, ..., W_N^i$ and $S_j = W_1^j, W_2^j, ..., W_M^j$, the similarity between $S_i$ and $S_j$ can be defined as (Mihalcea and Tarau,

2004):

$$Similarity(S_i, S_j) = \frac{|W_k|W_k \in S_i \& W_k \in S_j|}{log(|S_i|) + log(|S_j|)}$$

In our experiments we have used a slightly modified similarity measure which employs TF-IDF (Manning et al., 2008), as implemented by the open-source TextRank implementation that can be found at (Bohde, 2012).

### 3.2 Argumentative Component Identification

The main focus of this paper is to evaluate whether there is any overlap between argument mining and automatic summarisation. An automatic summarisation algorithm such as TextRank is expected to rank highly sentences that are "recommended" by the rest of the sentences in a document, where "recommendation" suggests that sentences address similar concepts, and the sentences recommended by other sentences are likely to be more informative (Mihalcea and Tarau, 2004), thus more suitable for summarising a document. In a similar manner, a claim is expected to share similar concepts with other text fragments that either support or attack the claim. At the same time, these fragments are related to the claim with relations such as "support" or "attack". Thus, there seems to exist some overlap between how arguments are expressed and how TextRank selects and scores sentences. In the work presented in this paper we will try to exploit this similarity, in order to use TextRank for identifying sentences that contain argumentation components.

In its initial form for the summarisation task, TextRank segments text into sentences, and uses sentences as the text unit to model the given text into a graph. In order to apply TextRank for claim identification, we assume that an argument component can be contained within a single sentence, essentially ignoring components that are expressed in more than one sentences. A component can also be expressed as a fragment smaller than a sentence: in this case we want to identify whether a sentence contains a component or not. As a result, we define the task of component identification as the identification of sentences that contain an argumentation component.

In order to identify the sentences that contain argumentation components, we tokenise a document into tokens and we identify sentences. Then we apply TextRank, and we extract a small number (one or two sentences) from the top scored sentences. If the document contains an argumentation component, we expect the sentence containing the component to be included in the small set of sentences extracted by TextRank.

## 4  Empirical Evaluation

In order to evaluate our hypothesis, that there is a potential overlap between automatic summarisation (as represented by extractive approaches such as TextRank) and argument mining (at least claim identification), we have applied TextRank on two corpora written in English. The first corpus has been compiled from online debate forums, containing user posts concerning four thematic domains (Hasan and Ng, 2014), while the second corpus contains 90 persuasive essays on various topics (Stab and Gurevych, 2014).

### 4.1  Experimental Setup

The first corpus that has been used in our study has been compiled and manually annotated as described in (Hasan and Ng, 2014). User generated content has been collected from an online debate forum[1]. Debate posts from four popular *domains* were collected: "abortion", "gay rights", "marijuana", and "Obama". These posts are either in favour or against the domain, depending on whether the author of the post supports or opposes abortion, gay rights, the legalisation of marijuana, or Obama respectively. The posts were manually examined, in order to identify the *reasons* for the stance (in favour or against) of each post. A set of 56 reasons were identified for the four domains, which were subsequently used for annotating the posts: for each post, segments that correspond to any of these reasons were manually annotated.

We have processed the aforementioned corpus, and we have removed the posts where the annotated segments span more than a single sentence, keeping only the posts where the annotated segments are contained within a single sentence. The resulting number of posts for each domain are shown in Table 1. The TextRank implementation used in the evaluation has been written in Python[2], and is publicly available through (Bohde, 2012).

Each post is associated with one (and in some cases more than one) segment that expresses the

main reason for the author to be in favour or against the domain. In order to examine whether there is an overlap between argument mining and summarisation, we have applied TextRank on each post, and we have examined whether the single, top ranked sentence by TextRank, contains the segment marked as the reason. In case the segment is contained in the top ranked sentence returned by TextRank, the post is classified as correctly identified. If the reason segment is not contained in the returned sentence, the post is characterised as an error. Evaluation results are reported through *accuracy* (proportion of true results among the total number of cases examined).

Finally, two experiments were performed, with the only difference being the number of sentences selected from TextRank to form the summary. During the first experiment (labelled as $E_1$), only a single sentence was selected (the top-ranked sentence as determined by TextRank), while during the second experiment (labelled as $E_2$) we have selected the *two* top-ranked sentences.

The main motivation for selecting the corpus compiled by Hasan and Ng (2014) was the fact that most of its documents have been manually annotated with a single claim, which was associated with a text fragment that most of the times is contained within a sentence. Having a single sentence as a target constitutes the evaluation of an approach such as the one presented in this paper easier, as the single sentence that represents the main claim of the document can be compared to the top-ranked sentence by the extractive summarisation algorithm. A corpus that has similar properties, in the sense that there is a "major" claim represented by a text fragment that is contained within a sentence, has been compiled by Stab and Gurevych (2014). This corpus contains 90 documents that are persuasive essays, and have been manually annotated with an annotation scheme that includes a "major" claim for each document, a series of arguments that support or attack the major claim, and series or premises that underpin the validity of an argument. Despite being a smaller corpus than the first corpus used for evaluation, having only 1675 sentences, that fact that it contains only 90 documents suggests that its documents are slightly larger than the posts of the first document by (Hasan and Ng, 2014). The average length of a persuasive essay is 18.61 sentences in this second evaluation corpus, which is larger than the aver-

---

[1] http://www.createdebate.com/
[2] http://www.python.org/

|  | "abortion" | "gay rights" | "marijuana" | "Obama" | all domains |
|---|---|---|---|---|---|
| Number of posts | 398 | 403 | 352 | 298 | 1451 |
| Mean post size (in sentences) | 11.15 | 8.22 | 6.52 | 6.50 | 8.25 |
| Mean argumentative sentences number | 1.80 | 1.65 | 1.97 | 1.39 | 1.71 |

Table 1: Number of posts per domain in the first corpus used for evaluation (Hasan and Ng, 2014).

| Domain | Total Posts | $E_1$ Correct Posts | $E_1$ Accuracy | $E_2$ Correct Posts | $E_2$ Accuracy |
|---|---|---|---|---|---|
| "abortion" | 398 | 150 | 0.37 | 226 | 0.57 |
| "gay rights" | 403 | 160 | 0.40 | 235 | 0.58 |
| "marijuana" | 352 | 168 | 0.47 | 239 | 0.68 |
| "Obama" | 298 | 159 | 0.53 | 208 | 0.70 |
| all domains | 1451 | 631 | 0.44 | 919 | 0.63 |

Table 2: Baseline results (for experiments $E_1$ and $E_2$) – first evaluation corpus (Hasan and Ng, 2014).

| Experiment | Total | Correct Essays | Accuracy |
|---|---|---|---|
| $E_1$ | 90 | 3 | 0.03 |
| $E_2$ | 90 | 10 | 0.11 |
| $E_1$ (all claims) | 90 | 30 | 0.33 |
| $E_2$ (all claims) | 90 | 48 | 0.53 |

Table 3: Baseline results (for experiments $E_1$ and $E_2$) – second evaluation corpus (Stab and Gurevych, 2014).

age post size of 8.25 sentences of the first corpus (Table 1). As a result, the second corpus that will be used for evaluation (Stab and Gurevych, 2014) provides the opportunity to evaluate TextRank on larger documents, where the selection of the sentence that represents the "major" claim is potentially more difficult, as the set of potential candidate sentences is larger. Finally, there is a single "major" claim for each persuasive essay, and the mean number of all claims (including the "major" claim) is 5.64 per persuasive essay.

## 4.2 Baseline

As a baseline approach, a simple random sentence extractor has been used. The sentences contained in each document (post for the first and essay for the second evaluation corpus respectively) were randomly shuffled by using the Fisher-Yates shuffling algorithm (Fisher and Yates, 1963). Then we extract a small number (the first or the two first sentences) from the sentences as randomly shuffled, simulating how we apply TextRank for identifying the sentences that contain argumentation components. The results obtained from this random shuffle baseline are shown in Table 2 for

the first evaluation corpus (Hasan and Ng, 2014), while the results for the second evaluation corpus (Stab and Gurevych, 2014) are presented in Table 3.

## 4.3 Evaluation Results

As described in the experimental setting, we have performed two experiments. During the first experiment ($E_1$) we have generated a "summary" of a single sentence (the top-ranked sentence by TextRank), while for the second experiment ($E_2$) we have selected the two top-ranked sentences as the generated "summary". In both experiments, each post is characterised as correct if the reason segment is contained in the extracted "summary"; otherwise the post is characterised as an error. The evaluation results are shown in Table 4 for experiment $E_1$ and Table 5 for experiment $E_2$.

As can be seen from Tables 4 and 5, TextRank has achieved better performance (as measured by accuracy) than our baseline in both experiments, $E_1$ and $E_2$. For experiment $E_1$, accuracy has increased from 0.44 (of the baseline) to 0.51, while in experiment $E_2$, accuracy has increased from 0.63 to 0.71, when considering all four domains. In addition, TextRank has achieved better performance for all individual domains than the baseline, which randomly selects sentences. Another factor is document size: the mean size of posts (measured as the number of contained sentences) seems to vary between the four domains, ranging from 6.5 sentences for domains "Obama" and "marijuana" to 11 sentences for domain "abortion". TextRank has exhibited better performance than the baseline even for the domains with larger

| Domain | Total Posts | Correct Posts | Accuracy | Accuracy (Baseline) |
| --- | --- | --- | --- | --- |
| "abortion" | 398 | 171 | 0.43 | 0.37 |
| "gay rights" | 403 | 201 | 0.50 | 0.40 |
| "marijuana" | 352 | 199 | 0.56 | 0.47 |
| "Obama" | 298 | 175 | 0.59 | 0.53 |
| all domains | 1451 | 746 | 0.51 | 0.44 |

Table 4: Evaluation Results (for experiment $E_1$) – first evaluation corpus (Hasan and Ng, 2014).

| Domain | Total Posts | Correct Posts | Accuracy | Accuracy (Baseline) |
| --- | --- | --- | --- | --- |
| "abortion" | 398 | 267 | 0.67 | 0.57 |
| "gay rights" | 403 | 269 | 0.67 | 0.58 |
| "marijuana" | 352 | 273 | 0.78 | 0.68 |
| "Obama" | 298 | 223 | 0.75 | 0.70 |
| all domains | 1451 | 1032 | 0.71 | 0.63 |

Table 5: Evaluation Results (for experiment $E_2$) – first evaluation corpus (Hasan and Ng, 2014).

| Experiment | Total Essays | Correct Essays | Accuracy | Accuracy (Baseline) |
| --- | --- | --- | --- | --- |
| $E_1$ | 90 | 14 | 0.16 | 0.03 |
| $E_2$ | 90 | 26 | 0.29 | 0.11 |
| $E_1$ (all claims) | 90 | 47 | 0.52 | 0.33 |
| $E_2$ (all claims) | 90 | 67 | 0.74 | 0.53 |

Table 6: Evaluation Results – second evaluation corpus (Stab and Gurevych, 2014).

posts, such as "abortion". Of course, as the size of documents increases the task of selecting one or two sentences becomes more difficult, and this is evident by the drop in performance (for both TextRank and the baseline) for domains "abortion" and "gay rights" when compared to the rest of the domains.

Results are similar for the second evaluation corpus of persuasive essays, as is shown in Table 6. Again TextRank has achieved better performance than the baseline for both experiments, $E_1$ and $E_2$. The overall performance of both TextRank and the baseline is lower than the first corpus, mainly due to the increased size of persuasive essays compared to posts (having an average size of 18.61 and 8.25 sentences respectively). For the second corpus an additional experiment has been performed, which expands the set of claims that have to be identified, from only the "major" claim, to all the claims (including the "major" one) in an essay. This experiment (labelled as "$E_1$ (all claims)" and "$E_2$ (all claims)" in Table 6) examines whether the top-ranked sentence (experiment "$E_1$ (all claims)") by TextRank is a claim, or whether the first two sentences as ranked

by TextRank contain a claim (experiment "$E_2$ (all claims)"). As expected, the performance of both TextRank and the baseline has been increased, as this is an easier task. The mean number of all claims (including the "major" claim) is 5.64 per persuasive essay.

Regarding the overall performance of the summarisation algorithm and its use for identifying a sentence containing an argumentation component, TextRank has managed to achieve a noticeable increase in performance over the baseline, despite the fact that it is an unsupervised algorithm, requiring no training or any form of adaptation to the domain. This suggests that an algorithm that models a document as a whole can provide positive information for argument mining, even if the algorithm has been designed for a different task, as is the case for TextRank variation used, which targets extractive summarisation. In addition, the evaluation results suggest that there is some overlap between argument mining and summarisation, leading to the conclusion that there are potential benefits for approaches performing argument mining through the synergy with approaches that perform document summarisation.

## 5 Conclusions

In this paper we have applied an unsupervised algorithm for extractive summarisation, TextRank, on a task that relates to argument mining, the identification of sentences that contain an argumentation component. Motivated by the need to better address relations and interactions that are not local within a document, we have applied a graph-based algorithm, which models a whole document having sentences as its basic text unit. Evaluation has been performed on two English corpora. The first corpus contains user posts from an on-line debating forum, which has been manually annotated with the reasons each post author uses to declare its stance, in favour or against, towards a specific topic. The second corpus contains 90 persuasive essays, which has been manually annotated with claims and premises, along with a "major" claim for each essay. Evaluation results suggest that graph-based approaches and approaches targeting extractive summarisation can have a positive effect on tasks of argument mining.

Regarding directions for further research, there are several axes that can be explored. Our evaluation results suggest that TextRank achieved better performance than the baseline for documents between 6 and 11 sentences, and it would be interesting to evaluate further its performance on longer documents. At the same time, the performance of TextRank depends on how "similarity" between its text units is defined; alternative "similarity" measures can be considered, even supervised ones that measure distance according to information obtained from a domain, or information obtained for a specific task. Even an external knowledge base can be explored, providing distances closer to semantic similarity. Finally, a third dimension is to examine alternative extractive summarisation algorithms, in order to clarify further whether other summarisation algorithms can have a positive impact for argument mining, similar to the results achieved by TextRank.

## References


Ehud Aharoni, Anatoly Polnarov, Tamar Lavee, Daniel Hershcovich, Ran Levy, Ruty Rinott, Dan Gutfreund, and Noam Slonim. 2014. A benchmark dataset for automatic detection of claims and evidence in the context of controversial topics. In *Proceedings of the First Workshop on Argumentation Mining*, pages 64–68, Baltimore, Maryland, June. Association for Computational Linguistics.

Philippe Besnard and Anthony Hunter. 2008. *Elements of argumentation*, volume 47. MIT press Cambridge.

Josh Bohde. 2012. Document Summarization using TextRank. `http://joshbohde.com/blog/document-summarization`. [Online; accessed 12-May-2016].

Filip Boltužić and Jan Šnajder. 2014. Back up your stance: Recognizing arguments in online discussions. In *Proceedings of the First Workshop on Argumentation Mining*, pages 49–58, Baltimore, Maryland, June. Association for Computational Linguistics.

Sergey Brin and Lawrence Page. 1998. The anatomy of a large-scale hypertextual web search engine. *Comput. Netw. ISDN Syst.*, 30(1-7):107–117, April.

Lucas Carstens and Francesca Toni. 2015. Towards relation based argumentation mining. In *Proceedings of the 2nd Workshop on Argumentation Mining*, pages 29–34, Denver, CO, June. Association for Computational Linguistics.

R.A. Fisher and F. Yates. 1963. *Statistical tables for biological, agricultural, and medical research.* Hafner Pub. Co.

Debanjan Ghosh, Smaranda Muresan, Nina Wacholder, Mark Aakhus, and Matthew Mitsui. 2014. Analyzing argumentative discourse units in online interactions. In *Proceedings of the First Workshop on Argumentation Mining*, pages 39–48, Baltimore, Maryland, June. Association for Computational Linguistics.

George Giannakopoulos, Jeff Kubina, Ft Meade, John M Conroy, MD Bowie, Josef Steinberger, Benoit Favre, Mijail Kabadjov, Udo Kruschwitz, and Massimo Poesio. 2015. Multiling 2015: Multilingual summarization of single and multi-documents, on-line fora, and call-center conversations. *16th Annual Meeting of the Special Interest Group on Discourse and Dialogue*, page 270.

Theodosis Goudas, Christos Louizos, Georgios Petasis, and Vangelis Karkaletsis. 2014. Argument extraction from news, blogs, and social media. In Aristidis Likas, Konstantinos Blekas, and Dimitris Kalles, editors, *Artificial Intelligence: Methods and Applications*, volume 8445 of *Lecture Notes in Computer Science*, pages 287–299. Springer.

Theodosis Goudas, Christos Louizos, Georgios Petasis, and Vangelis Karkaletsis. 2015. Argument extraction from news, blogs, and the social web. *International Journal on Artificial Intelligence Tools*, 24(05):1540024.

Heather Graves, Roger Graves, Robert Mercer, and Mahzereen Akter. 2014. Titles that announce argumentative claims in biomedical research articles. In *Proceedings of the First Workshop on Argumentation Mining*, pages 98–99, Baltimore, Maryland, June. Association for Computational Linguistics.

Nancy Green. 2014. Towards creation of a corpus for argumentation mining the biomedical genetics research literature. In *Proceedings of the First Workshop on Argumentation Mining*, pages 11–18, Baltimore, Maryland, June. Association for Computational Linguistics.

Kazi Saidul Hasan and Vincent Ng. 2014. Why are you taking this stance? identifying and classifying reasons in ideological debates. In *Proceedings of the 2014 Conference on Empirical Methods in Natural Language Processing (EMNLP)*, pages 751–762, Doha, Qatar, October. Association for Computational Linguistics.

Hospice Houngbo and Robert Mercer. 2014. An automated method to build a corpus of rhetorically-classified sentences in biomedical texts. In *Proceedings of the First Workshop on Argumentation Mining*, pages 19–23, Baltimore, Maryland, June. Association for Computational Linguistics.

Christian Kirschner, Judith Eckle-Kohler, and Iryna Gurevych. 2015. Linking the thoughts: Analysis of argumentation structures in scientific publications. In *Proceedings of the 2nd Workshop on Argumentation Mining*, pages 1–11, Denver, CO, June. Association for Computational Linguistics.

John Lawrence and Chris Reed. 2015. Combining argument mining techniques. In *Proceedings of the 2nd Workshop on Argumentation Mining*, pages 127–136, Denver, CO, June. Association for Computational Linguistics.

John Lawrence, Chris Reed, Colin Allen, Simon McAlister, and Andrew Ravenscroft. 2014. Mining arguments from 19th century philosophical texts using topic based modelling. In *Proceedings of the First Workshop on Argumentation Mining*, pages 79–87, Baltimore, Maryland, June. Association for Computational Linguistics.

Ran Levy, Yonatan Bilu, Daniel Hershcovich, Ehud Aharoni, and Noam Slonim. 2014. Context dependent claim detection. In *Proceedings of COLING 2014, the 25th International Conference on Computational Linguistics: Technical Papers*, pages 1489–1500. Dublin City University and Association for Computational Linguistics.

Christopher D. Manning, Prabhakar Raghavan, and Hinrich Schütze. 2008. *Introduction to Information Retrieval*. Cambridge University Press, New York, NY, USA.

Rada Mihalcea and Paul Tarau. 2004. Textrank: Bringing order into texts. In Dekang Lin and Dekai Wu, editors, *Proceedings of EMNLP 2004*, pages 404–411, Barcelona, Spain, July. Association for Computational Linguistics.

Niall Rooney, Hui Wang, and Fiona Browne. 2012. Applying kernel methods to argumentation mining. In G. Michael Youngblood and Philip M. McCarthy, editors, *Proceedings of the Twenty-Fifth International Florida Artificial Intelligence Research Society Conference, Marco Island, Florida. May 23-25, 2012.* AAAI Press.

Christian Stab and Iryna Gurevych. 2014. Annotating argument components and relations in persuasive essays. In Junichi Tsujii and Jan Hajic, editors, *Proceedings of the 25th International Conference on Computational Linguistics (COLING 2014)*, pages 1501–1510, Dublin, Ireland, August. Dublin City University and Association for Computational Linguistics.

Bianka Trevisan, Eva Dickmeis, Eva-Maria Jakobs, and Thomas Niehr. 2014. Indicators of argument-conclusion relationships. an approach for argumentation mining in german discourses. In *Proceedings of the First Workshop on Argumentation Mining*, pages 104–105, Baltimore, Maryland, June. Association for Computational Linguistics.

# Rhetorical structure and argumentation structure in monologue text


**Andreas Peldszus**
Applied Computational Linguistics
UFS Cognitive Science
University of Potsdam
`peldszus@uni-potsdam.de`

**Manfred Stede**
Applied Computational Linguistics
UFS Cognitive Science
University of Potsdam
`stede@uni-potsdam.de`



## Abstract

On the basis of a new corpus of short "microtexts" with parallel manual annotations, we study the mapping from discourse structure (in terms of Rhetorical Structure Theory, RST) to argumentation structure. We first perform a qualitative analysis and discuss our findings on correspondence patterns. Then we report on experiments with deriving argumentation structure from the (gold) RST trees, where we compare a tree transformation model, an aligner based on subgraph matching, and a more complex "evidence graph" model.


## 1 Introduction

Rhetorical Structure Theory (RST) (Mann and Thompson, 1988) was designed to represent the structure of a text in terms of coherence relations holding between adjacent text spans, where the same set of relations is being used to join the "elementary discourse units" (EDUs) and, recursively, the larger spans. The result is a tree structure that spans the text completely; there are no "gaps" in the analysis, and there are no crossing edges. The relations are being defined largely in terms of speaker intentions, so that the analysis is meant to capture the "plan" the author devised to influence his or her audience. The developers of RST had not explicitly targeted one particular text type or discourse mode (instructive, argumentative, descriptive, narrative, expository), but when we assume that the text is argumentative, the very nature of the RST approach suggests that it might in fact capture the underlying argumentation quite well.

Systems for automatic RST parsing have been built since the early 00s, with recent approaches including (Ji and Eisenstein, 2014) and (Joty et

al., 2015). Hence, a potentially useful architecture for argumentation mining could involve an RST parser as an early step that accomplishes a good share of the overall task. How feasible this is has so far not been determined, though.

On the theoretical side, different opinions have been voiced in the literature on the role of RST trees for argumentation analysis; we summarize the situation below in Section 2. All these opinions were based on the experiences that their authors had made with manually applying RST and with analyzing argumentation, but they were not based on systematic empirical evidence. In contrast, in this paper we use a new resource that we recently released (Stede et al., 2016), which offers annotations of both RST and argumentation structure analyses on a corpus of 112 short texts. Our previous paper presented a first rough analysis of the correlations between RST and argumentation. The present paper builds on those preliminary results and makes two contributions:

- We provide a qualitative analysis that examines the commonalities and differences between the two levels of representation in the corpus, and seeks explanations for them.

- We report on experiments in automatically mapping RST trees to argumentation structures, for now on the basis of the manually-annotated "gold" RST trees.

Following the discussion of related work in Section 2, Section 3 gives a brief introduction to the corpus and the annotation schemes that are used for argumentation and for RST. Then, Section 4 presents our qualitative (comparative) analysis, and Section 5 the results of our experiments on automatic analysis. Finally, Section 6 relates these two endeavours and draws conclusions.




*Proceedings of the 3rd Workshop on Argument Mining*, pages 103–112,
Berlin, Germany, August 7-12, 2016. ©2016 Association for Computational Linguistics

## 2   Related work

In this section, we summarize the positions that have so far been taken in the literature on the status of RST analyses for argumentation.

The view that performing an RST analysis essentially subsumes the task of determining argumentation structure was advanced by Azar (1999), who argued that RST's nucleus-satellite distinction is crucial for distinguishing the two roles in a dialectical argumentative relationship, and that, in particular, five RST relations should be regarded as providing argumentative support for different types of claims: Motivation for calls for action; Antithesis and Concession for increasing positive regard toward a stance; Evidence for forming a belief; Justify for readiness to accept a statement. Azar illustrated that idea with a few short sample texts that he analyzed in terms of RST trees using these relations. In one of these examples, however, Azar made the move of combining two non-adjacent text segments into a single node in the RST tree (representing the central claim), which is in conflict with a basic principle of RST. This indicates that Azar borrowed certain aspects from RST but ignored others. In our earlier work (Peldszus and Stede, 2013), we posited that the underlying phenomenon of non-adjacency creates a problem for RST-argumentation mapping in general, i.e., it is not limited to discontinuous claims: Both Support and Attack moves can be directed to material that occurs in non-adjacent segments.

A small portion of RST's ideas was incorporated into the annotation of argumentation performed by Kirschner et al. (2015) on student essays. The authors used standard argumentative Support and Attack relations, and to these added the coherence relations Sequence and Detail for capturing specific argumentative moves; the relation definitions are inspired by those used in RST.

Green (2010) proposed a "hybrid" tree representation called ArgRST, which combines RST's nuclearity principle and some of its relation definitions with additional annotations capturing aspects of argumentation: The analyst can add implicit statements to the tree (enthymemes in the argumentation), and in parallel to RST relations, the links between segments can also be labeled with relations from the scheme of Toulmin (1958) and with those proposed by Walton et al. (2008). Also, the representation allows for noncontiguous premises and conclusions. More recently, Green (2015) argued that the hybrid representation does not readily carry over to a different text genre (biomedical research articles), and she concluded that RST and argumentation structure operate on two levels that are subject to different motivations and constraints, and thus should be kept distinct.

We also subscribe to the view that (at least for many text genres) distinguishing rhetorical structure and argumentation structure is important for capturing the different aspects of a text's coherence on the one hand, and its pragmatic function on the other. Also, we wish to emphasize the conflict between segment *adjacency* (a central feature of RST's account of coherence) and *non-adjacency* (a pervasive phenomenon in argumentative function of portions of text). Still, it remains to be seen to what extent an RST analysis can in principle *support* an argumentation analysis, e.g. in a pipeline architecture; shedding light on this question is our goal for this paper.

## 3   The corpus

Below we provide a very brief description of the data and annotations that we provided in (Stede et al., 2016); for more details, see that paper. Notice that the layers of annotations had been produced independently by different people, thus inviting a posthoc comparison, which we will perform in the next sections. For reasons of space, we do not give further details on RST here; the interested reader should consult (Mann and Thompson, 1988) or (Taboada and Mann, 2006).

### 3.1   Data

The argumentative microtext corpus (Peldszus and Stede, 2016) is a freely available collection of 112 short texts that were collected from human subjects, originally in German. Subjects received a prompt on an issue of public debate, usually in the form of a yes/no question (e.g., Should shopping malls be open on Sundays?), and they were asked to provide their answer to the question along with arguments in support. They were encouraged to also mention potential objections. The target length suggested to the subjects was five sentences. After the texts were collected, they were professionally translated to English, so that the corpus is now available in two languages. An example of an English text is:

> Health insurance companies should naturally cover alternative medical treat-

ments. Not all practices and approaches that are lumped together under this term may have been proven in clinical trials, yet its precisely their positive effect when accompanying conventional western medical therapies thats been demonstrated as beneficial. Besides, many general practitioners offer such counselling and treatments in parallel anyway - and who would want to question their broad expertise?

In (Stede et al., 2016), two new annotation layers are introduced for the corpus: Discourse structure in terms of RST, and in terms of Segmented Discourse Representation Theory (Asher and Lascarides, 2003). Importantly, these two as well as the argumentation annotation use an identical segmentation into elementary discourse units (EDUs).

### 3.2 Argumentation structure representation

The annotation of argumentation structure follows the scheme outlined in (Peldszus and Stede, 2013), which in turn is based on the work of Freeman (1991). It posits that the argumentative text has a central claim (henceforth: CC), which the author can back up with statements that are in a Support relation to it; this is a transitive relation, leading to "serial support" in Freeman's terms. A statement can also have multiple Supports; these can be independent (each Support works on its own) or linked (only the combination of two statements provides the Support). Also, the scheme distinguishes between "standard" and "example" support, whose function originates from providing an illustration, or anecdotal evidence.

When the text mentions a potential objection, this segment is labeled as bearing the role of "opponent's voice"; this goes back to Freeman's insight that any argumentation, even if monological, is inherently dialectical. The segment will be in an Attack relation to another one (which represents the proponent's voice), and the scheme distinguishes between Rebut (denying the validity of a claim) and Undercut (denying the relevance of a premise for a claim). When the author proceeds to refute the attack, the attacking segment itself is subject to a Rebut or Undercut relation.

The building blocks of such an analysis are Argumentative Discourse Units, which often are larger than EDUs: Multiple discourse segments

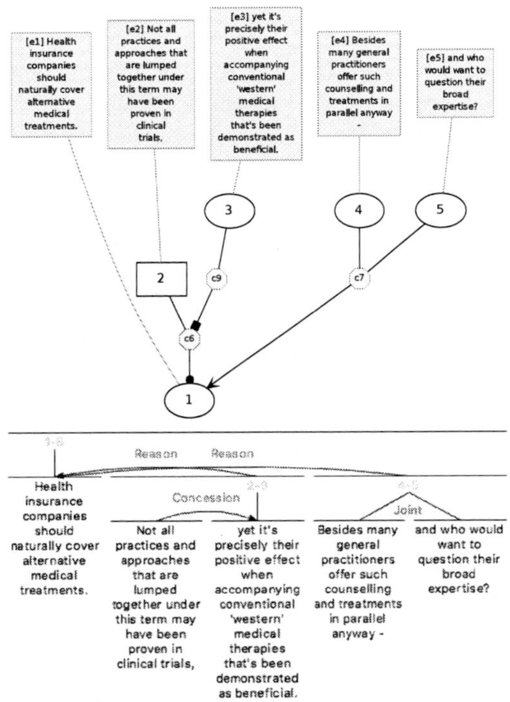


Figure 1: Example ARG and RST structure

play a common argumentative role. In such cases, the EDUs are linked together by a meta-relation called Join. The argumentation and RST analyses of the sample text are shown in Figure 1.

## 4 Matching RST and argumentation: Qualitative analysis

When introducing the corpus (Stede et al., 2016), we provided figures on how edges in the RST tree map to edges in the argumentation graph (which can be calculated straightforwardly, because both representations build on the same segmentation). We found that, ignoring the labels, 60% of the edges are common to both structures. As can be expected, argumentative Support mostly corresponds to Reason or Justification; however, 39% of the Supports do *not* have a corresponding RST edge. Furthermore, 72% of all Rebuts and 33% of Undercuts do not have a corresponding RST edge. Thus, the correspondences between the layers are certainly not trivial. In order to understand the mismatches, we undertook a qualitative analysis that focuses on the three central notions of the argumentation: the central claim and its mapping to RST nuclearity, the Support relations, and the configurations of Attack/Counterattack.

## 4.1 CC and Nuclearity

Recall that Azar (1999) already pointed out the importance of RST's notion of 'nucleus' for representing argumentation. To operationalize the analogy, it is important to make use of the "strong nuclearity principle" (Marcu, 2000), according to which the most important segment(s) of a text can be found by following the RST tree from its root down the nucleus links to the leaf nodes. If there are only mononuclear relations along the way, there is a single most important segment (henceforth: RSTnuc); otherwise, there are multiple ones. A natural first question therefore is whether the RSTnuc segment corresponds to the CC in argumentation. We found that for 95 texts, i.e., the vast majority of the 112 texts (85%), this is the case. Considering the goal of RST analysis, which is to capture the main intention of the writer, this is the expected default case.

But what happens in the 17 mismatches? In five cases, RSTnuc and ARGcc are indeed disjoint. Four of these are due to the thesis being stated early in the text and once again (as a paraphrase) later on. It is thus left to the annotator to decide which formulation s/he considers more apt to play the central role of the text – and these decisions happen to have lead to different results in the four texts. In the fifth, the thesis is not explicitly stated; here, too, there are two plausible options for choosing the most important segment of the text.

In 12 texts, RSTnuc and ARGcc overlap, which can be due to two reasons. (i) In five texts, ARGcc consists of two EDUs, with the RSTnuc being one of them. This is due to an RST relation that is not argumentatively relevant (mostly Condition). (ii) Seven texts show the reverse situation: A multinuclear RST relation induces >1 RSTnuc. In three of these cases, this seems due to an unclear text; the author's position remains somewhat ambiguous, and the RST annotator considered different statements as equally important. The ARG annotation, on the other hand, was committed to making a decision on the CC (as stated in the guidelines). In the remaining four cases, we find minor differences in interpretation, where the RST decision might well be influenced by surface features, in particular the presence of coordinating conjunctions, which suggest a parallel structure for a coherence-oriented analysis. ARG analysis, on the other hand, encourages the annotator to ab-

stract from linguistic realization and to consider the underlying pragmatic relationships.

## 4.2 Support

Of the 261[1] ARG-Supports, 132 have a corresponding edge in the associated RST tree, with a label that is clearly compatible with Support: Reason, Justify, Evidence, Motivation, or Cause. And of the 112 texts, 26 have only such canonical SUPPORTs (and three texts do not have Supports at all). Together these are 23% of the texts, so that 77% contain non-canonical Support. This calls for closer investigation, and we found two groups:

(i) 12 Support relations have a corresponding RST edge that is labeled with an "unexpected" relation: Elaboration, Background, Result, Interpretation, Antithesis, Concession, or a multinuclear relation. These are instances of the dichotomy between accounting for the local coherence versus the underlying argumentation; in fact, this corresponds to a discussion that originated shortly after the introduction of RST and pointed out the potential conflict between an "informational" versus an "intentional" analysis (Moore and Pollack, 1992).

(ii) 117 Support relations do not have a coresponding edge in the RST tree. The reasons can be subclassified as follows, with the observed frequency given in parentheses. (These attributes can combine, so the numbers add to more than 117.)

- The RST segment participates in a multinuclear relation (List, Conjunction, Joint), or in the pseudo-relation Same-Unit. Hence it can be reached directly by following the respective edges. (70)
- Relation disagreement: The RST annotator did not see a Support-like relation, but used something else (most often Background or Elaboration). (21)
- Transitivity mismatch: ARG and RST annotations do not agree on serial versus joint support, i.e., whether a segment supports a claim directly or only indirectly. (16)
- Grain size: In a segment, RST uses a non-argumentative relation such as Condition, so that the nuclearity assignment does not match that of the segmentation in the ARG-Join relation. (9)

---

[1]This number diverges by 25 from that given by Stede et al. (2016), because for technical reasons they excluded from their statistics 10 texts that have discontinuous segments.

- Consequence of the different nuclearity structures we mentioned in the previous subsection. (5)
- Different or same reason: RST and ARG annotators differed in whether two segments constitute the same Reason/Support, or separate ones. (4)

### 4.3 Attack

Finally, we study what RST constellations correspond to attack configurations in the ARG tree. For the time being, we do not distinguish Rebut from Undercut.[2] We discuss the cases in increasing order of complexity and give the number of texts where the instance occurs (which is almost identical to the number of instances).

1. Text does not have any attacks in ARG. (16)
2. A single attack node in ARG, or a joined pair; these are leaf nodes. This is the situation where an attack is not being countered – the author considers his other Supports to implicitly outweigh the attack. (24) – Variant: The attack is not a leaf but supported by another opponent-voice node. (7) – We treat these together, and of the 31, 24 have a "canonical" RST counterpart: The attacking segment is also a leaf node, and its is connected via one of the RST relations Antithesis, Contrast, Concession. The remaining 7 have a "non-canonical" RST counterpart: The opponent voice is not reflected in the RST tree, or a local attachment of an attacking subordinate segment leads to a non-canonical relation.
3. Similar to (2), but instead of one there are two separate attack nodes in ARG. In all of these cases, the RST tree combines the two attacks in a Conjunction relation. (7)
4. The attack is being countered: An opponent-voice-segment has both an outgoing and an incoming attack. For illustration, consider Figure 1 above (the "incoming" attack of node 2 there is an undercut). In general, there are three structural subclasses. (i): Both attack and counterattack are individual segments (36), as is the case in Fig. 1. The structures can be straightforwardly compared to their RST correspondents as follows:
   - Canonical-a: The counterattack corresponds to a backward Conces-

sion/Antithesis, and the whole is the satellite of a canonical support relation (Reason, Justify, ...). (22) This is shown in Fig. 1.
   - Canonical-b: Likewise, but the whole participates first in some multinuclear relation (List, Joint), which in turn is the satellite of a canonical support. (6)
   - Non-canonical: RST annotator did not see argumentative function as most important for capturing local coherence. (8)

(ii) Slightly more complex: The counterattack has $>1$ segment. (16)
   - Canonical: The counterattack subtree gets some RST analysis, and the overall construction is as described in the previous category. (13)
   - Noncanonical: reason as in (i). (3)

(iii) More complex: The attack has $>1$ segment. (8)
   - Canonical: overall construction is as described above. (6)
   - Noncanonical: Support corresponds to Interpretation/Elaboration. (2)

### 4.4 Summary

We found a large proportion of CC, Support and Attack confgurations to correspond to "canonical" configurations in RST trees – i..e, subtrees that intuitively reflect the argumentative functions (under the definitions of the RST relations). While so far we looked at the correspondence only in the direction ARG→RST, this result still suggests that an automatic mapping from RST to ARG tree can be feasible; this will be the topic of the next section. Furthermore, a central purpose of the manual analysis was to determine the reasons for mismatches, which can inform theoretical considerations on the relationship between RST and argumentation. For reasons of space, we cannot go into detail, but our central observation is that RST analysis is subject to a tension between accounting for the *local* coherence or for the *global* one using underlying intentions, i.e., the argumentation. As we noted earlier, this has been discussed in the RST community early on — but it has never been resolved. The issue is likely to be much more pronounced in longer texts than in the microtexts we are studying here. In principle, the specific RST annotation guidelines could ask annotators to clearly prefer

---

[2]Intuitively, we see no evidence that this distinction is reflected in RST, but it needs to be determined quantitatively.

one or the other perspective; this would shift the original goal of the theory, but probably would do better justice to the data.

Considering the option of annotating an "argumentation-oriented" RST tree, the question arises to what extent it can be theoretically adequate. Of central importance is the correspondence between RSTnuc and ARGcc; we found that for all the mismatches in the corpus, it is possble to construct a plausible alternative RST tree such that the two are identical or at least overlapping (when the granularities of the analyses don't match exactly). Another issue is the presence of crossing edges, which occur in seven ARG graphs in the corpus. Since this is likely to occur more often in longer texts, it remains a fundamental issue; we will return to it at the end.

## 5 Deriving argumentation structure from rhetorical structure automatically

In order to automatically map between RST and argumentation, it is very helpful to have both layers in the same technical format. To that end, our joint work with colleagues in Toulouse supplied a common dependency structure representation (Stede et al., 2016). In the following, we use that version of the corpus. For illustration, see Figure 2 for the dependency conversion of the example text.

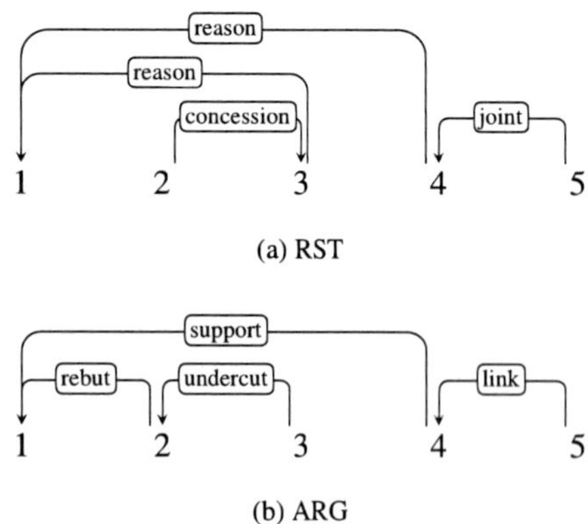



Figure 2: Dependency conversion example

### 5.1 Models

We have implemented three different models: A simple heuristic tree-transformation serves as a baseline, against which we compare two data-driven models. All models and their parameters are described in the following subsections.

In our study, we follow the experimental setup of (Peldszus and Stede, 2015). We use the same train-test splits, resulting from 10 iterations of 5-fold cross validation, and adopt their evaluation procedure, where the correctness of predicted structures is assessed in four subtasks:

- **attachment (at)**: Given a pair of EDUs, are they connected? [yes, no]
- **central claim (cc)**: Given an EDU, is it the central claim of the text? [yes, no]
- **role (ro)**: Given an EDU, is it in the [proponent]'s or the [opponent]'s voice?
- **function (ro)**: Given an EDU, what is its argumentative function? Here, we use the fine-grained relation set available in the data. [support, example, rebut, undercut, link, join]

Note that the argumentative role of each segment is not explicitly coded in the structures we predict below, but is inferred from the chain of supporting (role preserving) and attacking (role switching) relations from the central claim (by definition in proponent's voice) to the segment of interest.

#### 5.1.1 Heuristic baseline

The baseline model (**BL**) produces an argumentation structure that is isomorphic to the RST tree. RST relations are mapped to argumentative functions, based on the most frequently aligning class as reported in (Stede et al., 2016) – see Figure 3. For the two relations marked with an asterisk, no direct edge alignments could be found, and thus we assigned them to the class of the non-argumentative *join*-relation. The argumentative *example* and *link*-relations were not frequent enough to be captured in this mapping.

We expect this baseline to be not an easy one to beat. It will predict the central claim correctly already for 85% of the texts, due to the correspondence described in Section 4.1. Also, as we saw above, 60% of the unlabelled edges should be mappable. Finally, the argumentative role is covered quite well, too: The chain of supporting and attacking relations determining the role is likely to be correct on an EDU basis, if the relation mapping is correct, and even if attachment is wrongly predicted.

#### 5.1.2 Naive aligner

Our naive aligner model (**A**) learns the probability of subgraphs in the RST structure mapping to

| |
|---|
| **support**: background, cause, evidence, justify, list, motivation, reason, restatement, result<br>**rebut**: antithesis, contrast, unless<br>**undercut**: concession<br>**join**: circumstance, condition, conjunction, disjunction, e-elaboration, elaboration, evaluation-s, evaluation-n, interpretation*, joint, means, preparation, purpose, sameunit, solutionhood* |

Figure 3: Mapping of RST relations to ARG relations, used in the heuristic baseline.

| |
|---|
| **base features incl. 2-node subgraph features:**<br>- absolute and relative position of the segment in the text<br>- binary feature whether it is the first or the last segment<br>- binary feature whether it has incoming/outgoing edges<br>- number of incoming/outgoing edges<br>- binary feature for each type of incoming/outgoing edge<br>**3-node subgraph features:**<br>- all relation chains of length 2 involving this segment<br>**4-node subgraph features:**<br>- all relation chains of length 3 involving this segment |

Figure 4: Segment feature sets

| |
|---|
| - direction of the potential link (forward or backward)<br>- distance between the segments<br>- whether there is a RST relation between the segments<br>- type of the RST relation between the segments or None |

Figure 5: Segment-pair features

subgraphs of the argumentative structure.

For training, this model applies a subgraph alignment algorithm yielding connected components with $n$ nodes occurring in the undirected, unlabelled version of both the RST and the argumentative structures. It extracts the directed, labelled subgraphs for these common components for both structures and learns the probability of mapping one to the other over the whole training corpus.

For prediction, all possible subgraphs of size $n$ in the input RST tree are extracted. If one maps to an argumentation subgraph according to the mapping learned on the training corpus, the corresponding argumentation subgraph is added to an intermediary multi-graph. After all candidate subgraphs have been collected, all equal edges are combined and their individual probabilities accumulated. Finally, a tree structure is decoded from the intermediary graph using the minimum spanning tree (MST) algorithm (Chu and Liu, 1965; Edmonds, 1967).

The model can be instantiated with different subgraph sizes $n$. Choosing $n = 2$ only learns a direct mapping between RST and ARG edges. Choosing larger $n$ can reveal larger structural patterns, including edges that cannot be directly aligned. Most importantly, the model can be trained with more than one subgraph size $n$: for example, model **A-234** simultaniously extracts subgraphs of the size $n = [2, 3, 4]$, so that the edge probabilities of differently large subgraphs add up.

The collected edges of all candidate subgraphs do not necessarily connect all possible nodes. In this case, no spanning tree can be derived. We thus initialize the intermediary multi-graph as a total graph with low-scored default edges of the type *unknown*. These should only be selected by the MST algorithm when there is no other evidence for connecting to unconnected subgraphs. The number of predicted unknown edges thus serves as an indicator of the coverage of the learnt model. In

evaluation, unknown edges are interpreted as the majority relation type, i.e. as support.

Finally, we added an optional root-constraint (**+r**) to the model: It forbids outgoing edges from the node corresponding to the RST central nucleus, and therefore effectively enforces the ARG structure to have the same root as the RST tree.

### 5.1.3 Evidence graph model

We implemented a variant of the evidence graph model (**EG**) of (Peldszus and Stede, 2015). In this model, four base classifiers are trained for the four levels of the task (cc, ro, fu and at). For each possible edge, the predictions of these base classifiers are combined into one single edge score. Again, MST decoding is used to select the globally optimal tree structure.

The combined edge score reflects the probability of attachment, the probability of not being the central claim (similar to the root constraint in the alignment model), the probability of a role switch between the connected nodes and the probability of the corresponding edge type. Jointly predicting these different levels has been shown to be superior over the single prediction of the base classifiers.

Our model differs from the original one in two respects: First, our model is trained on the new version of the corpus, featuring a finer segmentation into EDUs, and it considers the full relation set (in contrast to the reduced relation set of just Support and Attack). Second and more importantly, our base classifiers are trained exclusively on a new feature set reflecting aspects of the input RST tree, and do not use any linguistic features.

The segment features are shown in Figure 4. We distinguish three feature groups: base features including edges (EG-2), base features plus 3-node subgraph features (EG-23), and the latter plus 4-node subgraph-features (EG-234). Base classifiers for the cc, ro, and fu-level are trained on segment features. The at-level base classifier is trained on segment features for the source and the target node, as well as on relational features, shown in Figure 5.

As in the original model, the base classifiers perform an inner cross-validation on the training data to optimize the hyperparameters of the log-linear SGD classifier (Pedregosa et al., 2011). We do not optimize the weighting of the base classifiers for score combination here, because we had shown in the original experiments that an equal weighting yields competitive results (Peldszus and Stede, 2015).

## 5.2 Results on gold RST trees

Scores are reported as averages over the 50 train-test-splits, with macro-averaged F1 as the metric. For significance testing, we apply the Wilcoxon signed-rank test on the macro-averaged F1 scores and assume a significance level of $\alpha = 0.01$. The evaluation results are shown in Table 1.

All alignment models including at least subgraphs of size n=3 (A-23*) improve over the baseline (BL) in predicting the relation type (fu) and the attachment (at). Considering larger subgraphs helps even more, and it decreases the rate of unknown edges.[3] On the role level, the baseline is unbeaten. For central claim identification, the alignment model performs poorly. Adding the root constraint yields exactly the baseline prediction for the central claim, but also improves the results on all other levels, with the cost of an increased rate of unknown edges. The clear improvement over the baseline for the relation type (fu) indicates that the probability estimates of the alignment models capture the relations better than the heuristic mapping to the most frequently aligning class in the baseline. Furthermore, extraction of larger subgraphs gradually increases the result on both the fu and the at level, showing us that there are subgraph regularities to be learnt which are not captured when assuming isomorphic trees.

---

[3] Note that when testing the A-234 model on training data, only very few unknown edges are predicted (less than 1%), which indicates that more data might help to fully cover all of them.

| model | cc | ro | fu | at | unknown |
|---|---|---|---|---|---|
| BL | .861 | **.896** | .338 | .649 | |
| A-2 | .578 | .599 | .314 | .650 | 10.6% |
| A-23 | .787 | .744 | .398 | .707 | 7.5% |
| A-234 | .797 | .755 | .416 | .719 | 7.0% |
| A-2345 | .794 | .762 | .424 | .721 | 6.8% |
| A-2+r | .861 | .681 | .385 | .682 | 13.9% |
| A-23+r | .861 | .783 | .420 | .716 | 11.3% |
| A-234+r | .861 | .794 | .434 | .723 | 10.8% |
| A-2345+r | .861 | .800 | .443 | .725 | 10.7% |
| EG-bc-2 | .899 | .768 | .526 | .747 | |
| EG-bc-23 | .907 | .845 | .525 | .749 | |
| EG-bc-234 | .906 | .847 | .526 | .750 | |
| EG-2 | .918 | .843 | .522 | .744 | |
| EG-23 | **.919** | .869 | .526 | **.755** | |
| EG-234 | .918 | .868 | **.530** | .754 | |

Table 1: Evaluation scores of all models on the gold RST input trees reported as macro-avg. F1

For the evidence graph model, we will first investigate the performance of the base classifiers (EG-bc-*), before we discuss the results of the decoder. The difference between the three feature sets is most important here. Comparing the classifier that only uses the basic feature set (EG-bc-2) against the one with extra features for 3-node subgraphs (EG-bc-23), we find the greatest improvement on the argumentative role level with an extra +7.7 points macro F1 score. Central claim identification also profits with a minor gain of +0.8 points. Interestingly, the local models for function and attachment are not effected by the richer feature sets. Extending the features even to 4-node subgraphs (EG-bc-234), does not further improve the results on any level.

The evidence graph decoding models (EG-*) combine the predictions of the base classifiers to a global optimal structure. The model using the base classifiers with the smallest feature set (EG-2) already outperforms the best alignment model on all levels significantly and beats the baseline on all levels but argumentative role. We attribute this improvement to three aspects of the model: First, the learning procedure of the base classifiers is superior to that of the alignment model. Second, the base classifiers not only learn regularities between RST and ARG but also positional properties of the target structures. Finally, the joint prediction of the different levels in the evidence graph model helps to compensate weaknesses of the local models by enforcing constraints in the combination of the individual predictions: Comparing the base classifier's predictions (EG-bc-2) with the decoded predictions (EG-2), we observe a boost of +7.5 points macro F1 on the role level and a small boost of +1.9 points for central claim through joint prediction.

Adding features for larger subgraphs further improves the results: EG-23 beats EG-2 on all levels, but the improvement is significant only for role and attachment. EG-234, though, differs from EG-23 only marginally and on no level significantly. Note, that the gain from joint prediction is less strong with better base classifiers, but still valuable with +2.4 points on the role level and +1.2 points for central claim.

In conclusion, the baseline model remained unbeaten on the level of argumentative role. This was already expected, as the sequence of contrastive relations in the RST tree is very likely to map to a correct sequence of proponent and opponent role assignments. On all other levels, the best results for mapping gold RST trees to fine-grained argumentation structures are achieved by the EG-23(4) model.

## 6   Summary and Outlook

We presented the first empirical study on the relationship between discourse structure (here in terms of Rhetorical Structure Theory) and argumentation structure. In the qualitative analysis, we found a large proportion of "canonical" correspondences between RST subtrees and the central notions of argumentation, with the remaining mismatches being due to an inherent ambiguity of RST analysis (informational versus intentional) and to more technical aspects of granularity (multinuclear relations). By using annotation guidelines that "drive" the annotator toward capturing underlying argumentation, the correspondence could be considerably higher. There remain problems with non-adjacency in the ARG structure, however. These are likely to increase when texts are larger than our microtexts.

For mapping the gold RST trees to ARG structure, we compared three mapping mechanisms: A heuristic baseline, transforming RST trees to isomorphic trees with corresponding argumentative relations; a simple aligner, extracting matching subgraph pairs from the corpus and applying them to unseen structures; and one fairly elaborate evidence graph model, which trains four classifiers and combines their predictions for decoding globally optimal structures. The latter achieved promising results (with the exception of *prima facie* low numbers for argumenative function, but recall we are using a much larger tag set than all the related work). This confirms the conclusion from the qualitative study, and it invites the next step, which is to use our mapping procedure on the predictions of state-of-the-art RST parsers.


## References

Nicholas Asher and Alex Lascarides. 2003. *Logics of Conversation*. Cambridge University Press.

M. Azar. 1999. Argumentative text as rhetorical structure: An application of Rhetorical Structure Theory. *Argumentation*, 13:97–114.

Y. J. Chu and T. H. Liu. 1965. On the shortest arborescence of a directed graph. *Science Sinica*, 14:1396–1400.

Jack Edmonds. 1967. Optimum Branchings. *Journal of Research of the National Bureau of Standards*, 71B:233–240.

James B. Freeman. 1991. *Dialectics and the Macrostructure of Argument*. Foris, Berlin.

Nancy Green. 2010. Representation of argumentation in text with Rhetorical Structure Theory. *Argumentation*, 24:181–196.

Nancy Green. 2015. Annotating evidence-based argumentation in biomedical text. In *Proceedings of the IEEE Workshop on Biomedical and Health Informatics*.

Yangfeng Ji and Jacob Eisenstein. 2014. Representation learning for text-level discourse parsing. In *Proceedings of the 52nd Annual Meeting of the Association for Computational Linguistics*, Baltimore, Maryland, June. Association for Computational Linguistics.

Shafiq Joty, Giuseppe Carenini, and Raymond Ng. 2015. Codra: A novel discriminative framework for rhetorical analysis. *Computational Linguistics*, 41(3):385–435.

Christian Kirschner, Judith Eckle-Kohler, and Iryna Gurevych. 2015. Linking the thoughts: Analysis of argumentation structures in scientific publications. In *Proceedings of the 2015 NAACL-HLT Conference*. Association for Computational Linguistics, June.

William Mann and Sandra Thompson. 1988. Rhetorical structure theory: Towards a functional theory of text organization. *TEXT*, 8:243–281.

Daniel Marcu. 2000. *The theory and practice of discourse parsing and summarization*. MIT Press, Cambridge/MA.

Johanna Moore and Martha Pollack. 1992. A problem for RST: The need for multi-level discourse analysis. *Computational Linguistics*, 18(4):537–544.

F. Pedregosa, G. Varoquaux, A. Gramfort, V. Michel, B. Thirion, O. Grisel, M. Blondel, P. Prettenhofer, R. Weiss, V. Dubourg, J. Vanderplas, A. Passos, D. Cournapeau, M. Brucher, M. Perrot, and E. Duchesnay. 2011. Scikit-learn: Machine learning in Python. *Journal of Machine Learning Research*, 12:2825–2830.

Andreas Peldszus and Manfred Stede. 2013. From argument diagrams to automatic argument mining: A survey. *International Journal of Cognitive Informatics and Natural Intelligence (IJCINI)*, 7(1):1–31.

Andreas Peldszus and Manfred Stede. 2015. Joint prediction in mst-style discourse parsing for argumentation mining. In *Proceedings of the 2015 Conference on Empirical Methods in Natural Language Processing*, pages 938–948, Lisbon, Portugal, September. Association for Computational Linguistics.

Andreas Peldszus and Manfred Stede. 2016. An annotated corpus of argumentative microtexts. In *Argumentation and Reasoned Action: Proceedings of the 1st European Conference on Argumentation, Lisbon 2015 / Vol. 2*, pages 801–816, London. College Publications.

Manfred Stede, Stergos Afantenos, Andreas Peldszus, Nicholas Asher, and Jérémy Perret. 2016. Parallel discourse annotations on a corpus of short texts. In *Proceedings of the International Conference on Language Resources and Evaluation (LREC)*, Portoroz.

Maite Taboada and William Mann. 2006. Rhetorical Structure Theory: Looking back and moving ahead. *Discourse Studies*, 8(4):423–459.

Stephen Toulmin. 1958. *The Uses of Argument*. Cambridge University Press, Cambridge.

D. Walton, C. Reed, and F. Macagno. 2008. *Argumentation schemes*. Cambridge University Press, Cambridge.

# Recognizing the Absence of Opposing Arguments in Persuasive Essays

**Christian Stab**[†] and **Iryna Gurevych**[†‡]
[†]Ubiquitous Knowledge Processing Lab (UKP-TUDA)
Department of Computer Science, Technische Universität Darmstadt
[‡]Ubiquitous Knowledge Processing Lab (UKP-DIPF)
German Institute for Educational Research
www.ukp.tu-darmstadt.de

## Abstract

In this paper, we introduce an approach for recognizing the absence of opposing arguments in persuasive essays. We model this task as a binary document classification and show that adversative transitions in combination with unigrams and syntactic production rules significantly outperform a challenging heuristic baseline. Our approach yields an accuracy of 75.6% and 84% of human performance in a persuasive essay corpus with various topics.

## 1 Introduction

Developing well-reasoned arguments is an important ability and constitutes an important part of education programs (Davies, 2009). A frequent mistake when writing argumentative texts is to consider only arguments supporting the own standpoint and to ignore opposing arguments (Wolfe and Britt, 2009). This tendency to ignore opposing arguments is known as *myside bias* or *confirmation bias* (Stanovich et al., 2013). It has been shown that guiding students to include opposing arguments in their writings significantly improves the argumentation quality, the precision of claims and the elaboration of reasons (Wolfe and Britt, 2009). Therefore, it is likely that a system which automatically recognizes the absence of opposing arguments effectively guides students to improve their argumentation. For the same reason, the writing standards of the *common core standard*[1] require that students are able to clarify the relation between their own standpoint and opposing arguments on a controversial topic.

Existing *structural approaches* on argument analysis like the argumentation structure parser

presented by Stab and Gurevych (2016) or the approach introduced by Peldszus and Stede (2015a) recognize the internal microstructure of arguments. Although these approaches can be exploited for identifying opposing arguments, they require several consecutive analysis steps like separating argumentative from non-argumentative text units (Moens et al., 2007), recognizing the boundaries of argument components (Goudas et al., 2014) and classifying individual arguments as support or oppose (Somasundaran and Wiebe, 2009). Certainly, an advantage of structural approaches is that they recognize the position of opposing arguments in text. However, knowing the position of opposing arguments is only relevant for positive feedback to the author and irrelevant for negative feedback, i.e. pointing out that opposing arguments are missing. Therefore, it is reasonable to model the recognition of missing opposing arguments as a document classification task.

The contributions of this paper are the following: first, we introduce a corpus for detecting the absence of opposing arguments that we derive from argument structure annotated essays. Second, we propose a novel model and a new feature set for detecting the absence of opposing arguments in persuasive essays. We show that our model significantly outperforms a strong heuristic baseline and an existing structural approach. Third, we show that our model achieves 84% of human performance.

## 2 Related Work

Existing approaches in computational argumentation focus primarily on the identification of arguments, their components (e.g. claims and premises) (Rinott et al., 2015; Levy et al., 2014) and structures (Mochales-Palau and Moens, 2011; Stab and Gurevych, 2014b). Among these, there

---

[1]www.corestandards.org



*Proceedings of the 3rd Workshop on Argument Mining*, pages 113–118,
Berlin, Germany, August 7-12, 2016. ©2016 Association for Computational Linguistics

are few approaches which distinguish between supporting and opposing arguments.

Peldszus and Stede (2015b) use lexical, contextual and syntactic features to classify argument components as support or oppose. They experiment with pro/contra columns of a German newspaper and German microtexts. Similarly, their minimum spanning tree (MST) approach identifies the structure of arguments and recognizes if an argument component belongs to the proponent or opponent (Peldszus and Stede, 2015a). However, both approaches presuppose that the components of an argument are already known. Thus, they omit important analysis steps and cannot be applied directly for recognizing the absence of opposing arguments. Stab and Gurevych (2016) present an argumentation structure parser that includes all required steps for identifying argument structures and supporting and opposing arguments. First, they separate argumentative from non-argumentative text units using conditional random fields (CRF). Second, they jointly model the argument component types and argumentative relations using integer linear programming (ILP) and finally they distinguish between supporting and opposing arguments. We employ this parser as a structural approach and compare it to our document classification approach for recognizing the absence of opposing arguments in persuasive essays.

Another related area is *stance recognition* that aims at identifying the author's stance on a controversy by labeling a document as either "for" or "against" (Somasundaran and Wiebe, 2009; Hasan and Ng, 2014). Consequently, stance recognition systems are designed to identify the predominant stance of a text instead of recognizing the presence of less conspicuous opposing arguments.

Other approaches on argumentation in essays focus on thesis clarity (Persing and Ng, 2013), argumentation schemes (Song et al., 2014) or argumentation strength (Persing and Ng, 2015). We are not aware of any approach that focuses on recognizing the absence of opposing arguments.

## 3 Data

For our experiments, we employ an argument structure annotated essay corpus (Stab and Gurevych, 2014a; Stab and Gurevych, 2016). To the best of our knowledge, this corpus is the only available resource that exhibits an appropriate size and class distribution for detecting the absence of opposing arguments at the document-level. Each essay in this corpus is annotated with argumentation structures that allow to derive document-level annotations. The argumentation structures include arguments supporting or opposing the author's stance. Accordingly, we consider an essay as *negative* if it solely includes supporting arguments and as *positive* if it includes at least one opposing argument. Note that the manual identification of opposing arguments is a subtask of the argumentation structure identification. Both require that the annotators identify the author's stance, the individual arguments and if an argument supports or opposes the author's stance. Thus, deriving document-level annotations from argumentation structures is a valid approach since the decisions of the annotators in both tasks are equivalent.

### 3.1 Inter-Annotator Agreement

To verify that the derived document-level annotations are reliable, we compare the annotations derived from the argumentation structure annotations of three independent annotators. In particular, we determine the inter-annotator agreement on a subset of 80 essays. The comparison shows an observed agreement of 90%. We obtain substantial chance-corrected agreement scores of Fleiss' $\kappa = .786$ (Fleiss, 1971) and Krippendorff's $\alpha = .787$ (Krippendorff, 2004). Thus, we conclude that the derived annotations are reliable since they are only slightly below the "*good reliability threshold*" proposed by Krippendorff (2004).

### 3.2 Statistics

Table 1 shows an overview of the corpus. It includes 402 essays. On average each essay includes 18 sentences and 366 tokens.

| | |
|---|---|
| Tokens | 147,271 |
| Sentences | 7,116 |
| Documents | 402 |
| Negative | 251 (62.4%) |
| Positive | 151 (37.6%) |

Table 1: Size and class distribution of the corpus.

The class distribution is skewed towards negative essays. The corpus includes 251 (62.4%) essays that do not include opposing arguments and 151 (37.6%) positive essays. For encouraging future research, the corpus is freely available.[2]

---

[2]https://www.ukp.tu-darmstadt.de/data

## 4 Approach

We consider the recognition of opposing arguments as a binary document classification. Due to the size of the corpus and to prevent errors in model assessment stemming from a particular data splitting (Krstajic et al., 2014), we employ a stratified and repeated 5-fold cross-validation setup. We report the average evaluation scores and the standard deviation over 100 folds resulting from 20 iterations. For model selection, we randomly sampled 10% of the training set of each run as a development set. We report accuracy, macro precision, macro recall and macro F1 scores as described by Sokolova and Lapalme (2009, p. 430).[3] We employ Wilcoxon signed-rank test on macro F1 scores for significance testing (significance level = .005).

We preprocess the essays using several models from the DKPro framework (Eckart de Castilho and Gurevych, 2014). For tokenization, sentence and paragraph splitting, we employ the language tool segmenter[4] and check for line breaks. We lemmatize each token using the mate tools lemmatizer (Bohnet et al., 2013) and apply the Stanford parser (Klein and Manning, 2003) for constituency and dependency parsing. Finally, we use a PDTB parser (Lin et al., 2014) and sentiment analyzer (Socher et al., 2013) for identifying discourse relations and sentence-level sentiment scores. As a learner, we choose a support vector machine (SVM) (Cortes and Vapnik, 1995) with polynomial kernel implemented in Weka (Hall et al., 2009). For extracting features, we use the DKPro TC framework (Daxenberger et al., 2014).

### 4.1 Features

We experiment with the following features:

**Unigrams (uni):** In order to capture the lexical characteristics of an essay, we extract binary and case sensitive unigrams.

**Dependency triples (dep):** The binary dependency features include triples consisting of the lemmatized governor, the lemmatized dependent and the dependency type.

**Production rules (pr):** We employ binary production rules extracted from the constituent parse trees (Lin et al., 2009) that occur at least five times.

**Adversarial transitions (adv):** We assume that opposing arguments are frequently signaled by lexical indicators. We use 47 adversative transitional phrases that are compiled as a learning resource[5] and grouped in the following categories: concession (18), conflict (12), dismissal (9), emphasis (5) and replacement (3). For each of the five categories, we add two binary features set to true if a phrase of the category is present in the surrounding paragraphs (introduction or conclusion) or in a body paragraph.[6] Note that we consider lowercase and uppercase versions of these features which results in a total of 20 binary features.

**Sentiment Features (sent):** We average the five sentiment scores of all essay sentences for determining the global sentiment of an essay. In addition, we count the number of negative sentences and define a binary feature indicating the presence of a negative sentence.

**Discourse relations (dis):** The binary discourse features include the type of the discourse relation and indicate if the relation is implicit or explicit. For instance, "*Contrast_imp*" indicates an implicit contrast relation. Note that we only consider the discourse relations of body paragraphs since the introduction frequently includes a description of the controversy which is not relevant to the author's argumentation and whose discourse relations could be misleading for the learner.

### 4.2 Baselines

For model assessment, we use the following two baselines: First, we employ a *majority baseline* that classifies each essay as negative (not including opposing arguments). Second, we employ a rule-based *heuristic baseline* that classifies an essay as positive if it includes the case-sensitive term "*Admittedly*" or the phrase "*argue that*" which often indicate the presence of opposing arguments.[7]

### 4.3 Results

In order to select a model and to analyze our features, we conduct feature ablation tests (lower part of Table 2) and evaluate our system with individual features. The adversative transitions and unigrams are the most informative features. Both show the best individual performance and a sig-

---

[3] Since the macro F1 score assigns equal weight to classes, it is well-suited for evaluating experiments with skewed data.

[4] www.languagetool.org

[5] www.msu.edu/~jdowell/135/transw.html

[6] We identify paragraphs by checking for line breaks and consider the first paragraph as introduction, the last as conclusion and all remaining ones as body paragraphs.

[7] We recognized these indicators by ranking n-grams using information gain.

| | Accuracy | Macro F1 | Precision | Recall | F1 Negative | F1 Positive |
|---|---|---|---|---|---|---|
| *Model assessment on test data* | | | | | | |
| Human Upper Bound* | .900±.010 | .894±.011 | .895±.011 | .014±.892 | .865±.016 | .921±.008 |
| Baseline Majority | .624±.001 | .384±.000 | .312±.001 | .500±.000 | .769±.001 | 0 |
| Baseline Heuristic | .711±.039 | .679±.050 | .715±.059 | .646±.045 | .797±.027 | .497±.083 |
| SVM uni+pr+adv † | **.756**±.044 | **.734**±.048 | **.747**±.049 | **.721**±.050 | **.814**±.034 | **.639**±.075 |
| *Model selection and feature ablation on development data* | | | | | | |
| SVM all w/o uni ‡ | .733±.060 | .708±.087 | .768±.110 | .660±.073 | .817±.038 | .496±.151 |
| SVM all w/o dep | .765±.077 | .745±.087 | .762±.092 | .731±.086 | .822±.059 | .649±.125 |
| SVM all w/o pr | .760±.062 | .738±.082 | **.781**±.097 | .701±.074 | **.830**±.042 | .583±.138 |
| SVM all w/o adv ‡ | .736±.066 | .709±.090 | .756±.108 | .670±.079 | .816±.044 | .524±.151 |
| SVM all w/o sent | .756±.064 | .733±.085 | .778±.100 | .696±.076 | .828±.043 | .572±.146 |
| SVM all w/o dis | .757±.061 | .734±.082 | .780±.097 | .696±.075 | .829±.041 | .571±.143 |
| SVM uni+pr+adv | **.770**±.071 | **.750**±.081 | .767±.086 | **.735**±.080 | .825±.055 | **.656**±.118 |
| SVM all features | .755±.064 | .732±.086 | .776±.102 | .695±.077 | .827±.044 | .569±.149 |

Table 2: Results of the best performing model on the test data and selected results of the model selection experiments on the development data († significant improvement over *Baseline Heuristic*; ‡ significant difference compared to *SVM all features*; *determined on a subset of 80 essays).

nificant decrease if removed from the entire feature set. Thus, we conclude that lexical indicators are the most predictive features in our feature set. The sentiment and discourse features do not perform well. Individually they do not achieve better results than the majority baseline and the accuracy increases slightly when removing them from the entire feature set. By experimenting with various feature combinations, we found that combining unigrams, production rules and adversative transitions yields the best results (*SVM uni+pr+adv*).

For model assessment, we evaluate the best performing model on our test data and compare it to the baselines (upper part of Table 2). The heuristic baseline considerably outperforms the majority baseline and achieves an accuracy of 71.1%. Our best system significantly outperforms this challenging baseline with respect to all evaluation measures. It achieves an accuracy of 75.6% and a macro F1 score of .734. We determine the human upper bound by comparing pairs of annotators and averaging the results of the 80 independently annotated essays (cf. Section 3). Compared to the upper bound, our system achieves 14.4% less accuracy and 84% of human performance.

We compare our system to an argumentation structure parser that recognizes opposing components on a designated 80:20 train-test-split (Stab and Gurevych, 2016). We consider essays with predicted opposing arguments as positive, and negative if the parser does not recognize an opposing argument. This yields a macro F1 score of .648. Our document-level approach considerably outperforms the component-based approach with a macro F1 score of .710. Thus, we can confirm our assumption that modeling the task as document classification outperforms structural approaches.

## 4.4 Error Analysis

To analyze frequent errors of our system, we manually investigate essays that are misclassified in all 100 runs of the repeated cross-validation experiment on the development set. In total, 29 positive essays are consistently misclassified as negative. As reason for these errors, we found that the opposing arguments in these essays lack lexical indicators. In addition, we found 14 negative essays which are always misclassified as positive. Among these essays, we observe that the majority includes opposition indicators (e.g. *"but"*) which are used in another sense (e.g. expansion). Therefore, the investigation of both false negatives and false positives shows that most errors are due to misleading lexical signals. Consequently, word-sense disambiguation for identifying senses or the integration of domain and world knowledge in the absence of lexical signals could further improve the results.

## 5 Conclusion

We introduced the novel task of recognizing the absence of opposing arguments in persuasive essays. In contrast to existing structural approaches, we model this task as a document classification which does not presuppose several complex analysis steps. The analysis of several features showed that adversative transitions and unigrams are most indicative for this task. We showed that our best model significantly outperforms a strong heuristic baseline, yields a promising accuracy of 75.6%, outperforms a structural approach and achieves 84% of human performance. For future work, we plan to integrate the system in writing environments and to investigate its effectiveness for fostering argumentation skills.

## Acknowledgments

This work has been supported by the Volkswagen Foundation as part of the Lichtenberg-Professorship Program under grant No. I/82806 and by the German Federal Ministry of Education and Research (BMBF) as a part of the Software Campus project AWS under grant No. 01|S12054. We thank Anshul Tak for his valuable contributions.

## References

Bernd Bohnet, Joakim Nivre, Igor Boguslavsky, Richárd Farkas, Filip Ginter, and Jan Hajič. 2013. Joint morphological and syntactic analysis for richly inflected languages. *Transactions of the Association for Computational Linguistics*, 1:415–428.

Corinna Cortes and Vladimir Vapnik. 1995. Support-vector networks. *Machine Learning*, 20(3):273–297.

Peter Davies. 2009. Improving the quality of students' arguments through 'assessment for learning'. *Journal of Social Science Education (JSSE)*, 8(2):94–104.

Johannes Daxenberger, Oliver Ferschke, Iryna Gurevych, and Torsten Zesch. 2014. DKPro TC: A Java-based framework for supervised learning experiments on textual data. In *Proceedings of the 52nd Annual Meeting of the Association for Computational Linguistics. System Demonstrations*, ACL '14, pages 61–66, Baltimore, MD, USA.

Richard Eckart de Castilho and Iryna Gurevych. 2014. A broad-coverage collection of portable NLP components for building shareable analysis pipelines. In *Proceedings of the Workshop on Open Infrastructures and Analysis Frameworks for HLT (OIAF4HLT) at COLING 2014*, pages 1–11, Dublin, Ireland.

Joseph L. Fleiss. 1971. Measuring nominal scale agreement among many raters. *Psychological Bulletin*, 76(5):378–382.

Theodosis Goudas, Christos Louizos, Georgios Petasis, and Vangelis Karkaletsis. 2014. Argument extraction from news, blogs, and social media. In *Artificial Intelligence: Methods and Applications*, volume 8445 of *Lecture Notes in Computer Science*, pages 287–299. Springer International Publishing.

Mark Hall, Eibe Frank, Geoffrey Holmes, Bernhard Pfahringer, Peter Reutemann, and Ian H. Witten. 2009. The weka data mining software: An update. *SIGKDD Explor. Newsl.*, 11(1):10–18.

Kazi Saidul Hasan and Vincent Ng. 2014. Why are you taking this stance? identifying and classifying reasons in ideological debates. In *Proceedings of the 2014 Conference on Empirical Methods in Natural Language Processing*, EMNLP '14, pages 751–762, Doha, Qatar.

Dan Klein and Christopher D. Manning. 2003. Accurate unlexicalized parsing. In *Proceedings of the 41st Annual Meeting on Association for Computational Linguistics - Volume 1*, ACL '03, pages 423–430, Sapporo, Japan.

Klaus Krippendorff. 2004. *Content Analysis: An Introduction to its Methodology*. Sage, 2nd edition.

Damjan Krstajic, Ljubomir J. Buturovic, David E. Leahy, and Simon Thomas. 2014. Cross-validation pitfalls when selecting and assessing regression and classification models. *Journal of Cheminformatics*, 6(10):1–15.

Ran Levy, Yonatan Bilu, Daniel Hershcovich, Ehud Aharoni, and Noam Slonim. 2014. Context dependent claim detection. In *Proceedings of the 25th International Conference on Computational Linguistics*, COLING '14, pages 1489–1500, Dublin, Ireland.

Ziheng Lin, Min-Yen Kan, and Hwee Tou Ng. 2009. Recognizing implicit discourse relations in the Penn Discourse Treebank. In *Proceedings of the 2009 Conference on Empirical Methods in Natural Language Processing: Volume 1*, EMNLP '09, pages 343–351, Stroudsburg, PA, USA.

Ziheng Lin, Hwee Tou Ng, and Min-Yen Kan. 2014. A pdtb-styled end-to-end discourse parser. *Natural Language Engineering*, 20(2):151–184.

Raquel Mochales-Palau and Marie-Francine Moens. 2011. Argumentation mining. *Artificial Intelligence and Law*, 19(1):1–22.

Marie-Francine Moens, Erik Boiy, Raquel Mochales Palau, and Chris Reed. 2007. Automatic detection of arguments in legal texts. In *Proceedings of the 11th International Conference on Artificial Intelligence and Law*, ICAIL '07, pages 225–230, Stanford, CA, USA.

Andreas Peldszus and Manfred Stede. 2015a. Joint prediction in mst-style discourse parsing for argumentation mining. In *Proceedings of the 2015 Conference on Empirical Methods in Natural Language Processing*, EMNLP '15, pages 938–948, Lisbon, Portugal.

Andreas Peldszus and Manfred Stede. 2015b. Towards detecting counter-considerations in text. In *Proceedings of the 2nd Workshop on Argumentation Mining*, pages 104–109, Denver, CO.

Isaac Persing and Vincent Ng. 2013. Modeling thesis clarity in student essays. In *Proceedings of the 51st Annual Meeting of the Association for Computational Linguistics (Volume 1: Long Papers)*, ACL '13, pages 260–269, Sofia, Bulgaria.

Isaac Persing and Vincent Ng. 2015. Modeling argument strength in student essays. In *Proceedings of the 53rd Annual Meeting of the Association for Computational Linguistics and the 7th International Joint Conference on Natural Language Processing (Volume 1: Long Papers)*, ACL '15, pages 543–552, Beijing, China.

Ruty Rinott, Lena Dankin, Carlos Alzate Perez, Mitesh M. Khapra, Ehud Aharoni, and Noam Slonim. 2015. Show me your evidence - an automatic method for context dependent evidence detection. In *Proceedings of the 2015 Conference on Empirical Methods in Natural Language Processing*, EMNLP '15, pages 440–450, Lisbon, Portugal.

Richard Socher, Alex Perelygin, Jean Wu, Jason Chuang, Christopher D. Manning, Andrew Y. Ng, and Christopher Potts. 2013. Recursive deep models for semantic compositionality over a sentiment treebank. In *Proceedings of the 2013 Conference on Empirical Methods in Natural Language Processing*, EMNLP '13, pages 1631–1642, Seattle, WA, USA.

Marina Sokolova and Guy Lapalme. 2009. A systematic analysis of performance measures for classification tasks. *Information Processing & Management*, 45(4):427–437.

Swapna Somasundaran and Janyce Wiebe. 2009. Recognizing stances in online debates. In *Proceedings of the 47th Annual Meeting of the ACL and the 4th IJCNLP of the AFNLP*, ACL '09, pages 226–234, Suntec, Singapore.

Yi Song, Michael Heilman, Beata Beigman Klebanov, and Paul Deane. 2014. Applying argumentation schemes for essay scoring. In *Proceedings of the First Workshop on Argumentation Mining*, pages 69–78, Baltimore, MA, USA.

Christian Stab and Iryna Gurevych. 2014a. Annotating argument components and relations in persuasive essays. In *Proceedings of the 25th International Conference on Computational Linguistics*, COLING '14, pages 1501–1510, Dublin, Ireland.

Christian Stab and Iryna Gurevych. 2014b. Identifying argumentative discourse structures in persuasive essays. In *Proceedings of the 2014 Conference on Empirical Methods in Natural Language Processing*, EMNLP '14, pages 46–56, Doha, Qatar.

Christian Stab and Iryna Gurevych. 2016. Parsing argumentation structures in persuasive essays. *arXiv preprint arXiv:1604.07370*.

Keith E. Stanovich, Richard F. West, and Maggie E. Toplak. 2013. Myside bias, rational thinking, and intelligence. *Current Directions in Psychological Science*, 22(4):259–264.

Christopher R. Wolfe and M. Anne Britt. 2009. Argumentation schema and the myside bias in written argumentation. *Written Communication*, 26(2):183–209.

# Expert Stance Graphs for Computational Argumentation


**Orith Toledo-Ronen**     **Roy Bar-Haim**     **Noam Slonim**

IBM Research - Haifa

{oritht,roybar,noams}@il.ibm.com



## Abstract

We describe the construction of an *Expert Stance Graph*, a novel, large-scale knowledge resource that encodes the stance of more than 100,000 *experts* towards a variety of controversial *topics*. We suggest that this graph may be valuable for various fundamental tasks in computational argumentation. Experts and topics in our graph are Wikipedia entries. Both automatic and semi-automatic methods for building the graph are explored, and manual assessment validates the high accuracy of the resulting graph.


## 1 Introduction

Background knowledge plays an important role in many NLP tasks. However, *computational argumentation* is one area where little work has been done on developing specialized knowledge resources.

In this work we introduce a novel knowledge resource that may support various tasks related to argumentation mining and debating technologies. This large-scale resource, termed *Expert Stance Graph*, is built from *Wikipedia*, and provides background knowledge on the stance of experts towards debatable topics.

As a motivating example, consider the following *stance classification* setting, where the polarity of the following expert opinion on *Atheism* (*Pro* or *Con*) should be determined:

*Dawkins sums up his argument and states, "The temptation (to attribute the appearance of a design to actual design itself) is a false one, because the designer hypothesis immediately raises the larger problem of who designed the designer. The whole problem we started out with was the problem of*

*explaining statistical improbability. It is obviously no solution to postulate something even more improbable." (Dawkins, 2006, p. 158)*

Inferring the stance directly from the above text is a difficult and complex task. However, this complexity may be circumvented by utilizing background knowledge about (Richard) Dawkins, who is a well-known atheist. Dawkins' page in Wikipedia[1] includes various types of evidence for his stance towards atheism:

1. *Categories:* Dawkins belongs to the following Wikipedia categories: *Antitheists, Atheism activists, Atheist feminists* and *Critics of religions*[2].

2. *Article text:* The article text contains statements such as *"Dawkins is a noted atheist"* and *"Dawkins is an outspoken atheist"*.

3. *Infobox:* Dawkins has a *known-for* relation with *"criticism of religion"*.

## 2 Expert Stance Graphs

The *Expert Stance Graph (ESG)* is a directed bipartite graph comprising two types of nodes: (a) *concept* nodes, which represent debatable topics such as *Atheism, Abortion, Gun control* and *Same-sex marriage*, and (b) *expert* nodes, representing persons whose stance towards one or more of the concepts can be inferred from Wikipedia. Stance is represented as labeled directed edges from an expert to a concept, e.g. *Richard Dawkins* $\xrightarrow{Pro}$ *Atheism*. Each concept and each expert have their own article in Wikipedia. We use the term *Experts* inclusively to refer to academics,

---

[1] https://en.wikipedia.org/wiki/
Richard_Dawkins

[2] Inferring *Pro* stance for *Atheism* from *Critics of religions* depends on knowing the contrast relation between *Atheism* and *Religion*.

119


*Proceedings of the 3rd Workshop on Argument Mining*, pages 119–123,
Berlin, Germany, August 7-12, 2016. ©2016 Association for Computational Linguistics

writers, religious figures, politicians, activists, and so on.

## 3 Applications

Expert opinions are highly valuable for making persuasive arguments, and expert evidence (premise) is a commonly used type of argumentation scheme (Walton et al., 2008). Rinott et al. (2015) describe a method for automatic evidence detection in Wikipedia articles. Three common evidence types are explored: *Study, Expert,* and *Anecdotal*. The proposed method uses type-specific features for detecting evidence. For instance, in the case of expert evidence, a lexicon of words describing persons and organizations with relevant expertise is used.

The process of incorporating expert opinions on a given topic into an argument involves several steps. First, we need to retrieve from our corpus articles that contain expert opinions related to the given topic. Second, the exact boundaries of these opinions should be identified. Finally, the stance of the expert opinion towards the topic (Pro or Con) should be determined, to ensure it matches the stance of the argument we are making. Each of these steps is a challenging task by itself.

The expert stance graph may facilitate each of the above subtasks. If an expert $E$ is known to be a supporter or an opponent of some topic $T$, then the Wikipedia page of $E$ is likely to contain relevant opinions on $T$. Furthermore, a mention of $E$ can be a useful feature for identifying relevant expert opinions for $T$ in a given article.

Finally, perhaps the most important use of the graph for expert evidence is stance classification. Previous work on stance classification has shown that it can be much improved by utilizing external information beyond the text itself. For example, posts by the same author on the same topic are expected to have the same stance (Thomas et al., 2006; Hasan and Ng, 2013). Similarly, as shown in the previous example, external knowledge on expert stance towards a topic can improve stance classification of expert opinions.

## 4 Building the Graph

We consider two complementary settings for building the graph: (a) *Offline*, in which the set of concepts is predefined, and minimal human supervision is allowed, and (b) *Online*, where our goal is to find ad-hoc *Pro* and *Con* experts for an unseen concept, in a fully-automatic fashion.

For both settings, our approach is based on Wikipedia categories and lists, which have several advantages: (a) they provide an easy access to large collections of experts, (b) their stance classification is relatively easy, and (c) their hierarchical structure can be exploited.

### 4.1 Concepts

Offline construction of the graph starts with deriving the set of concepts. We started with Wikipedia's list of controversial issues[3], which contains about 1,000 Wikipedia entries, grouped into several top-level categories. We manually selected a subset of 12 categories , and filtered out the remaining 3 categories.[4]

One of the authors selected from the remaining list concepts that represent a two-sided debate (*Meaning of life*, for instance, is a controversial topic but does not represent a two-sided debate). Persons and locations were filtered out as well. This list was expanded manually by identifying relevant concepts in Wikipedia article titles that contain the words "Debate" or "Controversy". Finally, two annotators assessed the resulting list according to the above guidelines. Concepts that were rejected by both annotators were removed. The final list contained 201 concepts.

### 4.2 Candidate Expert Categories

Next, we search relevant Wikipedia categories and lists for each concept. The process starts with creating search terms. The concept itself is a search term, as well as any lexical derivation of the concept that represents a person (e.g. *Atheism→Atheist*), which we term *person derivations*. Person derivations are found using WordNet (Miller, 1995; Fellbaum, 1998): we look for lexical derivations of the concept that have *"person"* as a direct or inherited hypernym.

We then find all Wikipedia categories and lists[5] that contain the search terms. For example, given the search terms *atheism* and *atheist*, some of the categories found are *Atheism activists, American*

---

[3] `https://en.wikipedia.org/wiki/`
`Wikipedia:List_of_controversial_issues`

[4] The selected categories were *Politics and economics, History, Religion, Science biology and health, Sexuality, Entertainment, Environment, Law and order, Philosophy, Psychiatry, Technology,* and *Sports*. The excluded categories were *Linguistics, Media and culture,* and *People*.

[5] Lists are Wikipedia pages whose title begins with "List of".

*atheists, List of atheist authors, Converts to Christianity from atheism or agnosticism* and *Critics of atheism*. The set of categories is further expanded with subcategories of the categories found in the previous step. This step adds more relevant categories that do not contain the search terms, such as *Antitheists* for *Atheism*. To avoid topic drifting, we only add one level of subcategories.

Next, the persons associated with each category[6] are identified by considering outgoing links from the category page which are of type "Person", based on DBPedia's `rdf:type` property for the page (Lehmann et al., 2014). Categories with fewer than five persons are discarded. We also removed three concepts, for which the number of categories was too large: *Christianity*, *Catholicism*, and *Religion*. The resulting set included 4,603 categories containing 121,995 persons. Categories were found for 132 of the 198 concepts.

### 4.3 Category Stance Annotation

Finally, category names are manually annotated for stance. The annotation process has two stages: first, determine whether the category explicitly defines membership in a group of persons. For instance, *Swedish women's rights activists* and *Feminist bloggers* meet this criterion, but *Feminism and history* does not. We apply this test since we observed that it is much easier to predict with confidence the stance of persons in these categories.

Categories that do not pass this filter are marked as *Irrelevant*. Otherwise, the annotators proceed to the second stage, where they are asked to determine the stance of the persons in the given category towards the given concept, based on the category name. Possible labels are:

1. *Pro:* supporting the concept.

2. *Con:* opposing the concept.

3. *None:* The stance towards the concept cannot be determined based on the category name.

For instance, for the concept *Communism* we will have *British communists* and *Canadian Trotskyists* classified as *Pro*, *Moldovan anticommunists* classified as *Con*, and *Western writers about Soviet Russia* classified as *None*. Annotators may also consider direct parent categories for determining stance. In the previous example, knowing that *Canadian communists* is a parent category

---



| Polarity | Concepts | Categories | Experts |
|---|---|---|---|
| Pro | 105 | 3,221 | 93,570 |
| Con | 40 | 272 | 10,666 |

Table 1: Statistics on the Expert Stance Graph

of *Canadian Trotskyists* may help classifying the latter as *Pro* for *Communism*.

The categories were labeled by a team of six annotators, with each category labeled by two annotators. The overall agreement was 0.92, and the average inter-annotator Cohen's kappa coefficient was 0.79, which corresponds to *substantial agreement* (Landis and Koch, 1997). Cases of disagreement were labeled by a third annotator and were assigned the majority label. Category annotation was completed rather quickly - about 260 categories were annotated per hour. The total number of annotation hours invested in this task was 37.

The resulting ESG is composed of all experts in the categories labeled as *Pro* and *Con*. A total of 104,236 experts were found for 114 out of the 132 concepts, and for 31 concepts, both *Pro* and *Con* experts were found. The number of concepts, categories and experts for each stance is given in Table 1. As shown in the table, the vast majority of categories and experts found are *Pro*. Overall, our method efficiently constructs a very large ESG, while only requiring a small amount of human annotation time.[7]

### 4.4 Category Stance Classification

The offline list of concepts we started with is unlikely to be complete. Therefore, we would like to be able to find on-the-fly *Pro* and *Con* experts also for new, unseen concepts. This requires the development of a stance classifier for categories. We randomly split the 198 concepts into two equal-size subsets and used one subset for development and the other for testing. As a result, the 132 concepts for which categories were found are split into a development set, containing 69 concepts and their associated 2,069 categories, and a test set, containing 63 concepts and 2,534 categories. The development set was used for developing a simple rule-based classifier.

The logic of the rule-based classifier is sum-

---

[6]For convenience, we will refer in the following to categories and lists collectively as "categories".

[7]The IBM Debating Technologies group in IBM Research has already released several data resources, found here: `https://www.research.ibm.com/haifa/dept/vst/mlta_data.shtml`. We aim to release the resource presented in this paper as well, as soon as we obtain the required licenses.

```
Input: category CAT ; concept C ; person derivation PD for
    the concept
Output: stance classification of CAT into PRO/CON/NONE
    if CAT =~ critics of C then
        return CON
    else if CAT =~ anti|former|... PD then
        return CON
    else if CAT =~ PD dissident|... then
        return CON
    else if CAT =~ PD then
        return PRO
    else if CAT =~ anti|former|... C PERSON then
        return CON
    else if CAT =~ C PERSON then
        return PRO
    else
        return NONE
```

**Algorithm 1:** Category stance classification

|  | Predicted | Correct | Labeled | P | R |
|---|---|---|---|---|---|
| Categories | | | | | |
| Pro | 1,298 | 1,182 | 1,738 | 91.1 | 68.0 |
| Con | 144 | 140 | 186 | 97.2 | 75.3 |
| Experts | | | | | |
| Pro | 28,693 | 25,754 | 41,701 | 89.8 | 61.8 |
| Con | 4,113 | 4,016 | 6,912 | 97.6 | 58.1 |

Table 2: Category stance classification results

|  | Predicted | Correct | Labeled | P | R |
|---|---|---|---|---|---|
| Manual Annotation | | | | | |
| Pro | 200 | 181 | 189 | 90.5 | 95.8 |
| Con | 200 | 173 | 178 | 86.5 | 97.2 |
| Classifier | | | | | |
| Pro | 76 | 60 | 189 | 78.9 | 31.7 |
| Con | 87 | 81 | 178 | 93.1 | 45.5 |

Table 3: Expert stance assessment

marized in Algorithm 1. "=~" denotes pattern matching, and PERSON is any hyponym of the word "person" in WordNet, e.g. *activist, provider,* and *writer*. "..." denotes omission of some lexical alternatives.

The algorithm is first applied to the category itself, and if it fails to make a *Pro* or *Con* prediction (i.e returns *None*), it is applied to its direct parent categories, and the classification is made based on the majority of their *Pro* and *Con* predictions.

Table 2 shows the performance of the classifier on the test set, with respect to both categories and experts. Expert-level evaluation is done by labeling all the experts in each category with the category label. The following measures are reported for *Pro* and *Con* classes: number of predictions, number of correct predictions, number of labeled instances for this class, precision (P) and recall (R). Overall, the classifier achieves high precision for Pro and Con, both at the category and at the expert level, while covering most of the labeled instances. Yet, the coverage of the classifier is incomplete. As an example of its limitations, consider the categories *American pro-choice activists* and *American pro-life activists*, which are *Pro* and *Con* abortion, respectively. Their stance cannot be determined from the category itself according to our rules, because they do not contain the concept *Abortion*, and both were added as subcategories of *Abortion in the United States*, a category that does not have a clear stance (and indeed has both *Pro* and *Con* subcategories).

## 5   Expert-Level Assessment

So far we assumed that experts' stances can be predicted precisely from their category names. In this section we put this assumption to the test. We sampled 200 Pro experts and 200 Con experts from the test set. The polarity of the experts was derived from the manual labeling of their category. For each sampled instance, we first randomly selected one of the concepts in the test set, and then randomly picked an expert with the requested polarity. If the concept did not have any experts with that polarity, the above procedure was repeated until such an expert was found.

We then asked three human annotators to determine the stance of the experts towards their associated concept (*Pro/Con/None*), based on any information found on their Wikipedia page, and considered the majority label. As with the previous task, the annotators achieved *substantial agreement* (average kappa of 0.65). We evaluated the expert stance inferred from the category labeling by both the manual annotation and the rule-based classifier against these 400 labeled experts. The results are summarized in Table 3.

For the manual annotation, we see that the category name indeed predicts the expert's stance with high precision. In most of the misclassifications cases, the annotators could not determine the stance from the expert's web page. This discrepancy is partially due to the fact that the expert's page shows categories containing the expert, but does not display lists and parent categories containing the expert, which are available for category-based stance annotation. The precision of the classifier on this sample is also quite good (better for *Con*), but while we are able to identify a substantial part of the experts, recall still leaves much room for improvement.

## 6 Conclusion and Future Work

We introduced *Expert Stance Graphs*, a novel, large scale knowledge resource that has many potential use cases in computational argumentation. We presented an offline method for constructing the graph with minimal supervision, as well as a fully-automated method for finding experts for unseen concepts. Both methods show promising results.

In future work we plan to improve coverage by considering additional sources of information, such as the text of the expert's page in Wikipedia. We will also apply the graph in different tasks related to the detection and stance classification of expert evidence.

We also plan to enrich the graph with additional types of knowledge, which may be utilized to predict missing stance edges. Semantic relations between concepts, such as contrast (e.g. *Atheism* vs. *Religion*), may support such inferences, as experts are expected to have opposite stances towards contrasting concepts. Another possible extension of the graph is *influence* links between experts, which may indicate similar stances for these experts. Influence information is available from Wikipedia infoboxes.

Finally, we would like to apply collaborative filtering techniques to predict missing expert-concept stance relations. This is based on the intuition that experts who tend to have same (or opposite) stances on a set of topics, are likely to follow a similar pattern on topics for which we only have partial stance information.


## References

Richard Dawkins. 2006. *The God Delusion*. Bantam Press.

Christiane Fellbaum, editor. 1998. *WordNet: An Electronic Lexical Database*. Language, Speech and Communication. MIT Press.

Kazi Saidul Hasan and Vincent Ng. 2013. Stance classification of ideological debates: Data, models, features, and constraints. In *Proceedings of IJCNLP*.

J. R. Landis and G. G. Koch. 1997. The measurements of observer agreement for categorical data. *Biometrics*, 33:159–174.

Jens Lehmann, Robert Isele, Max Jakob, Anja Jentzsch, Dimitris Kontokostas, Pablo N. Mendes, Sebastian Hellmann, Mohamed Morsey, Patrick van Kleef, Sören Auer, and Christian Bizer. 2014. DBpedia - a large-scale, multilingual knowledge base extracted from Wikipedia. *Semantic Web Journal*.

G. A. Miller. 1995. WordNet: A lexical database for English. *Communications of the ACM*, pages 39–41.

Ruty Rinott, Lena Dankin, Carlos Alzate Perez, Mitesh M. Khapra, Ehud Aharoni, and Noam Slonim. 2015. Show me your evidence - an automatic method for context dependent evidence detection. In *Proceedings of EMNLP*.

Matt Thomas, Bo Pang, and Lillian Lee. 2006. Get out the vote: Determining support or opposition from Congressional floor-debate transcripts. In *Proceedings of EMNLP*.

Douglas Walton, Christopher Reed, and Fabrizio Macagno. 2008. *Argumentation Schemes*. Cambridge University Press.

# Fill the Gap! Analyzing Implicit Premises between
# Claims from Online Debates

**Filip Boltužić** and **Jan Šnajder**
University of Zagreb, Faculty of Electrical Engineering and Computing
Text Analysis and Knowledge Engineering Lab
Unska 3, 10000 Zagreb, Croatia
`{filip.boltuzic,jan.snajder}@fer.hr`

## Abstract

Identifying the main claims occurring across texts is important for large-scale argumentation mining from social media. However, the claims that users make are often unclear and build on implicit knowledge, effectively introducing a gap between the claims. In this work, we study the problem of matching user claims to predefined main claims, using implicit premises to fill the gap. We build a dataset with implicit premises and analyze how human annotators fill the gaps. We then experiment with computational claim matching models that utilize these premises. We show that using manually-compiled premises improves similarity-based claim matching and that premises generalize to unseen user claims.

## 1 Introduction

Argumentation mining aims to extract and analyze argumentation expressed in natural language texts. It is an emerging field at the confluence of natural language processing (NLP) and computational argumentation; see (Moens, 2014; Lippi and Torroni, 2016) for a comprehensive overview.

Initial work on argumentation mining has focused on well-structured, edited text, such as legal text (Walton, 2005) or scientific publications (Jiménez-Aleixandre and Erduran, 2007). Recently, the focus has also shifted to argumentation mining from social media texts, such as online debates (Cabrio and Villata, 2012; Habernal et al., 2014; Boltužić and Šnajder, 2014), discussions on regulations (Park and Cardie, 2014), product reviews (Ghosh et al., 2014), blogs (Goudas et al., 2014), and tweets (Llewellyn et al., 2014; Bosc et al., 2016). Mining arguments from social media can uncover valuable insights into peoples' opinions;

in this context, it can be thought of as a sophisticated opinion mining technique – one that seeks to uncover the reasons for opinions and patterns of reasoning. The potential applications of social media mining are numerous, especially when done on a large scale.

In comparison to argumentation mining from edited texts, there are additional challenges involved in mining arguments from social media. First, social media texts are more noisy than edited texts, which makes them less amenable to NLP techniques. Secondly, users in general are not trained in argumentation, hence the claims they make will often be unclear, ambiguous, vague, or simply poorly worded. Finally, the arguments will often lack a proper structure. This is especially true for short texts, such as microbloging posts, which mostly consist of a single claim.

When analyzing short and noisy arguments on a large scale, it becomes crucial to identify identical but differently expressed claims across texts. For example, summarizing and analyzing arguments on a controversial topic presupposes that can identify and aggregate identical claims. This task has been addressed in the literature under the name of *argument recognition* (Boltužić and Šnajder, 2014), *reason classification* (Hasan and Ng, 2014), *argument facet similarity* (Swanson et al., 2015; Misra et al., 2015), and *argument tagging* (Sobhani et al., 2015). The task can be decomposed into two subtasks: (1) identifying the main claims for a topic and (2) matching each claim expressed in text to claims identified as the main claims. The focus of this paper is on the latter.

The difficulty of the claim matching task arises from the existence of a gap between the user's claim and the main claim. Many factors contribute to the gap: linguistic variation, implied commonsense knowledge, or implicit premises from the beliefs and value judgments of the person making the



*Proceedings of the 3rd Workshop on Argument Mining*, pages 124–133,
Berlin, Germany, August 7-12, 2016. ©2016 Association for Computational Linguistics

| **User claim:** | *Now it is not taxed, and those who sell it are usually criminals of some sort.* |
| **Main claim:** | *Legalized marijuana can be controlled and regulated by the government.* |
| **Premise 1:** | *If something is not taxed, criminals sell it.* |
| **Premise 2:** | *Criminals should be stopped from selling things.* |
| **Premise 3:** | *Things that are taxed are controlled and regulated by the government.* |

Table 1: User claim, the matching main claim, and the implicit premises filling the gap.

claim; the latter two effectively make the argument an *enthymeme*. In Table 1, we give an example from the dataset of Hasan and Ng (2014). Here, a user claim from an online debate was manually matched to a claim previously identified as one of the main claims on the topic of marijuana legalization. Without additional premises, the user claim does not entail the main claim, but the gap may be closed by including the three listed premises.

Previous annotation studies (Boltužić and Šnajder, 2014; Hasan and Ng, 2014; Sobhani et al., 2015) demonstrate that humans have little difficulty in matching two claims, suggesting that they are capable of filling the premise gap. However, current machine learning-based approaches to claim matching do not account for the problem of implicit premises. These approaches utilize linguistic features or rely on textual similarity and textual entailment features. From an argumentation perspective, however, these are shallow features and their capacity to bridge the gap opened by implicit premises is limited. Furthermore, existing approaches lack the explanatory power to explain why (under what premises) one claim can be matched to the other. Yet, the ability to provide such explanations is important for apprehending arguments.

In this paper, we address the problem of claim matching in the presence of gaps arising due to implicit premises. From an NLP perspective, this is a daunting task, which significantly surpasses the current state of the art. As a first step in better understanding of the task, we analyze the gap between user claims and main claims from both a data and computational perspective. We conduct two studies. The first is an annotation study, in which we analyze the gap, both qualitatively and quantitatively, in terms of how people fill it. In the second study, we focus on the computational models for claim matching with implicit premises, and gain preliminary insights into such models could benefit from the use of implicit premises.

To the best of our knowledge, this is the first work that focuses on the problem of implicit premises in argumentation mining. Besides reporting on the experimental results of the two studies, we also describe and release a new dataset with human-provided implicit premises. We believe our results may contribute to a better understanding of the premise gap between claims.

The remainder of the paper is structured as follows. In the next section, we briefly review the related work on argumentation mining. In Section 3 we describe the creation of the implicit premises dataset. We describe the results of the two studies in Section 4 and Section 5, respectively. We conclude and discuss future work in Section 6.

## 2 Related Work

Work related to ours comes from two broad strands of research: argumentation mining and computational argumentation. Within argumentation mining, a significant effort has been devoted to the extraction of argumentative structure from text, e.g., (Walton, 2012; Mochales and Moens, 2011; Stab and Gurevych, 2014; Habernal and Gurevych, 2016)). One way to approach this problem is to classify the text fragments into *argumentation schemes* – templates for typical arguments. Feng and Hirst (2011) note that identifying the particular argumentation scheme that an argument is using could help in reconstructing its implicit premises. As a first step towards this goal, they develop a model to classify text fragments into five most frequently used Walton's schemes (Walton et al., 2008), reaching 80–95% pairwise classification accuracy on the Araucaria dataset.

Recovering argumentative structure from social media text comes with additional challenges due to the noisiness of the text and the lack of argumentative structure. However, if the documents are sufficiently long, argumentative structure could in principle be recovered. In a recent study on social media texts, Habernal and Gurevych (2016) showed that (a slightly modified) Toulmin's argumentation model may be suitable for short documents, such as article comments or forum posts. Using sequence labeling, they identify the claim, premise, backing, rebuttal, and refutation components, achieving a token-level F1-score of 0.25.

Unlike the work cited above, in this work we do not consider argumentative structure. Rather, we focus on short (mostly single-sentence) claims, and the task of matching a pair of claims. The task of claim matching has been tackled by Boltužić and Šnajder (2014) and Hasan and Ng (2014). The former frame the task as a supervised multi-label problem, using textual similarity- and entailment-based features. The features are designed to compare the user comments against the textual representation of main claims, allowing for a certain degree of topic independence. In contrast, Hasan and Ng frame the problem as a (joint learning) supervised classification task with lexical features, effectively making their model topic-specific.

Both approaches above are supervised and require a predefined set of main claims. Given a large-enough collection of user posts, there seem to be at least two ways in which main claims can be identified. First, they can be extracted manually. Boltužić and Šnajder (2014) use the main claims already identified as such on an online debating platform, while Hasan and Ng (2014) asked annotators to group the user comments and identify the main claims. The alternative is to use unsupervised machine learning and induce the main claims automatically. A middle-ground solution, proposed by Sobhani et al. (2015), is to first cluster the claims, and then manually map the clusters to main claims. In this work, we assume that the main claims have been identified using any of the above methods.

Claim matching is related to the well-established NLP problems: *textual entailment* (TE) and *semantic textual similarity* (STS), both often tackled as shared tasks (Dagan et al., 2006; Agirre et al., 2012). Boltužić and Šnajder (2014) explore using outputs from STS and TE in solving the claim matching problem. Cabrio and Villata (2012) use TE to determine support/attack relations between claims. Boltužić and Šnajder (2015) consider the notion of *argument similarity* between two claims. Similarly, Swanson et al. (2015) and Misra et al. (2015) consider *argument facet similarity*.

The problem of implicit information has also been tackled in the computational argumentation community. Work closest to ours is that of Wyner et al. (2010), who address the task of inferring implicit premises from user discussions. They annotate implicit premises in *Attempto Controlled English* (Fuchs et al., 2008), define propositional logic axioms with annotated premises, and extract and explain policy stances in discussions. In our work, we focus on the NLP approach and work with implicit premises in textual form.

| Topic | # claim pairs | # main claims |
|---|---|---|
| Marijuana (MA) | 125 | 10 |
| GayRights (GR) | 125 | 9 |
| Abortion (AB) | 125 | 12 |
| Obama (OB) | 125 | 16 |

Table 2: Dataset summary.

## 3 Data and Annotation

The starting point of our study is the dataset of Hasan and Ng (2014). The dataset contains user posts from a two-side online debate platform on four topics: "Marijuana" (MA), "Gay rights" (GR), "Abortion" (AB), and "Obama" (OB). Each post is assigned a stance label (*pro* or *con*), provided by the author of the post. Furthermore, each post is split up into sentences and each sentence is manually labeled with a single claim from a predefined set of main claims, different for each topic. Note that all sentences in the dataset are matched against exactly one main claim. Hasan and Ng (2014) report substantial levels of inter-annotator agreement (between 0.61 and 0.67, depending on the topic).

Our annotation task extends this dataset. We formulate the task as a "fill-the-gap" task. Given a pair of previously matched claims (a user claim and a main claim), we ask the annotators to provide the premises that bridge the gap between the two claims. No further instructions were given to the annotators; we hoped that they would resort to common-sense reasoning and effectively reconstruct the deductive steps needed to entail the main claim from the user claim. The annotators were also free to abstain from filling the gap, if they felt that the claims cannot be matched; we refer to such pairs as *Non-matching*. If no implicit premises are required to bridge the gap (the two claims are paraphrases of each other), then the claim pair is annotated as *Directly linked*.

We hired three annotators to annotate each pair of claims. The order of claim pairs was randomized for each annotator. We annotated 125 claims pairs for each topic, yielding a total of 500 gap-filling premise sets. Table 2 summarizes the dataset statistics. An excerpt from the dataset is given in Table 3. We make the dataset freely available.[1]

---

[1] Available under the CC BY-SA-NC license from `http://takelab.fer.hr/argpremises`

| Claim pair | Annotation |
|---|---|
| **User claim:** *Obama supports the Bush tax cuts. He did not try to end them in any way.* <br> **Main claim:** *Obama destroyed our economy.* | **P1:** *Obama continued with the Bush tax cuts.* <br><br> **P2:** *The Bush tax cuts destroyed our economy.* |
| **User claim:** *What if the child is born and there is so many difficulties that the child will not be able to succeed in life?* <br> **Main claim:** *A fetus is not a human yet, so it's okay to abort.* | Non-matching |
| **User claim:** *Technically speaking, a fetus is not a human yet.* <br> **Main claim:** *A fetus is not a human yet, so it's okay to abort.* | Directly linked |

Table 3: Examples of annotated claim pairs.

## 4 Study I: Implicit Premises

The aim of the first study is to analyze how people fill the gap between the user's claim and the corresponding main claim. We focus on three research questions. The first concerns the variability of the gap: to what extent do different people fill the gap in different ways, and to what extent the gaps differ across topics. Secondly, we wish to characterize the gap in terms of the types of premises used to fill it. The third question is how the gap relates to the more general (but less precise) notion of textual similarity between claims, which has been used for claim matching in prior work.

### 4.1 Setup and Assumptions

To answer the above questions, we analyze and compare the gap-filling premise sets in the dataset of implicit premises from Section 3. We note that, by doing so, we inherit the setup used by Hasan and Ng (2014). This seems to raise three issues.

First, the main claim to which the user claim has been matched to need not be the correct one. In such cases, it would obviously be nonsensical to attempt to fill the gap. We remedy this by asking our annotators to abstain from filling the gap if they felt the two claims do not match. Moreover, considering that the agreement on the claim matching task on this dataset was substantial (Hasan and Ng, 2014), we expect this to rarely be the case.

The second issue concerns the granularity of the main claims. Boltužić and Šnajder (2015) note that the level of claim granularity is to a certain extent arbitrary. We speculate that, on average, the more general the main claims are, the fewer the number of main claims for a given topic and the bigger the

|  | A1 | A2 | A3 | Avg. |
|---|---|---|---|---|
| Avg. # premises | 3.6 | 2.6 | 2.0 | 2.7 ± 0.7 |
| Avg. # words | 26.7 | 23.7 | 18.6 | 23.0 ± 3.4 |
| Non-matching (%) | 1.2 | 3.6 | 14.5 | 6.4 ± 5.8 |

Table 4: Gap-filling parameters for the three annotators.

gaps between the user-provided and main claims.

Finally, we note that each gap was not filled by the same person who identified the main claim, which in turn is not the original author of the claim. Therefore, it may well be that the original author would have chosen a different main claim, and that she would commit to a different set of premises than those ascribed to by our annotators.

Considering the above, we acknowledge that we cannot analyze the *genuine* implicit premises of the claim's author. However, under the assumption that the main claim has been correctly identified, there is a gap that can be filled with *sensible* premises. Depending on how appropriate the chosen main claim was, this gap will be larger or smaller.

### 4.2 Variability in Gap Filling

We are interested in gauging the variability of gap filling across the annotators and topics. To this end, we calculate the following quantitative parameters: the average number of premises, the average number of words in premises, and the proportion of non-matched claim pairs.

Table 4 shows that there is a substantial variance in these parameters for the three annotators. The average number of premises per gap is 2.7 and the average number of words per gap is about 23, yielding the average length of about 9 words per premise. We also computed the word overlap between the three annotators: 8.51, 7.67, and 5.93 for annotator pairs A1-A2, A1-A3, and A2-A3, respectively. This indicates that, on average, the premise sets overlap in just 32% of the words. The annotators A1 and A2 have a higher word overlap and use more words to fill the gap. Also, A1 and A2 managed to fill the gap for more cases than A3, who much more often desisted from filling the gap. An example where A1 used more premises than A3 is shown in Table 5.

Table 6 shows the gap-filling parameters across topics. Here the picture is more balanced. The least number of premises and the least number of words per gap are used for the AB topic. The GR

| | |
|---|---|
| **User claim:** | *It would be loads of empathy and joy for about 6 hours, then irrational, stimulant-induced paranoia. If we can expect the former to bring about peace on Earth, the latter would surely bring about WWIII.* |
| **Main claim:** | *Legalization of marijuana causes crime.* |

| | |
|---|---|
| **A1 Premise 1:** | *Marijuana is a stimulant.* |
| **A1 Premise 2:** | *The use of marijuana induces paranoia.* |
| **A1 Premise 3:** | *Paranoia causes war.* |
| **A1 Premise 4:** | *War causes aggression.* |
| **A1 Premise 5:** | *Aggression is a crime.* |
| **A1 Premise 6:** | *"WWIII" stands for the Third World War.* |

| | |
|---|---|
| **A3 Premise 1:** | *Marijuana leads to irrational paranoia which can lead to commiting a crime.* |

Table 5: User claim, the matching main claim, and the implicit premise(s) filling the gap provided by two different annotators.

| | Topic | | | | |
|---|---|---|---|---|---|
| | MA | GR | AB | OB | Avg. |
| Avg. # premises | 2.8 | 2.8 | 2.5 | 2.8 | $2.7 \pm 0.1$ |
| Avg. # words | 23.6 | 24.9 | 19.1 | 23.4 | $22.8 \pm 2.2$ |
| Non-matching (%) | 5.9 | 6.8 | 4.6 | 4.3 | $5.4 \pm 1.0$ |

Table 6: Gap-filling parameters for the four topics.

topic contained the most (about 7%) claim pairs for which the annotators desisted from filing the gap.

### 4.3 Gap Characterization

We next make a preliminary inquiry into the of nature of the gap. To this end, we characterize the gap in terms of the individual premises that are used to fill it. At this point we do not look at the relations between the premises (the argumentative structure); we leave this for future work.

Our analysis is based on a simple ad-hoc typology of premises, organized along three dimensions: premise type (fact, value, or policy), complexity (atomic, implication, or complex), and acceptance (universal or claim-specific). The intuition behind the latter is that some premises convey general truths or widely accepted beliefs, while others are specific to the claim being made, and embraced only by the supporters of the claim in question.

We (the two authors) manually classified 50 premises from the MA topic into the above categories and averaged the proportions. The kappa-agreement is 0.42, 0.62, and 0.53 for the premise type, complexity, and acceptance, respectively. Factual premises account for the large majority (85%) of cases, value premises for 9%, and policy premises for 6%. Most of the gap-filling premises

are atomic (77%), while implication and other complex types constitute 16% and 7% of cases, respectively. In terms of acceptance, premises are well-balanced: universal and claim-specific premises account for 62% and 38% of cases, respectively.

We suspect that the kind of the analysis we did above might be relevant for determining the overall strength of an argument (Park and Cardie, 2014). An interesting venue for future work would be to carry out a more systematic analysis of premise acceptance using the complete dataset, dissected across claims and topics, and possibly based on surveying a larger group of people.

### 4.4 Semantic Similarity between Claims

Previous work addressed claim matching as a semantic textual similarity task (Swanson et al., 2015; Misra et al., 2015; Boltužić and Šnajder, 2015). It is therefore worth investigating how the notion of semantic similarity relates to the gap between two claims. We hypothesize that the textual similarity between two claims will be negatively affected by the size of the gap. Thus, even though the claims are matching, if the gap is too big, similarity will not be high enough to indicate the match.

To verify this, we compare the semantic similarity score between each pair of claims against its gap size, characterized by the number of premises required to fill the gap, averaged across the three annotators. To obtain a reliable estimate of semantic similarity between claims, instead of computing the similarity automatically, we rely on human-annotated similarity judgments. We set up a crowd-sourcing task and asked the workers to judge the similarity between 846 claim pairs for the MA topic. The task was formulated as a question *"Are two claims talking about the same thing?"*, and judgments were made on a scale from 1 ("not similar") to 6 ("very similar"). Each pair of claims received five judgments, which we averaged to obtain the gold-similarity score. The average standard deviation is 1.2, indicating good agreement.

The Pearson correlation coefficient between the similarity score and the number of premises filling the gap for annotators A1, A2, and A3 is $-0.30$, $-0.28$, and $-0.14$, respectively. The correlation between the similarity score and the number of premises averaged across the annotators is $-0.22$ ($p<0.0001$). We conclude that there is a statistically significant, albeit weak negative relationship between semantic similarity and gap size.

# 5 Study II: Claim Matching Model

In this section we focus on claim matching models with implicit premises. In the previous section, we demonstrated that the degree of similarity between matched claims varies and is negatively correlated with the number of gap-filling premises. This result directly suggests that the similarity scores for matched claims could be increased by reducing the size of the gap. Furthermore, we expect that the size of the gap can be effectively reduced by including premises in the similarity computation.

Motivated by these insights, we conduct a preliminary study on the use of implicit premises in claim matching. The study is also motivated by our long-term goal to develop efficient models for recognizing main claims in social media texts. Given a user's claim, the task is to find the main claim from a predefined set of claims to which the user's claim matches the best. We address three research questions: (1) whether and how the use of implicit premises improves claim matching, (2) how well do the implicit premises generalize, and (3) could the implicit premises be retrieved automatically.

## 5.1 Experimental Setup

The claim matching task can be approached in a supervised or unsupervised manner. We focus here on the latter, based on semantic similarity between the claims and the premises. We think unsupervised claim matching provides a more straightforward and explicit way of incorporating the implicit premises. Furthermore, the unsupervised approach better corresponds to the very idea of argumentation, where claims and premises are compared to each other and combined to derive other claims.

**Dataset.** We use the implicit premise dataset from Section 3, consisting of 125 claim pairs for each of the four topics. We use the gap-filling premise sets from annotator A1, who on average has provided the largest number of implicit premises. We refer to this dataset as the *development set*. In addition, we sample and additional *test set* consisting of 125 pairs for each topic from the dataset of Hasan and Ng (2014); for claim pairs from this set we have no implicit premises.

**Semantic similarity.** We adopt the distributional semantics approach (Turney and Pantel, 2010) to computing semantic textual similarity. We rely on distributed representation based on the neural network skip-gram model of Mikolov et al.

(2013a).[2] We represent the texts of the claims and the premises by summing up the distributional vectors of their individual words, as the semantic composition of short phrases via simple vector addition has been shown to work well (Mikolov et al., 2013b). We measure claim similarity using cosine distance between two vectors.

Inspired by (Cabrio et al., 2013; Boltužić and Šnajder, 2014), we also attempted to model claim matching using textual entailment. However, our results, obtained using the *Excitement Open Platform* (Padó et al., 2015), were considerably worse than that of distributional similarity models, hence we do not consider them further in this paper.

**Baselines.** We employ two baselines. First, an unsupervised baseline, which simply computes the similarity between the user claim and main claim vectors without using the implicit premises. Each user claim is matched to the most similar main claim. The other is a supervised baseline, which uses a support vector machine (SVM) classifier with an RBF kernel, trained on the user comments, to predict the label corresponding to the main claim. We train and evaluate the model using a nested $5 \times 3$ cross-validation, separately for each topic. The hyperparameters $C$ and $\gamma$ are optimized using grid search. We use the well-known LibSVM implementation (Chang and Lin, 2011).

**Premise sets and combination with claims.** To obtain a single combined representation of a premise set, we simply concatenate the premises together before computing the distributional vector representation. We do the same when combining the premises with either of the claims. This is exemplified in Table 7. In what follows, we denote the user claim, the main claim, and the gap-filling premise set with $U_i$, $M_j$, and $P_{ij}$, respectively.

## 5.2 Matching with Implicit Premises

To answer the first research question – whether using premise sets can help in matching claims – we use gold-annotated premise sets and combine these with either the main claim or the user claim. The main idea is that, by combining the premises with a claim, we encode the information conveyed by the premises into the claim, hopefully making the two claims more similar at the textual level.

We consider four models: the unsupervised baseline, denoted "$U_i \leftrightarrow M_j$", the supervised baseline,

---

[2]We use the pre-trained vectors available at
`https://code.google.com/p/word2vec/`

| Type | Text content |
|---|---|
| $U_i$ | *Marijuana has so many benefits for sick people.* |
| $M_j$ | *Marijuana is used as a medicine for its positive effects.* |
| $P_{ij}$ | *Marijuana helps sick people. Sick people use marijuana.* |
| $U_i+P_{ij}$ | *Marijuana has so many benefits for sick people. Marijuana helps sick people. Sick people use marijuana.* |
| $M_j+P_{ij}$ | *Marijuana is used as a medicine for its positive effects. Marijuana helps sick people. Sick people use marijuana.* |

Table 7: Combination of premise sets and claims.

|  | Topic | | | | |
|---|---|---|---|---|---|
| Model | MA | GR | AB | OB | Avg. |
| $U_i \leftrightarrow M_j$ | 7.39 | 12.52 | 24.59 | 10.87 | 13.84 |
| $U_i \leftrightarrow M_j$ (S) | 35.26 | 27.81 | 33.30 | 20.92 | 29.32 |
| $U_i+P_{ij} \leftrightarrow M_j$ | 22.73 | **46.03** | 47.22 | 21.41 | 34.35 |
| $U_i \leftrightarrow M_j+P_{ij}$ | **48.05** | 28.23 | **49.34** | **64.11** | **47.43** |

Table 8: Performance of claim matching baselines and oracle performance of the claim matching models utilizing implicit premises from annotator A1 (macro-averaged F1-score).

denoted "$U_i \leftrightarrow M_j$ (S)", the model in which the premises are combined with the user claim, denoted "$U_i+P_{ij} \leftrightarrow M_j$", and the model in which the premises are combined with the main claim, denoted "$U_i \leftrightarrow M_j+P_{ij}$". The latter two predict the main claim as the one that maximizes the similarity between two claims, after one of the claims is combined with the premises. The $U_i+P_{ij} \leftrightarrow M_j$ model considers all pairs of the user claim $U_i$ and the gold-annotated premise sets $P_{i*}$ for that user claim. In contrast, the $U_i \leftrightarrow M_j+P_{ij}$ model considers all pairings of the main claim $M_j$ and the gold-annotated premise sets $P_{*j}$ for that main claim. In effect, this model tries to fill the gap using different premise sets linked to the given main claim. In this oracle setup, we always use the gold-annotated premise set for the main claim.

In Table 8, we show the claim matching results in terms of the macro-averaged F1-score on the development set. Results demonstrate that using the implicit premises helps in selecting the most similar main claim, as the models with added implicit premises outperform the unsupervised baseline by 20.5 and 33.6 points of F1-score. Furthermore, the model that combines the premises with the main claim considerably outperforms the two baselines and the model that combines the premises with the user claim. An exception is the GR topic, on which the the latter model works best. Our analysis revealed this to be due to the presence of very general (i.e., lexically non-discriminative) premises in some of the premise sets (e.g., *"Straight people have the right to marry"*), which makes the corresponding main claim more similar to user claims. Another interesting observation is the very good performance on the OB topic. This is because only one of the 16 main claims contains the word *Obama*, also making it more similar to user claims.

However, after the premise sets get combined with all the main claims, this difference diminishes and the matching performance improves.

We obtained the above results using premises compiled by annotator A1. To see how model performance is influenced by the differences in premise sets, we re-run the same experiment with the best-performing $U_i \leftrightarrow M_j+P_{ij}$ model, this time using the premises compiled by annotators A2 and A3. Although we obtained a lower macro-averaged F1-score (33.97 for A2 and 32.91 for A3), the model still outperforms both baselines. On the other hand, this suggest that the performance very much depends on the quality of the premises.

The claim matching problem bears resemblance with query matching in information retrieval. A common way to address the lexical gap between the queries and the documents is to perform query expansion (Voorhees, 1994). We hypothesize that human-compiled premises are more useful for claim matching than standard query expansion. To verify this, we replicate setups $U_i+P_{ij} \leftrightarrow M_j$ and $U_i \leftrightarrow M_j+P_{ij}$, but instead of premise sets, use (1) WordNet synsets and (2) top $k$ distributionally most similar words (using word vectors from Section 5.1 and $k=\{1, 3, 5, 7, 9\}$) to expand the user or the main claim. We obtained no improvement over the baselines, suggesting that the lexical information in the premises is indeed specific.

### 5.3 Premise Generalization

From a practical perspective, we are interested to what extent the premises generalize, i.e., whether it is possible to reuse the premises compiled for the main claims, but different user claims. We choose the best-performing model from the previous section ($U_i \leftrightarrow M_j+P_{ij}$), and apply this model and the baseline models on the test set. This means that the model uses the premise sets $P_{ij}$ for pairs of claims

| Model | MA | GR | AB | OB | Avg. |
|---|---|---|---|---|---|
| | | Topic | | | |
| $U_k \leftrightarrow M_j$ | 9.60 | 19.68 | 27.70 | 12.39 | 17.35 |
| $U_k \leftrightarrow M_j$ (S) | 29.01 | **29.39** | 21.09 | 18.22 | 24.43 |
| $U_k \leftrightarrow M_j+P_{ij}$ | **30.63** | 23.00 | **32.72** | **23.87** | **27.55** |

Table 9: Performance of claim matching baselines and the models utilizing the implicit premises on the test set (macro-averaged F1-score).

| Model | MA | GR | AB | OB | Avg. |
|---|---|---|---|---|---|
| | | Topic | | | |
| $U_i \leftrightarrow M_j$ | 7.39 | 12.52 | 24.59 | **10.87** | 13.84 |
| $U_i+P \leftrightarrow M_j$ (WT) | **8.95** | **19.54** | **29.32** | 7.30 | **16.28** |
| $U_i+P \leftrightarrow M_j$ (XT) | 8.56 | 19.01 | 28.73 | 7.07 | 15.84 |
| $U_k \leftrightarrow M_j$ | **9.60** | **19.68** | **27.70** | 12.39 | **17.35** |
| $U_k \leftrightarrow M_j$ (XT) | 5.69 | 17.75 | 15.38 | **12.43** | 12.82 |

Table 10: Performance of the claim matching model with premise retrieval on the dev. set (upper part) and test set (lower part); macro-avg. F1-score.

$U_i$ and $M_j$ from the training set, and the hope is that the same premise sets will be useful for unseen user claims $U_k$. Results are shown in Table 9. The model again outperforms the baselines, except on the GR topic. The performance improvement varies across topics: the average improvement over the unsupervised and supervised baselines is 10.2 and 3.12 points of F1-score, respectively. This result suggests that the premises that fill the gap generalize to a certain extent, and thus can be reused for unseen user claims.

### 5.4 Premise Retrieval

In a realistic setting, we would not have at our disposal the implicit premises for each main claim, but try to generate or retrieve them automatically. We preliminary investigate the feasibility of this option with our third research question – could the implicit premises be retrieved automatically?

To retrieve the premise set P and then perform claim matching, we use a simple heuristic: given a user claim as input, we choose $N$ premises most similar to the user claim, and then combine them with the user claim. We next compute the similarity between the premise-augmented claim vector and all the main claims. If the average similarity to main claims has increased, we increment $N$ and repeat the procedure, otherwise we stop. The main idea is to retrieve as many premises as needed to bring the user claim "closer" to the main claims. We run this with $N$ ranging from 1 to 5. In cases when combining the user claim with additional premises makes the claim less similar to the main claims, no combination takes place.

We consider two setups: one in which the pool of premises to retrieve from comes from the topic in question (within-topic), and the other in which the premises from all four topics are considered (cross-topic). Results are shown in Table 10. We evaluate on both the development set the test set, as well as within-topic (WT) and cross-topic (XT) premise retrieval. Results suggest that our simple method for within-topic premise retrieval improves claim matching over the baseline for all topics except the OB topic. On the other hand, results on the test set indicate that the model does not generalize well, as it does not outperform the baseline.

## 6 Conclusion

We addressed the problem of matching user claims to main claims. Implicit premises introduce a gap between two claims. This gap is easily filled by humans, but difficult to bridge for natural language processing methods.

In the first study, we compiled a dataset of implicit premises between matched claims from online debates. We showed that there is a considerable variation in the way how human annotators fill the gaps with premises, and that they use premises of various types. We also showed that the similarity between claims, as judged by humans, negatively correlates with the size of the gap, expressed in the number of premises needed to fill it.

In the second study, we experimented with computational models for claim matching. We showed that using gap-filling premises effectively reduces the similarity gap between claims and improves claim matching performance. We also showed that premise sets generalize to a certain extent, i.e., we can improve claim matching on unseen user claims. Finally, we made a preliminary attempt to retrieve automatically the gap-filling premises.

This paper is a preliminary study of implicit premises and their relevance for argumentation mining. For future work, we want to further study the types of implicit premises, as well as relationships between them. We also intend to experiment with more sophisticated premise retrieval models.

**Acknowledgments.** We thank the reviewers for their many insightful comments and suggestions.

# References

Eneko Agirre, Mona Diab, Daniel Cer, and Aitor Gonzalez-Agirre. 2012. SemEval-2012 task 6: A pilot on semantic textual similarity. In *Proceedings of the First Joint Conference on Lexical and Computational Semantics-Volume 1: Proceedings of the main conference and the shared task, and Volume 2: Proceedings of the Sixth International Workshop on Semantic Evaluation*, pages 385–393. Association for Computational Linguistics.

Filip Boltužić and Jan Šnajder. 2014. Back up your stance: Recognizing arguments in online discussions. In *Proceedings of the First Workshop on Argumentation Mining*, pages 49–58. Association for Computational Linguistics.

Filip Boltužić and Jan Šnajder. 2015. Identifying prominent arguments in online debates using semantic textual similarity. In *Proceedings of the 2nd Workshop on Argumentation Mining*, pages 110–115. Association for Computational Linguistics.

Tom Bosc, Elena Cabrio, and Serena Villata. 2016. DART: A dataset of arguments and their relations on Twitter. In *Proceedings of the Tenth International Conference on Language Resources and Evaluation (LREC 2016)*. European Language Resources Association.

Elena Cabrio and Serena Villata. 2012. Combining textual entailment and argumentation theory for supporting online debates interactions. In *Proceedings of the 50th Annual Meeting of the Association for Computational Linguistics: Short Papers-Volume 2*, pages 208–212. Association for Computational Linguistics.

Elena Cabrio, Serena Villata, and Fabien Gandon. 2013. A support framework for argumentative discussions management in the web. In *The Semantic Web: Semantics and Big Data*, pages 412–426. Springer.

Chih-Chung Chang and Chih-Jen Lin. 2011. LIBSVM: A library for support vector machines. *ACM Transactions on Intelligent Systems and Technology (TIST)*, 2(3):27.

Ido Dagan, Oren Glickman, and Bernardo Magnini. 2006. The PASCAL recognising textual entailment challenge. In *Machine Learning Challenges. Evaluating Predictive Uncertainty, Visual Object Classification, and Recognising Tectual Entailment*, pages 177–190. Springer.

Vanessa Wei Feng and Graeme Hirst. 2011. Classifying arguments by scheme. In *Proceedings of the 49th Annual Meeting of the Association for Computational Linguistics: Human Language Technologies-Volume 1*, pages 987–996. Association for Computational Linguistics.

Norbert E Fuchs, Kaarel Kaljurand, and Tobias Kuhn. 2008. Attempto controlled english for knowledge representation. In *Reasoning Web*, pages 104–124. Springer.

Debanjan Ghosh, Smaranda Muresan, Nina Wacholder, Mark Aakhus, and Matthew Mitsui. 2014. Analyzing argumentative discourse units in online interactions. In *Proceedings of the First Workshop on Argumentation Mining*, pages 39–48. Association for Computational Linguistics.

Theodosis Goudas, Christos Louizos, Georgios Petasis, and Vangelis Karkaletsis. 2014. Argument extraction from news, blogs, and social media. In *Hellenic Conference on Artificial Intelligence*, pages 287–299. Springer.

Ivan Habernal and Iryna Gurevych. 2016. Argumentation mining in user-generated web discourse. *arXiv preprint arXiv:1601.02403*.

Ivan Habernal, Judith Eckle-Kohler, and Iryna Gurevych. 2014. Argumentation mining on the web from information seeking perspective. In *Proceedings of the Workshop on Frontiers and Connections between Argumentation Theory and Natural Language Processing*.

Kazi Saidul Hasan and Vincent Ng. 2014. Why are you taking this stance? Identifying and classifying reasons in ideological debates. In *Proceedings of the 2014 Conference on Empirical Methods in Natural Language Processing (EMNLP)*, pages 751–762. Association for Computational Linguistics.

María Pilar Jiménez-Aleixandre and Sibel Erduran. 2007. Argumentation in science education: An overview. In *Argumentation in Science Education*, pages 3–27. Springer.

Marco Lippi and Paolo Torroni. 2016. Argumentation mining: State of the art and emerging trends. *ACM Transactions on Internet Technology (TOIT)*, 16(2):10.

Clare Llewellyn, Claire Grover, Jon Oberlander, and Ewan Klein. 2014. Re-using an argument corpus to aid in the curation of social media collections. In *Proceedings of the Nineth International Conference on Language Resources and Evaluation (LREC 2014)*, pages 462–468. European Language Resources Association.

Tomas Mikolov, Kai Chen, Greg Corrado, and Jeffrey Dean. 2013a. Efficient estimation of word representations in vector space. In *Proceedings of ICLR*, Scottsdale, AZ, USA.

Tomas Mikolov, Ilya Sutskever, Kai Chen, Greg S Corrado, and Jeff Dean. 2013b. Distributed representations of words and phrases and their compositionality. In *Advances in Neural Information Processing Systems*, pages 3111–3119.

Amita Misra, Pranav Anand, JEF Tree, and MA Walker. 2015. Using summarization to discover argument facets in online idealogical dialog. In *Proceedings of* the 2015 Annual Conference of the North American Chapter of the ACL*, pages 430–440. Association for Computational Linguistics.

Raquel Mochales and Marie-Francine Moens. 2011. Argumentation mining. *Artificial Intelligence and Law*, 19(1):1–22.

Marie-Francine Moens. 2014. Argumentation mining: Where are we now, where do we want to be and how do we get there? In *Post-proceedings of the forum for information retrieval evaluation (FIRE 2013)*.

Sebastian Padó, Tae-Gil Noh, Asher Stern, Rui Wang, and Roberto Zanoli. 2015. Design and realization of a modular architecture for textual entailment. *Natural Language Engineering*, 21(02):167–200.

Joonsuk Park and Claire Cardie. 2014. Identifying appropriate support for propositions in online user comments. In *Proceedings of the First Workshop on Argumentation Mining*, pages 29–38. Association for Computational Linguistics.

Parinaz Sobhani, Diana Inkpen, and Stan Matwin. 2015. From argumentation mining to stance classification. In *Proceedings of the 2nd Workshop on Argumentation Mining*, pages 67–77. Association for Computational Linguistics.

Christian Stab and Iryna Gurevych. 2014. Annotating argument components and relations in persuasive essays. In *Proceedings of COLING 2014, the 25th International Conference on Computational Linguistics: Technical Papers*, pages 1501–1510.

Reid Swanson, Brian Ecker, and Marilyn Walker. 2015. Argument mining: Extracting arguments from online dialogue. In *Proceedings of 16th Annual Meeting of the Special Interest Group on Discourse and Dialogue (SIGDIAL 2015)*, pages 217–227. Association for Computational Linguistics.

Peter D Turney and Patrick Pantel. 2010. From frequency to meaning: Vector space models of semantics. *Journal of artificial intelligence research*, 37(1):141–188.

Ellen M Voorhees. 1994. Query expansion using lexical-semantic relations. In *Proceedings of the 17th annual international ACM SIGIR conference on Research and development in information retrieval*, pages 61–69. Springer-Verlag New York, Inc.

Douglas Walton, Christopher Reed, and Fabrizio Macagno. 2008. *Argumentation schemes*. Cambridge University Press.

Douglas Walton. 2005. *Argumentation methods for artificial intelligence in law*. Springer.

Douglas Walton. 2012. Using argumentation schemes for argument extraction: A bottom-up method. *International Journal of Cognitive Informatics and Natural Intelligence (IJCINI)*, 6(3):33–61.

Adam Wyner, Tom van Engers, and Anthony Hunter. 2010. Working on the argument pipeline: Through flow issues between natural language argument, instantiated arguments, and argumentation frameworks. In *Proceedings of the Workshop on Computational Models of Natural Argument*.

# Summarising the points made in online political debates


**Charlie Egan**
Computing Science
University of Aberdeen
c.egan.12@aberdeen.ac.uk

**Advaith Siddharthan**
Computing Science
University of Aberdeen
advaith@abdn.ac.uk

**Adam Wyner**
Computing Science
University of Aberdeen
azwyner@abdn.ac.uk



## Abstract

Online communities host growing numbers of discussions amongst large groups of participants on all manner of topics. This user-generated content contains millions of statements of opinions and ideas. We propose an abstractive approach to summarize such argumentative discussions, making key content accessible through 'point' extraction, where a point is a verb and its syntactic arguments. Our approach uses both dependency parse information and verb case frames to identify and extract valid points, and generates an abstractive summary that discusses the key points being made in the debate. We performed a human evaluation of our approach using a corpus of online political debates and report significant improvements over a high-performing extractive summarizer.


## 1 Introduction

People increasingly engage in and contribute to online discussions and debates about topics in a range of areas, e.g. film, politics, consumer items, and science. Participants may make points and counterpoints, agreeing and disagreeing with others. These online argumentative discussions are an untapped resource of ideas. A high-level, summarised view of a discussion, grouping information and presenting points and counter-points, would be useful and interesting: retailers could analyse product reviews; consumers could zero in on what products to buy; and social scientists could gain insight on social treads. Yet, due to the size and complexity of the discussions and limitations of summarisers based on sentence extraction, much of the useful information in discussions is inaccessible.

In this paper, we propose a fully automatic and domain neutral unsupervised approach to abstractive summarisation which makes the key content of such discussions accessible. At the core of our approach is the notion of a 'point' - a short statement, derived from a verb and its syntactic arguments. Points (and counter-points) from across the corpus are analysed and clustered to derive a summary of the discussion. To evaluate our approach, we used a corpus of political debates (Walker et al., 2012), then compared summaries generated by our tool against a high-performing extractive summariser (Nenkova et al., 2006). We report that our summariser improves significantly on this extractive baseline.

## 2 Related Work

Text summarisation is a well established task in the field of NLP, with most systems based on sentence selection and scoring, with possibly some post-editing to shorten or fuse sentences (Nenkova and McKeown, 2011). The vast majority of systems have been developed for the news domain or on structured texts such as science (Teufel and Moens, 2002).

In related work on mailing list data, one approach clustered messages into subtopics and used centring to select sentences for an extractive summary (Newman and Blitzer, 2003). The concept of recurring and related subtopics has been highlighted (Zhou and Hovy, 2006) as being of greater importance to discussion summarisation than the summarisation of newswire data. In 'opinion summarisation', sentences have also been grouped based on the




*Proceedings of the 3rd Workshop on Argument Mining*, pages 134–143,
Berlin, Germany, August 7-12, 2016. ©2016 Association for Computational Linguistics

feature discussed, to generate a summary of all the reviews for a product that minimised repetition (Hu and Liu, 2004). There has also been interest in the summarisation of subjective content in discussions (Hu and Liu, 2004; Lloret et al., 2009; Galley et al., 2004).

In addition to summarisation, our work is concerned with argumentation, which for our purposes relates to expressions for or against some textual content. Galley et al. (2004) used adjacency pairs to target utterances that had been classified as being an agreement or disagreement. Others have investigated arguments raised in online discussion (Boltuzic and Šnajder, 2015; Cabrio and Villata, 2012; Ghosh et al., 2014). A prominent example of argument extraction applies supervised learning methods to automatically identify claims and counter-claims from a Wikipedia corpus (Levy et al., 2014).

In this paper, we explore the intersection of text summarisation and argument. We implement a novel summarisation approach that extracts and organises information as points rather than sentences. It generates structured summaries of argumentative discussions based on relationships between points, such as counterpoints or co-occurring points.

## 3  Methods

Our summariser is based on three components. The first robustly identifies and extracts points from text, providing data for subsequent analysis. Given plain text from a discussion, we obtain (a) a pattern or signature that could be used to link points – regardless of their exact phrasing – and (b) a short readable extract that could be used to present the point to readers in a summary. A second component performs a number of refinements on the list of points such as removing meaningless points. The third component builds on these extracted points by connecting them in different ways (e.g., as point and counterpoint, or co-occurring points) to model the discussion. From this, it formulates a structured summary that we show to be useful to readers.

### 3.1  Point Extraction

We use the notion of a 'point' as the basis for our analysis – broadly speaking it is a verb

and its syntactic arguments. Points encapsulate both a human-readable 'extract' from the text as well as a pattern representing the core components that can be used to match and compare points. Extracts and patterns are stored as attributes in a key-value structure that represents a point.

Consider the sentence from a debate about abortion: *"I don't think so, an unborn **child** (however old) **is** not yet a **human**."* Other sentences may also relate to this idea that a child is not human until it is born; e.g. *"So you say: children are not complete humans until birth?"* Both discuss the point represented by the grammatically indexed pattern: `child.subject be.verb human.object`. Note that we are at this stage not concerned with the stance towards the point being discussed; we will return to this later. To facilitate readability, the extracted points are associated with an 'extract' from the source sentence; in these instances, *"an unborn child is not yet a human"* and *"children are not complete humans until birth?"* Generation of points bears a passing resemblence to Text Simplification (Siddharthan, 2014), but is focussed on generating a single short sentence starting from a verb, rather than splitting sentences into shorter ones.

Points and extracts are derived from a dependency parse graph structure (De Marneffe et al., 2014). Consider:

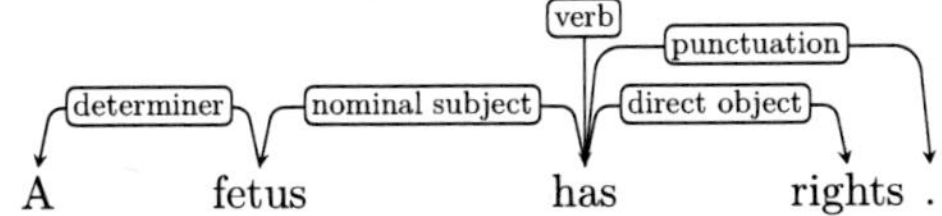


Here, the nominal subject and direct object relations form the pattern, and relations are followed recursively to generate the extract. To solve the general case, we must select dependency relations to include in the pattern and then decide which should be followed from the verb to include in the extract.

### 3.1.1  Using Verb Frames

We seek to include only those verb dependencies that are required by syntax or are optional but important to the core idea. While this often means using only subject and object relations, this is not always the case. Some dependencies, like adverbial modifiers or parataxis, which do not introduce information relevant to

```
<FRAME>
  <DESCRIPTION primary="NP V NP"
       secondary="Basic Transitive"/>
  <EXAMPLES>
    <EXAMPLE>
      Brutus murdered Julius Cesar.
    </EXAMPLE>
  </EXAMPLES>
  <SYNTAX>
    <NP value="Agent"><SYNRESTRS/></NP>
    <VERB/>
    <NP value="Patient"><SYNRESTRS/></NP>
  </SYNTAX>
  <SEMANTICS>...</SEMANTICS>
</FRAME>
```

Figure 1: VerbNet frame for 'murder'

the point's core idea are universally excluded. For the rest, we identify valid verb frames using FrameNet, available as part of VerbNet, an XML verb lexicon (Schuler, 2005; Fillmore et al., 2002). Represented in VerbNet's 274 'classes' are 4402 member verbs. For each of these verb classes, a wide range of attributes are listed. FrameNet frames are one such attribute, these describe the verb's syntactic arguments and the semantic role of each in that frame. An example frame for the verb 'murder' is shown in Figure 1. Here we see that the verb takes two Noun Phrase arguments, an Agent ('murderer') and Patient ('victim').

We use a frame's syntactic information to determine the dependencies to include in the pattern for a given verb. This use of frames for generation has parallels to methods used in abstractive summarisation for generating noun phrase references to named entities (Siddharthan and McKeown, 2005; Siddharthan et al., 2011). To create a 'verb index', we parsed the VerbNet catalogue into a key-value structure where each verb was the key and the list of allowed frames the value. Points were extracted by querying the dependency parse relative to information from the verb's frames.

With an index of verbs and their frames, all the information required to identify points in parses is available. However, as frames are not inherently queriable with respect to a dependency graph structure, queries for each type of frame were written. While frames in different categories encode additional semantic information, many frames share the same basic syntax. Common frames such as `NounPhrase Verb NounPhrase` cover a high

percentage of all frames in the index. We have manually translated such frames to equivalent dependency relations to implement a means of querying dependency parses for 17 of the more common patterns, which cover 96% of all frames in the index. To do this, we used the dependency parses for the example sentences listed in frames to identify the correct mappings. The remaining 4% of frames, as well as frames not covered by FrameNet, were matched using a 'Generic Frame' and a new query that could be run against any dependency graph to extract subjects, objects and open clausal complements.

### 3.1.2 Human Readable Extracts

Our approach to generating human readable extracts for a point can be summarised as follows: recursively follow dependencies from the verb to allowed dependents until the sub-tree is fully explored. Nodes in the graph that are related to the verb, or (recursively) any of its dependents, are returned as part of the extract for the point. However, to keep points succinct the following dependency relations are excluded: *adverbial clause modifiers, clausal subjects, clausal complement, generic dependencies and parataxis*. Generic dependencies occur when the parser is unable to determine the dependency type. These either arise from errors or long-distance dependencies and are rarely useful in extracts. The other blacklisted dependencies are clausal in nature and tend to connect points, rather than define them. The returned tokens in this recursive search, presented in the original order, provide us with a sub-sentence extract for the point pattern.

### 3.2 Point Curation

To better cluster extracted points into distinct ideas, we curated points. We merged subject pronouns such as 'I' or 'she' under a single 'person' subject as these were found to be used interchangeably and not reference particular people in the text; for example, points such as `she.nsubj have.verb abortion.dobj` and `I.nsubj have.verb abortion.dobj` were merged under a new pattern: `PERSON.nsubj have.verb abortion.dobj`. Homogenising points in this way means we can continue to rely on a cluster's size as a measure of importance in the summarisation task.

A number of points are also removed using a series of 'blacklists'. Based on points extracted from the Abortion debate (1151 posts, ~155000 words), which we used for development, these defined generic point patterns were judged to be either of little interest or problematic in other ways. For example, patterns such as `it.nsubj have.verb rights.dobj` contain referential pronouns that are hard to resolve. We excluded points with the following subjects: *it_PRP, that_DT, this_DT, which_WDT, what_WDT*. We also excluded a set of verbs with a `PERSON` subject; certain phrases such as "*I think*" or "*I object*" are very common, but relate to attribution or higher argumentation steps rather than point content. Other common cue phrases such as "*make the claim*" were also removed.

### 3.3 Summary Generation

Our goal is the abstractive summarisation of argumentative texts. Extracted points have 'patterns' that enable new comparisons not possible with sentence selection approaches to summarisation, for instance, the analysis of counter points. This section describes the process of generating an abstractive summary.

#### 3.3.1 Extract Generation

**Extract Filtering:** In a cluster of points with the same pattern there are a range of extracts that could be selected. There is much variation in extract quality caused by poor parses, punctuation or extract generation. We implemented a set of rules that prevent a poor quality extract from being presented.

Predominantly, points were prevented from being presented based on the presence of certain substring patterns tested with regular expressions. Exclusion patterns included two or more consecutive words in block capitals, repeated words or a mid-word case change. Following on from these basic tests, there were more complex exclusion patterns based on the dependencies obtained from re-parsing the extract. Poor quality extracts often contained (on re-parsing) clausal or generic dependencies, or multiple instances of conjunction. Such extracts were excluded.

**Extract Selection:** Point extracts were organised in clusters sharing a common pattern of verb arguments. Such clusters contained all the point extracts for the same point pattern and thus all the available linguistic realisations to express the cluster's core idea. Even after filtering out some extracts, as described above, there was still much variation in the quality of the extracts. Take this example cluster of generated extracts about the Genesis creation narrative:

> "The world was created in six days."
> "The world was created in exactly 6 days."
> "Is there that the world could have been created in six days."
> "The world was created by God in seven days."
> "The world was created in 6 days."
> "But, was the world created in six days."
> "How the world was created in six days."

All of these passed the 'Extract Filtering' stage. Now an extract must be selected to represent the cluster. In this instance our approach selected the fifth point, "*The world was created in 6 days.*" Selecting the best extract was performed every time a cluster was selected for use in a summary. Selections were made using a length-weighted, bigram model of the extract words in the cluster, in order to select a succinct extract that was representative of the entire cluster.

**Extract Presentation:** Our points extraction approach works by selecting the relevant components in a string for a given point, using the dependency graph. While this has a key advantage in creating shorter content units, it also means that extracts are often poorly formatted for presentation when viewed in isolation (not capitalised, leading commas etc.). To overcome such issues we post-edit the selected extracts to ensure the following properties: first character is capitalised; ends in a period; commas are followed but not preceded by a space; contractions are applied where possible; and consecutive punctuation marks condensed or removed. Certain determiners, adverbs and conjunctions (because, that, therefore) are also removed from the start of extracts. With these adjustments, extracts can typically be presented as short sentences.

#### 3.3.2 Content Selection:

A cluster's inclusion in a particular summary section is a function of the number of points in the cluster. This is based on the idea that larger clusters are of greater importance (as the point is made more often). Frequency is a commonly used to order content in summarisation research for this reason; however in argumentative texts, it could result in the suppression of minority viewpoints. Identifying such views might be an interesting challenge, but is out of scope for this paper.

Our summaries are organised as sections to highlight various aspects of the debate (see below). To avoid larger clusters being repeatedly selected for each summary section, a list of used patterns and extracts is maintained. When an point is used in a summary section it is 'spent' and added to a list of used patterns and extracts. The point pattern, string, lemmas and subject-verb-object triple are added to this list. Any point that matches any element in this list of used identifiers cannot be used later in the summary.

### 3.3.3 Summary Sections:

A summary could be generated just by listing the most frequent points in the discussion. However, we were interested in generating more structured summaries that group points in different ways, i.e. counterpoints & co-occurring points.

**Counter Points:** This analysis was intended to highlight areas of disagreement in the discussion. Counterpoints were matched on one of two possible criteria, the presence of either negation or an antonym. Potential, antonym-derived counterpoints, for a given point, were generated using its pattern and a list of antonyms. Antonyms were sourced from WordNet (Miller, 1995). Taking `woman.nsubj have.verb right.dobj` as an example pattern, the following potential counterpoint patterns are generated:

- `man.nsubj have.verb right.dobj`
- `woman.nsubj lack.verb right.dobj`
- `woman.nsubj have.verb left.dobj`

Where there were many pattern words with antonym matches, multiple potential counter point patters were generated. Such hypothesised antonym patterns were rejected if the pattern did not occur in the debate. From the example above, only the first generated pat-

tern: `man.nsubj have.verb right.dobj` appeared in the debate.

Negation terminology was not commonly part of the point pattern, for example, the `woman.nsubj have.verb right.dobj` cluster could include both *"A woman has the right"* and *"A woman **does not** have the right"* as extracts. To identify negated forms within clusters, we instead pattern matched for negated words in the point extracts. First the cluster was split into two groups, extracts with negation terminology and those without. The Cartesian product of these two groups gave all pairs of negated and non-negated extracts. For each pair a string difference was computed, which was used to identify a pair for use in summary. Point-counterpoint pairs were selected for the summary based on the average cluster size for the point and counterpoint patterns. In the summary section with the heading "people disagree on these points", only the extract for the point is displayed, not the counterpoint.

**Co-occurring Points:** As well as counterpoints we were also interested in presenting associated points, i.e. those frequently raised in conjunction with one another. To identify co-occurring points, each post in the discussion was first represented as a list of points it made. Taking all pairwise combinations of the points made in a post, for all posts, we generated a list of all co-occurring point pairs. The most common pairs of patterns were selected for use in the summary. Co-occurring pairs were rejected if they were too similar – patterns must differ by more than one component. For example, `woman.nsubj have.verb choice.dobj` could not be displayed as co-occurring with `woman.nsubj have.verb rights.dobj` but could be with `fetus.nsubj have.verb rights.dobj`.

**Additional Summary Sections:** First, points from the largest (previously) unused clusters were selected. Then we organised points by topic terms, defined here as commonly used nouns. The subjects and objects in all points were tallied to give a ranking of topic terms. Using these common topics, points containing them were selected and displayed in a dedicated section for that topic.

Figure 2: Examples of Layout vs Plain Summaries

Most large clusters have a pattern with three components. Points with longer patterns are less common but often offer more developed extracts (e.g. *"The human life cycle begins at conception."*) Longer points were selected based on the number of components in the pattern. An alternative to selecting points with a longer pattern is to instead select points that mention more than one important topic word. Extracts were sorted on the number of topic words they include. Extracts were selected from the top 100 to complete this section using the extract selection process.

As a final idea for a summary section we included a list of questions that had been asked a number of times. Questions were much less commonly repeated and this section was therefore more an illustration than a summary.

## 4 Evaluation

Studies were carried out using five political debates from the Internet Argument Corpus (Walker et al., 2012): creation, gay rights, the existence of god, gun ownership and healthcare (the 6th, abortion rights, was used as a development set). This corpus was extracted from the online debate site 4forums (www.4forums.com/political) and is a large collection of unscripted argumentative dialogues based on 390,000 posts.

25 Study participants were recruited using Amazon Mechanical Turk who had the 'Masters' qualification. Each comparison required a participant to read a stock summary and exactly one of the other two (plain and layout) in a random order. Figure 2 provides examples of these, which are also defined below.

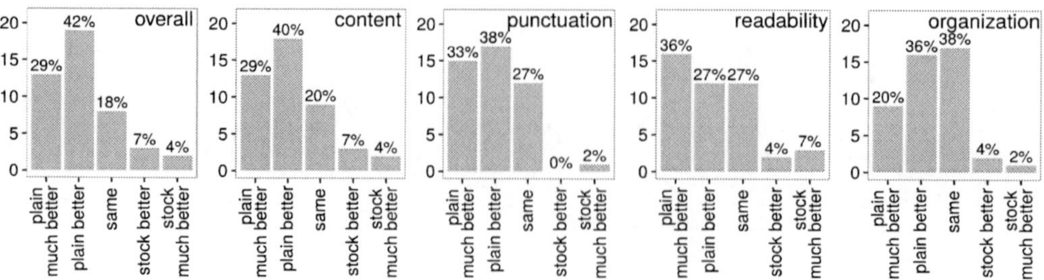

Figure 3: Counts of participant responses when comparing of Plain & Stock.

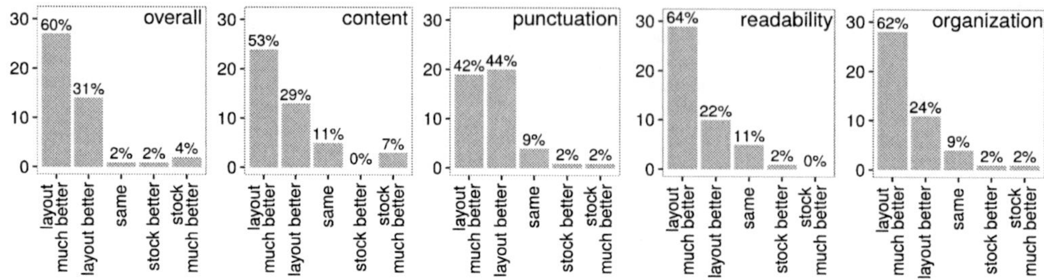

Figure 4: Counts of participant responses when comparing of Layout & Stock.

- **Stock**: A summary generated using an implementation of the state of the art sentence extraction approach described by Nenkova et al. (2006)
- **Plain**: A collection of point extracts with the same unstructured style and length as the Stock summary.
- **Layout**: A summary adds explanatory text that introduces different sections of points.

The Stock summaries were controlled to be the same length as other summary in the comparison for fair comparison. Participants were asked to compare the two summaries on the following factors:

- **Content Interest / Informativeness**: The summary presents varied and interesting content
- **Readability:** The summary contents make sense; work without context; aren't repetitive; and are easy to read
- **Punctuation & Presentation**: The summary contents are correctly formatted as sentences, punctuation, capital letters and have sentence case
- **Organisation:** Related points occur near one another

Finally they were asked to give an overall rating and justify their response using free text. 9 independent ratings were obtained for each pair of summaries for each of the 5 debates using a balanced design.

## 4.1 Results

The study made comparisons between two pairs of summary types: Plain vs. Stock and Layout vs. Stock.

All of the five comparison factors presented in Figure 3 show a preference for our Plain summaries. These counts are aggregated from all Plain vs. Stock comparisons for all five political debates. Each histogram represents 45 responses for a question comparing the two summaries on that factor. The results were tested using Sign tests for each comparison factor, with 'better' and 'much better' aggregated and 'same' results excluded. The family significance level was set at $\alpha = 0.05$; with $m = 5$ hypotheses - using the Bonferroni correction $(\alpha/m)$; giving an individual significance threshold of $0.05/5 = 0.01$. 'overall', 'content', 'readability', 'punctuation' and 'organisation' were all found to show a significant difference $(p < 0.0001$ for each); i.e. even unstructured summaries with content at the point level was overwhelmingly preferred to state of the art sentence selection.

Similarly, when Layout was also compared against Stock on the same factors, we observed an even stronger preference for Layout summaries (see Figure 4). To test the increased

| | Plain (A) vs. Stock (B) | Layout (A) vs. Stock (B) | Row Total |
|---|---|---|---|
| A much better | 13 | 27 | 40 |
| A better | 19 | 14 | 33 |
| A same | 8 | 1 | 9 |
| B better | 3 | 1 | 4 |
| B much better | 2 | 2 | 4 |
| Column Total | 45 | 45 | 90 |

Table 1: Plain & Layout vs Stock responses contingency table

preference for Layout vs. Stock, compared to Plain, we used a One-sided, Fisher's Exact Test. Taking the 45 responses for 'overall' ratings from both comparisons, the test was performed on the contingency table (Table 1). The p-value was found to be significant ($p = 0.008$); i.e the structuring of points into sections with descriptions is preferred to the flat representation.

## 4.2 Discussion

The quantitative results above show a preference for both Plain and Layout point-based summaries compared to Stock. We had also solicited free textual feedback; these comments are summarised here.

Multiple comments made reference to Plain summaries having fewer questions, less surplus information and more content. Comments also described the content as being "proper English" and using "complete sentences". Comments also suggested some participants believed the summaries had been written by a human. References were also made to higher level properties of both summaries such as "logical flow", "relies on fallacy", "explains the reasoning" as well as factual correctness. In summary, participants acknowledged succinctness, variety and informativeness of the Plain summaries. This shows points can form good summaries, even without structuring into sections or explaining the links.

For comments left about preferences for Layout summaries, references to organisation doubled with respect to preferences for Plain. Readability and the idea of assimilating information were also common factors cited in justifications. Interestingly, only one comment made a direct reference to 'categories' (sections) of the summary. We had expected more references to summary sections. Fewer comments in this comparison referenced human

authors; sections perhaps hint at a more mechanised approach.

## 5  Conclusions and Future Work

We have implemented a method for extracting meaningful content units called points, then grouping points into discussion summaries. We evaluated our approach in a comparison against summaries generated by a statistical sentence extraction tool. The comparison results were very positive with both our summary types performing significantly better. This indicates that our approach is a viable foundation for discussion summarisation. Moreover, the summaries structure the points; for instance by whether points are countered, or whether they link different topic terms. We see this project as a step forward in the process of better understanding online discussion.

For future work, we think the approach's general methods can be applied to tasks beyond summarisation in political debate, product reviews, and other areas. It would be attractive to have a web application that would take some discussion corpus as input and generate a summary, with an interface that could support exploration and filtering of summaries based on the user's interest, for example, using a discussion-graph built from point noun component nodes connected by verb edges.

Currently the approach models discussions as a flat list of posts — without reply/response annotations. Using hierarchical discussion threads opens up interesting opportunities for Argument Mining using points extraction as a basis. A new summary section that listed points commonly made in response to other points in other posts would be a valuable addition. There is also potential for further work on summary presentation. Comments by participants in the evaluation also suggested that it would be useful to present the frequencies for points to highlight their importance, and to be able to click on points in an interactive manner to see them in the context of the posts.

## Acknowledgements

This work was supported by the Economic and Social Research Council [Grant number ES/M001628/1].

## References

[Boltuzic and Šnajder2015] Filip Boltuzic and Jan Šnajder. 2015. Identifying prominent arguments in online debates using semantic textual similarity. In *Proceedings of the 2nd Workshop on Argumentation Mining*, pages 110–115.

[Cabrio and Villata2012] Elena Cabrio and Serena Villata. 2012. Combining textual entailment and argumentation theory for supporting online debates interactions. In *Proceedings of the 50th Annual Meeting of the Association for Computational Linguistics: Short Papers-Volume 2*, pages 208–212. Association for Computational Linguistics.

[De Marneffe et al.2014] Marie-Catherine De Marneffe, Timothy Dozat, Natalia Silveira, Katri Haverinen, Filip Ginter, Joakim Nivre, and Christopher D Manning. 2014. Universal stanford dependencies: A cross-linguistic typology. In *LREC*, volume 14, pages 4585–4592.

[Fillmore et al.2002] Charles J Fillmore, Collin F Baker, and Hiroaki Sato. 2002. The framenet database and software tools. In *LREC*.

[Galley et al.2004] Michel Galley, Kathleen McKeown, Julia Hirschberg, and Elizabeth Shriberg. 2004. Identifying agreement and disagreement in conversational speech: Use of bayesian networks to model pragmatic dependencies. In *Proceedings of the 42nd Annual Meeting on Association for Computational Linguistics*, page 669. Association for Computational Linguistics.

[Ghosh et al.2014] Debanjan Ghosh, Smaranda Muresan, Nina Wacholder, Mark Aakhus, and Matthew Mitsui. 2014. Analyzing argumentative discourse units in online interactions. In *Proceedings of the First Workshop on Argumentation Mining*, pages 39–48.

[Hu and Liu2004] Minqing Hu and Bing Liu. 2004. Mining and summarizing customer reviews. In *Proceedings of the tenth ACM SIGKDD international conference on Knowledge discovery and data mining*, pages 168–177. ACM.

[Levy et al.2014] Ran Levy, Yonatan Bilu, Daniel Hershcovich, Ehud Aharoni, and Noam Slonim. 2014. Context dependent claim detection. In *COLING 2014, 25th International Conference on Computational Linguistics, Proceedings of the Conference: Technical Papers, August 23-29, 2014, Dublin, Ireland*, pages 1489–1500.

[Lloret et al.2009] Elena Lloret, Alexandra Balahur, Manuel Palomar, and Andrés Montoyo. 2009. Towards building a competitive opinion summarization system: challenges and keys. In *Proceedings of Human Language Technologies: The 2009 Annual Conference of the North American Chapter of the Association for Computational Linguistics, Companion Volume: Student Research Workshop and Doctoral Consortium*, pages 72–77. Association for Computational Linguistics.

[Miller1995] George A. Miller. 1995. Wordnet: A lexical database for english. *Commun. ACM*, 38(11):39–41, November.

[Nenkova and McKeown2011] Ani Nenkova and Kathleen McKeown. 2011. Automatic summarization. *Foundations and Trends in Information Retrieval*, 5(2-3):103–233.

[Nenkova et al.2006] Ani Nenkova, Lucy Vanderwende, and Kathleen McKeown. 2006. A compositional context sensitive multi-document summarizer: exploring the factors that influence summarization. In *Proceedings of the 29th annual international ACM SIGIR conference on Research and development in information retrieval*, pages 573–580. ACM.

[Newman and Blitzer2003] Paula S Newman and John C Blitzer. 2003. Summarizing archived discussions: a beginning. In *Proceedings of the 8th international conference on Intelligent user interfaces*, pages 273–276. ACM.

[Schuler2005] Karin Kipper Schuler. 2005. *VerbNet: A broad-coverage, comprehensive verb lexicon*. Ph.D. thesis, University of Pennsylvania.

[Siddharthan and McKeown2005] Advaith Siddharthan and Kathleen McKeown. 2005. Improving multilingual summarization: using redundancy in the input to correct mt errors. In *Proceedings of the Conference on Human Language Technology and Empirical Methods in Natural Language Processing*, pages 33–40. Association for Computational Linguistics.

[Siddharthan et al.2011] Advaith Siddharthan, Ani Nenkova, and Kathleen McKeown. 2011. Information status distinctions and referring expressions: An empirical study of references to people in news summaries. *Computational Linguistics*, 37(4):811–842.

[Siddharthan2014] Advaith Siddharthan. 2014. A survey of research on text simplification. *ITL-International Journal of Applied Linguistics*, 165(2):259–298.

[Teufel and Moens2002] Simone Teufel and Marc Moens. 2002. Summarizing scientific articles: experiments with relevance and rhetorical status. *Computational linguistics*, 28(4):409–445.

[Walker et al.2012] Marilyn A. Walker, Jean E. Fox Tree, Pranav Anand, Rob Abbott, and Joseph King. 2012. A corpus for research on deliberation and debate. In *Proceedings of the Eighth International Conference on Language Resources and Evaluation (LREC-2012), Istanbul, Turkey, May 23-25, 2012*, pages 812–817.

[Zhou and Hovy2006] Liang Zhou and Eduard H Hovy. 2006. On the summarization of dynamically introduced information: Online discussions and blogs. In *AAAI Spring Symposium: Computational Approaches to Analyzing Weblogs*, page 237.

# What to Do with an Airport? Mining Arguments in the German Online Participation Project Tempelhofer Feld


Matthias Liebeck[1]    Katharina Esau[2]    Stefan Conrad[1]

[1] Institute of Computer Science, Heinrich Heine University Düsseldorf, Germany
{liebeck,conrad}@cs.uni-duesseldorf.de

[2] Institute of Social Sciences, Heinrich Heine University Düsseldorf, Germany
katharina.esau@uni-duesseldorf.de



## Abstract

This paper focuses on the automated extraction of argument components from user content in the German online participation project *Tempelhofer Feld*. We adapt existing argumentation models into a new model for decision-oriented online participation. Our model consists of three categories: major positions, claims, and premises. We create a new German corpus for argument mining by annotating our dataset with our model. Afterwards, we focus on the two classification tasks of identifying argumentative sentences and predicting argument components in sentences. We achieve macro-averaged $F_1$ measures of 69.77% and 68.5%, respectively.


## 1 Introduction

In the last few years in Germany, more and more cities are offering their citizens an internet-based way to participate in drafting ideas for urban planning or in local political issues. The administrations utilize websites to gather the opinions of their citizens and to include them in their decision making. For example, the German town Ludwigshafen has an elevated highway that is damaged and has to be demolished. Experts created four variants for a replacement and Ludwigshafen asked[1] its citizens to discuss them and to gather arguments for and against each variant, which were considered in the final political decision. Other cities such as Lörrach[2] tap into ideas of their citizens for a sustainable urban development and

cities such as Darmstadt[3] and Bonn[4] also gather proposals in participatory budgetings. In general, these platforms are accompanied by offline events to inform residents and to allow for discussions with citizens who cannot or do not want to participate online. In the following, the term *online participation* refers to the involvement of citizens in relevant political or administrative decisions.

A participation process usually revolves around a specific subject area that is determined by the organizer. In a city, the administration might aim to collect ideas to improve a certain situation (e.g. how it can beautify a park). Aside from politics, companies or institutions can use online participation for policy drafting, for example, in universities (Escher et al., 2016).

By contrast, there are also platforms whose purpose is to report defects (e.g., such as a road in need of repair or a street lamp that needs replacing), which we do not regard further because they are only used for reporting issues and do not encourage discussions between citizens. In the scope of this paper, we focus only on the subset of online participation projects that aim to gather options for actions or decisions (e.g., "*We should build an opera.*" or "*Should we close the golf course or the soccer field?*"). Given a large number of suggestions and comments from citizens, we want to automatically identify options for actions and decisions, extract reasons for or against them (e.g., "*This would improve the cultural offerings of our city.*") and detect users' stances (e.g., "*I totally agree!*").

As far as we know, it is rather rare in a municipal administration that such participation processes can be attended to by full-time employees, because they have other responsibilities as well. If

---

[1] https://www.ludwigshafen-diskutiert.de

[2] https://gestalten.loerrach.de

[3] https://da-bei.darmstadt.de/discuss/Buergerhaushalt2014

[4] https://bonn-macht-mit.de

144


*Proceedings of the 3rd Workshop on Argument Mining*, pages 144–153,
Berlin, Germany, August 7-12, 2016. ©2016 Association for Computational Linguistics

a process is well received by the general public, it might attract hundreds of suggestions and thousands of comments. The manual analysis of this data is time consuming and could take months. Due to budgetary reasons, it might also not be possible to outsource the analysis. Is it therefore possible that an online participation process was a success and a large amount of text contributions has been created, but not all content can be taken into account. To avoid that huge amounts of text content become unprocessable, it is necessary to utilize automated techniques to ensure a contemporary processing. To the best of our knowledge, the automated extraction of argument components in the form of mining decision options and pro and contra arguments from German online participation projects in a political context is a research gap that we try to fill.

The remainder of the paper is structured as follows: Section 2 describes related work in argument mining. Section 3 explains our data, our annotation model and the annotation process. Our argument mining approach is described in section 4. We conclude and outline future work in section 5.

## 2   Related Work

Argumentation mining is an evolving research topic that deals with the automatic extraction of argument components from text. Most research focuses on English text, but there is also research for German (Houy et al., 2013; Habernal et al., 2014; Eckle-Kohler et al., 2015) and for the Greek language (Goudas et al., 2014).

Previous research spans a variety of domains, such as the legal domain (Palau and Moens, 2009; Houy et al., 2013), eRulemaking (Park and Cardie, 2014), student essays (Stab and Gurevych, 2014b), news (Eckle-Kohler et al., 2015), and web content (Goudas et al., 2014; Habernal and Gurevych, 2015). Most of the papers share common tasks, such as separating text into argumentative and non-argumentative parts, classifying argumentative text into argument components and identifying relations between them. Currently, there is no argument model that most researchers agree upon. The chosen argument model often depends on the tasks and the application domain. However, most of the recent research agrees that the two argument components *claim* and *premise* are usually part of the chosen argument models.

Most of the researched domains offer a high text quality. For instance, in the news domain, the text content is usually editorially reviewed before publishing. Since our text content is from the web, it partially lacks proper spelling or grammar and is sometimes difficult to understand. Nevertheless, it is important to develop methods for processing web content because everyone's opinion should be considered, especially in a political context.

Another characteristic of our application domain is the presence of discourse between different users. In an online participation platform, users often write comments that refer to other people's suggestions or justifications. This differs from other domains, such as newspaper articles and student essays, where text content is rather monologic.

To evaluate the performance of an argumentation mining system, datasets are humanly annotated (which results in a gold standard), for instance with argument components. More recent publications (Stab and Gurevych, 2014a; Park and Cardie, 2014; Habernal et al., 2014; Eckle-Kohler et al., 2015) report inter-annotator agreement values of how well multiple annotators agree on their annotations. Due to different available inter-annotator agreement measures and different annotation lengths (tokens, sentences or freely assignable spans), there is currently no standardized single measure for inter-annotator agreement in the argumentation mining community. As a result, we report multiple values to ensure better comparability in the future. A detailed overview of annotation studies can be found in (Habernal and Gurevych, 2016).

There has been previous research on automatically mining people's opinions in the context of political decisions named as *policy making* (Florou et al., 2013) and as *eRulemaking* (Park and Cardie, 2014; Park et al., 2015a), which relate to our application domain *online participation*.

Florou et al. (2013) web crawled Greek web pages and social media. The authors aim to extract arguments that are in support or in opposition of public policies. As a first step, they automatically classify text segments as argumentative or non-argumentative, although they do not describe what they consider as argumentative and they do not refer to argumentation theory. In our approach, we use text content from a specific platform (instead of crawling multiple sources); we define three different argument components and their practical use; we relate to existing argumentation theory; and we further distinguish argument components in argumentative sentences.

Park and Cardie (2014) focus on English comments in the eRulemaking website *Regulation Room*. In their approach, they propose a model for eRulemaking that aims at verifiability by classifying propositions as *unverifiable*, *verifiable experiential*, and *verifiable non-experiential*. With their best feature set, they achieve a macro-averaged $F_1$ of 68.99% with a support vector machine. (Park et al., 2015b) discuss the results of conditional random fields as a machine learning approach. In our approach, we aim at identifying components and leave the issue of evaluability up to experts or to the wisdom of the crowd.

## 3 Data

This section discusses the data from the online participation project Tempelhofer Feld, presents our argumentation model, and describes our annotation process.

### 3.1 Background

The *Tempelhofer Feld*[5] project is an online participation project that focuses on the former airport *Berlin-Tempelhof (THF)* and its future use. Air traffic at the airport ceased in 2008. Until today, the 300 hectare area of the airport is mostly open space, which can be used for recreation.

In 2014, the *ThF-Gesetz (ThF law)* entered into force. It protects the large open space of the field, which is unique in Berlin, and limits structural changes, for example by prohibiting the construction of new buildings on the field.[6] The participation process was commissioned by Berlin's Senate Department for Urban Development and the Environment.

The project aims to collect ideas that improve the field for visitors while adhering to the ThF law, like settings up drinking fountains.

### 3.2 Discussion platform

The *Tempelhofer Feld* project uses the open-source policy drafting and discussion platform Adhocracy[7]. In Adhocracy, users can create proposals, which are text-based ideas or suggestions that contain a title and text content. To encourage discussions, users can comment on proposals and respond to previous comments, which results in a tree structured discussion per proposal. Adhocracy provides a voting system to upvote and downvote content. Therefore, users with limited time can follow *the wisdom of the crowd* by sorting proposals by their votes.

In the *Tempelhofer Feld* online participation process, users can register anonymously. Their voting behavior is public (it is possible to see which content was upvoted or downvoted by a specific user) and their text content is licensed under the Creative Commons License, which makes it attractive for academic use.

The official submission phase for proposals was from November 2014 until the end of March 2015. Afterwards, the proposals were condensed in offline events between May 2015 and July 2015. Until 2015-07-07, the users proposed 340 ideas and wrote 1389 comments. The comments vary in length. On average, they contain 3.56 sentences ($\sigma = 3.36$) and 58.7 tokens ($\sigma = 65.7$).

Each proposal is tagged with one out of seven categories. We excluded two categories because they mostly contain meta-discussions or serve as a "doesn't-fit-anywhere-else" category. This leaves the remaining five categories: *Bewirtschaftung* (cultivation), *Erinnerung* (memory), *Freizeit* (leisure), *Mitmachen* (participate), and *Natur* (nature).

The excluded categories are still important for the participation project, but, for the time being, we focus on proposals that contain ideas or suggestions that can potentially be realized. We do not judge whether it makes sense to realize the proposal or not. If someone wants to construct a roof over the whole area or wants to scatter blue pudding on the lawn, we leave it up to the other users to judge the proposal by voting and commenting on reasons for or against the realization, which we want to automatically extract.

We observed that the users occasionally did not use the platform correctly, by replying to a comment and referring to another previous comment.

It is worth mentioning that the participation process is not legally binding and that the most upvoted proposals do not become realized automatically. Although the participation process is encouraged by the politicians, the final decision which proposals will be realized is still up to them.

---

[5] https://tempelhofer-feld.berlin.de

[6] There are a few exceptions, like lighting, sanitary facilities, seating, and waste bins.

[7] https://github.com/liqd/adhocracy

### 3.3 Argumentation Model

We have a practical point of view on text content
in political online participation processes: To allow politicians to include the opinions expressed
in the platform into their decision making, we need
to extract three different components: (i) what do
people want to be built or decided upon, (ii) how
do people argue for and against these ideas, and
(iii) how many people in the discussion say that
they agree or disagree with them.

First, we tried to apply existing argumentation
models that are commonly used in argument mining to our dataset, namely Toulmin's model (Toulmin, 1958) and the claim-premise model (based
on (Freeman, 1991)). We quickly realized that attacks on logical conclusions are rather rare, that
users frequently express their wishes and participate by providing reasons for and against other
suggestions, and that we have to consider this behavior in the choice of an argumentation model.

Toulmin differentiates between six argument
components: *claim, ground / data, warrant, backing, qualifier* and *rebuttal*. The model revolves
around the claim, the statement of the argument
which has to be proven or, in Toulmin's words,
*"whose merits we are seeking to establish"* (Toulmin, 2003, p. 90). Grounds are the data that support the claim and serve *"as a foundation for the
claim"* (Toulmin, 2003, p. 90). A ground is connected to the claim by a warrant, which justifies
why the ground supports the claim. A warrant
can be supported by a backing which establishes
*"authority"* (Toulmin, 2003, p. 96) as to why the
warrant is to be accepted. A qualifier specifies the
degree of certainty or the *"degree of force"* (Toulmin, 2003, p. 93) of the claim, in respect of the
ground. Rebuttals are conditions which *"might
be capable of defeating"* (Toulmin, 2003, p. 94)
the claim. With Toulmin's model, we come to the
same conclusion as Habernal et al. (2014) that it
is difficult to apply the model to online-generated
discussions, especially when the users argue on a
level where most of Toulmin's categories can only
be applied very rarely.

The commonly used claim-premise model
(Palau and Moens, 2009; Peldszus and Stede,
2013; Stab and Gurevych, 2014a; Eckle-Kohler et
al., 2015) consists of the two components claim
and premise. A *claim "is the central component of
an argument"* (Stab and Gurevych, 2014a), whose
merit is to be established. *Premises* are reasons

that either support or attack a claim. According
to Stab and Gurevych (2014a), a claim *"should
not be accepted by readers without additional support."* Palau and Moens (2009) describe a claim as
*"an idea which is either true or false"* and Stab
and Gurevych (2014a) as a *"controversial statement that is either true or false."*

We share the opinion of Habernal et al. (2014)
that there is no one-size-fits-all argumentation theory for web data and follow the recommendation
that the argumentation model should be chosen
for the task at hand. In our participation project,
we are primarily interested in mining suggestions.
This differs from the common focus on mining
claims as the central component, because the definition of a claim stated above does not apply to our
dataset: suggestions cannot be classified as true or
false and they can be accepted without additional
support, although justifications are commonly provided by the users.

We adapted the claim-premise family and its
modification for persuasive essays in Stab and
Gurevych (2014a) to a three-part model for modeling arguments in online participation processes:
(i) major positions, (ii) claims, and (iii) premises

**Major positions** are options for actions or decisions that occur in the discussion (e.g., *"We should
build a playground with a sandbox."* or *"The
opening hours of the museum must be at least two
hours longer."*). They are most often someone's
vision of something new or of a policy change.
If another user suggests a modified version by
changing some details, the new suggestion is a
new major position (e.g. *"We should build a playground with swings."*). In our practical view, major positions are unique suggestions from citizens
that politicians can decide on.

A **claim** is a pro or contra stance towards a major position (e.g. *"Yes, we should definitely do
that!"*). In our model, claims are text passages
in which users express their personal positionings
(e.g., *"I dislike your suggestion."*). For a politi-
cian, the text content of a claim in our definition does not serve as a basis for decision making
because claims do not contain justifications upon
which decisions can be backed up. The purpose
behind mining these claims is a conversion into
two numbers that indicates how many citizens are
for or against a suggestion.

The term **premise** is defined as a reason that
attacks or supports a major position, a claim or

another premise. Premises are used to make an argumentation comprehensible for others, by reasoning why a suggestion or a decision should be realized or why it should be avoided (e.g. *"This would allow us to save money."*). We use the term premise in the same way as the claim-premise model and as Toulmin with *grounds*.

We do not evaluate if a reason is valid. We only determine the user's intent: If an annotator perceives that a user is providing a reason, we annotate it as such. Otherwise, we would have to evaluate each statement on a semantic level. For example, if a user argues that a suggestion violates a building law, the annotators would need to check this statement. A verification of all reasons for correctness would require too much expertise from annotators or a very large knowledge database. In our application domain, we leave the evaluation up to human experts who advise politicians.

Our argumentation model is illustrated in Figure 1.

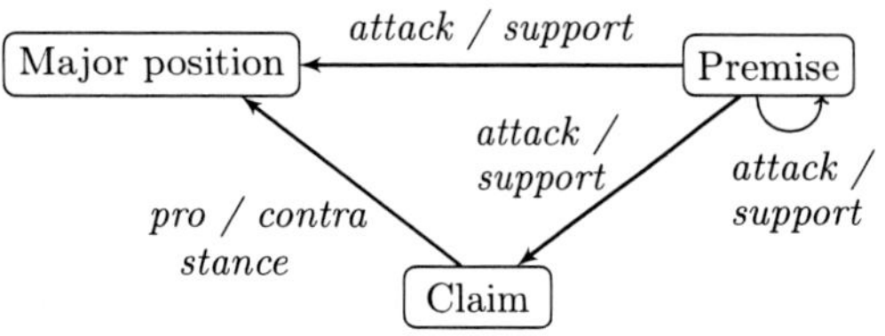


Figure 1: Our argumentation model for political online participation

If a sentence contains only one argument component, we annotate the whole sentence. If there is more than one argument component in a sentence, we annotate the different components separately, like in the following example: [*claim*: We don't need a new playground] [*premise*: because we already have one.]

Depending on the writing style of a user, a thought or idea might be expressed in more than one sentence. In such a case, we combine all successive sentences of the same thought into a group: [*major position*: The city should build a public bath. It should contain a 50 meter pool and be flooded with daylight.] The boundaries of these groups are based on the content and, therefore, are subjective. Thus, in our evaluation, we first focus on a sentence-based classification of argument components and consider the identification of the group boundaries as future work. Freeman (1991,

p. 106) uses the term *linked* for premises that consist of multiple statements, each of which does not separately constitute a support, but together produce *"a relevant reason"*.

Major positions are very similar to the concept of *policy claims* which *"advocate a course of action"* and are about *"deciding what to do"* (Schiappa and Nordin, 2013, p. 101).

## 3.4 Annotation

We developed annotation guidelines and refined them over the course of multiple iterations. Our dataset was annotated by three annotators of which two are authors of this publication. The third annotator was instructed after the annotation guidelines were developed.

OpenNLP[8] was used to split each proposal and comment into individual sentences. Errors were manually corrected. We also removed embedded images that occur sporadically because we focus on text content. Afterwards, we used the *brat rapid annotation tool* (Stenetorp et al., 2012) for the annotation of the dataset. The text content also contains non-argumentative sentences which we did not annotate. These include salutations, valedictions, meta-discussions (for instance, comments about the participation process), and comprehension questions.

In our annotation process, we further divide claims into *pro claims* and *contra claims* by classifying the most dominant positioning, based on the content and the wording in order to report a simplified "level of agreement / disagreement" in preparation for a future user behavior study. More observations of our annotation process are detailed in section 6.

### 3.4.1 Inter-Annotator Agreement

Before annotating the data set, we took a subset of 8 proposals with 74 comments to measure the inter-annotator-agreement, consisting of 261 sentences and 4.1k tokens. The subset was randomly drawn from 67 proposals that have between 5 and 40 comments.

As in recent research (Stab and Gurevych, 2014a; Park and Cardie, 2014; Habernal et al., 2014; Eckle-Kohler et al., 2015), we also report inter-annotator agreement (IAA) values to quantify the consensus of our annotators and to make our annotation study more comparable. As there is

---

[8]https://opennlp.apache.org

| | $A_{o,t}$ | $\kappa_t$ | $\alpha_u$ |
|---|---|---|---|
| all | 76.4 | 62.6 | 78.0 |
| major positions | 89.3 | 71.9 | 79.8 |
| claims pro | 96.3 | 66.1 | 59.0 |
| claims contra | 95.6 | 52.3 | 57.2 |
| premises | 80.9 | 61.5 | 80.1 |
| AU / non-AU | 90.7 | 49.1 | 92.4 |

Table 1: Inter-annotator agreement scores in percentages: $A_{o,t}$ token-based observed agreement, $\kappa_t$ token-based Fleiss' kappa, and $\alpha_u$ Krippendorff's unitized alpha

currently no standardized single measure in the argumentation mining community, we report multiple IAA values. We use *DKPro Agreement* (Meyer et al., 2014) to report our inter-annotator agreement values. Table 1 summarizes our IAA values for three scenarios: (i) joint measures over all categories, (ii) category-specific values, and (iii) argumentative vs. non-argumentative units.

Since we asked the annotators to assign *labels* to *freely assignable spans*, we use *Krippendorff's unitized alpha* $\alpha_u$ (Krippendorff, 2004). We have to keep in mind that several comments only contain one sentence and are, therefore, much easier to annotate. An average over IAA values from all comments would be biased. Hence, we follow the proposed approach in (Habernal and Gurevych, 2016) to concatenate all text content into a single document and measure a single Krippendorff's $\alpha_u$ value instead of averaging $\alpha_u$ for each document.

We also report the token-based *observed agreement* $A_{o,t}$ and the token-based *Fleiss' kappa* $\kappa_t$ (Fleiss, 1971). The token-based distribution of the annotions of all three annotators is as follows: 1278 non-argumentative tokens and 11220 argumentative tokens (3214 major positions, 730 claims pro, 583 claims contra, 6693 premises)

We do not report a sentence-based inter-annotator agreement because more than one annotation per sentence is possible (e.g., a claim followed by a premise in a subordinate clause) and the IAA measures are for single-label annotation only.

The measures of $\alpha_u = 0.924$ for argumentative versus non-argumentative spans and the joint measure for all categories of $\alpha_u = 0.78$ indicate a reliable agreement between our three annotators. Therefore, we should be able to provide good annotations for automated classification tasks.

### 3.4.2 Corpus

For our corpus, we randomly drew 72 proposals that each contain at least one major position. These proposals were commented with 575 comments. In total, our annotated dataset consists of 2433 sentences and 40177 tokens. We annotated 2170 argumentative spans. They comprise 548 major positions, 378 claims (282 pro claims and 96 contra claims), and 1244 premises. Our annotated corpus consists of 4646 (11.6%) non-argumentative and 35531 (88.4%) argumentative tokens. This indicates that the text content is highly argumentative. Exactly 88 (3.6%) of the sentences were annotated with more than one argument component.

We plan to release our dataset along with our annotations under an open-source license to allow reproducibility.

## 4 Evaluation

This section discusses our initial approach to automatically identify argumentative sentences and to classify argument components.

### 4.1 Preprocessing

First, we tokenize all sentences in our dataset with *OpenNLP* and use *Mate Tools* (Björkelund et al., 2010) for POS-tagging and dependency parsing.

### 4.2 Features

For our classification problems, we evaluate different features and their combinations. They can be divided into three groups: (i) n-grams, (ii) grammatical distributions, and (iii) structural features. N-grams are an obvious choice to capture the text content because several words are used repeatedly in different argument components, like *"agree"* or *"disagree"* in the case of claims. We use unigrams and bigrams as binary features.

**Grammatical Distributions** Based on our observations, we identified that users use different tenses and sentences structures for our three categories. For instance, claims are often stated in the present tence (e.g., *"I agree!"*). Therefore, we use an $L_2$-normalized POS-Tag distribution of the STTS tags (Schiller et al., 1999) and an $L_2$-normalized distribution of the dependencies in the TIGER annotation scheme (Albert et al., 2003).

**Structural Features** We also capture multiple structural features: token count, percent-

| Feature Set | AU / non-AU | | | Argument Components | | |
|---|---|---|---|---|---|---|
| | SVM | RF | k-NN | SVM | RF | k-NN |
| Unigram | 65.99 | 68.13 | 61.00 | 64.40 | 59.41 | 40.30 |
| Unigram, lowercased | 66.69 | 64.53 | 62.26 | 65.32 | 53.35 | 38.25 |
| Bigram | 41.79 | 50.48 | 16.25 | 46.62 | 50.42 | 11.51 |
| Grammatical | 55.88 | 52.24 | 48.52 | 59.54 | 47.89 | 46.81 |
| Unigram + Grammatical | **69.77** | 58.39 | 64.87 | **68.50** | 57.13 | 35.90 |
| Unigram + Grammatical + Structural | 67.50 | 61.14 | 54.07 | 65.99 | 59.46 | 47.27 |

Table 2: Macro-averaged $F_1$ scores for the two classification problems: (i) classifying sentences as argumentative and non-argumentative, (ii) classifying sentences as major positions, claims, and premises.

age of comma tokens in the sentence, percentage of dot tokens in the sentence, and the last token of a sentence as an one-hot encoding ('.', '!', '?', 'OTHER'). Furthermore, we use the index of the sentence since we have noticed that users often start their comment with a pro or contra claim. Moreover, we use the number of links in a sentence as a feature.

### 4.3 Results

We report results for two classification problems. Subtask A is the classification of sentences as argumentative or non-argumentative and in subtask B we automatically classify argument components in sentences with exactly one annotated argument component. Macro-averaged $F_1$ was chosen as evaluation metric. For each subtask, we randomly split the respective annotated sentences into a 80% training set and 20% test set.

Different feature combinations were evaluated with three classifiers: Support vector machine (SVM) with an RBF kernel, random forest (RF), and k-nearest neighbor (k-NN). We use *scikit-learn* (Pedregosa et al., 2011) as machine learning library. The required parameters for our classifiers (SVM: penalty term $C$ and $\gamma$ for the kernel function; random forest: number of trees, maximal depth of the trees, and multiple parameters regarding splits; k-NN: number of neighbors $k$ and weight functions) were estimated by a grid search on a 10-fold cross-validation on the training set.

The results of both subtasks are listed in Table 2. k-NN almost always achieved the worst results in comparison with the two classifiers. The results of bigrams as features are worse than the results of unigrams. Lowercasing words has different effects, depending on the classifier: The results of unigrams improve for SVMs but decline for random forests and k-NN. The addition of the struc-

tural features also had different effects on the classifiers, depending on the subtask. Additionally, we experimented with lemmatized words by Mate Tools (combined with *IWNLP* (Liebeck and Conrad, 2015)) but our results were slightly lower. In our future work, we will work on better ways to incorporate lemmatization into our classification tasks.

#### 4.3.1 Subtask A

For identifying argumentative sentences, the best result of 69.77% was achieved by a support vector machine with unigrams and grammatical features. It is interesting to see that *unigrams* work better with the random forest classifier than with an SVM, but, with the additional *grammatical* features, the SVM outperforms the random forest. The training set for subtask A contains 1667 argumentative and 280 non-argumentative sentences, whereas the test set comprises 411 argumentative and 75 non-argumentative sentences.

#### 4.3.2 Subtask B

For the classification of argument components, we do not further differentiate between pro and contra claims because both of them occur rarer than major positions and premises. Therefore, we have grouped pro and contra claims. The training set for subtask B contains 1592 sentences (951 premises, 399 major positions, and 242 claims), whereas the test set comprises 398 sentences (219 premises, 110 major positions, and 69 claims).

The best result for subtask B with a macro-averaged $F_1$ score of 68.5% was again achieved by a support vector machine as classifier with unigrams and grammatical features. In subtask B, the gap between the results of the k-NN classifier and the results of the two classifiers is much larger than in subtask A.

<table>
<tr><td></td><td></td><td colspan="4" align="center">Predicted</td></tr>
<tr><td></td><td></td><td>MP</td><td>C</td><td>P</td><td>∑</td></tr>
<tr><td rowspan="4">Actual</td><td>MP</td><td>63</td><td>4</td><td>43</td><td>110</td></tr>
<tr><td>C</td><td>9</td><td>48</td><td>12</td><td>69</td></tr>
<tr><td>P</td><td>27</td><td>20</td><td>172</td><td>219</td></tr>
<tr><td>∑</td><td>99</td><td>72</td><td>227</td><td>398</td></tr>
</table>

Table 3: Confusion matrix for our best result of identifying argument components with a support vector machine and *"unigram + grammatical"* as features

In order to better understand our results, we report the confusion matrix for the best classifier in Table 3. The confusion matrix shows that the classification of premises works well and that major positions are often misclassified as premises. In our future work, we will try to find better semantic features to differentiate major positions from premises.

We initially tried to solve subtask B as a four class problem but our features do not allow for a good distinction between pro and contra claims with our small training size for claims yet. In our future work, we will treat their distinction as a further classification task and will integrate more polarity features.

## 5 Conclusion and Future Work

In this paper we have presented a new corpus for German argumentation mining and a modified argumentation scheme for online participation. We described the background of our data set, our annotation process, and our automated classification approach for the two classification tasks of identifying argumentative sentences and identifying argument components. We evaluated different feature combinations and multiple classifiers. Our initial results for argument mining in the field of German online participation are promising. The best results of 69.77% in subtask A and 68.5% in subtask B were both achieved by a support vector machine with unigrams and grammatical features.

While working with our dataset, we realized that citizens argue not only with rational reasons and that they are not always objective. They often express their positive and negative emotions and use humor to convince other participants or just to avoid conflicts. This makes an automatic approach more difficult.

In our future work, we want to experiment with additional features to further increase our classification results. We will identify specific emotions in the argumentation among citizens. We will try to find humor as a predictor for enjoyment and sociability.

So far, we have only worked on a sentence level. We would like to automatically detect tokens that form a group, based on the content. For this, we could use the token-based BIO scheme used in Goudas et al. (2014) and Habernal and Gurevych (2016), which divides tokens into beginning (B), inner (I), and other (O) tokens of an argument component. This would also allow us to find more than one argument component in a sentence.

Furthermore, we will work on the distinction of claims into pro and contra claims. Additionally, we aim to identify more freely available corpora for online participation to which we can apply our model for a comparative study.

## 6 Observations

**Background knowledge** Some proposals and comments require background knowledge in order to fully comprehend them. For an automated approach, this is much more difficult, especially if existing buildings on the field or city districts are referred to by name.

**Edge annotation** We chose not to annotate outgoing edges in our corpus. In a single label approach, ambiguity might occur because a premise might support one claim and attack another one. We tried an approach with multiple outgoing edges but it became very difficult to evaluate every possible edge in discussions with more than 30 comments and multiple major positions. In order to avoid an incomplete edge annotation, we completely omitted the annotation of edges for the time being.

**Contextual differentiation** During the annotation, we noticed some situations where it became difficult to decide which argument component is the best fit. For instance, *"Vertical vegetable gardens are an enrichment for our perception."* contains a slight positioning, but in the context of the comment, the sentence was used as a reason and, therefore, annotated as a premise.

## Acknowledgments

This work was funded by the PhD program *Online Participation*, supported by the North Rhine-

Westphalian funding scheme *Fortschrittskollegs*. The authors want to thank the anonymous reviewers for their suggestions and comments.

# References

Stefanie Albert, Jan Anderssen, Regine Bader, Stephanie Becker, Tobias Bracht, Sabine Brants, Thorsten Brants, Vera Demberg, Stefanie Dipper, Peter Eisenberg, Silvia Hansen, Hagen Hirschmann, Juliane Janitzek, Carolin Kirstein, Robert Langner, Lukas Michelbacher, Oliver Plaehn, Cordula Preis, Marcus Pussel, Marco Rower, Bettina Schrader, Anne Schwartz, Smith George, and Hans Uszkoreit. 2003. TIGER Annotationsschema. Technical report, Universität Potsdam, Universität Saarbrücken, Universität Stuttgart.

Anders Björkelund, Bernd Bohnet, Love Hafdell, and Pierre Nugues. 2010. A High-Performance Syntactic and Semantic Dependency Parser. In *Proceedings of the 23rd International Conference on Computational Linguistics: Demonstrations*, COLING '10, pages 33–36. Association for Computational Linguistics.

Judith Eckle-Kohler, Roland Kluge, and Iryna Gurevych. 2015. On the Role of Discourse Markers for Discriminating Claims and Premises in Argumentative Discourse. In *Proceedings of the 2015 Conference on Empirical Methods in Natural Language Processing, EMNLP 2015*, pages 2236–2242.

Tobias Escher, Dennis Friess, Katharina Esau, Jost Sieweke, Ulf Tranow, Simon Dischner, Philipp Hagemeister, and Martin Mauve. 2016. Online Deliberation in Academia: Evaluating the Quality and Legitimacy of Co-Operatively Developed University Regulations. *Policy & Internet*, (in press).

Joseph L. Fleiss. 1971. Measuring Nominal Scale Agreement Among Many Raters. *Psychological Bulletin*, 76(5):378 – 382.

Eirini Florou, Stasinos Konstantopoulos, Antonis Koukourikos, and Pythagoras Karampiperis. 2013. Argument extraction for supporting public policy formulation. In *Proceedings of the 7th Workshop on Language Technology for Cultural Heritage, Social Sciences, and Humanities*, pages 49–54. Association for Computational Linguistics.

James Freeman. 1991. *Dialectics and the Macrostructure of Arguments: A Theory of Argument Structure*, volume 10 of *Pragmatics and Discourse Analysis Series*. de Gruyter.

Theodosios Goudas, Christos Louizos, Georgios Petasis, and Vangelis Karkaletsis. 2014. Argument Extraction from News, Blogs, and Social Media. In *Artificial Intelligence: Methods and Applications*, pages 287–299.

Ivan Habernal and Iryna Gurevych. 2015. Exploiting Debate Portals for Semi-supervised Argumentation Mining in User-Generated Web Discourse. In *Proceedings of the 2015 Conference on Empirical Methods in Natural Language Processing (EMNLP)*, pages 2127–2137. Association for Computational Linguistics.

Ivan Habernal and Iryna Gurevych. 2016. Argumentation Mining in User-Generated Web Discourse. *Computational Linguistics*, (in press).

Ivan Habernal, Judith Eckle-Kohler, and Iryna Gurevych. 2014. Argumentation Mining on the Web from Information Seeking Perspective. In *Proceedings of the Workshop on Frontiers and Connections between Argumentation Theory and Natural Language Processing*, pages 26–39. CEUR-WS.

Constantin Houy, Tim Niesen, Peter Fettke, and Peter Loos. 2013. Towards Automated Identification and Analysis of Argumentation Structures in the Decision Corpus of the German Federal Constitutional Court. In *7th IEEE International Conference on Digital Ecosystems and Technologies (IEEE DEST)*. IEEE Computer Society.

Klaus Krippendorff. 2004. *Content Analysis: An Introduction to Its Methodology*. Sage Publications, second edition.

Matthias Liebeck and Stefan Conrad. 2015. IWNLP: Inverse Wiktionary for Natural Language Processing. In *Proceedings of the 53rd Annual Meeting of the Association for Computational Linguistics and the 7th International Joint Conference on Natural Language Processing (Volume 2: Short Papers)*, pages 414–418. Association for Computational Linguistics.

Christian Meyer, Margot Mieskes, Christian Stab, and Iryna Gurevych. 2014. DKPro Agreement: An Open-Source Java Library for Measuring Inter-Rater Agreement. In *Proceedings of COLING 2014, the 25th International Conference on Computational Linguistics: System Demonstrations*, pages 105–109.

Raquel Palau and Marie-Francine Moens. 2009. Argumentation Mining: The Detection, Classification and Structure of Arguments in Text. In *Proceedings of the 12th International Conference on Artificial Intelligence and Law, ICAIL '09*, pages 98–107. ACM.

Joonsuk Park and Claire Cardie. 2014. Identifying Appropriate Support for Propositions in Online User Comments. In *Proceedings of the First Workshop on Argumentation Mining*, pages 29–38. Association for Computational Linguistics.

Joonsuk Park, Cheryl Blake, and Claire Cardie. 2015a. Toward Machine-assisted Participation in eRulemaking: An Argumentation Model of Evaluability. In *Proceedings of the 15th International Conference on Artificial Intelligence and Law*, ICAIL '15, pages 206–210. ACM.

Joonsuk Park, Arzoo Katiyar, and Bishan Yang. 2015b. Conditional Random Fields for Identifying Appropriate Types of Support for Propositions in Online User Comments. In *Proceedings of the 2nd Workshop on Argumentation Mining*, pages 39–44. Association for Computational Linguistics.

Fabian Pedregosa, Gaël Varoquaux, Alexandre Gramfort, Vincent Michel, Bertrand Thirion, Olivier Grisel, Mathieu Blondel, Peter Prettenhofer, Ron Weiss, Vincent Dubourg, Jake Vanderplas, Alexandre Passos, David Cournapeau, Matthieu Brucher, Matthieu Perrot, and Édouard Duchesnay. 2011. Scikit-learn: Machine Learning in Python. *Journal of Machine Learning Research*, 12:2825–2830.

Andreas Peldszus and Manfred Stede. 2013. Ranking the annotators: An agreement study on argumentation structure. In *Proceedings of the 7th Linguistic Annotation Workshop and Interoperability with Discourse*, pages 196–204. Association for Computational Linguistics.

Edward Schiappa and John Nordin. 2013. *Argumentation: Keeping Faith with Reason*. Pearson Education.

Anne Schiller, Simone Teufel, Christine Stöckert, and Christine Thielen. 1999. Guidelines für das Tagging deutscher Textcorpora mit STTS (kleines und großes Tagset). Technical report, Universität Stuttgart, Universität Tübingen.

Christian Stab and Iryna Gurevych. 2014a. Annotating Argument Components and Relations in Persuasive Essays. In *Proceedings of the 25th International Conference on Computational Linguistics (COLING 2014)*, pages 1501–1510.

Christian Stab and Iryna Gurevych. 2014b. Identifying Argumentative Discourse Structures in Persuasive Essays. In *Proceedings of the 2014 Conference on Empirical Methods in Natural Language Processing (EMNLP 2014)*, pages 46–56.

Pontus Stenetorp, Sampo Pyysalo, Goran Topić, Tomoko Ohta, Sophia Ananiadou, and Jun'ichi Tsujii. 2012. BRAT: a Web-based Tool for NLP-Assisted Text Annotation. In *Proceedings of the Demonstrations at the 13th Conference of the European Chapter of the Association for Computational Linguistics*, EACL '12, pages 102–107. Association for Computational Linguistics.

Stephen Toulmin. 1958. *The Uses of Argument*. Cambridge University Press.

Stephen Toulmin. 2003. *The Uses of Argument, Updated Edition*. Cambridge University Press.

# Unshared task: (Dis)agreement in online debates


**Maria Skeppstedt**[1,2] **Magnus Sahlgren**[1] **Carita Paradis**[3] **Andreas Kerren**[2]
[1]Gavagai AB, Stockholm, Sweden
{maria, mange}@gavagai.se
[2]Computer Science Department, Linnaeus University, Växjö, Sweden
andreas.kerren@lnu.se
[3]Centre for Languages and Literature, Lund University, Lund, Sweden
carita.paradis@englund.lu.se


## Abstract


Topic-independent expressions for conveying agreement and disagreement were annotated in a corpus of web forum debates, in order to evaluate a classifier trained to detect these two categories. Among the 175 expressions annotated in the evaluation set, 163 were unique, which shows that there is large variation in expressions used. This variation might be one of the reasons why the task of automatically detecting the categories was difficult. F-scores of 0.44 and 0.37 were achieved by a classifier trained on 2,000 debate sentences for detecting sentence-level agreement and disagreement.


## 1 Introduction

Argumentation mining involves the task of automatically extracting an author's argumentation for taking a specific stance. This includes, e.g., to extract premises and conclusion, or the relationship between arguments, such as argument and counter-argument (Green et al., 2014; Habernal and Gurevych, 2015). In a corpus containing dialog, e.g., different types of web fora or discussion pages, the argumentation often involves a reaction to arguments given by previous authors in the discussion thread. The author might, for instance, give a counter-argument to an argument appearing earlier in the thread, or an argument supporting the stance of a previous author. A sub-task of detecting the argument structure of a dialogic corpus is, therefore, to detect when the author conveys agreement or disagreement with other authors.

The aim of this study was to investigate this sub-task, i.e., to automatically detect posts in a dialogic corpus that contain agreement or disagreement.

## 2 Previous research

Dis/agreement has been the focus of conversational analysis (Mori, 1999), and is linked to Speech Act Theory (Searle, 1976). The categories have been annotated and detected in transcribed speech, e.g., in meeting discussions (Hillard et al., 2003; Galley et al., 2004; Hahn et al., 2006), congressional floor-debates (Thomas et al., 2006), and broadcast conversations (Germesin and Wilson, 2009).

Online discussions in form of Wikipedia Talk have been annotated for *dis/agreement* (Andreas et al., 2012), for *positive/negative* attitude towards other contributors (Ferschke, 2014), and for subclasses of *positive/negative* alignment, e.g. explicit agreement/disagreement, praise/thanking, and critic/insult (Bender et al., 2011).

For online debate fora, there is a corpus of posts with a scalar judgment for their level of *dis/agreement* with a previous post (Walker et al., 2012). Misra et al. (2013) used frequently occurring uni/bi/trigrams from the non-neutral posts in this corpus for creating a lexicon of topic-independent expressions for *dis/agreement*. This lexicon was then used for selecting features for training a topic-independent classifier. The approach resulted in an accuracy of 0.66 (an improvement of 0.6 points compared to standard feature selection) for distinguishing the classes *agreement/disagreement*, when evaluating the classifier on debate topics not included in the training data.

Despite this usefulness of the lexicon for creating a topic-independent dis/agreement classifier, there are, to the best of our knowledge, no debate forum corpora annotated with the focus of topic-independent expressions of dis/agreement. Here, the first step towards creating such a resource was, therefore, taken.




*Proceedings of the 3rd Workshop on Argument Mining*, pages 154–159,
Berlin, Germany, August 7-12, 2016. ©2016 Association for Computational Linguistics

## 3  Method

The study was conducted on discussions from a debate forum. The data originates from createde-bate.com, which is a debate forum that hosts debates on a variety of topics. The data used as evaluation set was provided for task *Variant A* in the 3rd Workshop on Argument Mining, and consists of 27 manually collected discussion threads.[1] The debates start with a question, e.g., "Should the age for drinking be lowered?", which users then debate, either by posting an independent post, or by supporting/disputing/clarifying a previous post.

The same division into topic-specific/topic-independent means for conveying dis/agreement as previously used by Misra et al. (2013) was adopted. Instead of using it for creating a lexical resource, it was, however, used as a guideline for annotation. A preliminary analysis of posts tagged as *support/dispute* in 8 discussion threads showed that typical topic-specific strategies for conveying dis/agreement were reformulations/expansions/elaborations of what was stated in a previous post. A new argument for or against the initial debate question could, however, also be given, without references to the content of the previous post. Topic-independent means for conveying dis/agreement were typically either explicit statements such as "I (dis)agree", "NO way!", or critical follow-up questions, "A: Alcohol should be forbidden. B: *Should it then* also be illegal with cell phones?". All means of conveying dis/agreement independent of debate topic were, however, included in the task, e.g., as exemplified by Bender et al. (2011), topic-independent explicit dis/agreement, (sarcastic) praise/thanking, positive reference, doubt, criticism/insult, dismissing.

The preliminary analysis also showed that the *support/dispute* tagging provided in the unshared task data would not suffice for distinguishing agreement from disagreement, as there were posts tagged as *support* that consisted mainly of expressions of disagreement.

### 3.1  Annotation of task data (evaluation set)

All instances in which agreement or disagreement were conveyed using topic-independent expressions were annotated in the unshared task data set. The annotation was performed by marking a relevant scope of text, in the form of the longest pos-

---



Figure 1: Two of the chunks in the unshared task data that were annotated as dis/agreement.

sible chunk that was still a topic-independent expression conveying dis/agreement. For instance, in Figure 1, "fighting a war" is specific to the topic of the debate, whereas the annotated chunk, "is a good thing?", is topic-independent and could be used for expressing disagreement in other cases.

The annotation was performed by one annotator, with Brat as the annotation tool (Stenetorp et al., 2012).

### 3.2  Annotation/classification of training set

Identifying and annotating relevant chunks in running text is a time-consuming task, which also requires a large amount of attention from the annotator. Classifications of individual sentences is, however, an easier task, and to classify a limited corpus of 2,000 sentences is feasible in a relatively short amount of time. For creating a larger (but still relatively limited) training set of discussion sentences conveying dis/agreement, the chunk annotation task was reformulated as a text classification task, and individual sentences were manually classified according to the categories *agreement*, *disagreement* or *neutral*. As for the previous annotation set-up, sentences containing topic-independent expressions for conveying the two categories of interest were classified as containing *agreement* or *disagreement*.

The 2,300 most popular threads, i.e., those containing the largest number of posts, were downloaded from the createdebate.com website (excluding threads present in the evaluation data). The posts are provided with author tagging that states what posts are *disputing* or *clarifying* previous posts. Among posts for which no such tag was attached (the *other* posts), and among posts tagged as *disputing* a previous post, 2,000 first-sentences were randomly selected for manual classification. Only first-sentences of posts were included to make it possible to classify each individual sentence without context, since it is likely that their agreement/disagreement classification is less dependent on the context of the post. For sentence segmentation, the standard functionality in NLTK (Bird, 2002) was used.

---

[1]https://github.com/UKPLab/argmin2016-unshared-task.

### 3.3 Training a classifier

As the final step, linear support vector machines were trained to perform the binary text classification tasks of detecting sentences containing *agreement* and *disagreement*. The LinearSVC class included in Scikit learn (Pedregosa et al., 2011) was trained with uni/bigrams/trig-rams as features, with the requirement of a uni/bigram/trigram to having occurred at least twice in the training data to be included. The $n$ best features were selected by the built-in $\chi^2$-based feature selection, and suitable values of $n$ and the support vector machine penalty parameter $C$ were determined by 10-fold cross-validation. The text was not transformed into lower-case, as the use of case is one possible way of expressing or emphasising dis/agreement, e.g., 'NO way!'. The settings that achieved the best results were used for training a model on the entire training data set, which was then evaluated on the data provided for the unshared task. The annotations in the unshared task data were transformed into an evaluation set by transforming the text chunk annotations into sentence-level classifications of whether a sentence contained *agreement* or *disagreement*.

Two versions of the classifiers were trained, one in which neutral sentences were included and one with the same set-up as used by Misra et al. (2013), i.e., to train a classifier to distinguish *agreement* from *disagreement* and thereby not including neutral sentences.

## 4   Results and discussion

| # of chunks annotated in total: 175 (163 unique) | |
|---|---|
| # *agreement:* 43 | # *disagreement:* 132 |

Table 1: Statistics of unshared task annotated data.

Statistics of the annotated data (Tables 1, 2) shows that expressions for disagreement are more frequently occurring than expressions for agreement. This is most likely explained by the typical style used in debate fora, in which debating often is conducted by disputing other debaters, but it could also be due to a more frequent use of topic-independent expressions for this category.

A large variation in the expressions used was observed during annotation. This observation is supported by the data, as 163 unique expressions

| | Disputed | Other | Total |
|---|---|---|---|
| # *agreement* | 36 | 73 | 109 |
| # *disagreement* | 420 | 92 | 512 |
| # *sentences in total* | 1,000 | 1,000 | 2,000 |

Table 2: The training data statistics shows the number of sentences annotated as *agreement* and *disagreement*, extracted from posts tagged as *disputing* a previous post or as *other*. *# sentences in total* is the total number of annotated sentences. The corpus also included 57 sentences, for which it could not be determined without context whether disagreement or agreement was expressed. These were classified as *neutral*. The 25 sentences that contained both agreement and disagreement were classified as belonging to the *agreement* category.

were annotated. This shows that the approach used by Misra et al. (2013), i.e., to classify frequently occurring n-grams, is not sufficient for creating a high-coverage lexicon of expressions, and it also indicates that automatic detection of these expressions might be a difficult task.

The most important features used by the classifiers (Figure 2) are topic-independent, which indicates that the aim to create topic-independent classifiers was reached. Among less important features, there were, however, also topic-specific expressions, which shows that the trained classifiers were not entirely topic-independent.

The classifier results are shown in Table 3. For the training set, an F-score of around 0.47 was obtained for *agreement* and around 0.55 for *disagreement*. Results were, however, substantially lower for *disagreement* on the evaluation set. This decrease in results could be explained by overfitting to the training data, and by uncertainty of the results due to the small evaluation set. There might, however, also be a difference between what is considered as an expression of disagreement when it occurs in the first sentence of a post (which was the case for the training data) and when it occurs somewhere else in the text (which was the case for many sentences in the evaluation data).

To distinguish agreement from disagreement was an easier task, resulting in F-scores of 0.60 for *agreement* and 0.92 for *disagreement* on the training set and F-scores of 0.55 and 0.81, respectively on the evaluation set. The recall for *agreement* was, however, low also for this task, proba-

? admit agree-that agree-with are-right as-well be-it but-in but-it But-no but-there but-with clarified correct decent **don-agree** doubt easier figured good-points guess-you Hear hear however idea-as is-correct it-is-the lol love misunderstood my-argument myself nice of-an ok okay on-here people-can point points puts right round said supported **they-would** this-idea to-keep True true-that upvote ur Well what-you-said win yeah yes Yes your-point Yup

?? Actually **agree** all-and anything argument arguments-you **bad** because-if bother bullshit But **choice** claim disagree disputing don-believe-in Dude evidence flawed foolish fuck generalization half how ignorant Ignoring in-hell Is-it is-so Is-that it-does **lead** like-to-see lying **many** No NO no-but Nope nothing obviously of-evidence on-it once peacefully permission-to point pointless proof **should-be** So sorry stop stupid think-so think-that-you understand Well-thats What what what-is which-should Why **yes** You you-have-the you-know you-saying yourself

Figure 2: The most important features for detecting *agreement* (green) and *disagreement* (red). Font size corresponds to the importance of the feature, and negative features (in black) are underlined.

| | Including neutral sentences | | Agreement vs. disagreement (no neutral sent.) | |
| | Precision | Recall | Precision | Recall |
|---|---|---|---|---|
| Training-set (10-fold) *agreement* | 0.46 | 0.47 | 0.64 | 0.56 |
| *disagreement* | 0.54 | 0.56 | 0.91 | 0.93 |
| Evaluation-set *agreement* | 0.45±0.15 | 0.44±0.15 | 0.70±0.17 | 0.46±0.15 |
| *disagreement* | 0.29±0.06 | 0.50±0.09 | 0.84±0.06 | 0.93±0.04 |

Table 3: Machine learning results obtained on the corpus annotated in this study.

bly due to the few occurrence of this class in the training data.

Previous machine learning approaches were generally more successful. In Wikipedia Talk, F-scores of 0.69 and 0.53 were achieved for detecting *positive* and *negative* attitudes (Ferschke, 2014), and F-scores of 0.61 and 0.84 for detecting *explicit agreement/disagreement* (Opitz and Zirn, 2013). In other types of online debates, F-scores of 0.65 and 0.77 have been achieved for detecting dis/agreement (Yin et al., 2012), and an F-score of 0.75 for detecting disagreement (Allen et al., 2014). Including a neutral category, however, has resulted in agreement/disagreement F-scores of 0.23/0.46 for Wikipedia Talk and 0.26/0.57 for debate forums (Rosenthal and McKeown, 2015). Not all of these previous studies are, however, directly comparable, e.g., since more narrowly or broadly defined categories were used and/or larger training data sets or external lexical resources.

The next step includes an expansion of the training and evaluation sets, as well as to involve a second annotator to measure inter-annotator agreement and to create a gold standard. Without this measure of reliability, the annotated corpus cannot be considered complete. However, as a snapshot of its current status, the annotations have been made publicly available.[2] Future work also includes studying to what extent a topic-independent classifier detects dis/agreement in general. If dis/agreement is frequently conveyed by means specific to the topic of the debate, relations between the content of the debate posts need to be modelled, to be able to analyse reformulations/expansions/elaborations of previous posts.

## 5   Conclusion

To be able to train a topic-independent classifier for detecting dis/agreement in online debate fora, a corpus annotated for topic-independent expressions of dis/agreement is a useful resource. Here, the first step towards creating such a resource was taken. A debate forum corpus consisting of 27 discussion threads was annotated for topic-independent expressions conveying dis/agreement. Among the 175 annotated expressions (43 for *agreement* and 132 for *disagreement*), 163 were unique, which shows that there is a large variation in expressions used.

This variation might be one of the reasons why the task of detecting *dis/agreement* was difficult. 10-fold cross-validation on an additional set of 2,000 randomly selected sentences annotated for sentence-level *dis/agreement* resulted in a precision of 0.46 and a recall of 0.47 for *agreement* and a precision of 0.54 and a recall 0.56 for *disagreement*. Results for *disagreement*, however, decreased when the model was applied on held-out data (precision 0.29, recall 0.50). Better results were achieved for the task of distinguishing agreement from disagreement, i.e., not including neutral sentences, but recall for the more infrequently occurring category *agreement* was still low.

---

[2]http://bit.ly/1Ux8o7q

## Acknowledgements

This work was funded by the StaViCTA project, framework grant "the Digitized Society – Past, Present, and Future" with No. 2012-5659 from the Swedish Research Council (Vetenskapsrådet).

## References

Kelsey Allen, Giuseppe Carenini, and Raymond T. Ng. 2014. Detecting disagreement in conversations using pseudo-monologic rhetorical structure. In *Proceedings of the 2014 Conference on Empirical Methods in Natural Language Processing, EMNLP 2014, October 25-29, 2014, Doha, Qatar, A meeting of SIGDAT, a Special Interest Group of the ACL*, pages 1169–1180, Stroudsburg, PA, USA. Association for Computational Linguistics.

Jacob Andreas, Sara Rosenthal, and Kathleen McKeown. 2012. Annotating agreement and disagreement in threaded discussion. In *Proceedings of the Eighth International Conference on Language Resources and Evaluation (LREC-2012), Istanbul, Turkey, May 23-25, 2012*, pages 818–822.

Emily M. Bender, Jonathan T. Morgan, Meghan Oxley, Mark Zachry, Brian Hutchinson, Alex Marin, Bin Zhang, and Mari Ostendorf. 2011. Annotating social acts: Authority claims and alignment moves in wikipedia talk pages. In *Proceedings of the Workshop on Languages in Social Media*, LSM '11, pages 48–57, Stroudsburg, PA, USA. Association for Computational Linguistics.

Steven Bird. 2002. Nltk: The natural language toolkit. In *Proceedings of the ACL Workshop on Effective Tools and Methodologies for Teaching Natural Language Processing and Computational Linguistics*, Stroudsburg, PA, USA. Association for Computational Linguistics.

Oliver Ferschke. 2014. *The Quality of Content in Open Online Collaboration Platforms: Approaches to NLP-supported Information Quality Management in Wikipedia*. Dissertation, Technische Universität Darmstadt, July.

Michel Galley, Kathleen McKeown, Julia Hirschberg, and Elizabeth Shriberg. 2004. Identifying agreement and disagreement in conversational speech: Use of bayesian networks to model pragmatic dependencies. In *Proceedings of the 42Nd Annual Meeting on Association for Computational Linguistics*, ACL '04, Stroudsburg, PA, USA. Association for Computational Linguistics.

Sebastian Germesin and Theresa Wilson. 2009. Agreement detection in multiparty conversation. In *Proceedings of the 2009 International Conference on Multimodal Interfaces*, ICMI-MLMI '09, pages 7–14, New York, NY, USA. ACM.

Nancy Green, Kevin Ashley, Diane Litman, Chris Reed, and Vern Walker, editors. 2014. *Proceedings of the First Workshop on Argumentation Mining*. Association for Computational Linguistics, Stroudsburg, PA, USA.

Ivan Habernal and Iryna Gurevych. 2015. Exploiting debate portals for semi-supervised argumentation mining in user-generated web discourse. In *Proceedings of the 2015 Conference on Empirical Methods in Natural Language Processing*, pages 2127–2137, Stroudsburg, PA, September. Association for Computational Linguistics.

Sangyun Hahn, Richard Ladner, and Mari Ostendorf. 2006. Agreement/disagreement classification: exploiting unlabeled data using contrast classifiers. In *Proceedings of the Human Language Technology Conference of the North American Chapter of the ACL*, pages 53–56, Stroudsburg, PA, USA. Association for Computational Linguistics.

Dusting Hillard, Mari Ostendorf, and Elisabeth Shriberg. 2003. Detection of agreement vs. disagreement in meetings: Training with unlabeled data. In *Proceedings of the Human Language Technology Conference of the North American Chapter of the ACL*, Stroudsburg, PA, USA. Association for Computational Linguistics.

Amita Misra and Marilyn Walker. 2013. Topic independent identification of agreement and disagreement in social media dialogue. In *Proceedings of the SIGDIAL 2013 Conference*, pages 41–50, Stroudsburg, PA, USA, August. Association for Computational Linguistics.

Junko Mori. 1999. *Negotiating agreement and disagreement in Japanese : connective expressions and turn construction*. J. Benjamins Pub. Co, Amsterdam.

Bernd Opitz and Cäcilia Zirn. 2013. Bootstrapping an unsupervised approach for classifying agreement and disagreement. In *Proceedings of the 19th Nordic Conference of Computational Linguistics (NODALIDA)*. Linköping Univ. Electronic Press, Linköping.

Fabian Pedregosa, Gaël Varoquaux, Alexandre Gramfort, Vincent Michel, Bertrand Thirion, Olivier Grisel, Mathieu Blondel, Peter Prettenhofer, Ron Weiss, Vincent Dubourg, Jake Vanderplas, Alexandre Passos, David Cournapeau, Matthieu Brucher, Matthieu Perrot, and Edouard Duchesnay. 2011. Scikit-learn: Machine learning in Python. *Journal of Machine Learning Research*, 12:2825–2830.

Sara Rosenthal and Kathleen McKeown. 2015. I couldn't agree more: The role of conversational structure in agreement and disagreement detection in online discussions. In *SIGDIAL 2015 Conference*, pages 168–177, Stroudsburg, PA, USA. Association for Computational Linguistics.

John R. Searle. 1976. A Classification of Illocutionary Acts. *Language in Society*, 5(1):1–23.

Pontus Stenetorp, Sampo Pyysalo, Goran Topic, Tomoko Ohta, Sophia Ananiadou, and Jun'ichi Tsujii. 2012. brat: a web-based tool for nlp-assisted text annotation. In *EACL 2012, 13th Conference of the European Chapter of the Association for Computational Linguistics*, pages 102–107, Stroudsburg, PA, USA. Association for Computational Linguistics.

Matt Thomas, Bo Pang, and Lillian Lee. 2006. Get out the vote: Determining support or opposition from Congressional floor-debate transcripts. In *Proceedings of the 2006 Conference on Empirical Methods in Natural Language Processing*, pages 327–335, Stroudsburg, PA, USA. Association for Computational Linguistics.

Marilyn A. Walker, Pranav An, Jean E. Fox Tree, Rob Abbott, and Joseph King. 2012. A corpus for research on deliberation and debate. In *In Proceedings of the Eighth International Conference on Language Resources and Evaluation, LREC 2012*, pages 23–25.

Jie Yin, Paul Thomas, Nalin Narang, and Cecile Paris. 2012. Unifying local and global agreement and disagreement classification in online debates. In *Proceedings of the 3rd Workshop in Computational Approaches to Subjectivity and Sentiment Analysis*, WASSA '12, pages 61–69, Stroudsburg, PA, USA. Association for Computational Linguistics.

# Unshared Task at the 3rd Workshop on Argument Mining:
# Perspective Based Local Agreement and Disagreement in Online Debate


**Chantal van Son, Tommaso Caselli, Antske Fokkens, Isa Maks, Roser Morante,**
**Lora Aroyo** and **Piek Vossen**
Vrije Universiteit Amsterdam
Boelelaan 1105, 1081 HV Amsterdam, The Netherlands
{c.m.van.son, t.caselli, antske.fokkens, isa.maks,
r.morantevallejo, lora.aroyo, piek.vossen}@vu.nl



## Abstract

This paper proposes a new task in argument mining in online debates. The task includes three annotations steps that result in fine-grained annotations of agreement and disagreement at a propositional level. We report on the results of a pilot annotation task on identifying sentences that are directly addressed in the comment.


## 1 Introduction

Online debate (in its broadest sense) takes an increasingly prominent place in current society. It is at the same time a reflection and a shaping factor of the different beliefs, opinions and perspectives that exist in a certain community. Online debate characterizes itself by the dynamic interaction between its participants: they attack or support each other's stances by confirming or disputing their statements and arguments, questioning their relevance to the debate or introducing new arguments that are believed to overrule them. In fact, as Peldszus and Stede (2013, p. 4) point out, all argumentative text is of dialectic nature: "an argument always refers to an explicitly mentioned or at least supposed opponent, as for instance in the rebutting of possible objections." Therefore, these (implicit) interactions between participants should be given a central role when performing argument mining.

In recent years, several studies have addressed the annotation and automatic classification of *agreement* and *disagreement* in online debates. The main difference between them is the annotation unit they have targeted, i.e. the textual units that are in (dis)agreement. Some studies focused on *global* (dis)agreement, i.e. the overall stance towards the main debate topic (Somasundaran and Wiebe, 2010). Other studies focused on *local* (dis)agreement, comparing pairs of posts (Walker

et al., 2012), segments (Wang and Cardie, 2014) or sentences (Andreas et al., 2012). Yin et al. (2012) propose a framework that unifies local and global (dis)agreement classification.

This paper describes an argument mining task for the Unshared Task of the 2016 ACL Workshop on Argument Mining,[1] where participants propose a task with a corresponding annotation model (scheme) and conduct an annotation experiment given a corpus of various argumentative raw texts. Our task focuses on local (dis)agreement. In contrast to previous approaches, we propose *micro-propositions* as annotation targets, which are defined as the smallest meaningful statements embedded in larger expressions. As such, the annotations are not only more informative on exactly *what* is (dis)agreed upon, but they also account for the fact that two texts (or even two sentences) can contain both agreement and disagreement on different statements. The micro-propositions that we use as a basis have the advantage that they are simple statements that can easily be compared across texts, whereas overall propositions can be very complex. On the other hand, creating a gold-standard annotations of micro-propositions is time consuming for long texts. We therefore propose an (optional) additional annotation step which identifies relevant portions of text. This results in a three-step annotation procedure: 1) identifying relevant text, 2) identifying micro-propositions and 3) detecting disagreement. We report on a pilot study for the first subtask.

We selected a combination of two data sets provided by the organizers: i) Editorial articles extracted from Room for Debate from the N.Y. Times website (Variant C), each of which has a debate title (e.g. *Birth Control on Demand*), debate description (e.g. *Should it be provided by the gov-*

---

[1] http://argmining2016.arg.tech/index.
php/home/call-for-papers/unshared-task




*Proceedings of the 3rd Workshop on Argument Mining*, pages 160–165,
Berlin, Germany, August 7-12, 2016. ©2016 Association for Computational Linguistics

*ernment to reduce teen pregnancies?*) and article title describing the author's stance (e.g. *Publicly Funded Birth Control Is Crucial*); and ii) Discussions (i.e. collections of comments from different users) about these editorial articles (Variant D).

The remainder of this paper is structured as follows. Section 2 introduces the theoretical framework the task is based on. The annotation task is described in Section 3. Section 4 discusses the results of an annotation experiment, and we conclude and present future work in Section 5.

## 2 Perspective Framework

We consider any (argumentative) text to be a collection of propositions (statements) associated with some *perspective values*. In our framework (van Son et al., 2016), a *perspective* is described as a relation between the source of a statement (i.e. the author or, in the case of quotations, another entity introduced in the text) and a target in that statement (i.e. an entity, event or proposition) that is characterized by means of multiple perspective values expressing the attitude of the source towards the target. For instance, the commitment of a source towards the factual status of a targeted event or proposition is represented by a combination of three perspective values expressing *polarity* (AFFIRMATIVE or NEGATIVE), *certainty* (CERTAIN, PROBABLE, POSSIBLE) and *time* (FUTURE, NON-FUTURE). Other perspective dimensions, such as sentiment, are modeled in the same way with different sets of values.

Our assumption is that participants in an online debate interact with each other by attacking or supporting the perspective values of any of the propositions in a previous text. In this framework, we define *agreement* as a correspondence between one or more perspective values of a proposition attributed to one source and those attributed to another source; *disagreement*, on the other hand, is defined as a divergence between them. For example, consider the following pair of segments, one from an editorial article and the other from a comment in the context of *Teens Hooked on Screens*:

> **ARTICLE:** The bullies have moved from the playground to the mobile screen, and there is no escaping harassment that essentially lives in your pocket.
>
> **COMMENT:** Ms. Tynes: The bullies haven't moved from the playground to the screen.

This is a clear example of disagreement on the perspective values of a proposition present both in the editorial article and in the comment. As represented in Figure 1, the article's author commits to the factual status of the proposition, whereas the commenter denies it. In this example, the disagreement concerns the whole proposition ("no moving took place at all"). However, we assume that (dis)agreement can also target specific arguments within a proposition (i.e. hypothetically, someone could argue that it is not the bullies that moved from the playground to the screen, but someone else). We call these smallest meaningful propositional units in a text *micro-propositions*.

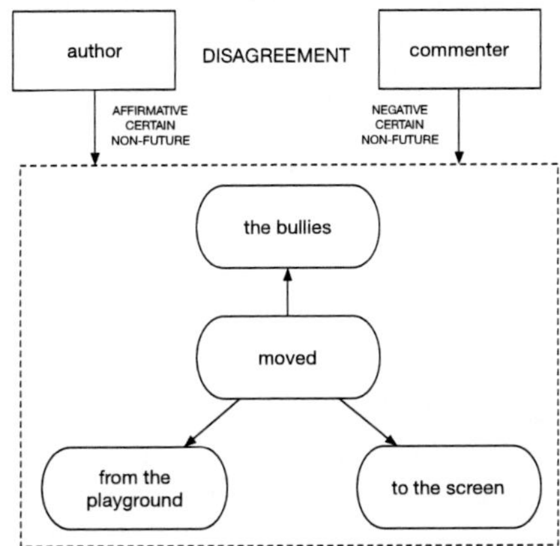


Figure 1: Representation of disagreement in the perspective framework.

## 3 Task Definition

Based on the perspective framework, we propose a task that aims at determining whether authors agree or disagree on the perspective values associated with the propositions contained in debate texts. Rather than trying to model the full debate comprehensively, we propose to start from the smallest statements made (i.e. micro-propositions) and derive more overall positions from the perspectives on these statements. This requires a detailed analysis of the texts. We optimize the annotation process by dividing the task into three subtasks described below: (1) Related Sentence Identification, (2) Proposition Identification, and (3) Agreement Classification.

### 3.1 Task 1: Related Sentence Identification

In an online debate, people often do not respond to each and every statement made in previous texts, but instead tend to support or attack only one or a few of them. The aim of the first task is to identify those sentences in the editorial article that are

COMMENTED_UPON in the comment. A sentence is defined to be COMMENTED_UPON if:

- the comment **repeats** or **rephrases** (part of) a statement made in the sentence;
- the comment **attacks** or **supports** (part of) a statement made in the sentence.

The main purpose of this task is to eliminate the parts of the editorial article that are irrelevant for (dis)agreement annotation. In the data set we use in this paper, the average number of sentences in the editorial articles is 19 (in the comments, the number of sentences ranges from 1 to 16). Without this first task, all propositions of the article including the irrelevant ones would have to be identified and annotated for (dis)agreement, which is neither efficient nor beneficial for the attention span of the annotators. With other data consisting of short texts, however, this subtask may be skipped.

Deciding whether a statement is COMMENTED_UPON may require some reasoning, which makes the task inherently subjective. Instead of developing overdetailed annotation guidelines simply to improve inter-annotator agreement, we adopt the view of Aroyo and Welty (2014) that annotator disagreement can be an indicator for language ambiguity and semantic similarity of target annotations. We considered using crowdsourcing for this task, which is particularly useful when harnessing disagreement to gain insight into the data and task. However, platforms like CrowdFlower and MTurk are not suitable for annotation of long texts and eliminating context was not an option in our view. Therefore, the task is currently designed to be performed by a team of expert annotators, and we will experiment with different thresholds to decide which annotations should be preserved for Tasks 2 and 3. In the future, we might experiment with alternative crowdsourcing platforms.

### 3.2 Task 2: Proposition Identification

A sentence can contain many propositions. For instance, the article sentence discussed earlier in this paper (repeated below) contains three propositions centered around the predicates marked in bold:[2]

> **ARTICLE:** The bullies have **moved** from the playground to the mobile screen, and there is no **escaping** harassment that essentially **lives** in your pocket.

[2]We do not consider *is* to express a meaningful proposition in this sentence.

In Task 2 we annotate the (micro-)propositions in the sentences that have been annotated as being COMMENTED_UPON. We first identify predicates that form the core of the proposition (e.g. *moved*, *escaping* and *lives*). Next, we relate them to their arguments and adjuncts. For the first predicate *moved*, for example, we obtain the following micro-propositions:

- moving
- the bullies moved
- moved from the playground
- moved to the screen

In this task, we annotate linguistic units. Though we will experiment with obtaining crowd annotations for this task, we may need expert annotators for creating the gold standard. We expect to be able to identify micro-propositions automatically with high accuracy.

### 3.3 Task 3: Agreement Classification

The final goal of the task is to identify the specific micro-propositions in the editorial article that are commented upon in a certain comment, and to determine whether the commenter agrees or disagrees with the author of the article on the perspective values of these micro-propositions. Thus, the final step concerns classifying the relation between the comment and the micro-propositions in terms of agreement and disagreement. For example, there is disagreement between the author and the commenter about the factual status of *moving*. We aim to obtain this information by asking the crowd to compare micro-propositions in the original text to those in the comment.

Even though most irrelevant micro-propositions have been eliminated in Task 1, we need an IRRELEVANT tag to mark any remaining micro-propositions for which (dis)agreement cannot be determined (e.g. all those obtained for *escaping* and *lives* in our example).

### 3.4 Interaction between Subtasks

The first two subtasks are primarily used to provide the necessary input for the third subtask. The relation between the second and third task is clear. In the second task, we create the units of comparison and in the third task we annotate the actual (dis)agreement. Similarly, the first task directly provides the input for the second task. The relation between the first and third task is more complex. In order to establish whether a comment comments upon a specific sentence, we need to determine if there is any (dis)agreement with the sentence in question. A natural question may be how this can be done if this information is only made explicit in subtask 3 or why we need to carry out subtasks 2 and 3 if we already established (dis)agreement in subtask 1. The main difference lies in the level of specificity of the two tasks. In subtask 1, annotators are asked if a comment addresses a given sentence in any way. Subtask 3 dives deeper into the interpretation by asking for each micro-proposition in the sentence whether the commenter agrees or disagrees with it.

There may be cases where one of the subtasks assumes that there is (dis)agreement and the other that there is no relation. We use the following strategies to deal with this. When no (dis)agreement is found on a detailed level, subtask 3 provides an option to indicate that there is no relation between a micro-proposition and the comment (the IRRELEVANT tag). This captures cases that were wrongly annotated in subtask 1. If subtask 1 misses a case of (dis)agreement, this cannot be corrected in subtask 3. We can, however, maximize recall in the first subtask by using multiple annotators and a low threshold for selecting sentences (e.g. requiring only one annotator to indicate whether the sentence is commented upon). We will elaborate on this in Section 4.

## 4 Task 1: Pilot annotation

This section reports on a pilot annotation experiment targeted at the first subtask. Five expert annotators were asked to identify those sentences in the editorial article that were COMMENTED_UPON in the comment. A set of eight editorial articles (152 unique sentences, including titles) and a total of 62 comments were provided. In total, this came down to 1,186 sentences to be annotated. We used the Content Annotation Tool (CAT) (Lenzi et al., 2012) for the annotations.

The experiment was performed in two rounds. First, simple instructions were given to the annotators to explore the data and task. For the second round, the instructions were refined by adding two simple rules: exclude titles (they are part of the meta-data), and include cases where a proposition is simply 'mentioned' rather than functioning as part of the argumentation. For example, the fact that the closing of Sweet Briar College is repeated in the comment below without its factual status be-

ing questioned most likely means that there is an agreement about it, so we do need to annotate it:

> **ARTICLE:** Despite a beautiful campus, dedicated faculty, loyal alumnae and a significant endowment, Sweet Briar College is closing after 114 years.
>
> **COMMENT:** Anyway, there's something ineffably sad to me about Sweet Briar's closing.

Figure 2 shows the distribution of the annotations in both rounds. Only the sentences that were annotated by at least one annotator (29% in Round 2) are included in the graph. We explained in Section 3.1 that identifying whether a sentence is commented upon or not is an inherently subjective task. We analyze the distribution of annotations, because distributions are more insightful for tasks where disagreement is expected than measurements for inter-annotator agreement.

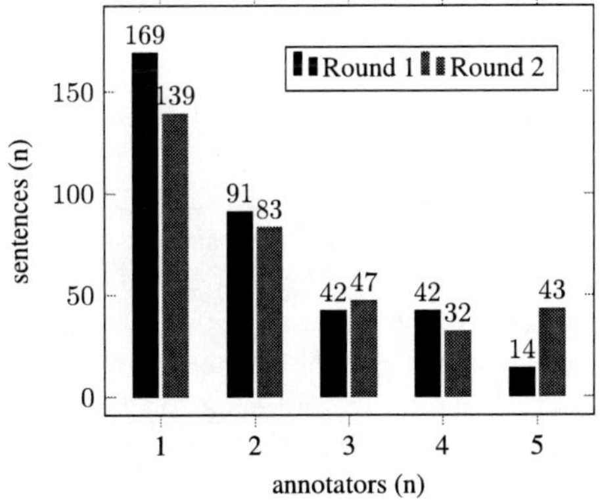


Figure 2: Distribution of annotations.

A deeper analysis of the annotated data and the annotation distribution shows the different degrees of connectivity between the annotated sentences and the comments. The sentences that were annotated by 4 or 5 annotators clearly were strongly and unambiguously related to the comment. For example, the following sentence was annotated by all of the annotators:

> **ARTICLE:** But allowing children and teens to regulate their behavior like adults gives them room to naturally modify their own habits.
>
> **COMMENT:** I empathize with your argument that allows children to regulate their behavior like adults.

In addition, the above sentence is one example of those that were annotated as being COM-MENTED_UPON in multiple comments. What these sentences seem to have in common is that they express an important argument or a concluding statement in the editorial article. In the above case, the author of the article uses this argument in an online debate about *Teens Hooked on Screens* to argue why you should not limit your teen's screen time. Comparing this example to one where only a minority of the annotators agreed (i.e. 2 out of 5), a difference can be noticed in the amount of inference that is required to understand a relation between the sentence and the comment (i.e. the article sentence specifies *how* access to birth control is a win-win for young women):

> **ARTICLE:** Giving poor young women easy access to birth control is about exactly that - control.
>
> **COMMENT:** This is a rational argument for how access to birth control is a win-win for young women, their partners, and the taxpaying public who might otherwise foot the welfare bill.

The choice to annotate the sentence as being COMMENTED_UPON or not depends on the question: how strong or obvious is the inference? The answer is ambiguous by nature and seems to partly depend on the annotator, given the number of total annotated sentences ranging from 123 to 212 (indicating that some annotators are more likely to annotate inference relations than others). Partly, however, it depends on the specific instance, indicated by the fact that all annotators had annotated multiple relations between sentences and comments that none of the others did.

The sentences that were not annotated at all (by none of the annotators and for none of the comments) typically included (personal) anecdotes or other background information to support or introduce the main arguments in the article. For example, the following four subsequent sentences introduce and illustrate the statements about the freeing powers of single-sex education that follow:

> **ARTICLE:** Years ago, during a classroom visit, I observed a small group of black and Latino high school boys sitting at their desks looking into handheld mirrors. They were tasked with answering the question, "What do you see?" One boy said, "I see an ugly face." Another said, "I see a big nose."

A major advantage of asking multiple annotators is that we can use different thresholds for selecting data. If we want to create a high quality set of clearly related sentences and comments, we can use only those sentences annotated by all. As suggested in Section 3, we can also select all sentences annotated by one or more person to aim for high recall. Nevertheless, this will not guarantee that no sentences are missed. Our results show that each additional annotator led to more candidate sentences, indicating that five annotators may

be too few and new sentences would be added by a sixth annotator. If we want to find out how many relevant micro-proposition we miss, we can address this through a study where we apply the last two subtasks on complete texts and verify how many (dis)agreement pairs are missed in subtask 1.

## 5 Conclusion

We described a new task for argument mining based on our perspective framework and provided the results of a pilot annotation experiment aimed at identifying the sentences of an editorial article that are COMMENTED_UPON in a comment. Although a functional classification of statements was not part of our original goal, looking at argumentative texts from an interactive point of view did prove to shed new light on this more traditional argument mining task. Statements that are repeated, rephrased, attacked or supported by other debate participants seem to be the ones that are (at least perceived as) the main arguments of the text, especially when commented upon by multiple users. In contrast, statements that are not commented upon are likely to provide background information to support or introduce these arguments. We argued that annotator disagreement is not so much undesirable as it is insightful in tasks like this and reported on the distribution of the annotations. In our case, annotator disagreement appeared to be an indicator for the amount of inference that is needed to understand the relation between the sentence and the comment.

In the future, we plan to further experiment with the other two defined subtasks using a combination of expert annotation, semi-automatic approaches (textual similarity and entailment, generation of propositional relations) and crowdsourcing. Furthermore, we will include comment–comment relations (where one comment is a response to another) next to article–comment relations. The annotations and code for the experiment described in this paper are publicly available. [3]

## References

Jacob Andreas, Sara Rosenthal, and Kathleen McKeown. 2012. Annotating agreement and disagreement in threaded discussion. In *Proceedings of the 8th International Conference on Language Re-*

---

[3]`github.com/ChantalvanSon/`
`UnsharedTask-ArgumentMining-2016`

*sources and Evaluation (LREC 2012)*, pages 818–822, Istanbul, Turkey.

L. Aroyo and C. Welty. 2014. The three sides of CrowdTruth. *Human Computation*, 1:31–34.

Valentina Bartalesi Lenzi, Giovanni Moretti, and Rachele Sprugnoli. 2012. CAT: the CELCT Annotation Tool. In *Proceedings of the 8th International Conference on Language Resources and Evaluation (LREC 2012)*, pages 333–338, Istanbul, Turkey, May.

Andreas Peldszus and Manfred Stede. 2013. From argument diagrams to argumentation mining in texts: A survey. *International Journal of Cognitive Informatics and Natural Intelligence (IJCINI)*, 7(1):1–31.

Swapna Somasundaran and Janyce Wiebe. 2010. Recognizing stances in ideological on-line debates. In *Proceedings of the NAACL HLT 2010 Workshop on Computational Approaches to Analysis and Generation of Emotion in Text*, pages 116–124, Los Angeles, California, June. Association for Computational Linguistics.

Chantal van Son, Tommaso Caselli, Antske Fokkens, Isa Maks, Roser Morante, Lora Aroyo, and Piek Vossen. 2016. GRaSP: A multilayered annotation scheme for perspectives. In *Proceedings of the 10th International Conference on Language Resources and Evaluation (LREC 2016)*, Portorož, Slovenia, May.

Marilyn A Walker, Jean E Fox Tree, Pranav Anand, Rob Abbott, and Joseph King. 2012. A corpus for research on deliberation and debate. In *Proceedings of the 8th International Conference on Language Resources and Evaluation (LREC 2012)*, pages 812–817, Istanbul, Turkey.

Lu Wang and Claire Cardie. 2014. Improving agreement and disagreement identification in online discussions with a socially-tuned sentiment lexicon. In *Proceedings of the 5th Workshop on Computational Approaches to Subjectivity, Sentiment and Social Media Analysis (ACL 2014)*, Baltimore, Maryland, USA, June. Association for Computational Linguistics.

Jie Yin, Paul Thomas, Nalin Narang, and Cecile Paris. 2012. Unifying local and global agreement and disagreement classification in online debates. In *Proceedings of the 3rd Workshop in Computational Approaches to Subjectivity and Sentiment Analysis*, pages 61–69. Association for Computational Linguistics.

# A Preliminary Study of Disputation Behavior in Online Debating Forum

**Zhongyu Wei**[1,2], **Yandi Xia**[1], **Chen Li**[1], **Yang Liu**[1]
**Zachary Stallbohm**[1], **Yi Li**[1] and **Yang Jin**[1]
[1]Computer Science Department, The University of Texas at Dallas
Richardson, Texas 75080, USA
[2]School of Data Science, Fudan University, Shanghai, P.R.China
{zywei,yandixia,chenli,yangl,stallbohm,yili,yangjin}@hlt.utdallas.edu

## Abstract

In this paper, we propose a task for quality evaluation of disputing argument. In order to understand the disputation behavior, we propose three sub-tasks, detecting disagreement hierarchy, refutation method and argumentation strategy respectively. We first manually labeled a real dataset collected from an online debating forum. The dataset includes 45 disputing argument pairs. The annotation scheme is developed by three NLP researchers via annotating all the argument pairs in the dataset. Two under-graduate students are then trained to annotate the same dataset. We report annotation results from both groups. Then, another larger dataset was annotated and we show analysis of the correlation between disputing quality and different disputation behaviors.

## 1 Introduction

With the popularity of the online debating forum such as idebate[1], convinceme[2] and createdebate[3], researchers have been paying increasing attention to analyze debating content, including identification of arguing expressions in online debate (Trabelsi and Zaiane, 2014), recognition of stance in ideological online debates (Somasundaran and Wiebe, 2010; Hasan and Ng, 2014; Ranade et al., 2013b), and debate summarization (Ranade et al., 2013a). However, there is still little research about quality evaluation of debating content.

Tan et al. (2016) and Wei and Liu (2016) studied the persuasiveness of comments in sub-reddit *change my view* of Reddit.com. They evaluated

[1]http://idebate.org/
[2]http://convinceme.net
[3]http://www.createdebate.com/

Figure 1: A disputation example from createddebate.com (The debating topic is "Should the Gorilla have died?")

the effectiveness of different features for the prediction of highly voted comments in terms of delta score and karma score respectively. Although they considered some sorts of argumentation related features, such features are merely based on lexical similarity, without modeling persuasion behaviors.

In this paper, we focus on a particular action in the online debating forum, i.e., *disputation*. Within debate, disputation happens when a user disagrees with a specific comment. Figure 1 gives a disputation example from the online debating forum *createdebate*. It presents an original argument and an argument disputing it. Our study aims to evaluate the quality of a disputing comment given its original argument and the discussed topic. In order to have a deep understanding of disputation, we analyze disputation behavior via three sub-tasks, including disagreement hierarchy identification, refutation method identification and argumentation strategy identification.

We first manually labeled a small amount of data collected from createdebate.com. It includes 8 debate threads related to different topics. We

166

extracted all the 45 disputing pairs from these threads. Each pair contains two arguments and the second one disputes the first one. Three NLP researchers (the first three authors of the paper) first developed a rough version of annotation scheme and they annotated all the argument pairs. Based on the annotation feedback and discussioins, they modified the scheme. Two native English speakers are then trained to annotate the same dataset. Further, we asked one annotator with better performance in previous step to annotate a larger set of data. We then analyze the correlation between disputing quality and different disputation behaviors. We will introduce annotation schema in Section 2 and then report the annotation result in Section 3. We conclude the paper in Section 4.

## 2 Annotation Schema

Our annotation is performed on a pair of arguments from opposite sides of a specific topic. In each pair, the second argument disputes the first one. Any of them can hold the "supportive" stance to the discussed topic. We define four annotation tasks: disagreement hierarchy (DH), refutation method (RM), argumentation strategy (AS) and disputing quality (DQ). The first three are proposed to understand the disputation behavior. In the disputing comment, DH indicates how the disagreement is expressed, RM describes which part of the original argument is attacked, and AS shows how the argument is formed.

### 2.1 Disagreement Hierarchy

In order to identify how users express their disagreement to the opposite argument, we borrowed the disagreement hierarchy from Paul Graham[4]. We modified the original version of the theory by combining some similar categories and proposed a four-level hierarchy. The definition of different types of DH is shown below. Examples of disputing comments with different disagreement hierarchies are shown in Table 1.

a) **DH-LV1: Irrelevance**. The disagreement barely considers the content of the original argument.

b) **DH-LV2: Contradiction**. The disagreement simply states the opposing case, with little or no supporting evidence.

Table 1: Examples for disagreement hierarchy

| *original argument* |
| --- |
| I strongly feel age for smoking and drinking should not be lowered down as it can disturb the hormonal balance of the body! |

| *disputing argument* |
| --- |
| DH-LV1: Irrelevance |
| Wat???? You are an idiot! I would definitely give you a down vote! |
| DH-LV2: Contradiction |
| I do not think this correct, it is impossible to be accepted. |
| DH-LV3: Target Losing Argument |
| So this age 21 thing is really stupid cause like i said minors still get hold to alcoholic beverages. (Age limit is non-sense because teen-age can always have alcohol.) |
| DH-LV4: Refutation |
| Getting involved in a war will also hurt your body as drinking and smoking, but the age limit is 18 instead of 21. |

c) **DH-LV3: Target Losing Argument**. The disagreement is contradiction plus reasoning and/or evidence. However, it aims at something slightly different from the original argument.

d) **DH-LV4: Refutation**. Refutation is a counter-argument quoting content from the original argument. The quoting can be either explicit or implicit.

### 2.2 Refutation Method

When a disputing comment is labeled as *refutation*, we will further identify its refutation method. This sub-task is proposed to indicate what aspect of the original argument is attacked by the disputing one. Three categories are given for this sub-task according to the theory of *refutation methods* proposed by Freeley and Steinberg (2013). Examples for disputing comments using different refutation methods are shown in Table 2.

a) **RM-F: refute fallacy**. Refutation is performed by attacking the fallacy of the original argument. This usually happens when the target of the attack is the correctness of the claim itself in the original argument.

b) **RM-R: refute reasoning**. Refutation is performed by attacking the reasoning process demonstrated in the original argument.

c) **RM-E: refute evidence**. Refutation is performed by attacking the correctness of the evidence given in the original argument.

### 2.3 Argumentation Strategy

To dispute the original argument, the users will form their own argument. Argumentation strategies have been studies in both The Toulmin Model

---

Table 2: Examples for refutation methods (OA: original argument; DA: disputing argument)

| |
| --- |
| RM-F: refute fallacy |
| OA: Humans are not animal's and dont say that we evolved from monkeys because we did not<br>DA: dont say that we evolved from monkeys because we did not http://en.wikipedia.org/wiki/Human_evolution And there's a long list of references and further reading down there. |
| RM-R: refute reasoning |
| OA: There is supposed to be equal protection under the law. If we give some couples benefits for being together we need to give it to the rest.<br>DA: Talking about the 14th Amendment's Equal Protection Clause? That was talking about slavery. |
| RM-E: refute evidence |
| OA: Dont say that we evolved from monkeys because we did not http://en.wikipedia.org/wiki/Human_evolution And there's a long list of references and further reading down there.<br>DA: Evolution is fake God made you retard learn it. Also Wikipedia is soooooooooo wrong random people put stuff in there and the creator does not even care Yah Fools |

Table 3: Examples for argumentation strategy

| |
| --- |
| Generalization |
| Look at alan turing; government data collection on him and his homosexual tendencies led to his suicide. |
| Analogy |
| What has worked for drug decriminalization in the Netherlands should work in the United States. |
| Sign |
| Where there's fire, there's smoke. |
| Cause |
| Beer causes drunkenness, or that drunkenness can be caused by beer. |
| Authority |
| As stated by Wikipedia: human is evolved from animal. |
| Principle |
| As it says, "there is a will, there is a way". |

of Argumentation[5] and the work of Walton et al. (2008). In our research, we employ the classification version from Toulmin because it is much simpler. Six categories are used to indicate the argumentation strategy used in the disputing argument. Note that this label should be given based on user's intention instead of the quality of the argument. For example, users might choose inappropriate evidence to support the disputing claim. We will still treat it as *generalization*. Examples of arguments with different argumentation strategies are shown in Table 3.

a) **Generalization**. Argument by generalization assumes that a number of examples can be applied more generally.

b) **Analogy**. Argument by analogy examines alternative examples in order to prove that what is true in one case is true in the other.

c) **Sign**. Argument by sign asserts that two or more things are so closely related that the presence or absence of one indicates the presence or absence of the other.

d) **Cause**. Argument by cause attempts to establish a cause and effect relationship between two events.

e) **Authority**. Argument by authority relies on the testimony and reasoning of a credible source.

f) **Principle**. Argument by principle locates a principle that is widely regarded as valid and shows that a situation exists in which this principle applies.

g) **Other**. When no above-mentioned argumentation strategy is identified, we label it as other.

[5] http://www-rohan.sdsu.edu/~digger/305/toulmin_model.htm

## 2.4  Debating quality evaluation

We are also interested in the general quality of the disputing comment. We use three categories: *bad debate*, *reasonable debate* and *good debate*. The label should be assigned based on the content of the disputing argument instead of annotators' personal preference to the topic.

a) **Bad debate**. The disagreement is irrelevant or simply states its attitude without any support; the support or reasoning or fallacy is not reasonable.

b) **Reasonable debate**. The disagreement is complete including contradiction and related supportive evidence or reasoning. However, the argument might be attacked easily.

c) **Good debate**. The disagreement contains contradiction and related supportive evidence or reasoning. Besides, this argument is good and persuasive to some extent.

## 3  Annotation Result

The annotation is performed on the variantA dataset[6] provided by the 3rd workshop on argumentation mining collected from createdebate.com. In such forum, each debating thread is about a particular topic and users can initialize a comment with a specific stance. Besides starting a comment, users can also reply to a comment with an intention of supporting, disputing or clarifying.

We first work on one subset of the data, namely *dev* to develop our annotation scheme and analyze the annotation performance of two laymen annotators. The statistics of the original *dev* set are given in Table 4. As we can see, more than half of the comments are disputing ones. We extract all disputing comments together with their original comment to form argument pairs as the first batch of

[6] Please contact authors for the annotated dataset.

Table 4: Statistics of the dev dataset in VariantA from createdebate.com

| Thread # | 8 |
| --- | --- |
| avg comment # | 10.25 |
| avg initial comment # | 3.00 |
| avg disputation comment # | 5.63 |
| avg support comment # | 1.38 |
| avg clarify comment # | 0.25 |
| unique user # | 6.7 |
| avg length of initial comments | 87.16 |
| avg length of disputation comments | 67.02 |
| avg length of comments | 69.24 |

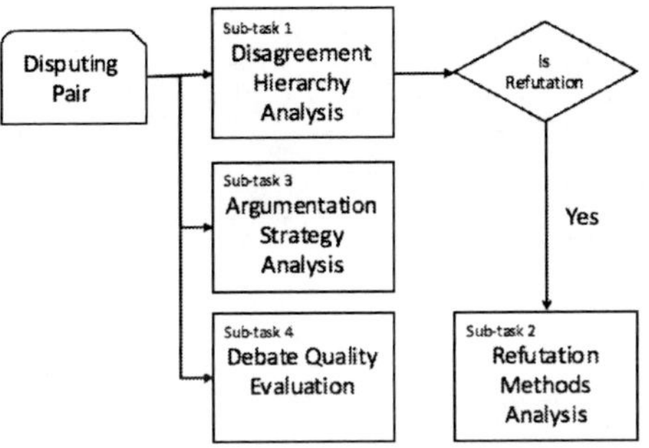


Figure 2: Workflow of the annotation task

our experiment dataset *batch-1*, 8 threads and 45 pairs of arguments in total.

We also analyze the relationship between different disputation behaviors and the quality of the disputing argument. To make this correlation analysis more convincible and also to motivate follow-up research for disputation analysis in the online forum, we collected another batch of annotation on the larger dataset *batch-2* from another two sub-sets of variantA (i.e., *test* and *crowdsourcing*). This batch contains 20 new topics including 93 pairs of disputing arguments. The correlation analysis is then performed on the combination of *batch-1* and *batch-2*.

### 3.1 Annotation Result of Expert and Layman on Batch-1

Three NLP researchers work together to define the annotation scheme via annotating all the argument pairs in *batch-1*. Two undergraduate students are then hired to annotate the same set of data given two days to finish all the annotation task. A half an hour training session is used for introducing the annotation scheme and demonstrating the annotation process via two samples. The work flow of the annotation is shown in Figure 2. Annotators are given the entire thread of the debating to have a

background of the discussion related to this topic.

We first look at the label distribution on all the four annotation tasks based on experts' opinion on *batch-1*. The annotation scheme changes during the annotation process via discussion, we thus are not able to provide agreement between experts. For the three disputation behavior annotation tasks, experts finalize the label after discussion. For the disputing quality evaluation, experts agree on the label for *bad debate* but had different opinions about *good* and *reasonable* ones, since these are subjective. Therefore, for general quality annotation we take the majority. Table 5 shows the detail of the annotation results. For disagreement hierarchy, 36 out 45 (80%) disputation are *refutation*. For refutation method, 20 (44%) disputing comments refute fallacy directly, while 7 (18%) and 9 (20%) refute evidence and reasoning respectively. For argumentation strategy, 20 (44%) disputing comments do not use any specified methods. *Generalization* is the most popular one while no *sign* and *principle* are found. For the disputing quality, more than half of the comments are labeled as reasonable. Only 10 (22%) are labeled as good.

We then analyze the annotation result for two laymen annotators using experts' opinion as ground truth on *batch-1*. Generally speaking, the disputation behavior annotation is difficult for laymen. With only half an hour training, the performance of both annotators is not very good for labeling the four tasks. For disagreement hierarchy, annotators seem to have problems to distinguish *target losing argument* and *refutation*. Annotator-1 mis-labels too many instances as *ttarget losing argument* while annotator-2 gives only 1 such annotation. The lowest accuracy comes from refutation method identification. This is because the task requires deep understanding and analysis of argument. For disputing quality evaluation, it is easier for annotators to identify the *bad* argument. Distinguishing *good* and *reasonable* disputing is much more difficult. This is because the difference between them is very subjective.

### 3.2 Correlation of Disputation Behavior and Disputing Quality

With the same strategy, we further construct and annotate the second batch of experiment dataset *batch-2*. *Annotator-1* worked for this. Before the annotation, we review the error annotation

Table 5: Annotation results

| Annotation Type | | Batch-1 | | | | | | | | | Batch-2 |
| --- | --- | --- | --- | --- | --- | --- | --- | --- | --- | --- | --- |
| | | Expert | Annotator-1 | | | | Annotator-2 | | | | Annotator-1 |
| | | # | # | precision | recall | F-1 | # | precision | recall | F-1 | # |
| DH | DH-LV1 | 2 (1%) | 3 | 0.667 | 1.000 | 0.800 | 1 | 1.000 | 0.500 | 0.667 | 4 (4%) |
| | DH-LV2 | 1 (2%) | 2 | 0.500 | 1.000 | 0.667 | 2 | 0.500 | 1.000 | 0.667 | 5 (5%) |
| | DH-LV3 | 6 (13%) | 12 | 0.417 | 0.833 | 0.556 | 1 | 0.000 | 0.000 | 0.000 | 12 (13%) |
| | DH-LV4 | 36 (80%) | 27 | 1.000 | 0.750 | 0.857 | 41 | 0.829 | 0.944 | 0.883 | 72 (77%) |
| RM | RM-E | 7 (18%) | 2 | 1.000 | 0.286 | 0.444 | 6 | 0.333 | 0.286 | 0.308 | 4 (4%) |
| | RM-R | 9 (20%) | 19 | 0.263 | 0.556 | 0.357 | 11 | 0.364 | 0.444 | 0.400 | 27 (29%) |
| | RM-F | 20 (44%) | 6 | 1.000 | 0.300 | 0.462 | 24 | 0.500 | 0.600 | 0.545 | 41 (44%) |
| AS | generalization | 9 (20%) | 6 | 0.667 | 0.667 | 0.667 | 6 | 0.167 | 0.167 | 0.167 | 5 (5%) |
| | analogy | 5 (11%) | 4 | 0.500 | 0.400 | 0.444 | 7 | 0.714 | 1.000 | 0.833 | 8 (9%) |
| | sign | 0 (0%) | 4 | 0.000 | 0.000 | 0.000 | 0 | 0.000 | 0.000 | 0.000 | 0 (0%) |
| | cause | 6 (13%) | 12 | 0.500 | 0.667 | 0.571 | 10 | 0.600 | 0.667 | 0.632 | 33 (35%) |
| | authority | 5 (11%) | 3 | 0.667 | 0.400 | 0.500 | 7 | 0.714 | 1.000 | 0.833 | 7 (8%) |
| | principle | 0 (0%) | 0 | 0.000 | 0.000 | 0.000 | 0 | 0.000 | 0.000 | 0.000 | 0 (0%) |
| | other | 20 (44%) | 16 | 0.813 | 0.650 | 0.722 | 15 | 0.800 | 0.600 | 0.686 | 40 (43%) |
| DQ | bad | 12 (27%) | 21 | 0.523 | 0.917 | 0.667 | 11 | 0.818 | 0.750 | 0.783 | 19 (20%) |
| | reasonable | 23 (51%) | 21 | 0.667 | 0.609 | 0.636 | 9 | 0.667 | 0.261 | 0.375 | 58 (62%) |
| | good | 10 (22%) | 3 | 0.000 | 0.000 | 0.000 | 25 | 0.280 | 0.700 | 0.400 | 16 (17%) |

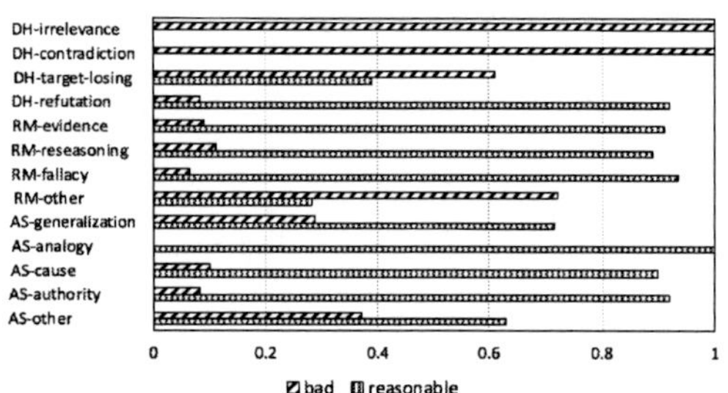


Figure 3: The correlation between disputation behaviors and disputing quality (binary setting) on *batch-1+batch-2*.

with the annotator to enhance his understanding about the annotation task. The annotation result of *batch-2* can be seen in Table 5. We then report the correlation result between disputation behaviors and disputing quality of the arguments on the combination of *batch-1* and *batch-2*.

For the correlation analysis, we report the label distribution in terms of disputing quality for arguments with different disputation labels. Considering the difference between a "good disputing" and a "reasonable disputing" is hard to decide, we treat both *reasonable* and *good* as *reasonable* to form a binary setting. Figure 3 shows the correlation between disputation behaviors and disputing quality. As we can see, all the arguments labeled as *DH-irrelevance* and *DH-contradiction* are *bad* ones, and 91.7% of *DH-refutation* arguments are *reasonable*. For argumentation strategy, *analogy* (100%), *cause* (89.7%) and *authority* (91.7%) are

good indicators for *reasonable* arguments.

## 3.3 Discussion

We identified two major reasons for annotation errors after result analysis on *batch-1*. First, some categories within sub-tasks are difficult to distinguish in nature (e.g. target losing argument and refutation). Second, some disputing comments contain multiple claims and premises. This makes it difficult to identify the essential claim of the disputation. We believe we can improve the annotation performance in future work by: a) extend the time for training session and pick some representative samples for demonstration; b) modify the annotation scheme to avoid the ambiguity between categories; c) preprocess the disputing comment to identify the essential argument for better annotation.

## 4 Conclusion

In this paper, we analyzed the disputation action in the online debate. Four sub-tasks were proposed including disagreement hierarchy identification, refutation method identification, argumentation strategy identification and disputing quality evaluation. We labeled a set of disputing argument pairs extracted from a real dataset collected in createddebate.com and showed annotation results.

## Acknowledgments

The work is partially supported by DARPA Contract No. FA8750-13-2-0041 and AFOSR award No. FA9550-15-1-0346.

## References

Austin Freeley and David Steinberg. 2013. *Argumentation and debate*. Cengage Learning.

Kazi Saidul Hasan and Vincent Ng. 2014. Why are you taking this stance? identifying and classifying reasons in ideological debates. In *EMNLP*, pages 751–762.

Sarvesh Ranade, Jayant Gupta, Vasudeva Varma, and Radhika Mamidi. 2013a. Online debate summarization using topic directed sentiment analysis. In *Proceedings of the Second International Workshop on Issues of Sentiment Discovery and Opinion Mining*. ACM.

Sarvesh Ranade, Rajeev Sangal, and Radhika Mamidi. 2013b. Stance classification in online debates by recognizing users? Intentions. In *SigDial*, pages 61–69.

Swapna Somasundaran and Janyce Wiebe. 2010. Recognizing stances in ideological on-line debates. In *Proceedings of the NAACL HLT 2010 Workshop on Computational Approaches to Analysis and Generation of Emotion in Text*, pages 116–124. Association for Computational Linguistics.

Chenhao Tan, Vlad Niculae, Cristian Danescu-Niculescu-Mizil, and Lillian Lee. 2016. Winning arguments: Interaction dynamics and persuasion strategies in good-faith online discussions. *arXiv preprint arXiv:1602.01103*.

Amine Trabelsi and Osmar R Zaıane. 2014. Finding arguing expressions of divergent viewpoints in on-line debates. In *Proceedings of the 5th Workshop on Language Analysis for Social Media (LASM)@ EACL*, pages 35–43.

Douglas Walton, Christopher Reed, and Fabrizio Macagno. 2008. *Argumentation schemes*. Cambridge University Press.

Zhongyu Wei and Yang Liu. 2016. Is this post persuasive? ranking argumentative comments in online forum. In *ACL*.

# Author Index


Addawood, Aseel, 1
Aroyo, Lora, 160
Ashley, Kevin D., 50

Bar-Haim, Roy, 119
Barker, Emma, 12
Bashir, Masooda, 1
Becker, Maria, 21
Beigman Klebanov, Beata, 70
Bollegala, Danushka, 31
Boltuzic, Filip, 124
Budzynska, Katarzyna, 40
Burstein, Jill, 70

Caselli, Tommaso, 160
Conrad, Stefan, 144

Duthie, Rory, 40

Egan, Charlie, 134
Esau, Katharina, 144

Fokkens, Antske, 160
Frank, Anette, 21

Gaizauskas, Robert, 12
Ghosh, Debanjan, 82
Gurevych, Iryna, 70, 113
Gyawali, Binod, 70

Jin, Yang, 166

Karkaletsis, Vangelis, 94
Kerren, Andreas, 154
Koreeda, Yuta, 76

Lawrence, John, 40
Li, Chen, 166
Li, Yi, 166
Liebeck, Matthias, 144
Liu, Yang, 166

Maks, Isa, 160
Mandya, Angrosh, 60
Morante, Roser, 160
Muresan, Smaranda, 82

Musi, Elena, 82

Niwa, Yoshiki, 76

Palmer, Alexis, 21
Paradis, Carita, 154
Parsons, Simon, 31
Peldszus, Andreas, 103
Petasis, Georgios, 94

Rajendran, Pavithra, 31
Reed, Chris, 40

Sahlgren, Magnus, 154
Sato, Misa, 76
Savelka, Jaromir, 50
Siddharthan, Advaith, 60, 134
Skeppstedt, Maria, 154
Slonim, Noam, 119
Šnajder, Jan, 124
Song, Yi, 70
Stab, Christian, 70, 113
Stallbohm, Zachary, 166
Stede, Manfred, 103

Toledo-Ronen, Orith, 119

van Son, Chantal, 160
Vossen, Piek, 160

Wei, Zhongyu, 166
Wyner, Adam, 60, 134

Xia, Yandi, 166

Yanai, Kohsuke, 76
Yanase, Toshihiko, 76